PENGUIN BOOKS

THE NATIONAL SOCIETY OF FILM CRITICS ON THE MOVIE STAR

Elisabeth Weis, secretary of the National Society of Film Critics, is an associate professor of film at Brooklyn College, City University of New York, and the author of *The Silent Scream: Alfred Hitchcock's Sound Track*. She co-edited, with Stuart Byron, *The National Society of Film Critics on Movie Comedy*, also published by Penguin Books.

The National Society of Film Critics is comprised of the country's leading critics for general-interest periodicals. Its aim is to promote the mutual artistic interests of filmmaking and film criticism. The best-known function of the society is its annual awards for best picture, director, actor and actress, supporting actor and actress, cinematographer, and screenplay. The society's anthologies were originally collections of annual reviews, from *Film 67/68* through *Film 73/74*. *The Movie Star* is the second in the society's new series of thematic anthologies, which began with *Movie Comedy*.

THE NATIONAL SOCIETY
OF FILM CRITICS ON

THE MOVIE STAR

EDITED BY
Elisabeth Weis

PENGUIN BOOKS

Penguin Books Ltd, Harmondsworth,
Middlesex, England
Penguin Books, 625 Madison Avenue,
New York, New York 10022, U.S.A.
Penguin Books Australia Ltd, Ringwood,
Victoria, Australia
Penguin Books Canada Limited, 2801 John Street,
Markham, Ontario, Canada L3R 1B4
Penguin Books (N.Z.) Ltd, 182–190 Wairau Road,
Auckland 10, New Zealand

First published in the United States of America in
simultaneous hardcover and paperback editions by
The Viking Press and Penguin Books 1981

LIBRARY OF CONGRESS CATALOGING IN PUBLICATION DATA
Main entry under title:
The National Society of Film Critics on the movie star.
Includes index.
1. Moving-picture actors and actresses—Addresses, essays, lectures.
2. Moving-pictures—Reviews.
I. Weis, Elisabeth. II. National Society of Film Critics.
PN1998.A2N35   1981b   791.43′028′0922   81-5153
ISBN 0 14 00.5947 4   AACR2

Printed in the United States of America by
Halliday Lithograph, West Hanover, Massachusetts
Set in CRT Baskerville

Pages 400–402 constitute an extension of this copyright page.

CONTENTS

II. THE STARS

Lillian Gish. (Courtesy of the Museum of Modern Art Film Stills Archive.)

INTRODUCTION

Most of us are a bit embarrassed to be reading about movie stars. We don't want to be dupes of the movie industry's image-hustlers. Or perhaps we feel that all articles about stars are tainted by association with fan magazines. But we should not have to conceal our fascination. The articles in this collection make a strong case for the value of the subject. To begin with, they argue persuasively about the indispensability of the performer. Now that directors, screenwriters, and others have finally gotten their due, William S. Pechter reminds us, it's worth reasserting that "there's probably been no other artistic medium in this century whose appeal rests so strongly on the human presence, and in which the human image has occupied a place of such primacy and centrality."

Because the pieces are written by a diverse group and in formats as varied as film reviews, book reviews, and even obituaries, they suggest a multiplicity of valid approaches for considering the role of the movie star. For one thing, many of the pieces show us how much a film depends on particular casting choices. By definition a star has an identifiable film persona that continues between and beyond particular movies. So we viewers meet the star halfway, bringing with us to the film a set of expectations about the performer which the film either depends on or plays against. The screenwriters do not have to devote much time to establishing the integrity of a Henry Fonda or a Jimmy Stewart. By contrast, to cast either actor in an unlikable role is to tamper with our sympathies in ways which may subtly extend our compassion for the character or which may provoke our hostility and backfire disastrously. This issue of casting against a preestablished type is raised in the Part I discussions of stars vs. actors. Many of today's serious actors (Jack Nicholson, Al Pacino), though they may have the charisma of the old-fashioned superstars, prefer to avoid star status precisely so that they can continue to extend themselves over a wide range of roles often denied to a star.

One way, then, to think about stars is to consider how much of a film's meaning depends on our previous familiarity with its leading players. That is one function of the career reviews in this anthology. On the one hand, they enable us to see the persona that continues even when a star appears to have assumed a variety of roles within a diversity of genres. On the other hand, some of the critics here answer charges that certain stars "merely" play themselves. Defenders of Clint Eastwood and Cary Grant, for example, suggest that there are greater subtlety and variation in the two actors' performances than are generally acknowledged, and, furthermore, that in some cases their roles are actually ironic comments on their previous film appearances.

Some of the pieces here dwell less on how star casting affects a given movie than on what the star represents to the nation that collectively worships him or her. This more sociological approach is based on the premise that our stars tell us a lot about ourselves and the national self-image. Charles Champlin has observed that "each generation alters the specifications for its stars, reflecting new currents and aspirations in the society at large." Many of these pieces propose reasons for a particular era's attention to its stars: during the Depression Astaire creates "the fantasy of an aristocracy based on charm and ability"; in the forties Crawford symbolizes "the American Dream of upward social mobility"; in the Eisenhower era Brando and Dean offer "an image of instinctive rebellion" that was otherwise repressed; and in the aftermath of Kent State and Watergate Jack Nicholson suggests "modern absurdism with a new whiff of heroism."

The analysis can't stop at national borders. What is it that makes yesterday's cowboy hero or today's Burt Reynolds the number-one box-office draw abroad? What made Hirohito, when he visited the United States in 1975, ask to meet John Wayne? (Jack Kroll suggests an answer.) Conversely, it's worth pondering, as we read the pieces on foreign actors, what characteristics the Italians, the French, and the English look for in their own stars, and what makes some of those stars internationally beloved, while others have tremendous, but only local, popularity.

In explaining the appeal of the stars, the critics here attempt to deal with the special relationship between viewer and screen actor. In the theater the magic comes from the reciprocal interaction between a live audience and a live actor in a shared space. But on the screen there is another kind of "presence"—an immediacy established by certain actors. For instance, Penelope Gilliatt speaks of Marilyn Monroe's "curious phosphorescence on film. . . . Her sheer gift of poignant physical presence is an essence of film acting."

Our physical, even sexual, attraction to film stars is something these critics do not slight. They recognize that our fascination with celebrities is made up of parts intellectual, curious (nosy?), emotional. While some of these pieces are the product of years of viewing and thinking, others are daily reviews that, if less reflective, capture instead the immediacy of performance and reaction. The critics may even acknowledge the trickiness of their situation—of that relation between star and critic which Richard Corliss has called one of "professional exhibitionist to professional voyeur."

If the nation's best film critics are no less vulnerable to star magnetism than the rest of us, they are nevertheless much more astute observers of the phenomenon and can help point out the particulars that make a star attractive and distinctive. They analyze the telling physical details: Gregory Peck's authoritative but vulnerable voice, John Wayne's "portentous but oddly delicate" walk, Barbra Streisand's "flaunting" use of makeup (right down to her unique way of painting fingernails!).

One of the central questions about film acting is: Who deserves credit for shaping a performance or a legend. There is the old-time studio, of course, which controlled not only publicity but which parts the contractees would play. There are the screenwriters, who may have invented a character from scratch or who may have written with the personality of the actor in mind as Ruth Gordon and Garson Kanin did for Katharine Hepburn and Judy Holliday. During the shooting the strongest force is likely to be the director, who might emphasize or even create certain aspects of a star's persona (see Andrew Sarris's discussion of James Stewart for some examples). At the other extreme we have the director chosen for having a nonassertive personality by a star, like Barbra Streisand, who wants to—literally—call the shots. Then there is the influence of the cameraman—the one constant in Garbo's Hollywood career. And in postproduction, it is the editor who can create or destroy a performance. Hence the struggle for rights of final cut (the released version of the film) among producer, director, and star. These articles do not pretend to settle the old dispute about who creates the role but they do help us appreciate the variety of influences.

All the problems of writing about actors are multiplied when critic meets star head on. And so some special remarks need to be made about interviews, which are, perhaps, the hardest pieces to write on stars. For, as Kirk Douglas tells Roger Ebert, an interview doesn't simply report what somebody said; it incorporates the point of view of the interviewer.

An interview involves a pact between writer and actor. The one needs publicity; the other needs fresh copy. On the one side is an actor who doesn't want his privacy violated. Yet he is also a star who must exercise considerable charm to preserve and promote his public image. But the critic is also wearing two hats. He is likely to be a fan meeting someone whom he has, like the rest of us, previously worshipped from afar. But the critic is also a journalist who can wield considerable word power. Despite the initial pact between writer and actor, there's a struggle for control over the actor's public image.

Some finished articles retain enough of their give-and-take to let us watch that struggle. (Occasionally a writer will exaggerate the tension, just to add some bite to the piece.) A critic may actually draw attention to the struggle by quoting something the star supposedly said off-the-record. If the writer then quotes the star as saying "Don't print that!" we can take it two ways. Either this is the playful result of a collaboration between critic and star, which lets the reader feel he has shared some relatively privy information, or the act is more malicious. If the critic wants to expose his subject, however, there is still an ethical problem—one of being honest without being irresponsible, critical without being cruel.

To be sure, any direct quotations are potentially dangerous. It is all too easy to let the subjects hang themselves by quoting them accurately but out of context. Most often, however, the interviews in this anthology that quote their subjects at great length (such as the interviews of Robert Mitchum and Kirk Douglas) use the conversational style to capture the vitality, integrity, or charm of the speaker. It is left for the reader to judge whether the personality that emerges is the real actor or just another role he puts on for interviews.

The fun in reading an interview comes from finding the subtext—the indications of the writer's true feelings even as he is being polite or even obsequious on the surface. To some extent the critic must be the pawn of the actor—especially the vintage movie king or queen who wants to exploit the critic to help perpetuate the legend. A sharp writer can undercut that manipulation. He can change the nature of the interview—get beyond the superficial—by establishing a rapport that enables the conversation to go beyond the star's oft-repeated clichés. Or, failing any cooperation, the writer can indicate his attitude through language. The critic can use an ironic tone that makes self-mockery of his own apparent deference to the star. It is up to the reader to determine, when critic meets glamorous star, whether the critic is responding with tongue hanging out or tongue in cheek—or both. The Bardot interview, for example, is an artful instance of writing style that captures the superficiality of the subject while commenting on it at the same time.

This is not to say that the pieces here are mostly negative. In fact, I have deliberately emphasized pieces of constructive criticism for this anthology. It is all too easy to denounce a performance, but it takes a discerning professional to show us why it's special.

Two short disclaimers: First, the inclusion or exclusion of certain stars and the length of pieces on them do not necessarily indicate the editor's or the society's opinion about their relative importance. (Names of actors and actresses who are discussed in other than separate entries can be found in the Index.) The aim here is to suggest, within limited space, the range and variety of approaches that may be validly applied to the subject of screen stardom. Second, the National Society of Film Critics is supported solely by the income from this series of anthologies, to which the writers contribute pieces that have usually appeared earlier in more ephemeral formats. Hence the number of pieces by a critic in each anthology depends mostly on his interest in a given subject and the format of the periodical for which he writes. The resulting diversity of perspectives should offer a broad view of the best writing on the topic and, in this case, an expanded appreciation of the nature and importance of screen acting.

Finally, special thanks to Herbert Hartig, Mary Corliss, Edwin Kennebeck, an editor for all seasons, and those critics who helped round out the anthology by writing new pieces for it: Richard Corliss, Dave Kehr, George Morris, and Peter Rainer.

—Elisabeth Weis

I.
THE STAR SYSTEM

Gary Cooper, Oscar, and James Stewart. Cooper receives
the award for his performance in *Sergeant York*.

THE DECLINE

Colin L. Westerbeck

STARS VS. ACTORS
The Importance of Being Oscar

In dusty little shops with names like "Memory Lane" or "High Camp, Inc.," one can still sometimes find prints of a remarkable photograph that was taken at M-G-M during World War II. The photograph looks as if it came from the yearbook of an unaccredited finishing school. Headmaster Louis B. Mayer is seated in the front-row center. Beside and behind him, like that year's doting senior class, are row upon row of M-G-M's top screen personalities: Jimmy Stewart, Katharine Hepburn, Greer Garson, Spencer Tracy, William Powell, et al. M-G-M's motto at the time was "More stars than there are in heaven . . ." and the picture confirms it. If the occasion was Mr. Mayer's birthday, as it may well have been, he'd awarded himself a star for each of his fifty-plus years, and at least a half dozen to grow on.

Were we not to recognize any of these people, however, the appointments in the room would still tell us unmistakably where the picture was taken. Off to one side of the assembled troupe is a dais, and on the dais is a giant Oscar. It's hard to say whether Oscar has been precariously balanced on the dais or crudely superimposed on the photograph. Either way, the effect is that Oscar seems to be present as a tribal apparition, a dream in the studio's collective unconscious. Like something in the funny papers, he should be framed by a thought balloon with trails of little bubbles streaming out to every head in the room. For many of those stars the dream had or would come true. But the star system in the M-G-M picture has become as much a collector's item as the picture itself, and perhaps Oscar has too.

Every once in a while there's an Academy Award nomination that tips you off Oscar is getting senile. It's like watching some elderly public figure go through momentary lapses where he mistakes an oak tree for his dearest friend. Just last year the Academy nominated Dustin Hoffman as best actor for *Midnight Cowboy*, and this year it's nominated George C. Scott for the title role in *Patton*. The embarrassing thing about both these nominations is that they seem to acknowledge the nominees' range as performers. Would a star have been allowed to go from the clean-cut and bewildered young man Hoffman played in *The Graduate* to the grubby, hustling Enrico Rizzo of *Midnight Cowboy*? Certainly not. Range is one thing that was forbidden to a star. Scott's *faux pas* is of even greater proportions, for he has shown extraordinary range within a single performance. The film's characterization of

Patton can only be described with oxymorons. Patton is an *idiot savant,* a cultured vulgarian, a preposterous and bellicose mystic. But Scott has made him credible anyway—has, indeed, made him all the more credible for his inconsistencies and contradictions.

By popping off at the Academy and disdaining its award, Scott has also accepted his nomination with a graciousness the Academy can hardly fail to appreciate. He's given the Academy a perfect (if irrelevant) excuse not to award him the Oscar. What could be more gracious than letting a rash and imprudently generous benefactor off the hook? The voting members of the Academy are fools if they don't accept Mr. Scott's magnanimous gesture and vote for someone else.

It may be clear that actors don't make suitable stars or Oscar recipients. But whether stars were capable of acting remains, in most cases, a moot question. In the *ancien régime* Cary Grant might have been cast as the Graduate, but if such a role had proved a big break for him, as it did for Hoffman, Mr. Grant could never have gone on to *Midnight Cowboy.* When he was cast as an ambiguous villain in Alfred Hitchcock's 1941 thriller *Suspicion,* RKO Pictures made Hitchcock change the film's ending so Grant could keep his star untarnished. Contrary to the implication of the entire plot, Grant had to be an innocent object of suspicion, and his roles haven't changed much since then. If we skip ahead twenty-two years in his career, we find him with Audrey Hepburn in *Charade,* still proving himself the innocent object of his heroine's suspicions.

Of course, it was Cary Grant, not Dustin Hoffman, who won an Academy Award last year. But that didn't surprise anyone. (None of the awards ever surprises anyone, except Richard Burton.) Mr. Grant was given a special award "for being Cary Grant," as Frank Sinatra pointed out in his presentation speech. Last year John Wayne was also given the best-actor award for being John Wayne, although nobody bothered to point that out. Perhaps it didn't need pointing out. All stars have received their Oscars for the same reason.

The Academy of Motion Picture Arts and Sciences was Louis B. Mayer's brainchild. He first conceived it in 1927 as a service to the industry's elite corps, especially the stars. Despite such contributions to the system, however, Mayer was preoccupied with forms of stardom that were far too primitive and rudimentary. His primary achievement at M-G-M during the 1930s was the production of a great many series films—films that tried to cash in on the popularity of a single role. Because these M-G-M products— the Andy Hardy comedies, for instance, which featured Mickey Rooney, and William Powell's Thin Man vehicles—are so literal-minded a use of the star system, they don't represent the system's best refinements.

A star doesn't have to play the same role in every film: he only has to be the same character no matter what the role is. When Universal put M-G-M graduate Marjorie Main through the Ma Kettle mill, a character actress was made into a star. When Mayer himself converted the Dr. Kildare series into a perambulator for Lionel Barrymore, a star was made into a character actor. But it's a different thing altogether to exploit fully the fact that every star is already a character actor by nature. Even in its use of the Katharine Hepburn–Spencer Tracy team M-G-M didn't realize the potential of stardom as well as one of the other Hollywood studios.

Jack Warner was the guy who knew what stardom was all about. A group portrait taken at Warner Brothers around the time of the one from M-G-M would have included people who were the very essence of stardom. It would have contained such luminaries as Bette Davis, Humphrey Bogart, Errol Flynn, and James Cagney. True to *his* wisdom that one well-defined convention is what makes a star, Warner put these performers through a grueling schedule of genre films. During the first two decades of the talkies, Bogart and Cagney made so many gangster movies so fast that neither of them could remember later which movie was which. It's no wonder, either. Their careers must have come to seem like endless rehearsals for a play that would never open.

There's a moment in *Public Enemy,* a gangster classic made in 1931, when Cagney smacks his moll with a half a grapefruit, "right in de kissah," as he would say. A wave of his hair drops over his forehead, he rolls his boozy-looking eyes up at the girl, and wields the grapefruit as if it were a pie and he were a Laurel-and-Hardy extra. It's a superb moment that hangs right in the balance, uncertain whether it's funny or disgracefully brutal. It's also a moment that *is* Cagney. The substantial acting in dozens of his movies amounts to no more than that one gesture.

After Bette Davis received an Academy Award for her 1935 performance in *Dangerous,* she let slip that the award was only a make-good: she should have received it the previous year, for *Of Human Bondage.* For a star born and bred at Warner Brothers, this egotism was a bit unprofessional. Any Warner talent should have known what Bogart and Cagney knew—that in the work of the ideal star, no particular film should be distinguishable from any other. In another sense, though, Miss Davis's slap at the Academy was quite proper and right in character for a star. The ultimate quality of stardom is that it's a state where art and life meet. If Miss Davis deserved an Oscar for playing a bitchy ingrate, then she should be a little bitchy and ungrateful. (In 1939, she would get the Oscar she deserved for a role that suited her, *Jezebel.*)

No star tried to live up to this highest standard of performance more sincerely than Errol Flynn. Bogart and Cagney may have confused one movie with another, but Flynn managed to confuse his movies with his life. *My Wicked, Wicked Ways,* which was a 1959 sequel to his first autobiography, recounts numerous improbable adventures straight out of the Warner Brothers story department. There is even some irony in the last true adventure he had before he died at age fifty. Sensing that one of the twentieth century's greatest epics was about to be shot on location in Cuba, he rushed off to join the revolution. He managed to get nicked in the crossfire, decorated by Fidel and sent home to a fanfare of press agents. The irony is that low-budget indies like the Cuban Revolution are where the current stars come from. After it leaves the theater, the audience doesn't need Errol Flynn's stardom. It has Che Guevara to believe in this year.

The thing about a Dustin Hoffman that disgusts the old-timers is the fact that he doesn't even try to be a star. If Hoffman ever writes his memoirs, the closest they will come to real-life adventure will probably be that day last year when the town house next to his Greenwich Village apartment blew up. As Hoffman arrived on the scene, the television interviewers crowded around him. "Well," he began, "I was up at the office and . . ." Need I go further? Nobody who has an office is going to be a star, let alone somebody who admits to the public that he has one. But it's instructive to go a little further: "I was up at the office, and when I heard what'd happened I came down to see whether I could save my turtles." Turtles? Faced with England's quarantine laws, a star like Elizabeth Taylor may rent a yacht in the Thames just to accommodate her poodle. But in an emergency real stars have to have pet leopards to rescue. Hoffman just isn't the kind of person whose private life is going to sell copies of *Silver Screen.*

If it's not dignifying camp too much, I think it's fair to say that audiences nowadays take mostly an anthropological interest in stardom. Guevaristas and Maoists may flock to Bogart festivals at the Brattle Theater in Cambridge or at the New Yorker. But if you ask about the Bogart legend, the only thing they know is that he copped out before the House Un-American Activities Committee.

As for the more recent comers who are trying to make it as stars, they're quickly turning into a vestigial part of the industry. Even compared to a dead and demythologized Bogart, a live Julie Andrews is a mummy in a glass display case. One of her more recent efforts, inauspiciously entitled *Star!,* should have been called *Fizzle*! It did so poorly Twentieth Century-Fox has had to rerelease it under the appropriate retitle *Those WERE the Happy Times* (emphasis added).

While no actor can be a star, it should be admitted that a few stars did get a chance to prove they could act. Though only perfecting her stardom in *Jezebel,* when Miss Davis played the naïve girl in *The Petrified Forest* she showed that she had range as an actress. Humphrey Bogart did the same thing in *The Treasure of the Sierra Madre* and *The African Queen.* But for many stars—John Wayne is a prime example—the most daring departure from the routine of stardom has been a few late films that are parodies of their own early work. An acid test for identifying a star, as opposed to a mere actor, is that any stand-up comic who's not tone deaf can do imitations of stars. Try doing an imitation of Dustin Hoffman.

In the early days movies were considered an infra-dig art form, and studio heads had terrible feelings of insecurity. Oscar's purpose was to compensate for this. The psychology behind Oscar was a sound one: if you want to dignify something, pin a medal on it. The English Crown made respectable culture heroes out of scores of charlatans and brigands just by giving them the OBE. Why couldn't Hollywood do the same? Oscar offered Hollywood some assurance of its own significance; and even if it was only self-assurance, it was effective for awhile. But in the long run Oscar was humiliated by the very industry he was supposed to help dignify. The trouble with him is that he's the archetypal Hollywood yes-man. The model who sat for that little bronze statuette wasn't some Greek god of excellence: he was the studio flunky, one of the omnipresent factotums with whom movie moguls surrounded themselves. Oscar was never a young man with great expectations. He was always just a retainer who would some day have to pay for all the privilege he'd had.

That day arrived sometime during the mid-fifties, even before Guevara upstaged Errol Flynn. Big-budget films began requiring that extra publicity only Oscar could provide. Otherwise, it was apparent, heavy investments were going to be lost at the box office. As a result, the star system Oscar was designed to enhance began depending on him just to survive. The Academy Awards became more like a Welfare Program than an investiture. Oscar was given as a form of Aid to Dependent Children—in recognition of need, not merit.

Now that Oscar has been so demeaned, it's a good question whether he's worth giving away at all, or worth receiving. George C. Scott obviously doesn't think he is. Of course, there's always a chance that the Academy will award the Oscar to Scott anyway. I said before that, out of gratitude for Scott's contempt, the Academy members ought to vote for someone else. But on second thought, I'm not sure. If they vote for Scott, everything may come right in the end, like the plot of an Elizabethan comedy of errors. Scott couldn't possibly accept the award now, after he's been so upset about merely being nominated. Accepting would damage his own reputation as well as Oscar's. So Scott will refuse, and thereby save both reputations. The perfect solution. If only every serious actor would behave in this churlish fashion, it might give stardom a chance to make a comeback. This would also give Oscar the one chance he has for survival.

[1971]

Richard Schickel

STARS vs. CELEBRITIES
The Deterioration of the Star System

Long before anyone saw it on film, it was a famous scene: the actor Rip Torn, without obvious provocation, attacking Norman Mailer with a hammer, taking him by surprise and, in the subsequent wrestle, getting his ear bitten by the startled writer, who was fighting back with whatever weapons the memory of former street brawls suggested.

The encounter came when Mailer thought he had finished principal photography on *Maidstone*, his latest home movie (it cost over a quarter of a million dollars), but it was recorded by D. A. Pennebaker, the *cinéma-verité* filmmaker, who was serving as Mailer's cinematographer. Without actually reviewing *Maidstone*, I want to use this, its final scene, as a point of departure for some thoughts it provoked in me about public performance—the art of it and the changing expectations all of us, actors and audience alike, now entertain for it.

Mailer is strongly committed to what, for want of a better term, we might call improvisatory moviemaking. Toward the end of *Maidstone*, when he was under the misapprehension that it was all over, he called together his cast—many of them not professional actors but friends he had managed to enlist—and tried to explain what he thought they had all been doing during the several days they had spent on Gardiner's Island, off Long Island, making the film's climactic scenes. In essence, he told them—while Pennebaker's cameras continued to run—that he sees filmmaking as analogous to a military operation. There is an objective, there are plans, but as the "army" begins to execute these plans, unexpected contingencies arise and new strategies must be invented, under pressure, to cope with the new developments. The objective—the film's meaning—remains clear, but the means of achieving it necessarily change, and, in the end, the movie defines itself as the classic "existential hero" does, not through whatever ideal it may aspire to, but through the process of trying to attain to that ideal. Mailer's point was similar to the point Harold Rosenberg has made in discussing Gide's *The Counterfeiters*; the true novel of our time, said Rosenberg, "must be improvised out of events that take place independently of the intentions of the actors, and . . . it can have no ending any more than events do."

This, precisely, was the point that Rip Torn failed to grasp. *Maidstone* is a fantasy in Mailer's presidential series and its purpose, other than as an episode in the continuing drama of Mailer's own celebrity (of which more later), is to examine the conditions under which, in our highly volatile society, a famous artist (in this case a movie director played by Mailer and, except for his occupation, indistinguishable from Mailer in viewpoint) might become a serious candidate for president and how such a figure might, simply by virtue of being a celebrity, also be a candidate for assassination, only slightly increasing the risk when he formally enters politics. (Informally, as Mailer understands, any celebrity is in politics whether he likes it or not, just as political figures are in art—or at least show business—as we now define it, whether *they* like it or not.)

If, however, Mailer gave his "army" to understand that their "objective" was to create a situation in which he (or the character he was playing) might believably be killed, his army—for reasons not entirely clear in the film itself—never quite managed to storm that position. Though some violence did occur in the scene where, logically, the Mailer character should have been killed, it was not directed at Mailer. Still, given his belief in the existentially self-defining work of art, that was all right with Mailer. In effect, the people had spoken and, perhaps, given a sign—that in times so desperately out of joint only an out-of-joint personality could hope to survive in public life.

But it was not all right with Torn. He is, after all, something of a celebrity himself and actors of repute take on projects, even such unstructured ones as this, in expectation of getting at least one good scene they can call their own. Throughout *Maidstone* Torn can be observed skulking around the edges of other people's scenes, but by the time he had confidently "wrapped" his film, Mailer had still not given Torn a fair chance to do his stuff, a chance to which, under all the laws and customs of his profession, he was entitled as the only "name" actor present. In fact, watching the film, the audience—conditioned to expect, no less than the stars themselves, star turns—is made dissatisfied by the underutilization of Torn. Tantalized by glimpses of him, one keeps waiting to see Torn cut that demented energy of his loose, and the longer he is prevented from doing so, the more anxious one becomes. Thus, when he finally does take matters into his own hands, one feels, among other less exalted feelings, a certain sense of relief.

Probably it was the ham in Rip Torn that forced itself out in the end. Yet in speculating about what he did and why, some attention should also be paid to the theatrical traditionalist who abides vestigially in all actors and especially in one who has had his share of antiheroic roles of late, is probably sick of the fashion for irresolute movies, and who may very well instinctively sense that men like Mailer, with their sophisticated understanding of the new celebrity game (which derives from the comparatively simple star system but is so much more complex to manage), are driving actors to the sidelines of public attention, just as Torn is driven to the fringes of this film.

Even if that reading imputes too much to Torn's sociological intelligence, he must still be given credit, at least, for keen theatrical professionalism, for understanding the dramatic imperative to prevent the movie from just sputtering out, as Mailer was apparently willing to let it do, by simply rationalizing his method and explaining how the very lack of a strong conclusion validated that method. Torn clearly sensed that *Maidstone* needed what he was prepared to supply: a highly dramatic resolution, a big finish. And so, indeed, he insists in justifying his action to Mailer after the wrestling match is concluded, and the director and the actor—with, of course, Pennebaker's camera still running—continue their argument verbally. One is aware, by this point, that Torn has been right all along. The scene does not "work" within the sketchy fictional framework Mailer has long since demolished (as Torn should probably have realized); yet it does provide the film with an ending and perhaps even with its chief rationale for existence. And Mailer now seems to agree that *Maidstone* needed this scene as much as Torn's aching ego did.

But when Torn picked up his hammer and started flailing away at an entirely astonished Mailer, I had the feeling that he was taking up the cudgels not only for himself but for his profession as well. He was a man in revolt against the definition of himself as a mere extension—a sort of unconscious plaything—of the *auteur,* who may talk about the freedom of the actors to improvise solutions to the problems encountered on the way to the objective he has defined for them, but who actually provides the sole organizing principle of the work himself—and usually much later in the cutting room when the actors have moved on to other concerns. This total surrender of self to director is growing in movie work, where, increasingly, directors improvise as they go along, or withhold knowledge of a script's resolution from their actors, or force them to repeat and repeat a scene (as John Cassavetes does) until they lose their bearings and begin to behave with unscripted craziness. As a result, the situation that had previously pertained, in which there were several power centers in the creation of a movie and the leading actor certainly commanded one of them, is replaced by a kind of centralization of power, an exclusive concentration of it into the mind and will of the director.

The point deserves some expansion: until very recently each film in which a particular star might appear was properly seen—if not by him, then by his fans—as but a single event in a much larger drama, namely, the star's career. He came to each new enterprise trailing behind him (and often tripping over) the wisps of former parts, and we were pleased or displeased in the degree that, in his new role, he fulfilled our unspoken expectations. If, in addition, he provided some small variation on his basic personal theme, some new characterological wrinkle (such as, for example, the self-parody that began to creep into John Wayne's performances long before it fully bloomed in *True Grit*), then we counted ourselves twice-blessed.

It might even be said hyperbolically that the movie star fulfilled some of the functions of the hero in classic drama. We grasped that his fate was predetermined, as though by the gods, in that he was limited by the very workings of genetics in the roles he might undertake; Wayne could not, for example, essay drawing-room comedy while Cary Grant (or Humphrey Bogart, for that matter) did not sit comfortably in a Western saddle. Moreover, we felt that, if the gods did not actually descend onto the stage at the end of the star's life to decree his fate, it was nevertheless, often as not, an inexorable one. Some actors, like Wayne, Henry Fonda, and James Stewart, proved to be durable types with extremely long careers. Others were momentary phenomena, whose vogue passed quickly. Still others were tragically flawed, like Marilyn Monroe, and were unable to deal successfully either with the peaks or the valleys of their careers and ended up drunks or suicides or the most pathetic kind of has-beens—doing small parts on television situation comedies or working in the soaps. It is not for nothing that one of the most enduring themes in our popular culture has been the one which was archetypically stated in *A Star Is Born*.

Recently, however, things have begun to change. Show business, which used to be rigged in favor of the star, is now largely rigged against him. This is not to say that many who are serious (or at least sober) about their work do not find the new arrangement more congenial. Nor is it to imply that all the reasons for the change in emphasis are sociopsychological. Economics has a great deal to do with the matter. Star salaries rose to such impossible heights in the last decade or so that few if any of the names billed above the title could any longer perform the economic function they once did, which was to guarantee box-office success for any project they appeared in. Then, too, with fewer big features being produced, fewer stars are presently needed. It has become almost impossible for young actors to work in three or four films a year—as was the case when studios would put young people under term contracts and build them into valuable properties by the simple process of repeatedly exposing them to the public gaze.

But even if none of these factors had come into play, and even if the movies had not been economically reduced by television, I think it likely that the institution of stardom would have undergone the radical alteration we have been witnessing. To begin with, it must be remembered that stars were created and existed in a highly stylized world, that of the sound stage and the back lot, and although Hollywood prided itself on its ability to re-produce reality in those confines, the fact is that it never really did. The best Western or suburban or small town or New York street (to name the most common permanent back lot installations) were never more than good generalizations. They lacked the feel of actuality. They lacked specificity. They looked like everywhere and nowhere. We applauded the miracle of how close they came to natural and architectural truth, all the while picking up, out of the corner of our eye, as it were, comforting reminders that it was all a clever, pleasing fake: and, of course, a perfect setting for stars who were, like the sets themselves, generalizations from types, so much like us in all the unimportant ways that we were carried, all unknowing and uncaring, over the line into fantasy when they suddenly became untypically brave or witty or romantically apt.

Thus the beginning of the decline of the star system coincides with Hollywood's abandonment of the back lot and the sound stage to television. Today one of the competitive edges the movies have over television is their ability not only to go out into our own streets for background but into any street, no matter how exotic or inaccessible, anywhere in the world. The fact that it is technologically now possible to pack cast, crew, and all the equipment they need into a Cinemobile Systems bus makes it easier and cheaper to borrow reality as a stage than to reproduce or simulate it. And so it is that for ten or fifteen years now most of the best films have been shot *en plein air* or on location.

But notice: the stars don't really fit here. Watching an essentially unreal figure like Kirk Douglas move around a New Jersey Italian neighborhood (*The Brotherhood*) or watching him drive on a Los Angeles freeway (*The Arrangement*), we are jarred by the inappropriateness. He belonged to a back-lot world and he now seems right only when set into a period as remote from living reality as his own star personality is—in something like *There Was a Crooked Man*, an exotic Western rendered even more exotic by its curious setting (a prison in the middle of a desert). For what we really want in the new, totally real settings are anonymous faces, somewhat familiar-looking but not excessively so. Against such backgrounds the faces of movie stars stick out like a sore thumb: what, we wonder, are *they* doing there?

Another reason why the star system is likely to continue its decline is that, as with every other cultural commodity, so with the stars—our attention span is shorter than ever. Thus we now see show-business phenomena like Elliott Gould, who has gone from discovery to stardom to decline in eighteen months—an entire career compressed into a wink of history's eye.

But far more damaging to the institution of stardom than the working of movie economics, technological change, and the shortening of the public's attention span, is the effect of democratization. Metaphorically, of course, movie stars have always rubbed shoulders with celebrities from other fields in the gossip columns, but it was not until television in general, and the talk shows in particular, began to force them into closer, often accidental, intimacy with figures of greater substantiality and substance, figures so often superior to them socially and intellectually if not in physical beauty, that the stars began to suffer by comparison. The fact is that movie stars, until recently, existed in, depended on, remoteness to achieve their hold upon us. The task of their press agents was, largely, to protect them from intrusion, and on those rare occasions when they were placed on public exhibition, to make sure it was a controlled situation—a premiere, for example, or the kind of large event (a war-bond rally, for instance) where distance lent enchantment.

In his pioneering chapter on celebrity in *The Power Elite,* C. Wright Mills quoted Gustave Le Bon to the effect that "From the moment prestige is called in question it ceases to be prestige. The gods and men who have kept their prestige for long have never tolerated discussion. For the crowd to admire, it must be kept at a distance." It follows that a discussion program on television, a medium the prime power of which is to reduce distance, is the worst possible place for a star to show himself—unless he happens to be uncommonly intelligent, aware of how the power of the medium works and how to disarm it. (A common ploy, used by veteran and especially prestigious stars, is to insist on being isolated with the host, as Fred Astaire, for example, did when an entire Dick Cavett show was devoted to him.)

But most stars, though they have insatiable egos, also have a sort of innocence about them, which is why when they are belatedly politicized they usually talk and behave like such idiots. Most of them have no understanding of the nature of the enterprise in which they are engaged, often naïvely clinging to the notion that they are just actors, stoutly insisting that their obligation to the public ends with performing roles, and not noticing that actors who are only role players are almost never stars—unless of course they are English and knighted. Many of them search all their lives for "different" parts, complaining bitterly about typecasting, never comprehending that for a star—each of whose roles is only a single episode in the larger drama of his entire career—gross novelty is likely to be disastrous. Who needs a hero turning suddenly into a villain in the middle of the play?

It is this strange, even self-destructive, insistence on an attenuated self-definition that gets them into trouble. They like to think they are just ordinary people, despite their wealth and their isolation (no true star travels without a herd of flunkies, their function being to condition the psychic air around him to the temperature he finds most comfortable). But naturally, when they descend to less rarefied atmospheres where breathe variety headliners, real working actors, major and minor politicians, and authors plugging their latest books, the situation becomes quite different. Plunged on a talk show into a set of conditions he does not control—that is, into a reality that has been defined by someone else, someone who has his own fish to fry and can't be bothered with protecting him—the star is often left gasping pitifully for breath.

To put the matter bluntly, it requires a more supple and intelligent awareness of self and world than the average movie star possesses to manage the modern celebrity game successfully—and manage it Norman Mailer has, as well as anyone and better than most. For it is, of course, in the business of defining reality to suit himself that Mailer is most a genius. The drama he has constructed revolves around the question of just how great a writer he is. Will he finally produce the great novel he has publicly and repeatedly announced as his goal? Or will he instead redefine this novel to suit his talents, as he has come very close to doing with his brilliant ventures into journalism? Might he actually write his novel on film or through one of his candidacies for public office? Will he succeed in imposing upon all of us a truly lively awareness that in our time the great literary form is autobiography, chapters of which are to be written in all the different media, and the ending and meaning of which remain unknown to the author himself?

It should in sum be clear, then, that we are: (a) in a period where intelligence of Mailer's order is necessary to survive within the celebrity system; that (b) the line between fiction and journalism is being blurred not only by the presentation of imaginary toads (the stars) in real—much too real—gardens, but by the *cinéma-verité* directors who increasingly deal not with reality as they discover it but as they restructure it (a good example being those movies about rock concerts that are set up primarily so that movies can be made of them); that (c) stars—and other actors too—are and will increasingly be subjected to experiences such as Rip Torn suffered in *Maidstone*, namely, engagements in films that deny them that sense of dramatic closure which they require both for their own instinctual satisfaction and for the creation—and re-creation—of an image that will resonate satisfactorily with the audience, stimulating a desire for replication in future films.

I doubt that there is much the star or the would-be star can do about this situation. For the director, as Truffaut once said, "is the only one to carry the whole film in his head." As such, he is always potentially the great creative hero of our culture and the middlebrow audience is bound to see those who work for him as mere extensions of his artistic will. Moreover, the more intellectually sophisticated directors, whether they be professionals like Godard or talented amateurs like Mailer, share a desire to make movies that have at least the look of being "advanced forms of art" in which, according to Harold Rosenberg, "the indeterminacy of the act" is an underlying principle. They must therefore deny to the star those actions from which, in the past, he (and the audience) derived—often falsely, of course—the feeling that it was the star who controlled events. They thus deny to the star his traditional melodramatic ability to achieve heroic stature simply by resolving conflicts, and thereby walling off the work of art from the ravages of ordinary experience and of ordinary time.

I am not, I discover, entirely happy with those "advanced forms" that stress "the indeterminacy of the act," and as I think about it I am grateful to Rip Torn for acting upon his primitive and no doubt irrational distrust of Mailer's rather too comfortable embrace of indeterminacy as a principle, for doing his violent damnedest not to let *Maidstone* be just another happening. If there is any hope to be derived from the movie, it is in Mailer's acceptance of Torn's contribution as the climax of his work.

Without it, at any rate, we would have been denied contemplation of a most delicious irony. This is that by asserting his rights as a public person, Torn yanked Mailer right out of *his* public *persona*. For in the argument they have in the aftermath of the assault Mailer ceases, for the moment, to play the role of the avant-garde film artist and multimedia celebrity, and becomes, instead, what any of us would likely be in the circumstances—an aggrieved parent. What is truly unforgivable, he says, is that Torn assaulted him "in front of the children." And as glimpses of their frightened faces attest, Mailer was right to be angry on this score. In fact, one has never seen Mailer more appealing in public than he is here as a middle-class family man trying to protect his brood from the ugly realities of adult existence. And so, in a further ironic twist, Torn accidentally enhances the writer's celebrity, providing one of those off-guard snapshots of the famous that have traditionally enlivened mass-magazine profiles and which have the effect not of diminishing the celebrity in size but of humanizing him for the audience.

As usual, then, Mailer has provided us with material that forces us to contemplate a matter of major significance in the realities of our time, even though—in still another ironic twist—he required on this occasion the assistance of an actor giving vent to an old-fashioned, unchic, and entirely hammy instinct. Lovely. I haven't wanted to think so much about a single movie scene in years.

[1971]

(CLOCKWISE FROM NEAR RIGHT)

John Travolta. (*Saturday Night Fever*.
Copyright © MCMLXXVII by
Paramount Pictures Corporation.
All rights reserved.)

Jack Nicholson. (*Chinatown*.
Copyright © MCMLXXIV by Long Road
Productions. All rights reserved.)

Robert Redford.

Lily Tomlin. (*The Late Show*.
© Warner Bros. Inc. All rights reserved.
Used by permission.)

THE
NEW
BREED

Peter Rainer

DEAN vs. PRYOR
Acting in the Seventies

Offscreen, in interviews and on the talk shows, some of America's most enduringly successful actors seem wised-up, dispirited. They're more cynical than their counterparts of a few generations ago. Typically, these actors are middle-aged men who made it in the fifties and sixties and are still snug in the saddle, riding into a new decade. The notion that acting is not a fit occupation for a grown man has been around a long time, but it's become almost a daily refrain on the talk-show circuit.

Actors like Robert Redford, George C. Scott, Marlon Brando, and Paul Newman publicly regard their acting as a necessary evil—it allows them the luxury of doing what really "matters" in their lives (politics, car-racing, ecology, etc.). Their phenomenal salary demands are a way of showing their contempt for Hollywood by sticking it to the bastards. When the demands are met, it only increases their contempt. Their faces grin back at us from the all-star block-buster movie posters like prize heads on a big-game hunter's trophy wall. The hunters' names may change from year to year (Joe Levine, Sir Lew Grade, Dino De Laurentiis, Irwin Allen, the Salkinds) but it's the same old floating crap game, with the same stars dealing from the same cold deck.

The successful middle-aged actor's cynicism rampant today can't all be blamed on male menopause; it has a lot to do with the increasing scarcity of movies being made—the scarcity of good roles. There were fewer than a hundred major studio projects released last year (with approximately the same number from independents); during the same time, the pool of "bankable" actors—actors with the name value to get a movie financed—has become a puddle. Formula plots in Hollywood have given way to formula financing. "It doesn't matter what the movie's about," goes the conventional wisdom. "Just get Charles Bronson or Steve McQueen and the rest will take care of itself."

But even the concept of star financing seems to have fallen through partway: Charles Bronson has been on a losing streak for the last few years (Lord knows, it has nothing to do with his acting; if anything, it's improved). Steve McQueen's crack at Ibsen, *An Enemy of the People*, remains in the can after a year; Paul Newman's last two—*Buffalo Bill and the Indians* and *Slapshot*—were box-office disappointments; so were Liza Minnelli's (*A Matter of Time* and *New York, New York*); Jack Nicholson's name didn't do much for *The Passenger* or *Missouri Breaks* or *Going South*; and George Segal and Elliott Gould have been in enough gobblers in the last five years to last each of them a lifetime. Instead of opening up the floodgates for the gifted but "unbankable," this trend seems to have made narrow-minded producers even narrower. In five years, the annual number of studio-financed films will be down to seven, and they will all star Barbra Streisand.

The open cynicism of the Newmans and the Scotts and the Brandos is a front for their creative frustrations. The proof is, when they have a decent role, they go all the way with it: Scott in *Hospital* and *Islands in the Stream* (and, on Broadway, *Death of a Salesman*); Newman in *Buffalo Bill* and *Slapshot*; Brando in *Last Tango in Paris*. These performances represent what is probably the best work of their careers. James Cagney and Cary Grant gave almost a lifetime of pleasure to audiences, but they probably were right to quit when they did; they were turning into less spry versions of what we always loved them for, and mealy-mouthed old-codger roles seemed just around the corner. Even if old age had made them deeper actors, I'm not sure that would have been what anyone wanted. (I like Cary Grant in *None but the Lonely Heart*, his "best" performance, but I love him in *North by Northwest*.)

But, after *Last Tango in Paris*, who would wish Marlon Brando into comfortable retirement? He may be aging to look ravaged, bloated, but he still has his danger. Even in the stills for *Apocalypse Now*, he carries more force than most actors do on screen. George C. Scott will soon be seen in Paul Schrader's *Hard Core*—no piece of fluff; Paul Newman, despite the commercial failure of *Buffalo Bill*, has already finished another movie for Robert Altman (*Quintet*). It's not the good roles which make these actors openly cynical; it's the humiliating work and the interminable wait in between. How horrible it would be for us all if one day these actors decided it wasn't worth the wait. Hollywood hasn't made it difficult for them to be actors (a star can always get work), but it's made it difficult for them to be artists. Laurence Olivier, the great actor of the century, wasn't "bankable" until just recently. And what has he been starring in? *Sleuth, Marathon Man*, cameos in the *The Seven-Per-Cent Solution* and *A Bridge Too Far, The Betsy*, and *The Boys from Brazil*. The big-game hunters like to have Olivier around; he gives their junk class.

Against all odds, Olivier is *still* terrific in these films, but other actors wade through a steady stream of junk without much effect at all. It's becoming painful to watch George Segal. *Fun with Dick and Jane* was bad enough, but *The Duchess and the Dirtwater Fox* and *Who's Killing the Great Chefs of Europe?*! What made Segal so interesting a few years back—in movies like *Born to Win, Loving, Where's Poppa?, Blume in Love,* and *California Split*—was the suggestion of pain inside his funny faces. Movies used to have one sustained tone throughout—funny or scary, upbeat, downbeat—but some of the best movies of the seventies—the films of Scorsese, DePalma, Altman, and others—are a deliberate jumble of disparate tones. Segal's actor's compression of sweet and funny and slapstick sad seemed to make him the ideal new movie star. He could express torment in a new way: he incarnated the emotionalism of the most progressive movies of the seventies. But the only torment Segal expresses now is the torment of a gifted actor getting rich off his own profligacy. How long will it be before he's entombed in a Hollywood Square?

Elliott Gould's record is even worse. After *The Long Goodbye* his career seemed ready to take off again but, except for *California Split*, there's been *I Will, I Will, For Now, Whiffs*, a real stinker about germ warfare, a dumb cameo in *A Bridge Too Far, Matilda*, a "comedy" about a boxing kangaroo, and *Capricorn One.* It's hard to believe now that he was the number one movie idol on college campuses in the early 1970s. Gould had a goofy athleticism in his early roles (*Bob & Carol & Ted & Alice, M*A*S*H*); he was grungy yet hip, and that appealed to students who saw themselves not only as bedraggled odd-men-out but as *winners*. Gould—like Woody Allen—was a winner who looked like a loser. Curled up inside the slouch and the loose jaw and the glassy eyes was a demon ready to spring, and when it did there was a rage upon the whole straight, uptight world. Gould seems to have slipped away from his own wild Twilight Zone, where he always did his hottest work, and joined that straight, uptight world. He acts willfully spaced out now, as if his vacancy could somehow float him above the awfulness of his recent movies and spare him shame.

In poignant contrast to these tired, hang-dog, going-through-the-motions, star-stoned trips is the work of young actors like Jeff Bridges, Richard Dreyfuss, Sissy Spacek, Harvey Keitel, John Travolta, Nick Nolte, and Gary Busey. What a collection of faces! Each new movie generation has its stars who repudiate the glossy image of those stars who came before them—and in turn become glossified. One can't help wondering whether it will be any different with these new kids in town. Or will they all George Segal-ize in ten years? (Perhaps Segal himself will revitalize, the way Brando did in the late sixties after a string of tired performances in dreadful movies.) There is probably more red-hot acting talent in American movies and television now than at any other time in our history. And, for most of these actors, their victories are the same old Hollywood victories of redeeming, through sheer force of talent, a counterfeit conception. What would *Somebody Killed Her Husband* be without Jeff Bridges? *The Goodbye Girl* without Richard Dreyfuss? *The Buddy Holly Story* without Gary Busey? Busey doesn't just impersonate Buddy Holly, he actively inhabits his spirit; he doesn't keep a respectful actor's distance from his character and so, like Bridges, Travolta, De Niro and others, he seems possessed on screen. (So did Sissy Spacek in *Carrie*. She looked like what came out of the Serpent's Egg.)

Some of the best actors work the least, and not always by choice. Blythe Danner's television performance in *Eccentricities of a Nightingale* is one of the finest on film but, except for *Lovin' Molly* (1974), the only starring role she's had in the movies has been opposite Peter Fonda in *Futureworld*, and that was three years ago. For those of us not close enough to New York to catch their stage work, there's been nothing from Lenny Baker or Ellen Greene since *Next Stop, Greenwich Village*. Why has Ronee Blakley appeared (and briefly) in only one Hollywood movie since *Nashville*? Shelley Duvall was terrific in *Bernice Bobs Her Hair* on television and in Altman's *3 Women;* she was even terrific playing a psychotic in a *Baretta* episode a few seasons ago. Don't performances like these *mean* anything to producers?

Everybody knows movies have become primarily a young person's entertainment (the vast majority of audiences are under thirty); but it's only recently that the problems of youth have become the main dramatic mode in movies. Character and conflict are expressed in coming-of-age terms. The tribal rituals of adolescents, and those just a bit older, have all the Hollywood juices now. An occasional *An Unmarried Woman* will lure adults into the triplex, but the other two screens will feature *Grease* and *Saturday Night Fever*. This is yet more bad news for the Paul Newmans and George C. Scotts— who wants to see them play *parents*—but it means that young actors have a chance to connect with prime moviegoers in a more vital way than ever before. Or does it?

I had large reservations about James Bridges' recent movie *September 30, 1955*, a period drama about an Arkansas college kid's infatuation with James Dean, but it made me wonder: Is it conceivable that a movie star today could have the impact on American youth that James Dean had on kids in the fifties? Dean is often spoken of as the last "real" star, the last movie actor to work his way into the collective national psyche. There's some truth in this. The Rebel Without a Cause was like a searing wound across the face of fifties movies. The directors and writers of movies like *The*

Wild One and *Rebel Without a Cause* may have tried to sentimentalize their rebels, make them part of a social "problem," but the presence of Dean and Brando was far more troubling, more *enigmatic* than the pulpy movies they figured in. There was something going on in a James Dean movie that often had very little to do with the movie itself: two of the three movies he made before he died—*East of Eden* and *Giant*—were set in the rural American past, and yet young urban audiences identified intensely with them. They identified with Dean's torment—and with his narcissism.

The Rebel Without a Cause may have been symptomatic of a national ailment—postwar youth stuck in the Eisenhower limbo between Korea and Vietnam, in a conservative society that had no way to deal with or absorb their anger—but, in movie terms, their problems were almost always simplified to the problems of growing up in a broken home. In the sixties and early seventies most of the new movie misfits had doting parents (when they were mentioned at all), the broken home became society at large, and psychic rebellion turned inward. Movies like Dennis Hopper's *Easy Rider* (1970) and Bob Rafelson's *Five Easy Pieces* (1971) expressed a prevailing mood: they summed it all for a generation that felt stifled by traditional culture and unwanted by the status quo. The movies' advice was to escape, but where to? Disaffected Americans—in Hopper's and Rafelson's terms, the "best" Americans, the ones who were in the best position to view the country's inner sickness—found themselves on the edge of a society that did not recognize or want them. Audiences felt protective toward James Dean, because he was really looking for love, but no one felt protective toward the counterculture movie antiheroes that followed him a decade later. Audiences identified less with a particular movie star (Jack Nicholson, Dustin Hoffman, et al.) than with the malaise he represented. This might not have happened if a star had come along with Dean's instinct to go for the emotional jugular, but, in any case, movies didn't rock the senses of the counterculture in the sixties. Rock music did. Stars like Bob Dylan, Janis Joplin, and Jimi Hendrix had an immediacy that was missing in American movies until very recently, and now the immediacy tends to come less from a particular star than from the obsessive visions of directors like Coppola, Scorsese, and Altman.

One of the real tragedies of American pop culture is that moviemakers did so little with the rock stars of the sixties. (It's almost as great a movie tragedy as the criminal, ongoing waste of black acting talent.) These stars might have invigorated movies and created a whole new audience. Instead, a great portion of that audience may have been lost to movies forever. They *did* turn out for *American Graffiti,* one of the last big predisco youth hits, but the atmosphere inside the theater was like a raucous high-school reunion. Significantly *American Graffiti* was one of the few youth hits which did not strike new attitudes with its audience. Or rather, its new attitudes were simply a hankering for the old fifties attitudes of its audiences—commercialized nostalgia. (The movie seemed to be saying, "Look at how poignant we were!" Really, we weren't all that poignant.) *American Graffiti* was the most inevitable movie of 1973: the fifties finally became Period for the generation that grew up with James Dean. (The year the film takes place, 1962, wasn't conceptually part of the sixties at all, just a closing out of the fifties.) The James Dean character in the film, Paul Le Mat's John Milner, the JD with a heart of gold, demonstrated how precious the rebel without a cause had become. The swagger of delinquency became a put-on and violence (like the wrecking of the police car by the local toughs) became slapstick.

In her 1964 essay *Notes on Camp*, Susan Sontag wrote: "Things are campy not when they become old—but when we become less involved in them, and can enjoy, instead of being frustrated by, the failure of the attempt. . . . But the effect of time is unpredictable. Maybe 'Method' Acting (James Dean, Rod Steiger, Warren Beatty) will seem as camp some day as Ruby Keeler does now. . . . And maybe not." But it's not only failure that has the potential for camp, it's also success as defined by values that we are no longer share. There's a tendency among filmgoers my age (twenty-seven), and a generation older, to approach Dean or Brando revivals with trepidation. What if all that once meant so much to us now seems laughably camp? But it's been my experience that such revivals hold up quite well. James Dean movies, despite their large inadequacies, come alive whenever he's on screen because he upped the emotional stakes so high. He gave the loss of love tragic overtones, and his acting rhythm—chaotic, fragmentary, driven— moved us kinesthetically. Dean didn't have the technical *simplicity* of most great actors; he fussed and carried on, he dripped narcissism. But even when his self-indulgence was awful you felt protective, which meant you *cared*. Part of this protection grew from the fact that it was often difficult to separate Dean's acting from what we knew about his offscreen life. His personae onscreen and off merged, which, in Method terms, made him the compleat actor. No other actor of his generation, not even Brando or Clift, and certainly few actors before him, gave you the feeling that if he didn't break through to the fundament of his feelings, he would go crazy. Dean's inarticulateness seemed more eloquent than the rhythmed, polished acting of his predecessors. For better or worse, he made them seem phony. His death at twenty-four, in an automobile accident, was the capper to his legend—

Dean, the flaming angel of his generation, finally flew over the cliff he was heading for all along.

If Dean had survived, he might have grown as an actor (like Brando in *Last Tango*) but, given the changing times and the commerce of the film business, his legend probably would have been fatally compromised. I once asked Nicholas Ray, the director of *Rebel Without a Cause*, what Dean might have become had he lived. His answer: "A tired movie director." That statement probably reveals more about Ray than Dean, but it confirms our own suspicions about the inappropriateness of the rebel—worse, perhaps *any* galvanizing persona—in the confused modern world of movies. Norman Mailer has written that "Part of the crisis of the 20th century is that nothing like a coherent view of personality is able to prevail. We live in every concept of human motivation and they are all at odds." Until recently, this did not really apply to most movie stars, many of whom, like Gary Cooper, Bette Davis and Clark Gable, had unambiguous movie personae. To paraphrase Mailer, their legend survived because they were *comprehensible*. We may be entering a new movie-acting age now, where Mailer's crisis situation does indeed apply; that is, in the absence of the comprehensible core of character that an actor's star persona thrives on, the actor himself, not tied into concept of character, may become the real star. Robert De Niro, for example, is a star despite the fact that he has absolutely no categorizable persona. In the fifties, De Niro might have been in the rebel front line, but his spooky transformations from role to role now, his newly stamped spirit each time out, seem to fit in with the uncategorizable seventies. In the same way, no one talks, except in verbal shorthand, about "the new Al Pacino movie." What is there to link *The Godfather I* and *II*, *Serpico*, *Scarecrow*, *Dog Day Afternoon*, and *Bobby Deerfield*?

It was easier to build star roles in the days when actors were more of a known quantity, when the motivations for their actions could be fit into a neat dramatic system. One of the reasons there aren't more women stars right now (there's certainly no shortage of good actresses) is because the popular values that might have formed a base for a female star persona in the past are outdated, or at least in flux. It's perhaps no accident that the two biggest female stars—Barbra Streisand and Liza Minnelli—have scored their biggest hits in stylized period pieces (*Funny Girl*, *Cabaret*) while their softer, more closely contemporary roles in movies like *Up the Sandbox* and *New York, New York* (the sexual dynamics of the latter were modern even if the period wasn't) have been rather bewilderingly received. Jill Clayburgh's performance as Erica, the bereft wife in Paul Mazursky's *An Unmarried Woman*, doesn't have the clarity of a star performance (probably because her life situation, by necessity, lacked clarity); but Erica may be the closest thing to a movie heroine of the seventies that we're likely to get.

I love watching Cagney or Bogart in their custom-fit roles, but on a deeper level I don't really believe in their characters as *people* the way I believe Al Pacino in *Dog Day Afternoon* or Robert De Niro in *Taxi Driver*. The tailoring of roles to fit performers is, among other things, a form of *protection*—the lesions of character are never exposed, the mysteries of personality are minimized. Some actors, of course, go to the tailor regularly. One of the big reasons Clint Eastwood is so extraordinarily popular is because, in the midst of this maelstrom, he's one of the few stars around who *stands for something*. What he stands for—ostensibly, the traditional four-square conservative virtues—may be almost beside the point. Or could it be that Eastwood is so popular with young, liberal, college audiences because he certifies their reactionary fantasies? (I certainly hope not.) Eastwood's lean, wolfish face and fighting trim make him a suitable-looking hero for both urban-contemporary and Western law-and-order fantasies. He's pared down—ideologically and physically—for action.

Audiences love Clint Eastwood's uncomplicatedness, the "pure" pleasure of his heroism in a world where Good and Evil are as carefully delineated as the colored bars in a Mondrian. And they love the humor of his deadpan in such a world. But, although Eastwood is always cast as the hero, unlike actors like Richard Harris and Sean Connery, he doesn't have a heroic presence. He also doesn't have the humor to kid the made-to-order heroism of his roles, like Burt Reynolds. Or, more exactly, he doesn't feel the *need* to kid his heroism because he's still a believer. The political climate in this country isn't as divisive as it was in Dirty Harry's heyday, when a homicidal maniac could be portrayed as a hippie with a peace-sign belt-buckle. The embarrassment of Eastwood's last cop movie, *The Gauntlet*, was that he was still lambasting Hell's Angels and Easy Riders; someone should have told him to turn his clock ahead. Dirty Harry has been left out in the cold in the Carter era, and my guess is that Eastwood's cop will operate in an increasingly political vacuum in the future. The ads for *The Gauntlet* were already uniquely "elemental" for this urban-cop genre; Eastwood is standing stalwart like Thor against the forces of evil while his lady lashes herself to his trunk like a frightened gazelle. Was Warner Brothers trying to pretest *Conan*? If Eastwood's new "comedy" *Every Which Way But Loose*—that hop-head *Hee-Haw*—is any indication, he may have decided to throw in his badge altogether.

Could the recent proliferation of newspapers and magazines and television shows devoted entirely to stardom be symptomatic of the uncategorizability of most of the few who really are stars? In the light-headed formats of these shows and journals, it's simpler to deal with pseudostars—there's no friction of thought involved. Suzanne Somers and Cheryl Ladd and Farrah Fawcett-Majors represent spic-and-span sex—sex as plastic—and so it's easy to promote them as celebrities. Celebrity is their true sexual attraction. It's harder to know what to do with an Al Pacino or a Robert De Niro. Rejection of commercial usage is built right into these actors. The avidity of the public for show-business icons has created a circuslike atmosphere in the media, and it's becoming almost impossible for a serious actor to pass through it unscathed. An older actor like Burt Reynolds solves the problem by playing the fool—the stud sellout cackling at his own improbable good fortune. Serious younger actors are afraid of the media juggernaut; on the talk shows, you can see them listening to themselves, trying not to drone on like the successful, rich wax-statue of an actor sitting next to them. These older stars rarely stay on the talk shows for long; they leave, amidst tumultuous applause, to tape a Dean Martin Roast—the younger actor's vision of Hell. It's hard to lift oneself above the media juggernaut but, if you don't, you get streamrolled. In recent times, the only group of performers who have played the media game and thrived creatively are the comics; and that may be only because so much contemporary comedy is so media and show-biz oriented. (The *Saturday Night Live* bunch are like surfers making fun of the wave that is carrying them along.) Maybe it's always been that way, but the new crop of comedians (along with precursors like Carol Burnett) are perhaps the first to create entire careers around the notion that an immersion in pop culture will drive you nuts. And that nuttiness is what makes them hip.

In show-biz terms, and as a form of American consciousness in general, hip used to mean black. Now what seems to have happened is that hip has lost its facial accoutrements (if it hasn't, then surely it must be moving toward middle-class white). Hip is no longer where you're from, it's where you're coming from, so to speak. And the hippest performers in movies and television now are the comics who seem to operate out of their own uncharticable craziness. These new comedians have the same immediacy for young audiences that rock stars had for kids in the sixties. (*Rolling Stone* has more cover stories on yockers than rockers these days.) After years of "socially conscious" humor, savage humor, the street satire of sixties radicalism, what we have now is the humor of personal idiosyncrasy—grounded in pop culture—and the two progenitors of the new hip are Lily Tomlin and Richard Pryor.

Crazies in the movies and television used to be on the periphery of the action. Now they're the coming order, heading for the center of the action.

They're not even crazy, exactly—they're screw-loose visionaries. The lament of Lily Tomlin's loony UFO watcher in Tomlin's Broadway show *Appearing Nitely* is the melancholic motto of the new hip: "In this world, if you don't got evidence you're nothing." That's because, in straight society, tangible evidence is all. *Appearing Nitely* was advertised as a one-woman show, but has there ever been an actress with as many different comic personalities as Lily Tomlin? What's so awe-inspiring, what's so frightening about her is that she doesn't slip in and out of her characters in the simple way that, say, a mime shifts faces with a wipe of the hand. She, too, seems possessed on screen. In *The Late Show*, she got so far inside her Hollywood weirdo role that what might have been conceived as a comic turn became almost soulful.

Richard Pryor is probably the most gifted stand-up comic in America, but he's been mostly hamstrung in the movies. Pryor and Tomlin—true soulmates—can get together on one of her television specials and swing off each other's zigzag rhythms like a fine jazz duo. Pryor's bugged-out, hallucinatory quality, his ambiguity, is enough to make the tube's eye blink. (A sound engineer trying to lay in canned laughter over a Pryor television performance would be befuddled, because the comic rhythms are so offbeat.)

Obscenity is Richard Pryor's comic propulsion and, onstage, in front of a live audience, he really cooks in a way that he can't on television. Pryor's nightclub humor is more savage and racially oriented than the other hip comics, but he really isn't lashing out at Whitey (that's small potatoes), he's battling private demons. Without obscenity, Pryor's whole character is defused. This is partly what's wrong with him in the movies. The roles he's been getting—except for *Blue Collar*—are too silly to accommodate his demons. They don't have the *substance* for obscenity and so they don't mean anything to him. He can be ingratiating, with the audience rapport of a devil, in films like *Bingo Long . . .* and *Silver Streak,* but when it comes time for some serious acting, he closes himself off. He wears his zonked baby face like an opaque mask throughout most of a movie like *Greased Lightning.* Maybe one of the reasons he could be taken seriously *as an actor* in *Blue Collar,* a movie where he plays a Detroit auto worker who sells out to the white bosses, is because he wanted his fans to know—he wanted *himself* to know—that he was only acting. He had to create a character and so, acting a man unlike himself, Pryor, paradoxically, appears unfettered on screen for perhaps the first time.

It's one of the characteristics of the new hip comics—not just Pryor and Tomlin but Steve Martin, Chevy Chase, Martin Mull, the *Saturday Night Live* bunch, Andy Kaufman, Robin Williams—that they are constantly *on,* constantly in character. They don't even crack up in the middle of one of their own skits to show they're only fooling. They're too *obsessed* to crack up.

They represent craziness without sentimentality. Their comic personalities are woven around the put-on, and improvisation becomes a way of scrounging for idiosyncrasies that will, hopefully, connect with their audience. Young people who don't personally identify with these comics still connect with their craziness.

Woody Allen, who may be the closest equivalent to a movie cult hero among young audiences in the seventies that James Dean was in the fifties, inspires a much closer personal identification. His craziness is really sanity—that's what's so funny about it. We can feel the frustrations it comes out of. Woody may look like a schlemiel but he's got his pride; he may hesitate on his way to the bedroom but—the point is made in every movie—he's good in bed ("I'm thin but fun"). Woody's flip absurdism fits right in with the new hip comics; his sentimentality, his obsessive New York Jewishness, link him with an earlier set of comics, even those just a bit earlier, like Robert Klein.

He can draw on the same depths of feeling that Lily Tomlin can, but he's not as spacy as she is. Woody is a hip comic with, at bottom, square values. That dichotomy may have accounted for the huge across-the-board appeal of *Annie Hall*, which was, after all, a traditional love story. For the first time, people started to take a Woody Allen film *personally*.

The lack of sentiment in the new hip comedians is a form of distancing, like those adolescents who make fun of everything to avoid getting serious. The *Saturday Night Live* bunch are not satirists exactly—that would imply a point of view. They're more like equal opportunity gagsters (Gilda Radner is the only regular whom one can take to heart, and that may have less to do with her material than with a certain personal sweetness and simplicity). Their routines are the brightest regular comedy on television, but watching the show can be a cool experience: The put-on isn't a very endearing technique. Now that the counterculture has grown up and melted into the Establishment, it's hard to know whom to trust (clothes and hair aren't the symbols they used to be). The new comics don't want to appear square, so they put *everyone* on—that way they don't leave themselves open. Their often straight-laced appearance is symptomatic of this: It's a fake-out. Dan Ackroyd and Jane Curtin could be the couple in the suburban tract home next door; Steve Martin, with his white three-piece suit and silver-toned hair, looks like a smiley, clean-cut young accountant; Chevy Chase might be the bright young Republican hopeful in a Democratic district—until they open their mouths. "Never Trust Anyone over Thirty" has changed to "Never Trust Anyone." These performers are digging for the comic possibilities in the paranoia.

There's one more point that should be made. Many of these comics are

—of all things—sexy. They're obsessed and they think well of themselves—they're narcissists; and narcissism is the new sex appeal in the movies. That's why the ad for the new Lily Tomlin–John Travolta disaster, *Moment by Moment*, is so unintentionally funny. The ad shows Tomlin and Travolta—in huge profile—looking adoringly into each other's eyes. They share such a facial resemblance they might be melting at their own mirror images. Lily Tomlin is hilarious in her one-woman show; she's also a turn-on. Her sexual radiation is inner-directed; her sleek, calisthenic movements are self-caresses. She's not only the most original comic presence in the movies, she's also the most ambiguous new sexual presence—and the two are perhaps not as far apart as one might imagine.

[1979]

Dave Kehr

TRAVOLTA vs. WINKLER
Transfers from Other Media

Auteurism's elevation of the director has spawned countercults on behalf of the screenwriter, the cameraman, the art director, and even the much maligned producer. But for all of the effort that has gone into assigning credit and blame on the most minute levels of filmmaking, there remains one species of Old Hollywood *auteur* whose work has gone almost entirely unnoticed—the men and women, faceless then and nameless now, who made up the studio publicity departments. They created not films, but stars. . . .

There are no more studio publicists to make our stars—for the simple reason that there are, for all practical purposes, no more studios. Depending on which source you care to credit, the last performer to receive a full-scale star buildup was either Kim Novak (at Columbia) or George Hamilton (at M-G-M), both of whom are now enjoying a benign obsolescence. The contract player is a thing of the past, and it is no longer possible, or economically sensible, to invest the kind of time and money that the star-making process requires. Since the assembly line broke down, production has been too erratic to permit a personality to develop naturally across a series of films: the impact must be immediate (*vide* Sylvester Stallone and *Rocky*). But the danger now, without Harry Cohn and a team of PR experts behind the wheel, is that the newborn star will take a wrong turn (*vide* Sylvester Stallone and *F.I.S.T.*), leaving his fans back at the intersection. Since the stars of the seventies seldom make more than one film a year, you'd think that a great deal of time and consideration would go into the planning of the annual outing, making sure that the vehicle presented the star in his best possible light, his most mythic configurations. But the trend, of late, has gone in exactly the opposite direction: in the name of versatility, even the most firmly established stars of the seventies seem to have become intent on dissipating their personalities in a variety of perversely chosen projects: Steve McQueen in *An Enemy of the People,* Dustin Hoffman as a cold-blooded killer in *Straight Time,* Al Pacino striking Robert Taylor profiles in *Bobby Deerfield,* Paul Newman dipping into absurdity with *Buffalo Bill and the Indians,* or signing up as a charter member of the proletariat in *Slapshot.* Even Clint Eastwood's annual Christmas film was, this year, a screwball comedy.

The rules of the game have changed beyond recognition, and almost beyond understanding. Only Universal, among the major producers, has maintained any semblance of the old order, but there are signs of a revolution brewing on their back lot, too—as the studio shies away from formula pulp designed to showcase in-house stars (*Two Minute Warning,* and the like) and gingerly tests the waters of New Hollywood with an investment in *The Deer Hunter.*

Perhaps the breakdown of the old system will eventually usher in a new Age of Enlightenment. The star system had its sinister side: not only were the performers dehumanized, stripped of their identities and transformed into units of commerce, but the audience was subtly victimized, as well —as the system forced an insidious form of cultural fascism on a star-worshipping public. Ostensibly, Hollywood has already entered an era of greater freedom. Given the power to choose their own projects, screen actors can stretch out, exercise their skills; they need no longer fear the wrath of reviewers who accuse them of only "playing themselves." And once the audience has been liberated from the oppressive oligarchy of stardom, we will, presumably, be free to understand films in a more mature, more active way, unburdened by naïve identification with a closed circle of heroes. For the first time since Carl Laemmle invented Florence Lawrence, stars are no longer a crucial ingredient in a film's appeal. *Jaws* and *Star Wars* shot to the top of the charts without the benefit of box-office names; the newspaper ads for the fall release of *Midnight Express* didn't bother to identify a single member of the cast. If the new age isn't quite upon us yet, there are, at least, unmistakable signs that stardom has become vaguely redundant.

Redundant, that is, in a strictly limited commercial sense. We still seem to want stars, need them, although we're not quite sure what we want them for. If stardom was always a semimystical concept, in the seventies it has become a confused and contradictory one as well. Robert De Niro, for example, is widely perceived as a star, but in what sense is that really true? De Niro, with apparent self-consciousness, has studiously avoided all of the traditional trappings of film stardom, refusing to play the same role twice, submerging his personality as completely as possible in his parts, and keeping his private life strictly private. If we sense that something is missing in De Niro's screen presence as compared to the stars of the past, it lies in his lack of a cultural identity. For all of the skill of his performances, he has no range of associations to draw upon, no extra, accumulated resonance to bring to his parts. Monroe Starr cancels out Travis Bickle, and De Niro must fill in the void with endless attenuations of the Method, beginning anew with every film. If he has any understandable image at all, it's grounded in his professional standing: we respect him as a technician, we do not respond to him as a personality. De Niro represents something new under the Hollywood sun—although he is a pure product of the movies (or at least as pure as anyone is these days), he isn't a movie star but another beast entirely. He's a movie actor, more on the European model, a product of and a contributor to the new, Europeanized American film.

De Niro is a star who has transcended personality in a cinema that has done away with genre; a perfect complement to the changing cultural role of American movies. As such, he's a special case, still somewhat unique. Shards of the American genre cinema still, of course, exist, and these genre films—much reduced in scope and altered in purpose—continue to require personalities and star images, as marketing shortcuts if nothing else. But if Hollywood is now incapable of developing its own stars, if the phantom hand of the studio publicist is no longer present to guide a career, where do these new personalities come from?

The answer, increasingly, is that they rise from the ranks of other forms of popular entertainment—television, most obviously; records, more and more frequently; and sports, most perversely. All of these erstwhile rivals to the movies have one thing in common: they retain extremely well-defined, hard-and-fast star systems.

Traditionally, stars from other media have meant certain death at the box office. James Garner, who is probably the most polished and natural television personality that the medium has ever produced, has never made a successful crossover to movies, despite several attempts. His relaxed underplaying and gentle self-irony, so well attuned to television's intimacy, vanish on the big screen. For years the film success of such recording stars as Bing Crosby and Doris Day were the wild exceptions to the rule: for every

Crosby, there were a dozen Dick Haymes; for every Day, a dozen Julie Londons, whose vocal expressiveness did not translate to the visual. During the first wave of rock movies in the fifties, the musicians were invariably relegated to walk-on parts, as "themselves," never granted the opportunity to advance the action. As for sports, the subject itself was long a taboo, the victim of an industry superstition, while the idea of allowing an unfinished performer on the screen, even to play himself, was considered bizarre enough to force such extremes as Paul Newman as Rocky Graziano in *Somebody Up There Likes Me.*

Suddenly all of that has changed. Muhammad Ali now plays himself in *The Greatest,* while Fred Williamson, Jim Brown, O. J. Simpson, and a number of other athletes have undertaken film careers with varying degrees of success. At the moment, three of the top (if not *the* top) female film stars—Barbra Streisand, Liza Minnelli, and Diana Ross—come to us directly through the courtesy of records and the concert stage. Even the sidelined rock stars of the fifties have managed to commandeer leading roles—definitively, if not memorably, in *Sgt. Pepper's Lonely Hearts Club Band.* Bridging the gap between records, nightclubs, and television are the two leading comic personalities of the seventies, Mel Brooks and Woody Allen.

Movies have become the drainage pool of pop culture, siphoning off the top talent of the other media. The old critical chestnut that categorizes movies as the seventh art, taking what they want from the others, has now become true in a commercial as well as an aesthetic sense. Few performers arrive in film without first achieving success in some other area; those who have not (Richard Gere is the most recent example) are finding the road to stardom increasingly rocky. Making it in the movies remains the most prestigious species of stardom, not because film is the most popular art (it isn't anymore, not by a long shot) but because it's the last rung on the ladder, the proof that a star is a star across the board.

If new stars do indeed come to movies with their talent proven, their images and identities honed from other fields, the system doesn't seem all that different from the glory days of the studios. Other media do the weeding and the winnowing, leaving the movies to harvest the results. But things aren't that straightforward. The step up to movies involves a number of pitfalls, some obvious (but can he act?), some more obscure, abstract, touching on the different ways in which star personalities are presented and perceived among the various media. Farrah Fawcett-Majors, arguably the most popular female performer in the United States in 1977, ends up fronting for one of the most conspicuous bombs of 1978, *Somebody Killed Her Husband.* Farrah's nose-dive wasn't entirely the fault of a rickety vehicle; whatever the film's flaws, she, at least, acquitted herself honorably, communicating a warmth and charm far beyond her centerfold television characterization. But from the day the film opened, no one went to see it. Somehow, the television Farrah and the movie Farrah are two different people: the public knew it, and wasn't buying.

The central paradox of stardom in the seventies can be read in the strange case of Henry Winkler and John Travolta. Strange, inasmuch as both performers began their careers under remarkably similar circumstances—playing Italian hoods in television sitcoms—but have since gone on to widely different destinies. Winkler remains one of the top television stars (although he's been feeling some heat lately, his *Happy Days* consistently places among the five highest-rated shows), but his film career has been no more than moderately successful. Travolta, on the other hand, has emerged as one of the few certifiably genuine film stars of the seventies, while his television program, *Welcome Back, Kotter*, stands in constant danger of being axed. After a summer full of *Grease* and second-runs of *Saturday Night Fever*, *Kotter* began the new fall season with an hour-long episode, featuring a highly allegorical plot line in which the Travolta character (Vinnie Barbarino) took leave of his high-school classmates and prepared to enter the real working world—if not as a movie star, at least as a hospital orderly. For sheer sentimentality and star bathos, the episode rivaled John Wayne's farewell in *The Shootist.* But even if Travolta has a claim on superstardom, the time period still belonged to *Little House on the Prairie*, which trounced his return to the tube nationwide.

Television looks so much like the bush league of movies—B films in weekly installments—that it's easy to assume that it is. But the resemblance is more apparent than real. Television works with a different set of structures, a different set of possibilities and limitations. Although it has largely usurped the role of film in America's national consciousness, television has substituted a new experience in the place of the old moviegoing habit, an experience that is at once more intense and more diffuse. More intense, in that the principle of repetition that served old Hollywood's star system has been extended to its outermost limit—instead of seeing your favorite star two or three times a year in a similar part, you can now see him/her/it fifty-two times a year in an identical part. But this endless repetition places certain requirements on what stories are told, and on the ways in which they are told. Television's most deadly enemy is the dramatic climax: nothing must ever really end, none of the characters must ever really change or grow. Television drama is light, trivial, and disengaged because the form demands it—we must discover the same people in the same situation every time we tune in a show, or we'll stop tuning in.

A purposefully superficial drama requires purposefully superficial characters—"likability" is valued more than psychological complexity, since the dramatic conflicts must be solved in a nonpsychological, symbolic way, in order to avoid upsetting the status quo. To that end, television has taken Hollywood's taste for archetypes to new heights of abstraction, and it's in that light that Winkler's television character, the Fonz, begins to look like a work of genius. The Fonz (*aka* Arthur Fonzarelli) is less a greaser, circa 1955, than the idea of a greaser, circa 1955. He exists almost entirely on the level of his iconography, with virtually no identity apart from his motorcycle, black leather jacket, white T-shirt, and sideburns. But the T-shirt is a little too clean, the hair a little too heat-styled, to allow the iconography the full force of its traditional threat. The Fonz, significantly unlike any other movie hoodlum in history, doesn't smoke: he's a domesticated greaser, which is to say, no greaser at all.

With his uniform, worn week after week with absolutely no variation, and his collection of catch phrases (holding both thumbs up, the Fonz emits a low "Ay-y-y" in moments of triumph), the character resembles nothing more than a modified version of a comic-book superhero, and that, indeed, is the role he plays on the program. Always swooping down to rescue his straight buddy, Ritchie Cunningham (Ron Howard) from whatever undomesticated greasers may be threatening, the Fonz steps into one of the most venerable superhero archetypes: the reformed outlaw, now fighting on the side of justice. But the Fonz's extraordinary powers go beyond the traditional skill in violence, and enter an area that the comic books have long shied away from: he's a sexual superhero, too. With swarms of teenage girls descending out of nowhere at a literal snap of his fingers, the Fonz runs through a dozen romances while his long-suffering friend Ritchie struggles with the ethical problems of kissing a girl on the first date. The Fonz's legendary sexual prowess is one of the program's running gags, compared and contrasted to Ritchie's endless fumbling. That's another brilliant bit of antidramatic television strategy: the disruptive specter of sex is raised, but then diffused, distanced, through satire and comic exaggeration.

The Fonz, remember, is technically a peripheral character on *Happy Days*. Ostensibly, the program centers on the trials and tribulations of the Cunningham family (Ritchie, his mother and father, and a younger sister), none of which are all that different from the epochal upheavals of *Leave It to Beaver*. It's the Fonz, standing to one side and entering the action only at crucial moments, who validates the triteness of the drama for seventies audiences, turning the clichés into an acceptable fantasy. He represents everything that the Cunningham family, in their by now mythical middle-class security, carefully represses: sex, violence, and freedom from an oppressive family structure (the Fonz's parents never appear and I've never heard them alluded to; he has been orphaned by the concept, if not by the plot). But his subversive activity is purely symbolic: a wholly synthetic creature, he poses no real threat to the family order, but actually supports it, demonstrating that the family can absorb, transform, and exploit his antisocial energy. While the Fonz functions as a simple superhero for the younger members of the audience, gliding through social and sexual problems with magical ease, he performs an equally valuable service for the adults, symbolically establishing a truce between the family structure (the fantasy of the fifties) and the leather-jacketed social forces that threaten it (the reality of the seventies).

Heroes, Winkler's first theatrical feature, continued the symbolic mode of his television work. If *Heroes* is a second-rate film, it's a brilliant television movie, a prime example of the evasions and displacements that television (much like the classic melodrama) prefers to deal in when it's faced with the prospect of presenting a "serious" social theme. *Heroes* is ostensibly addressed to the problem of the returning Vietnam veteran, but the issues are shrewdly couched in "personal," hence solvable, terms. Winkler's character escapes from a New York VA hospital in the first reel, spends some time chasing and/or dragging Sally Field through a cross-country journey (read: cross section of society) and ends up on the opposite coast in time to discover that his psychological scars can be cured by the love of a good woman. Winkler's performance embraces a few key elements of the Fonz's personality: aggression, egotism, pride in his position as an outsider. But the film, at least partly, seems motivated by the need to separate Winkler from the Fonz—either to showcase Winkler's skill as an actor, or to establish a newer, perhaps "truer" image of Winkler in the public eye. And so, the Fonz's perfect cool is discarded, leaving Winkler's aggressiveness to be attributed to a classic, heartrending case of manic-depression, a pop-psychological gambit that neatly serves to introduce a new element of vulnerability to his screen character. Before the film is over, Field has been transformed from mistress to mother, and the Fonz has been symbolically domesticated again.

The ploy was apparently enough to put the film over with Winkler's hard-core adolescent cult, making *Heroes* a modest success. But to the degree that the film served as an amplification (inadvertent, perhaps) of the Fonz, it pointed up Winkler's dilemma—the dilemma of every media-shifting star. If something extra is required to coax the folks out of their living rooms and into the theaters—why should they pay for what they've been getting for free?—then the Fonz, pure and simple, won't do in a movie. But it's the Fonz, of course, who remains the genuine star, not Winkler: the actor has no identity apart from the role. And so the vicious circle spins on. For Winkler, it stopped with *The One and Only*, a curious hybrid that attempted explicitly what *Heroes* did unknowingly, grafting a television-spawned character onto a movie narrative. The result was ghastly comedy that borrowed *Happy Days'* mythical middle-class–fifties setting, and set Winkler loose as a transcendentally obnoxious would-be actor who marries a prim and proper midwestern girl, and then proceeds to shock, scandalize, and variously outrage every member of her family on his way to becoming a star. Winkler's character now has all of the Fonz's comic self-confidence, along with a strong shot of *Heroes'* manic kineticism. But the combination is too much: Winkler's rampage goes far and fatally beyond the narrow bounds set for his character on *Happy Days*. The Fonz seems unable to operate in the marginally realistic context of a 1977 film, as Winkler's excesses of stylization gradually overpower the narrative, the other characters, and almost everything else in sight. *The One and Only* is the Fonz unleashed, television's repressed id running amok. The film might as well have been subtitled *The Fonz Rapes Mrs. Cunningham*, for all of the warmth, charm, and appeal it held for Winkler's television audience.

Henry Winkler's film career (which appears, for the moment, to be over) is the story of an actor at war with his image. Unable (or unwilling) to translate the Fonz into film terms, he falls back on an exaggeration of his television character. But on the big screen, the artifice shows; the stylization, unsupported by the context, crumbles into bombast. The actor-hero of *The One and Only* finally achieves success as a television star, playing a preposterous variation on Gorgeous George in weekly wrestling matches. For the Yale-trained Winkler, the Fonz is not so different a fate.

Winkler's classical acting style, building a character through a careful accumulation of gesture and inflection, is perfectly pitched to the representational requirements of television, but it is a style that has come to seem inauthentic (or, more simply, unfashionable) in films. The rise of behaviorism that began with Brando and Clift has made performers of Winkler's ilk seem too distant, too calculating, particularly in the context of unmitigated reality that American popular films now seek to present. John Travolta, clearly, belongs to the new school, and his low-key, instinctual style helps him in the movies as surely as it ruins him on television. Travolta is practically invisible on the small screen, an anonymous member of the *Welcome Back, Kotter* ensemble, reduced to milking his one practiced mannerism—his smile—for all it's worth. Travolta's Vinnie Barbarino is a creature of archetype no less pure than the Fonz (genus: urban youth; subclassification: cute but dumb), but he lacks even the superficial specification that

Winkler is able to give his role. By no means does Barbarino play a part in the structure of *Kotter* as crucial as Winkler's in *Happy Days*: he's just another interchangeable face in yet another indistinguishable television "family."

But that vagueness, perhaps, is what allows Travolta's television character to extend more naturally into movies. Barbarino's lack of definition makes the part a perfect showcase, granting Travolta a certain amount of freedom. The television performers who seem to have made the most successful transitions to movies—Goldie Hawn, Chevy Chase, Lily Tomlin—tend to come from the variety shows, where the review format allows the actor to develop a personality without the risk of losing it to a particular part. The loose structure of *Welcome Back, Kotter* (the show is hardly more than a collection of one-liners) offers the next best thing to *Saturday Night Live*: exposure without identification. And so, *Saturday Night Fever* has no trouble working as an expansion of *Kotter*, rather than a contradiction. The setting and the broad outlines of Travolta's character are borrowed from the program, leaving the filmmakers only to fill in the details of psychology and milieu that television forbids.

Still, Travolta gains something genuinely crucial from the movies—they give him back his body. *Saturday Night Fever* makes its priorities immediately clear with its opening shot of two disembodied legs striding down a Brooklyn street. The composition would be almost unthinkable on television, since it begins where most television images leave off: right at the waist. On television, Travolta may suffer from his limited vocal range—the medium, after all, remains largely verbal—but his problems of articulation disappear on film, thanks almost exclusively to the long shots that give him room to work full figure. Where Winkler relies on a trick voice (and tends to hold a static, arms-crossed pose), Travolta operates through a broad range of movement and gesture. He has a physical expressiveness that Winkler lacks, an expressiveness that is magnified on film into what remains the most mysterious of star qualities—sex appeal.

Travolta's sex appeal, though, is of a different sort than that traditionally allowed male stars. Although *Saturday Night Fever* seems to fall smoothly into the currently popular genre of urban realism (*Serpico*, *Dog Day Afternoon*, etc.), it ultimately bears more resemblance to the classic studio musical, specifically of the backstage, star-is-born variety. At the center of the spectacle is Travolta's Tony, working days in a hardware store and working out as a dancer at night, perfecting his moves and polishing his star image. His final ascension to Manhattan holds out the implicit promise of Broadway, a curiously romantic revival of one of the musicals' most venerable clichés.

The interior of the 2001 Disco is as stylized as the set of any M-G-M musical, an abstract assemblage of flashing lights, deep shadows, and odd distortions of space. During the dance numbers, John Badham's camera seems as slavishly·devoted to Tony as it might, thirty years ago, have been devoted to a Hayworth or a Charisse. This isn't the direct, head-on camera work preferred by Kelly and Astaire but an overtly romantic, adulatory technique, made up of off-angles, delirious lighting, and frenzied montage—an effect that abstracts, even fetishizes Travolta's performance. In no sense does Tony dance "with" his partners; he hardly even dances at them. There is no sexual exchange, as in the best of Astaire and Rogers, but rather a curious feeling of self-containment, as if Travolta's sexual expression were complete in and of itself. His partners are merely members of an abbreviated chorus line, backing up and setting off the star.

Tony's self-containment extends beyond the dance floor. He's the most passive romantic lead in film history, waiting for women to hit on him, and then not caring much when they do. The sole sexual contact in the film is an aborted oral sex scene in the back of a car; it's perfunctory, messy, and Tony hardly seems involved. Only when he meets a woman (Karen Lynn Gorney) who is as self-contained as he is does Tony's interest seem to perk, and then his only response is to return to the mirror, to (literally) continue working on his image. The grand romantic climax comes in the form of a shy handshake, and a promise of nothing more than friendship.

Danny, in *Grease*, could almost be the big Broadway role that Tony was born to play. The film is an extension of the principles established in *Saturday Night Fever*, as surely as *Saturday Night* was an extension of *Kotter*. A traditional (if unusually inept) musical, it's the only natural follow-up, for it is only here, in the hermetic world of the studio, that the newborn star can be baptized, ordained, and sent off to a glitzy Hollywood heaven of complete stylistic and sexual abstraction. Wearing the Fonz's patented black-leather uniform, Travolta is less of a character than an erotic principle, with little or nothing to do but pose. Where much of the frisson of *Saturday Night* resulted from the tension between Travolta's sexual expression and his apparent unavailability—a simultaneous come-on and rebuff—*Grease* carries the concept to its limit, going to remarkable lengths to keep its romantic leads apart: after a parodistic opening sequence (Travolta and Olivia Newton-John smooch in the sand à la *From Here to Eternity*) they hardly talk, see, or stand in the same room with each other until the conclusion. One exception is the drive-in sequence, in which Travolta makes a pass at Newton-John and is summarily rejected. Naturally, this singular lapse of self-containment leads into the most spectacularly stylized number in the film, Travolta's solo of "Alone at a Drive-In Movie," a lyrical evocation of sexual frustration that nearly deifies the performer by bathing him in the cosmic rays of a movie projector. When the romantic relationship is finally consummated (musically, at least) it comes in a form even more curious than *Saturday Night*'s handshake. In order to win Travolta, Newton-John must don his uniform—leather jacket, pants, and boots—and, in effect, become him. Their climactic duet, "You're the One That I Want," is so sublimely narcissistic that it can only be followed by a literal ascent into the clouds.

The fetishizing of Travolta's body, his narcissism, his passivity, and even his (apparent) virginity all draw Travolta into the narrow romantic role once exclusively reserved for female stars. The implications aren't necessarily gay; rather, Travolta's image seems almost antisexual. If the working women of the forties posed the last significant threat to American concepts of sex, touching off a wave of reactionary romanticism in films (the rise of the "glamour girl"), it would seem only natural that the gay and women's movements of the seventies would find an even more extreme response in popular culture. Indeed, Travolta's carefully cultivated glamour image could almost have been borrowed from the pin-up girls of World War II— an image of antiseptic, idealized, and impersonal sex, offered to everyone but available to no one. John Travolta is the Betty Grable of 1978: a pin-up boy whose displaced and abstracted sexuality speaks to a decade of desperate sexual confusion.

As in Old Hollywood, the star-making process still seems to depend on the creation of a readable, meaningful image. Here, Travolta has been helped immeasurably by the guidance and packaging provided by the Robert Stigwood Organization. Stigwood's carefully orchestrated multimedia campaigns for *Saturday Night Fever* and *Grease*—making extensive use of radio and records (and pin-up posters)—provide a seventies parallel for the old-fashioned star buildup. Exposure in other media replaces the gradual development, from part to part, film to film, of the studio system; saturation campaigns guarantee an immediate impact. Had Henry Winkler signed with Stigwood (he was, reportedly, the first choice for *Grease*), things might have turned out differently.

But now that television, records, and radio have become integral parts of the star system, the nature of the image and the nature of stardom have changed. John Travolta may have found a place for himself in American culture, circa 1978, but his place depends so strongly on the depressed notions of sex and romance peculiar to the latter half of the seventies that it's hard to imagine how Travolta will survive beyond the next decade. If, unlike some of the stars of the thirties and forties, Travolta was not made to order, he was, at least, the right man in the right place at the right time, giving voice and body to attitudes that would have existed without him. He is a product of his culture; he does not transcend or deepen it, as did Wayne and Bogart, Garbo and Hepburn. Only time will tell if Travolta will be able to weather the inevitable changes in cultural attitudes (Joan Crawford, after all, underwent four distinct shifts of image over the course of her forty-year career). But Hollywood, no longer independent, no longer self-contained, can no longer take care of its own. When it lost its self-sufficiency, its ability to reproduce and extend itself, the American cinema lost its privileged status among the popular arts. The world of myth, like that of Old Hollywood, is closed, separate, apart. Hollywood has now been dragged, kicking and screaming into the real world, and in the process it has lost its mythic base. Television has made John Travolta a creature of the here and now. He may survive; but will he endure?

[1979]

Molly Haskell

GOULD vs. REDFORD vs. NICHOLSON
The Absurdist as Box-Office Draw

They don't make movie stars like they used to . . . or do they? We assume that such deities as Valentino, Garbo, Gable, Cooper, and Monroe were the last of a monarchical line, stars who *behaved* like stars in a cinema devoted to their display. When star cinema went out, so did they. And we, as a country of moviegoers, purportedly grew up. We put away childish attachments, ceased to pattern our speech and hairstyles and personalities on Joan Crawford or Humphrey Bogart or Elizabeth Taylor or even James Dean. We no longer demanded "role models," and instead went to see real actors—or even "real people"—saying inaudible things in unpleasant films that would make us *think*. This was the sixties. Pop went the American Dream as it had been floated by Hollywood, and out of its rubble emerged the American art film. No more heroines awakening from an eight-hour slumber with fresh makeup and immaculate coiffures. No more stoical heroes with a tough-guy swagger, but slouching, sensitive boy-men.

During the last decade, big names—Paul Newman, Jane Fonda, Vanessa Redgrave, Dustin Hoffman—spent a great deal of energy establishing their credentials as concerned human beings rather than stars. And had they not made such an earnest effort to dispel the star mystique, the talk shows would have done it for them. (I am talking of the culturally prestigious stars, not the action heroes like John Wayne, Steve McQueen, Clint Eastwood, Charles Bronson, and Burt Reynolds, who have formed an unbroken line parallel to them.)

The intimacy, the conversational casualness, and the hungry silences of the television talk shows invited stars to come down from their pedestals and reveal their "true" selves, without the services of sparkling-dialogue writers and flattering cameramen. The camp mystique, as it flowered and festered in the Warhol factory of transvestites and superstars delivered the final coup de grace to Hollywood glamour by sending it up and out of sight.

Today's stars—Jack Nicholson, Robert Redford, Elliott Gould—are of a different order and magnitude. With the possible exception of Redford, nobody cares what they eat for breakfast. They work for one studio, then another, raising the question (which we must answer in the negative): Is a star without a studio like a ship without a sail? If they work for themselves, then, and take a dim view of Hollywood, aren't they therefore able to fashion their own images and change them at will? Not necessarily. For stardom itself is only one half of a binding contract, in which money and power are granted an actor on the basis of his fulfilling a certain fantasy, to be tampered with only at great peril. How different, and how much more alterable, are the images of a battered Nicholson, a tousled Redford, a schleppy Gould from what we think of as the shinier and more streamlined façades of their predecessors?

With the cultural myopia endemic to every age, we see our contemporary idols as tough and "realistic," even subversive, while those of even a decade ago seem impossibly artificial. It is easy *now* to see that in the early days, all stars—male and female—were like kept women. They were "owned" by the studios, they were squeezed into categories that had little to do with their natural inclinations. Take Gable, for instance. The "king"—who on the screen became the quintessence of the outdoorsman and man's man, whose irresistible appeal to women was rooted in cocky indifference—was the antithesis in real life. Serving as stud, escort, and (when necessary) husband to a series of older women, well-placed to assist him, his ascension was marked by a dependence on the opposite sex that could never be acknowledged in the American screen's great virility symbol. And obviously the confidence he finally projected was at least partly the result of the solicitous nurturing of these mother figures, whose contribution was thereafter carefully concealed, both onscreen and off.

Although it's tempting to make the studio heads the archvillains, they were, in a sense, acting on a mandate from the public expressed at the box office. It was the money-paying fans, after all, who refused to allow Mary Pickford to outgrow her little girlhood, or to accept Marilyn Monroe as an honest-to-goodness woman instead of a sexual parody. Ingrid Bergman was ostracized for doing what would be accounted swinging and chic in the sixties.

The public, as a star-making body, still exists, but the relationship is more tenuous. The star once appealed, within a common frame of reference, to a broad-base, homogeneous, mass audience (or rather, one that accepted a certain homogeneous, "American" vision of itself). They spoke the same language, and the star reached out to communicate, one on one, with each spectator. But for later, antiheroic tastes, such stars seemed too much in the mainstream. The antistar rebel aesthetic of the sixties stipulated location shooting, nonstar casting, actors who would inhabit their pictures more seamlessly—who would come, in fact, to sink into them. By the more ironic conventions of contemporary cinema, actors, instead of reaching out to the public, seemed rather to recede from it, snickering to themselves over the very idea of heroes and villains, good guys and bad guys.

The current studio thinking holds that stars don't make the picture and are more dispensable (or rather, interchangeable: "If we can't get X, we'll get Y") than ever. But, by a curious twist of fate, these same "nonstar" actors dominate films more than at any time since the twenties, and almost by default. In the absence of genre conventions, and of the whole range of secondary and bit players on which films used to draw, the leads really set the tone and ambience. Despite Altman's strong directorial personality, *The Long Goodbye* is far more of an emanation of Gould's personality than were the previous Chandler films of their Marlowes: Bogart in *The Big Sleep* and Dick Powell in *Murder My Sweet.*

Jack Nicholson's major roles, almost all written and/or directed by friends, are characters of a special, elliptical, even private sort. They never completely "explain" themselves motivationally, are never punished, or redeemed, or judged by the moral and ethical touchstones of earlier movies. Similarly, Gould, whether as the manic-destructive archaeologist of *The Touch,* or the mad monkey surgeon of *M*A*S*H,* absorbs his part into vicious or comic Gouldness, without referring to any common denominator held in sympathy with his audience. And even Redford, who with his regular features and glamorous WASP good looks, comes closest to our traditional idea of the star, is constantly recoiling from stardom like a shy virgin from sexual surrender. His guardedness, his apparent distaste for the public life in a film like *The Candidate*, seems as much a projection of Redford himself as of the role. We know by the cool way they handle themselves, by the ironic distance they generally keep from emotional commitment, that these guys are smart, smarter than the bosses, smarter than the system (which they may or may not beat). When they play bastards, they know they are bastards, so even when they lose, they win.

There is something as inescapably "now" about their aura of wiseacre innocence—as Jimmy Stewart's boy scout idealism was "now" in the thirties, and Dean's adolescent angst was "now" in the fifties. Gould, Nicholson, and Redford are stars—as George Segal, Donald Sutherland, Bruce Dern, and Ryan O'Neal are not—through some mystical combination of talent, luck, and an X quality that harmonizes with a current mood. They don't flaunt it, baby, don't ride in limousines, but then limousines would finish them faster than a drug rap. They challenge the system, don't play the game, but then maybe the game has changed and they're simply playing according to the new rules.

The rebel star, the absurdist star is in, and it was Brando who cut the mold. Defying everything to which Beverly Hills was a collective monument, Brando was the prototype for such future renegades as Gould, Nicholson, and Redford, but by the time those nose-thumbers came along there was little left to thumb their noses at. The "system" was nothing but a loose aggregate of long-haired, bead-wearing grandsons of moguls making separate deals, of which the counterculture (*Easy Rider*, et al.) figured to be very big business. But the image of rebelliousness, as it turned out, was preferred to the thing itself, and being branded as "difficult" could be as harmful as ever. It was one thing to *seem* to be spaced out on drugs or sixties' euphoria, but to actually flip out was quite another, as Elliott Gould discovered when, as a result of his own temporary breakdown, the picture he was working on was terminated, and he was blackballed in the industry. The era in which a star could shanghai a production came to a close with Marilyn Monroe.

Several people I talked to felt that Gould got what he deserved, but one, director Paul Mazursky, thought more compassion might have been shown. When I questioned him about the incident, he would say only that Gould had tried to make something like eight pictures at once, with his marriage to Barbra Streisand breaking up simultaneously, and the combination was too much.

Gould's (not so) private life is, from all reports, as debauched and undisciplined as any of the philanderers of old. He has left a wake of wrecked women and homes from Manhattan to Malibu, and sired offspring as casually as a prize bull. A controversial figure, he seems to inspire even greater antagonism in men than in women. A Los Angeles observer of the film scene who has never met him bristled at the mention of his name. "I can't stand him," he told me. "He's affluent, self-indulgent, self-serving, he's a piggy male whose screen image reflects that decadence. Unlike Nicholson, he can be bought. He's—well—frankly, he's a shit."

Undoubtedly there is some truth in this description, but these qualities are not entirely divorced from what makes Gould interesting as an actor. Unfortunately for our illusions, there is no direct correlation between talent and likability (nor is there, for the artist-as-bastard cult, necessarily an inverse one). Paul Mazursky, who gave Gould his first big role as Dyan Cannon's schnook husband in *Bob & Carol & Ted & Alice*, thinks he's a terrific actor and has improved since the 1969 film. "I hired him the minute I saw him," said Mazursky. "He had this incredible, ingenuous double-edged humor. Incidentally, I think if he'd played the lead in *Portnoy's Complaint*, it would have been a hit. But he has changed in the years since *Bob & Carol*, and he is more interesting. He started off as the classic schmuck, the castrated Jewish male, but he's gotten edges on him now. But the public, you know, expects actors to be the very thing they started out as."

I remember seeing Gould for the first time in a silly, short-lived Broadway musical called *Drat the Cat*. As a goony-looking policeman in love with a lady cat thief, he was the antithesis of the usual bland WASP baritone musical-comedy hero, the John Raitt type. He won me over, and he has never completely lost me. But the reviewers were less impressed. Actor Leo Bloom, who was also in the production, recalls the critics complaining that the musical might have succeeded if it had only had a more attractive hero. Bloom remembers Gould as an affectionate, unassuming guy who at the closing-night party gave every cast member a little gold whistle inscribed, "If you ever need me, just whistle." Bloom wonders how many of his colleagues have thought of redeeming the offer by sending Gould tape recordings of their whistles of help.

Gould was perhaps less striking in his first film, *The Night They Raided Minsky's*, than in *Drat the Cat*, where he first showed the comic-book quality that is transmitted in the outrageous, outsized gestures and expressions: the startled, goosed look in which the mouth and eyes turn into identically shaped Orphan Annie ovals, an expression that is succeeded without transition by a diabolical, laughing grin.

Gould further refined his manic antics in Robert Altman's *M*A*S*H*, the Army comedy in which he and Sutherland play a couple of prankster surgeons who send up Army protocol, and sabotage all the goody-goodies who live by the book. As funny as the twosome are, there is a cruel, elitist streak to their games. The humor is not so much that of subversion of meaningless routine as of the tricks smart schoolboys play on their less adept comrades.

The smart-aleck orphan in Gould as well as the resiliency and irony were obviously qualities that appealed to Altman, coincided with his own style, and that he was able to use. (Mazursky gives Altman, and former UA president David Picker, credit for giving Gould another chance to save his career.) Gould, as the surgeon in *M*A*S*H*, the detective with a cat for a roommate in *The Long Goodbye*, and the two-bit gambler in *California Split*, embodies the outsider's view of society that goes beyond sixties alienation to giddy seventies absurdism, and that is expressed in a personality that expects no connections, but nevertheless proceeds jauntily along the exposed wires. It's a self-absorbed and self-entertaining personality, one that is not only accountable to no one within the film but not even to the old-fashioned principles of plot and character. The roles are improbable at the outset: an ethnic from Brooklyn as an Army officer and surgeon; Chandler's weary existential gumshoe; a West Coast gambler; and, in Irvin Kershner's *S*P*Y*S*, a CIA operative! The incongruity is the point. He is "out of character" to begin with, and his presence becomes a wry commentary on the very existence of such absurd roles.

In *California Split*, he is one of the loser-addicts, yet, as a performer of comic bits, comfortably outside this wretched breed. His riffs are usually played against the foil of another, generally more phlegmatic male, who enables him to unleash a lunacy that a woman's presence would inhibit. At least four of his films (the aforementioned three plus *Busting*) center on male duets. The Army or fraternity creates a free "boys will be boys" environment that would meet opposition if a woman of any stature were introduced. Her requirements as a woman would impose a limit on Gould's goofing off, and expose its infantile nature.

If he is a brat and a bastard with women, he is not exactly a tower of strength with his own sex. His buddy films, unlike the smoother, more glamorous pairings of Newman and Redford, require no real sense of reciprocity between the two men. But because they are rooted in a context of fraternal foolishness rather than anything deeper, we don't miss the commitment whose absence is so striking in the films where he is paired with women: *Move*, with Paula Prentiss; *I Love My Wife*, with Brenda Vaccaro; *Getting Straight*, with Candice Bergen; *The Touch*, with Bibi Andersson.

Whereas, one can watch the fantasies of the buddy films with relative detachment, the neuroticism of Gould's boy-girl pictures makes us uneasy, as they document the collapse of the couple under the weight of one overbearing ego. In *I Love My Wife*, he allows his wife to support him through medical school but leaves her in the lurch when he "makes it"—after he has acquired the financial and psychological resources to stand on his own. Now—with that cultural-sexual mobility so symptomatic of our times—he has the self-confidence to make it with beautiful women, but neither the character nor the motivation to stick. In *The Touch*, Ingmar Bergman tapped, to an even greater degree, the harsh underside of Gould's egocentricity, the psychotic immaturity that is the other side of the coin of the manic playfulness. And he did this, if we believe Gould's self-deceptive account expressed on talk shows at the time, utterly without Gould's realizing what was going on. Perhaps the misunderstanding was not entirely one-sided. Wouldn't Bergman, if he had understood English and more fully appreciated Gould's comic image for American audiences, have allowed some trace of irony to creep in and "redeem" the character? Whereas it is precisely the utter charmlessness of the character that makes him, and Gould's performance, so fascinating.

Not surprisingly, neither of these films was a success, either commercially or with the critics, who seemed to recoil in unison from a side of Gould they couldn't accept. A funny son of a bitch they could handle, a psychotic one, never. And so although there was nothing of Gould in *The Touch* that hadn't been dormant, or expressed comically, before, it was judged a wild misapprehension of the Gould we-know-and-understand-if-we-don't-exactly-love. We would, apparently, rather see the man make a fool of himself on the Dick Cavett show, blurting out his biography in spasms of amateur self-therapy (or turn cautious-catatonic, in a later phase, on Merv Griffin), then see him use and refine some of his less attractive characteristics in a performance.

But then, perhaps it's because he plays the bastard so well that we respond so viscerally, looking for opportunities to ridicule him and remove ourselves from his threatening charms. What happened to Brenda Vaccaro and Bibi Andersson (and Jenny Bogart and all the rest) shouldn't happen to us!

I never made it over to East Seventy-seventh Street, where Redford has been shooting *Three Days of the Condor*, and where he ungallantly refused to pose with our current mayor for the local news (perhaps out of loyalty to his old tennis partner, the former mayor). But a month ago I tried to get in to our neighborhood seafood-and-hamburger joint, only to find the place jammed, and normally jaded Upper-East-Siders queued up on the sidewalk, panting with expectation. Redford was within.

Robert Redford is perhaps the only one of the new breed to generate the kind of instant electrical charge that we associate with the stars of a bygone era. He is the pure and total star (and, some would say condescendingly, only a star) rather than the Nicholson/Gould-type actor-star, or a character-actor-turned-star such as Dustin Hoffman or Gene Hackman. For them, stardom remains conditional and related to role. For Redford, the voltage is set and steady and no longer has much to do with performance. Obviously his fresh, square-jawed, blond handsomeness (what the *Daily News*, in a poll, called his "Joe Lifeguard image") has something to do with this, and with the kind of parts he can play. But it is more than just regular or perfect good looks—Loretta Young and John Boles had them. Redford possesses the kind of beauty that, on film, you simply can't take your eyes off. It's what Gary Cooper had, as Charlton Heston suggests in a sharp interview in *Film Heritage*. During *For Whom the Bell Tolls*, Akim Tamiroff apparently tried desperately—first overacting, then underacting—to "wipe Cooper off the screen" but he realized, with each day's rushes, the futility of his efforts.

There are those people to whom "something happens" when the camera turns on them. Because it is too mystical and primitive for our understanding, all we can do is say they are not actors because what they are "doing" is invisible. Our one consolation is that, minus the camera which enables them to ripen into perfection, they are singularly shrunken and unimposing. It's a process of magnification that is like, but more subtle than a microscope, under which some organisms, invisible to the naked eye, reveal extraordinary patterns, whereas those whose beauty lies in a total design suffer in close-up. Redford, on the screen, is an orgy of the senses. You can feel the blond peach fuzz on his cheeks, see the sun-bleached eyelash ends, look into the eyes full of yearning and disillusionment and humor, touch the wrinkles and freckles and hair that have carelessly exposed themselves to the sun. But as puritanical Americans, none of us can be content with this simple and sinfully delicious experience. He wants respect, and so must be a doer and an activist; we want a "total relationship" to redeem (and dispel) this illusion, and so we send in our surrogates, the interviewers, to investigate the "real man." And, of course, he is short. And guarded. And square. And proudly monogamous, which, romantic as it is in real life, is a downer for fantasy. And a good-cause–minded liberal, which is also an anaphrodisiac.

That interviews by such experts as Liz Smith and Martha Weinman Lear were as lively as they were testified to the creative powers of the writers rather than the fascination of the subject. Faced with a shortage of interesting primary material, they resorted to studies of the star mystique, or ingeniously varied repetitions of "Wow!" A lengthy, "candid" interview in *Playboy* took over two years to tape; it contains thousands of fragments of "truth," but there is nothing that could explain or evoke or that has anything to do with the palpable immediacy, the "total" turn-on of a couple of shots in *The Way We Were.*

That Redford is a star, there can be little doubt, whether we date his canonization from *Butch Cassidy and the Sundance Kid* or *The Way We Were.* There are those—friends and fans—who feel he has betrayed himself. But my question is: Was there any way in the world that a face (a head, a body, a smile, a shock of hair) that looked like that when the camera got hold of it could have avoided becoming a star?

An old and possibly erstwhile friend who thinks there was an alternate route for Redford is Richard Schickel, *Time* movie critic and the author of *His Picture in the Papers,* a study of Douglas Fairbanks that Schickel admits was partly inspired by his close association with a contemporary movie star like Redford.

"Redford made an absolute, conscious choice," says Schickel, "to be a movie star of the sort he is rather than the sort Jack Nicholson is. He is living out a forties and fifties fantasy of the ultimate star.

"He could have developed differently," Schickel insists. "He was a wonderful observer of other people and a great raconteur. He had this novelistic ability to shape an anecdote so that it came to a hilarious point. And all the time—he was a fantastic impersonator—he was acting out four different people. And he had a genuine 'fuck you' attitude, a bullshit meter that was clicking away at top speed. Implicit in this was a sense of irony and satire that should have gone into his roles, but never has. And now maybe it's too late.

"He's a primitive actor. He goes on feeling and on what he can 'bring up' at any given time. He despises technique, and consequently has very little to fall back on. You begin to see the same mannerisms crop up again and again, the little boy wraith and so on."

How about Redford the rebel? "A pose," said Schickel. "Oh, sure, he makes little gestures like walking out of meetings, and he disappears for a few weeks so everyone will ask 'Where the hell is he?'" (and apparently, say others close to him, these periods are growing shorter and shorter as more and more money rides on individual projects). . . .

"He would prefer," says Schickel, "that people go to a hell of a lot of trouble to get in touch with him.

"*The Way We Were* was painful for both of us. I said I didn't like it in my review, which may be one reason for the cooling of our friendship. [My wife] actually walked out of it. I came home and she had cold compresses on her forehead, literally. 'I can't stand to see him do stuff like that,' she said."

Well, I suppose it depends on your point of view, and if I were an intimate of Redford's I might feel he had sold out to the devil. But as a nonintimate and perhaps, in a pardonable lapse, a noncritic (for even by the most lenient aesthetic standards, *TWWW* is at best *haut* schlock), I would trade many an art-film classic for the final exchange between Redford and Streisand in the front of the Plaza. As the lovers take their last leave, charged with unspoken emotion and unslaked desire, we enjoy not just the double vision of Redford as the spoiled and unfulfilled WASP hero, and Redford as Redford who belongs to us all, but the third dimension of Redford as the stand-in for every lover, male or female, we've had and lost, lost too soon before we'd had a chance to grow tired of him. With the transparency of perfect beauty that Garbo and Cooper also had, Redford becomes the all-purpose lover—the weak drifter, the security-minded woman, the married man who "doesn't want to get involved." He takes the cliché, dusts it off, and makes it dazzle. He sums up the ecstatic anguish of separation, of "impossible love" (a much simpler and more dramatizable emotion than possible love) in a moment of pure cinema.

Perhaps the scene derives extra power, and sadness, because Katie Morovsky is saying, along with a number of women, good-bye to irrational love, to love's tyranny over a woman, and to reverence for a certain kind of man cast falsely in the image of God. Whatever its appeal, it is a thrilling moment, the kind that is usually dismissed as "sentimental" by serious critics because its sources and wellsprings are emotional, ritualistic, and nonverbal, and because it involves so little formal acting or conception. Unlike *The Great Gatsby*, in which Redford's performance can be measured against an original conception, there is a formulaic simplicity to the character architecture in *TWWW* which Streisand and Redford fulfill admirably . . . although Arthur Laurents, author of the novel and the screenplay, would disagree. Having had to watch while his work was pruned and "embellished," he is not one of Redford's most ardent fans, and blames the dilution of the story's political content on Redford's lack of interest in that aspect.

Redford, according to Laurents, is as vain as any old Hollywood star in his calculated concern with his image, and to this end, he requested certain "changes." One of the most fascinating cuts was a line he was to have said to Streisand after their first love scene: "It'll be better next time, I promise." He could look like a cad, a snob, a moral weakling, but to admit to even a pardonable and transitory moment of sexual inadequacy—never! In this, Redford places himself firmly in the tradition of the American screen lover, who—in subconscious compensation, perhaps, for a nation of poor and indifferent lovers with a virility complex—must pretend to inphallibility.

It's a shame he dropped the line, because not only does it make him more human but it fits the idea of the beautiful beloved—the sought-after rather than the seeker—who has never had to exert himself in the sexual arena. The line and its deletion could be read in a hundred different ways. Perhaps Redford felt it was not the implication of failure but of knowingness, of a kind of sexual sophistication, that was alien to him. Or perhaps the complete narcissist wouldn't be sensitive enough to another's needs to suspect that merely looking wasn't enough. (And indeed, for Katie it was.)

Perhaps Redford's destiny in life—and if it is not the noblest, neither is it as trivial as our puritan conscience tells us—is to be looked at, to be enjoyed visually with a promise of sensual pleasure that remains forever in the realm of possibility or missed opportunity. What is vulgar about *TWWW*, ironically, is not the romantic plot but the political message, an oversimplified morality tale that is trivialized by its status as filler to the central love interest. The former does an injustice to the complexities of the issues far more than the latter violates what Hawthorne called an imperative of fiction, "the truth of the human heart." Here, even the extra-filmic contest of egos—Redford wanting to make himself look good and Streisand, perhaps a little intimidated, complying—contributes to the couple's authenticity.

The man as "love object" is not such a novelty in movies as people seem to think. Remember Gary Cooper as the "blocked" writer in *Wedding Night*? He leaves his society wife and heads for the country, where he is released by the ministrations of Swedish earth-woman Anna Sten, Streisand's 1935 ethnic equivalent. He, not she, is the thing of beauty. And anybody who thinks the erotic magnet of *Red Dust* was Harlow and not Gable should have his/her erogenous zones X-rayed. Nevertheless, it is particularly appropriate that the romantic idol should be male at a time when women are discouraged from being "mere" creatures of glamour, valued for their lookableness rather than their accomplishments.

But Redford, like most red-blooded American actors, seems to consider lover roles sissy. We have had to import our great lovers from abroad: Valentino, Boyer—and how wonderful Olivier might have been, had he not felt artistically superior to such parts. Redford, in the Protestant ethic tradition, seems to prefer the films that celebrate the virile loner: the rugged Fenimore Cooper–style trapper (*Jeremiah Johnson*), the competitive sportsman (*Downhill Racer*), the misunderstood politician (*The Candidate*), and, batching it up with a buddy, the cowboy (*Butch Cassidy and the Sundance Kid*), and the gangster (*The Sting*), and, some time in the future, the barnstorming stunt pilot in *The Great Waldo Pepper*, and the investigative reporter in the Woodward-Bernstein saga.

The "problem" that a Redford character projects—and that is his real problem as an actor—is that he has no problem, that things come too easily. The Adonis that we see on the screen is so beautiful he has to be spoiled, and the movies that play on this voluptuous weakness are more interesting than those in which he plays the rugged male, or in *Gatsby*, the go-getter with rough edges. If Redford ever had any rough edges—and he has exposed a few in the *Playboy* interview—they were buried deep and smoothed over by the time he brought Fitzgerald's arriviste to the screen. As a movie aristocrat, a breed determined by looks rather than blood, he belongs in East rather than West Egg. Moreover, Redford lacks the drive, the daring, the competitive edge, the sense of having grappled and sweated to get there that Jack Nicholson might have given the part. Whatever his real origins, Redford, the golden boy, seems too preppy pure, too shadowless. If there is a shameful secret in his past, it is perhaps that he has cheated on his exams rather than trafficked with gangsters.

Redford's mystery, like Cooper's or Garbo's, is a natural mystery, the elemental miracle of human beauty. But Gatsby's mystery, like Nicholson's, is one of biography, of an unsavory past with dubious connections. Even their dazzling smiles tell of differences: Nicholson's is not quite so boyish, it has been more places and accumulated more meanings. Its message is not immediately apparent, and may extend beyond the moment or the person to whom it is directed, while Redford's less ambiguous smile is personal, playful, erotically inviting. It's an invitation one can't imagine any woman refusing, or, if she refused, Redford bothering to pursue. Nicholson, on the other hand, might conceivably give himself over to the memory of a lost love. Certainly the ambition that is an inseparable part of Gatsby's love of Daisy is something Nicholson can convey and has known. There is nothing of an aloof, hard-to-get Pimpernel in Nicholson, nor in a career of scrambling and smiling and hustling his way up the studio ladder, from mail clerk at M-G-M to *Time* cover boy.

If Redford is/plays the narcissist-loner, or one of a duo, Nicholson is the loner who likes and needs people, who is always hooked up with a bunch of kooks, stragglers—although they may not be the same ones for long. The group he ran and worked with in Hollywood—Monte Hellman, Bob Rafelson, Carol Eastman, Bruce Dern, Robert Towne—were the avatars of what might be called the New Hollywood, trying to do something different with varying degrees of success and originality. Like the New Wave, they looked like more of a movement at the time, as they were breaking out of the molds, than later, as they have diverged and dispersed.

At the moment, Nicholson appears to be the standout of the group, and one of the most versatile and original talents to come out of Hollywood in a long time. As an actor who combines both technique and "presence," and who is said to contribute an enormous amount to the details and design of his roles, he is perhaps the rightful successor to the late James Dean. But whereas Dean, the archetypal adolescent—wounded, sensitive, childlike—stood for a generation on the brink of a cultural revolution, Nicholson is the more guarded and mature emblem of a generation which has lived through the upheaval, taken drugs, been on the "outs" with the authorities, but somehow survived. There is a certain cynicism, a defensive shell, that will prevent his ever opening himself up to us and becoming the sacrificial figure of identification that Dean was. In a world pervaded by stupidity and corruption, the line between the young and the old, the virtuous and the immoral is no longer quite so clear. Dean was the morbid but luminous expression of pure Oedipal longing, a primal drama he could freely translate into the anguished cry for a father's love in *East of Eden*, whereas Nicholson would play out the same role in *Five Easy Pieces* with more reserve.

Of the current crop of movie actors, Nicholson is the one perhaps best equipped to bridge the new and the old, the funky and the traditional, to invest modern absurdism with a new whiff of heroism. It is no accident that the role that put him over was that of the small-town lawyer in *Easy Rider*, a member of the Establishment, who could identify with the young. Unlike the young cyclists/pushers, he could make the two-way passage from America to Amerika without losing his eccentricity and moral courage.

The freedom to slide between different worlds—while the citizens of those worlds are stuck—becomes a bit more slippery in *Five Easy Pieces*, where his refusal to develop the talent God gave him makes a less admirable figure. His chosen female counterpart is the lower-class tart, but whereas she is mired in the mud, he has chosen it and can always opt out.

He drifts and can never be pinned down, but even in his "slutting" we feel a quality of responsiveness to women. He redeems the piggishness of the "man's man," just as in *The Last Detail* he gives grace to the four-letter words so long forbidden on the screen. But it is not until *Chinatown* that we get the idea that a woman could form an important part of his life and the image of himself that he is continually arguing with and reshaping.

After a glut of antiheroes and glorified criminals, audiences may be ready for a hero again, someone who can give to virtue the imagination and excitement that villainy has claimed for so long. But it is crucial that the hero, when he comes, not announce himself as a hero, wearing his virtue on his sleeve. Perhaps he should be disguised as a cynic; or better still, as a two-bit detective making a living out of the improprieties of others. And perhaps, like J. J. Gittes, even when he does get on the track of truth, he will prove ineffectual, so powerful will be the forces of evil arrayed against him. Perhaps he will wear a bandage over his nose when he takes a woman in his arms, and perhaps the sign of his heroism will be that he can find himself in over his head, confounded by events, unassaulted and made ridiculous, and still not feel his manhood is threatened; that he can "save his face" by losing it; and that he can fall in love with a woman who is not a kitten or a Kewpie doll or even a conventionally alluring femme fatale.

Surely, for all its bleakness—and the ending of *Chinatown* is one of the most shattering ever—there is an exhilarating triumph which has preceded, and in some way redeemed, it: the discovery of mutual trust between a man and a woman. In the forties crime melodramas, the heroine generally appeared virtuous but was eventually unmasked as a creature of pure evil. Here, the opposite occurs: Faye Dunaway begins as a bizarre, artificial enigma, and reveals herself, under the probing, then loving gaze of Nicholson, as a tormented, complex, fighter of a woman. In a horrible irony, he sticks to her with a tenacity that, in pursuing the truth, will eventually cause her death. Not exactly a happily-ever-after ending, but, considering the current sexual stalemate, an unforgettable and honorably romantic one, suitable to the new myths, and the new stars.

[1974]

Vincent Canby

CHARACTER ACTORS VS. STARS
The Distinction Is Fading

Every now and then we should stop to take stock of some of the extraordinary contributions being made to current movies—some good, some not so good—by actors for whom there's seldom space enough in a daily newspaper's film reviews to do full justice. In many ways, the lives of supporting actors are charmed. They're seldom blamed for a movie's failure, but unless they have a show-stopping scene, one to equal Richard Widmark's murder of the little old lady years ago in *Kiss of Death*, they tend to be appreciated in anonymity. There are right now a number of comparatively new, very talented character and/or supporting actors who are making even second-rate American movies easier to tolerate than would otherwise be expected.

Back in the so-called Golden Days of Hollywood, when people like Louis B. Mayer, Darryl Zanuck, Harry Cohn, Jack Warner as well as Herbert J. Yates-types ruled their mini-empires by means of seven-year contracts, one could as easily identify a film's studio-of-origin from the character people one saw in the film as from the stars.

Lewis Stone, C. Aubrey Smith, Henry O'Neill, and Frank Morgan were strictly M-G-M. Edmund Gwenn, Lynn Bari, and Laird Cregar meant that the movie came from 20th Century-Fox. Warners owned Peter Lorre, Alan Hale, Ronald Reagan, and Frank McHugh. These people never stopped working. They never became stars in the grand tradition, but they made very good livings.

The situation today is a lot more fluid. No studios sign supporting actors to long-term exclusive contracts. Actors float from film to film, from theatrical movies to television and back again. Today's character actors don't have the security that John Qualen (ninety-three films in forty years) once had, but also they are not locked into the studio-sponsored public personalities that prevent such performers as Gale Sondergaard, Sydney Greenstreet, ZaSu Pitts, and Mr. Qualen from ever really demonstrating the full extent of their talents on the screen.

Today's actors take risks. Unless they are signed for a television series, they live much of the time on the brink of economic disaster. Yet they can pick the assignments that make a career rewarding. . . .

One of the salutary effects of the collapse of the old star system has been the erosion of the lines of demarcation between the position of the star and that of the character actor. I'm not only talking about the ease with which an actor of Olivier's status can move from a supporting role in *The Seven-Per-Cent Solution* (which he almost swipes from the rest of the cast) to a leading role in *Marathon Man*. In effect, both roles are character roles. I'm also talking about the new freedom that allows our young leading actors to play the sort of character roles that no leading actors thirty years ago would have been caught dead playing. Dustin Hoffman, one of today's major young stars, is also one of our leading character actors on the evidence of his performances in *Midnight Cowboy*, *Papillon*, and *Lenny*.

Roy Scheider, William Devane, and Gene Hackman are character actors as much as they are stars—perhaps more so. Among the dividends of *Alice Doesn't Live Here Anymore* and *Taxi Driver* was seeing Harvey Keitel, who also plays straight leads, doing brilliant work as a psychotic lover in *Alice* and as the East Village pimp in *Taxi Driver*.

Performers, I suspect, cherish this new freedom to do character work. It allows them to test themselves without necessarily having the fate of the entire film depend on them. Supporting-character roles also allow the actor to get on and off fast, leaving a vivid impression with the least amount of time and effort.

Though stars are frequently sought to do comparatively small, colorful character roles, like Jack Nicholson's union organizer in *The Last Tycoon*, supporting character people are not often asked to step into star roles.

Diane Ladd, who played the raucous waitress in *Alice Doesn't Live Here Anymore* and came close to stealing that film from Ellen Burstyn, barely survived a larger role in a sci-fi film called *Embryo*. Both she and the movie were dreadful. She recouped her reputation by fine reviews in Broadway's *A Texas Trilogy*, but she has yet to make it as a star in films. Maybe she shouldn't try. Stars can come and go very quickly. Good character people go on forever.

Here are some of the new character faces whose names you should remember.

Randy Quaid, currently to be seen as Woody Guthrie's Okie friend and inarticulate social conscience in *Bound for Glory*, made his film debut in Peter Bogdanovich's *The Last Picture Show* and was subsequently seen in *Paper Moon*, *The Apprenticeship of Duddy Kravitz*, and *Missouri Breaks*. Like many of the best character actors, Mr. Quaid has an appearance that seems to vary from film to film. He is puttylike. His moving, funny performance as the slightly dim-witted sailor, the fellow being escorted to prison, in *The Last Detail*, established him firmly in the consciousness of the critics.

Michael Murphy, who plays the Communist writer for whom Woody Allen fronts in *The Front*, has the bland good looks of an actor who, in another era, would have demanded to play straight leading roles right from the start, even if the films were terrible. Instead, Mr. Murphy has taken comparatively off-beat roles in films of consistent quality, including Robert Altman's *McCabe and Mrs. Miller*, in which he played the WASPy representative of Big Business, and *Nashville*, where he was seen as the advance man for the never-seen third party candidate for president. He also was the journalist in television's *The Autobiography of Miss Jane Pittman*.

Richard Pryor, who plays Daddy Rich, the founder-head of the Church of the Divine Economic Spirituality in *Car Wash* and the wise-talking thief in *Silver Streak*, has succeeded in being the best thing in every film I've so far seen him in, with the exception of *Lady Sings the Blues*, which starred Diana

Ross. (He was second best in that one.) Mr. Pryor specializes in comedy performances (in addition to acting he's written comedy material for Lily Tomlin and Flip Wilson and he is a coauthor of Mel Brook's *Blazing Saddles*), but one of these days he may give us an all-out dramatic performance. There's also the possibility that he'll suddenly become a star on his own.

Talia Shire, Sylvester Stallone's shy girlfriend in *Rocky*, received fine reviews for her performances as Al Pacino's hysterical sister in the two *Godfather* films, but *Rocky* is the first film to demonstrate that she has the range of a first-class character actress.

Burt Young, the beer-guzzling, none-too-bright buddy of the title character in *Rocky*, made his first mark as the Master-at-Arms in *Cinderella Liberty*. Playing characters who are society's short-changed—inarticulate, fuzzy-minded, optimistic when they should be despairing—Mr. Young creates immediately identifiable figures that are an essential part of the American landscape.

Robert Duvall, now sporting a hugely funny (and effective) English accent as Dr. Watson in *The Seven-Per-Cent Solution*, gives an equally spectacular but completely different sort of performance in *Network*, in which he plays an ice-cold New York television executive. Mr. Duvall appears to be ageless, his acting range limitless. He is so fine, in fact, that one of these days he may just become a star.

On second thought, he already is one. Though his name doesn't automatically bring people into the theater yet, nor does it take precedence on the marquee, he has the dramatic force of a star presence in every film he appears in.

[1976]

THE PRIMACY OF THE ACTOR

(LEFT TO RIGHT)

Sally Field. (*Stay Hungry*. Copyright © 1976 United Artists Corporation. All rights reserved.)

Gloria Swanson.

Woody Allen. (On the set of *Annie Hall*. Copyright © 1977 United Artists Corporation. All rights reserved.)

William S. Pechter

CAGNEY VS. ALLEN VS. BROOKS
On the Indispensability of the Performer

"He moved more gracefully than any other actor in Hollywood," Kenneth Tynan said of him, and, excluding only Chaplin, Keaton, and Astaire, he couldn't have been speaking about anyone but James Cagney. Though the actual televised award ceremony was mainly the embarrassment such things seem inevitably to be, the American Film Institute's recent bestowal of its second "Life Achievement Award" on Cagney was a gesture I approved as wholeheartedly as I did the giving of the first award to John Ford. Like Ford, however, Cagney really can't be grasped through film clips, and perhaps the most unfortunate aspect of the television presentation was the impression it might leave in the minds of those unfamiliar with Cagney's best work that the occasion was just another wallow in nostalgia, a sentimental tribute to the movies' original "tough guy," or more of those media events whose ostensible subject has somehow been mislaid, much as the actual film of *The Great Gatsby* now seems to be no more than the tail end of the fashion industry's "Gatsby look." Yet there's no discernible Cagney boom so far, at least not on the order of the recent Astaire revival, nor has there ever been a Cagney cult comparable to Bogart's. Some of the reasons for this seem fairly obvious, others rather less so.

Most obvious, perhaps, is the fact of Cagney having appeared in so few films which have themselves won the public's lasting enthusiasm and affection as have Bogart's *The Maltese Falcon*, *The Big Sleep*, *Casablanca*, etc. Among Cagney's films, though *The Public Enemy*, which rocketed him to stardom, retains much of its topical punch and vigor, it has generally aged less well than has *Scarface* (if better than *Little Caesar*); and of the other Cagney movies, many of them comedies, made in the early thirties (including such quite brilliant films as *Blonde Crazy*, *Taxi!*, *Hard to Handle*, *Lady Killer*, and *Jimmy the Gent*), only *Footlight Parade*, thanks mainly to the camp appeal of Busby Berkeley's production numbers, is much seen today. *G-Men*, a big Cagney hit of the mid-thirties, probably seems too naïvely reverential of the

FBI for today's tastes, while, of the films from the later thirties, *Angels with Dirty Faces* and *The Roaring Twenties*, the former a crisp genre piece and the latter a soggy one, get television play, largely owing, one suspects, to the presence in them of Bogart (playing characters gunned down by Cagney in both movies). *Yankee Doodle Dandy*, which, in 1942, provided Cagney with his biggest box-office success, his one Oscar, and his own favorite among his screen roles, also survives today chiefly on television: though enjoyable, its flag-waving schmaltz lacks *Footlight Parade*'s campiness, and its main appeal now is rather squarely nostalgic. Only the 1949 gangster film, *White Heat*, among Cagney's films early and late, has earned for itself a certain cult status, though its stripped-for-action briskness and its emotional reserve seem to insure that such status will remain minor.

Yet to attempt to speak of Cagney's films thus—that is, as films apart from what Cagney brings to them—is really close to impossible. I once wrote of Fred Astaire that he was, like Keaton and Chaplin, so fully expressive a kinetic object on the screen as to be in himself a movie, a metaphor I might want to apply to Cagney as well, did not another one even more forcefully suggest itself. For if one's sense of a Cagney performance is of a lightning-flash vividness of not only face but entire body (as well as of the electric charge of that singular voice), no less does one sense in it the creation of a distinctive persona, an authentic character; and if Cagney's acting draws, as the best acting in movies usually does, on certain natural properties he possesses as a person, by the time these raw materials find their way to the screen they have been refined to the utmost by an exacting art. No matter how flat the background, the Cagney character is able to emerge as a fully rounded creation. If Cagney is a movie, no less is he a novel.

In 1932, before, one might have thought, Cagney's persona could have made so firm an impression, Lincoln Kirstein wrote:

> In America there are men and boys lounging in front of drugstores, easing down off trucks, lifting up the hoods of their engines, sighting for a cue on a billiard table, tossing down their little pony of raw whiskey, or even shooting through the pocket of their double-breasted tuxedos. When Cagney gets down off a truck, or deals a hand of cards, or curses, or slaps his girl, or even when he affords himself and her the mockery of sweetness, he is, for the time being, the American hero, whom ordinary men and boys recognize as themselves, and women consider "cute." It is impossible to tell at once whether his handshake is cordial or threatening. He is "cute"—the way Abraham Lincoln said a certain trapper was "cute," that is quick, candid, and ambiguous.*

* "James Cagney and the American Hero," *Hound and Horn*, April–June 1932.

It is this "cuteness" that allows Cagney, unlike, say, Bogart, to be at home in musicals as in gangster films, and to be able to project in both very much the same characterological components. One might be tempted to say that this character grows darker over the years, but, though it's true that he's never envisioned more blackly than in *White Heat*, the spilling over into psychosis which one sees in that film seems always at least potentially there in the Cagney character even at its lightest. One senses it, for instance, in an early comedy, such as *Lady Killer* (in which a plot about a mobster who becomes a movie star toys boldly with the public's sense of the "real" Cagney), when Cagney, acting on the idle jest of his leading lady that he give her monkeys for a birthday present, actually has a crate of monkeys delivered to her birthday party, and then, as the animals run amok, laughs convulsively, with a disturbing obliviousness to the distress of everyone else, at the destructive pandemonium he thus unleashes.

And yet the opposite of this is also true. When, before blowing himself sky-high from atop a gas tank at the conclusion of *White Heat,* he drags his wounded body about while laughing delightedly to himself at his own invincible cunning, the laughter, terrible as it is in its expression of a ravaged mind, is nevertheless somehow contagious. Indeed, by this time we have been so disoriented by the film's black-comic twists and turns that his death can seem, in its very outsized extravagance, a kind of triumph. "Made it, Ma! Top of the world!" he shouts, with a commitment to the American dream of exalted self-realization scarcely short of Gatsby's. He is, in this apotheosis, as he's always been, the upwardly-mobile urban American achiever writ large, the manic go-getter; and his ambiguity lies not in how we are meant to take his character, but in the very essence of the character itself. Though his meaning may be unclear, everything there is to know about him is on the screen. There is no sense of Bogart-like interiority. Everything is externalized, everything, in this medium of moving pictures, animated and made visible: everything there in his image.

And so one turns, heart sinking, to the present—to, for instance, the latest Woody Allen. For if Cagney can be said to burn a hole in the screen, surely this isn't the same as having a hole there to start with. Though it's true that, "cinematically," *Sleeper* is an advance on Woody Allen's earlier films (it's been given, for instance, an art director's "look"), the problem with it, as with his earlier work, isn't really that of slovenly appearance, or lack of development, or even the wildly uneven mixture of good and bad. All that could be passed over. What can't be passed over is the fact that no one's *there.*

This probably wouldn't be worth saying if it weren't for the increasing noises being made both by and about Woody Allen as the heir to the great silent comedians. It's true that, physically, he reminds one a bit of Harry Langdon, and that he imagines his screen character in terms of a Harold Lloyd-like striving to succeed. But though I find Woody Allen funny as a monologist, and have found his films funny, too (if never as funny as one hopes they're going to be), somehow *he* isn't funny *in* them. To be sure, *Sleeper* does display a growing dexterity at slapstick, and provides perhaps the first occasion in his films (his cruising dopily in a wheelchair near the beginning) when I can actually recall him and not the lines as what was funny. Given that rate of progress toward comic charisma, Woody Allen might just inch his way past the Three Stooges by the year 2000. And since, for all its greater polish, *Sleeper* is probably less funny than his earlier film *Bananas,* one wonders if the effort is worth it.

Mel Brooks dreams not of Chaplin and Keaton but of Olsen and Johnson, and to say that *Blazing Saddles* hits its mark where *Sleeper* misses isn't saying much. And even this much can't honestly be said; *Blazing Saddles* is a mess, and its worst is far worse than the worst of the Woody Allen. But its mess is rather invigorating, even liberating, and there's nothing quite so audacious in *Sleeper* as the way *Blazing Saddles'* burlesque-Western plot is pulled out of near the end, and, before being resumed, lost for a bewildering length of time while we watch the depicted "filming" of another movie. (Characteristically, Brooks then does the movie-within-a-movie business to death.) And though the lead role, played by Cleavon Little, cries out to have Richard Pryor (who collaborated on the script) in it, what *Blazing Saddles* does have (where *Sleeper* has only funny lines) is funny people: Harvey Korman and Gene Wilder, though both could use better material, among them; and, funniest of all, Mel Brooks himself (at least in his raucous first scene as the governor). Whatever it is that makes one person able to hold the screen and another not, Mel Brooks has it and Woody Allen hasn't; and though it isn't enough, there's no substitute for it. Woody Allen stars in a movie, and the effect is rather like a movie equivalent of those "Music Minus One" records. Mel Brooks appears on screen, and there's a leap in the energy level.

Perhaps this antithesis which Allen and Brooks present in its most rudimentary form might strike one less forcibly at a different moment. But given all the cant now spoken about film being a director's medium, it seems to me worth insisting on the indispensability in film of the performer, and insisting especially during a time when directorial superstars (not to say, grown men) can spend a year of their lives making things like *The Day of the Dolphin.* For during a lean period like this one, it's often the performer's art that sustains the life of the medium. It's little more than a bad joke to hear a

Sidney Lumet speak of how *Serpico* relates to his other films as an expression of his vision, when *Serpico* can scarcely be said to exist apart from what Al Pacino contributes to it. Probably, there's nothing among all of last year's movies I recall with more admiration than the way Jeff Bridges drawls, grins, concentrates his attention, and relaxedly carries himself in Lamont Johnson's *The Last American Hero*, a good, solid genre movie which Bridges' work alone lifts consistently above the conventional. And probably the most artistically exciting thing in American movies since is Jack Nicholson's explosive (and strikingly Cagneyesque) performance as a pugnacious Navy lifer in Hal Ashby's *The Last Detail*, a small, ironic study of men and institutions to which Nicholson brings scale and dimension.

For, in reality, far from the movies not being an actor's medium, there's probably been no other artistic medium in this century whose appeal rests so strongly on the human presence, and in which the human image has occupied a place of such primacy and centrality. And so, especially at a time such as this, the American Film Institute's honoring of Cagney side by side with a director noted for his visual mastery provides a salutary reminder both of how impoverished our movies would be without what a Cagney (or Jeff Bridges or Jack Nicholson) brings to them, and of how narrowly we usually speak of movies as a medium of images. Because of John Ford's best films, we have a certain image of America. Because of Cagney's, we have a certain image of an American.

[1974]

Andrew Sarris

ACTORS vs. DIRECTORS
The Actor as *Auteur*

Sunset Boulevard and *In a Lonely Place* are two 1950 movies with tortured screenwriter-protagonists undone respectively by belated regeneration and advanced paranoia. What both characters have in common is a gut feeling that their craft is not taken seriously enough. In *Sunset Boulevard*, William Holden moodily meditates on the fact that people don't know you have to sit down to write a picture; they think the actors make it up as they go along. This attitude (from Charles Brackett and Billy Wilder as filtered through Holden) reflects traditional behind-the-scenes resentment of the actor (and particularly the star) in the cinema. *In a Lonely Place* presents a slightly more sophisticated view: The ill-fated Martha Stewart hatcheck girl confesses to Humphrey Bogart that she never knew pictures were written by screenwriters. She thought instead that the stars wrote their own dialogue. If the stars are big enough, Bogart reassures her, they do just that.

The truth, of course, is everywhere in between. Actors are clay, actors are sculptors, actors are images, actors are imagists. They are spurned by the animators and the documentarians and the abstractionists. They are only grudgingly tolerated by the academics and the visual purists, and they seem to have been slighted by both the sociological and auteurist schools of criticism ("In the cinema," Sarris himself once spake, "feelings are expressed *through* actors, not *by* actors.") We begin our moviegoing by being conscious of nothing else, and we end up by being self-conscious about everything else. It has thus become very difficult to continue focusing on the craftsmen behind the screen. Whereas the actor is alone on the screen, he is not alone on the set. The "production story" demystifies the actor's domain.

Whenever the actor "writes" or "directs" the picture without directorial portfolio, his or her participation in the production is almost invariably interpreted as interference. Stars have often been satirized for knowing all too well where the camera was situated at every stage of the shooting. The knowing movie-watcher can pick out the telltale patterns of light and shadow as they trace the path of the performer's ego across the screen and over the darkened features of the less-influential player.

One did not have to be a trivia hound to remember which was the favored profile of Claudette Colbert and Olivia de Havilland. Indeed, de Havilland once played a dual role of good and bad sisters (in *The Dark Mirror*) with the good sister shown in the good profile and the bad sister in the bad. In *Sunset Boulevard*, we are treated to a delirious expression of star psychosis in Gloria Swanson's much-mimicked line: "I'm ready for my close-up, Mr. De Mille." In this context, the lingering soft-focus close-up is associated with everything that is mushy about movies. Consequently, many directors and writers have come to view the star as the greatest menace to the art of the cinema.

Yet, many of the alleged evils of the star system seem to depend for their documentation upon a facile equation of film with theater. The actor is supposedly entrusted with a sacred text from which he or she may not deviate. The role is all; the performer's personality nothing. If we recognize the actor, the performance is an ego-ridden failure. This may explain the inordinate respect accorded to players who hide behind all forms of character makeup in the pursuit of their parts.

The confusion of the art of acting with the art of disguise is bad enough on the stage, but it is grotesque on the screen, where the revelatory realism of the camera lens exposes all such impostures. To a certain extent, therefore, all screen performances consist at least partly of documentaries of the performer's appearance. The movie actor collaborates with the character he or she plays in order to create an inseparable fusion of fact and fiction, a fusion which results also in making casting an indispensable part of creation. This has been true of dramatic live-action cinema in all nations and all ages. But somehow only the American cinema has been stigmatized as a star cinema, as if the Colmans and the Cagneys had not had their counterparts in the Mifunes and the Mastroiannis.

Hence, Jean Renoir (in *My Life and My Films*) is unaccountably chauvinistic on the subject of national cinemas: "But who is the maker of a film? In the heroic period of the American cinema, it was generally the actor who put his stamp on it. As the industry prospered it became a medium for the manufacture of stars. The cinema of recent years has brought about the acceptance of the idea that the maker of a film is the director—a happy change, and in line with present-day artistic and literary tendencies. Today we have films signed 'Truffaut' or 'Jean-Luc Godard' just as we have novels signed 'Simenon' or 'André Gide.' "

Curiously, Renoir stated in an interview about twenty years ago that he could not understand the professed preference of the Italian neorealists for "real people" off the streets as opposed to professional actors. Where on the streets, Renoir asked rhetorically, was a Jean Gabin to be found? Nonetheless, Renoir implies in his categorization of the "heroic" American cinema that an actor's stamp is a sign of immaturity. Robert Bresson is even more relentlessly antiactorish both in his films and in his *Notes on Cinematography:* "No actors. (No directing of actors.) No parts. (No learning of parts.) No staging. But the use of working models, taken from life. *Being* (models) instead of *seeming* (actors). Movement from the exterior to the interior. (Actors: movement from the interior to the exterior.) The thing that matters is not what they show me but what they hide from me, and, above all, *what they do not suspect is in them.* Between them and me: telepathic exchanges, divination."

Bresson's quasi-religious aversion to actors is reflected in his fastidiously antihistrionic films. In his penchant for never using a performer more than once, Bresson seems to imply that once a performer's purity is violated by the camera, he or she lapses irrevocably from a state of grace. As a result, there has never been a Bresson stock company, like Ingmar Bergman's or John Ford's or even Luis Buñuel's. Not only has Bresson prevented actors from building up a career in his own films, he has generally jinxed them for other filmmakers as well. Dominique Sanda is about the only Bressonian "being" to achieve an independent career in films. But Bresson has paid a high price for his "purity" in terms of audience acceptance. Many directors have paid lip service to Bresson's vision of an actorless cinema, but few have chosen to make the necessary sacrifices in public esteem.

On a different tack, an F. Scott Fitzgerald may choose to denigrate stars as puppets (in Aaron Latham's book *Crazy Sundays*): "The dinner party in fact looked just like a Metro movie—except for the lines. Since the writers could not balance the actors on their knees like ventriloquists and give them dialogue, everything was a bit flat—[William] Powell was facetious without wit—Norma [Shearer] heavy without emotion."

Joseph L. Mankiewicz has spoken on occasion of Joan Crawford's giving a dinner party in the thirties, and quoting lines (with supposed spontaneity) from a scene she had been shooting that day. The moral is quite clear: the stars are nothing without the "creative" people behind the screen. But over the years the "creative" people have protested too much, leading a disinterested observer to suspect that actors, and even stars, have made more of a contribution to the cinema than the more jaundiced chronicles would suggest.

For one thing, the full scope of film history depends in great measure on the acting cross-references. Indeed, more often than not, sitting through a bad movie can be justified culturally only by the composition of the cast. And as much as I have always believed in a director's cinema at the summit, I have never been able to escape the haunting presence of the actor in determining the range of my likes and dislikes. Unfortunately, so-called serious film criticism has been so shamed by unabashed fan-mag star-gazing that it has often lost contact with what is most visible and most vital in the cinema. After all, it is the actor that we see aging and dying on the screen, not the director, writer, or other behind-the-screen artist or craftsman. It is time that we acknowledged this fundamental fact.

Throughout the history of the cinema there have been many elaborate attempts to remove the actor from the rhetoric of film theory. In the early twenties, both Lev Kuleshov and Vsevolod Pudovkin wrote of experiments in which the facial expressions of an actor were intercut with contrasting images. Jay Leyda's *Kino* quotes Kuleshov thus: "We had had a difference of opinion on the degree to which the psychological state of the actor is linked to montage. Some said that montage cannot alter that. To an important film actor who held this view we said: Imagine this scene—a man starving in prison is brought a bowl of soup; he is wonderfully happy and devours the soup greedily. Another scene: The prisoner is now fed, but now he longs for freedom, for birds, for the sun, for cottages, for clouds; the door is opened; released, he now sees all he dreamed of. We asked this actor: The face reacting to the soup and the face reacting to the sun—will these in cinema, be the same? His answer was indignant: They *will* be different, for no one would have identical reactions to soup and freedom.

"Then we filmed these two shots and—no matter how often I transposed them or how many people examined them—no one could detect any difference in the face of the actor, although his playing of the two reactions had been quite different. An actor's play reaches the spectator just as the editor requires it to, because the spectator himself completes the connected shots and sees in it what has been suggested to him by the montage."

Curiously, a better-known editing exercise with Ivan Mozhukhin is cited by Pudovkin to prove a quite different point. In this instance, the Russian actor retains the same "neutral" expression in alternation with shots of a plate of soup, a coffin, and a little girl. (A French film historian characteristically revised his account of the experiment by making the little girl a nude woman.) Russian spectators reportedly marveled at the range of expressions in Mozhukhin's repertoire. The joke, of course, was on the spectators since the same expression had been altered by the context of the preceding shot. Taking the two experiments together, one deduces that the Russian montage theoreticians believed that with the proper sequence of shots, actors would not have to alter their expressions, and that if they did, the spectators would not even notice.

As extreme as this position seems today even to steadfast admirers of the Soviet silent film, it established for decades a strong argument against the actor in the theoretical consideration of the cinema. In this context, Sergei Eisenstein's *typage*—a casting of parts by the visual appropriateness of passersby—was regarded as a rejection of the theatrically trained actor with his vast range of roles. Thus did good old Hollywood typecasting sneak in through the back door of film aesthetics.

After World War II, the Italian neorealists conned international audiences into believing that ultraprofessional performers like Anna Magnani and Aldo Fabrizi had been picked up off the streets. Indeed, Vittorio De Sica actually displayed a flair for directing nonprofessional players in *The Bicycle Thief* and *Umberto D*. It did not matter that most movies, "realistic" or not, depended for their dramatic impact on a certain degree of acting expertise. What mattered was that even a very occasional artistic coup with nonprofessionals could be cited *ad infinitum* and *ad nauseam* as a reproof to the artifice of greasepaint. Overlooked was the fact that amateur actors from Nanook on were nothing more or less than gifted "naturals" with an intuitive "feel" for screen space, and an expressive "look" for the lens. By the same token, many illustrious stage presences—Paul Scofield, Lynn Fontanne, Katharine Cornell, John Gielgud (early in his career)—have lacked camera magic.

It might be noted that different snobberies operate in this situation. On the one hand, the theater crowd with its cultural seniority insists that the stage is the only proper arena for serious acting. On the other, the proponents of pure cinema prefer to ignore the subject of acting. In terms of this impasse, the role of film editing is extremely complex.

The fact that a movie performance can be spliced together out of bits and pieces of behaviorism makes it possible for players of limited talent and experience to create an impression of competence. Acting can be reduced to reacting, and producers can fall back on that last forlorn hope: "We'll save it in the editing room." Conversely, the magic of montage makes it impossible for experienced stage actors to control their screen performances. With most movies shot out of sequence for economy's sake, and with several takes of each scene, the film actor seldom has any clear conception of the size and shape of his completed performance.

Yet something remains that is irreducibly actorish: a face and a figure painted in time, a palpable presence in space, a sign by which a physical surface is translated into a spiritual essence, and a representative of our race and our age. It makes a difference that *Stagecoach* was made with John Wayne and Claire Trevor instead of Gary Cooper and Marlene Dietrich, as the producer had proposed earlier. With Cooper and Dietrich, Josef von Sternberg (of *Morocco* memory) would have been looking over Ford's shoulder. Even the genre would have been different as world-weary narcissism replaced rough-and-ready vulnerability. Similarly, the proposed casting of Claudette Colbert and June Allyson in Joseph L. Mankiewicz's *All About Eve* in place of Bette Davis and Anne Baxter would have lifted the pitch of the Broadway model bitchery from Tallulah Bankhead to Ina Claire. In both *Stagecoach* and *Eve,* and in all movies, for that matter, the casting constitutes a major portion of the writing. Because the text of a film is ultimately the film itself, and not a printed screenplay, however lavishly illustrated, one cannot detach the player from the part.

Is there any point, therefore, in trying to imagine what Margaret Sullavan would have been like in Joan Fontaine's role in *Rebecca,* or Vivien Leigh instead of Merle Oberon as Cathy in *Wuthering Heights*? Should we not accept all past casting decisions as divinely inspired faits accomplis? As a rule, we do not spend too much time speculating about what one director or writer would have done with another's project. Why should we try to imagine Greta Garbo's Juliet or Walter Huston's Ahab?

Of course, the currently much-abused movie buff can be accused of wanting his favorite stars to play every conceivable role on the screen. But the absolute buff of antibuff legend supposedly likes every movie, and is therefore unlikely to make the kind of value judgment that implies any degree of miscasting. Besides, if casting is to be construed as a form of writing, is not apparent miscasting actually a form of rewriting? To take an extreme example, let us say that *Hamlet* had been cast with Jack Benny instead of with Laurence Olivier. Is Jack Benny miscast, or is *Hamlet* being rewritten at the very moment of casting?

These questions are not nearly as frivolous as they may seem. Over the past sixty years, our notion of what constitutes good screen acting has fluctuated wildly. Even before World War I there was a critical tension between the rival camps of the art film and the popular movie. From the beginning the theater was both a vital influence and a pretentious distraction. Through the silent era, movie acting retained part of its autonomy simply through its lack of speech. Sight dominated casting without regard to sound, and theater people chortled at the cultural inferiority of movie dumb shows (*vide* Debbie Reynolds's put-down of Gene Kelly in the Broadway-oriented speech in *Singin' in the Rain*).

After sound, many pretty faces with ugly voices were eased out of pictures. Theater people were recruited en masse, and film theoreticians bemoaned the demise of "pure" cinema. Gradually, film regained its visual equilibrium at the expense of what Jean-Luc Godard much later described as the sacred sound of speech. Montage regained enough of its magic to enable players with limited theatrical training to become stars and even myths. Exit John Gilbert! Enter Clark Gable!

The plot thickened in the fifties and sixties when André Bazin's challenge to Eisenstein's montage aesthetics made us all reexamine the traditional notions of "progress" in film history. We had to go back to the very early silents and to the very early talkies to realize that every step forward was also a step backward, and that, often, we had gained fluidity at the expense of conviction. For a time it seemed that wide screens, long takes, and intricate compositions in depth would render the Kim Novaks and Lana Turners of this world obsolete.

Then along came Michelangelo Antonioni with his alienated characters framed against indifferent landscapes, and the old Germanic nightmares about somnambulists were reinstituted in broad daylight. In the new age of alienation and absurdism, accomplished players both here and abroad found themselves reduced on the screen to dedramatized figures in a landscape. By contrast, more limited players found themselves up to their ears in action and emotion for unabashed genre studies. Then gradually violence became the dominant metaphor for both the art film and the popular movie. Through all these changes, screen acting has come to be seen more and more clearly as a form of screenwriting, as both the theater types and the movie types have come together in a common language, which is to say that even an Olivier can be regarded partly as an art object, and a Schwarzenegger partly as a sentient being.

Though I still believe in a cinema of directors, I have come to believe also that the actor constitutes much of the language of the cinema, and that directors, writers, and technicians have always had to cope with that language as one of the conditions of creation. Where criticism has lagged is in not integrating acting with the stylistics of montage and mise-en-scène. I have long urged film schools to devote more attention to casting and acting, and less to the explorations and improvisations of an anarchic camera.

Two final points. There is a contradiction between the public's tendency to patronize movies with their favorite stars and their subconscious desire to see brand-new people up on the screen on every occasion. The respectable argument has to do with realism. How can you believe Katharine Hepburn as a Chinese peasant? That sort of thing. Deep down, however, moviegoers and even critics yearn to be free to fantasize without being distracted by overly familiar stars. I am convinced that if moviegoers and critics had their way there would be few sustained careers in the movies. We are beginning to get a sense of in-and-out acceleration already in television.

Actors are always urged to change their type, to seek out difficult and unsympathetic roles. Theatrical humbug! All actors are typed one way or another. Olivier, for example, has been typed as a change-type. And his mellifluous speaking voice makes him as much an art object as Sophia Loren's bosom makes her. The camera seeks out beauty even in the midst of the most studied drabness.

[1977]

Vincent Canby

THE PERFORMER vs. THE ROLE
Catherine Deneuve and James Mason

Two weeks ago I did not walk out on a particularly phony little French melodrama called *Act of Aggression*. . . . The thing that kept me in the theater, as riveted as one can be by a terrible film, was the spectacle of Catherine Deneuve trying desperately and with wit to give some life to the venture. Now Miss Deneuve is one of the world's great beauties but she is never very close to the top of anyone's list of the world's great actresses. More than competent she is, and stunning to behold, even in a Chanel ad, but she never gets the kind of notices that are heaped on Glenda Jackson, Ellen Burstyn, and Jane Fonda.

Miss Deneuve was so effective within the dismal context of *Act of Aggression* . . . that I began to worry all over again about the manner in which critics treat film acting and actors.

Miss Deneuve has been marvelously effective in some fascinating films— Polanski's *Repulsion,* Buñuel's *Belle de Jour* and *Tristana*, and Truffaut's *Mississippi Mermaid*—but I don't think anyone has ever suggested that her performance alone had made any film worth seeing. I'm not about to know. *Act of Aggression* is unsalvageable. Given the right material, however, she appears to be growing into an actress of just such stature. But will we ever know?

It's not, I think, a foolish question. All of us—critics as well as people who simply go to the movies because they like them—bring into the theater so many preconditioned responses that the way we react to the performances may have little to do with the performer or his talent.

From the point of view of the intelligent actor, movies must be the least rewarding experience there is, unless the actor has the clout to pick his associates and material and run the show. Bad lighting, an inappropriate directorial style, a cut-and-paste screenplay, lawn-mower editing, can make any good actor look imbecilic. Sometimes an actor stands away from the background. More often not. In those magical moments of fiddling around with material after it's been photographed, a performance that once made sense can be transformed into a double-talk joke.

Inappropriate—bad—casting is something we often blame on the actor when all he's trying to do is make a living. Take the recent work of Glenda Jackson, an actress who, for various reasons, is incapable of playing someone without brains and a good deal of spine. There's a certain amount of fun watching her in an overripe Italian tomato like *The Devil Is a Woman*, playing a sexually hung-up nun, but the subterranean personality that shapes her every performance throws Joseph Losey's *The Romantic Englishwoman* off the track.

The film is interesting as long as it's about Miss Jackson and her equally intelligent though troubled husband, played by Michael Caine. They seem made for each other. They are peers. But when the movie introduces the idea that a woman like Miss Jackson could throw herself at the feet of a gigolo of Helmut Berger's weightlessness, the movie becomes a solemn, overdressed fraud. We lose patience with everyone, including Miss Jackson. She's still the actress she always has been but we blame her for having gotten into bad company.

The best film performers (and some of the most enduring) are the most pliant, though pliancy is not meant to be synonymous with versatility. Pliancy has something to do with talent and even more to do with the personality of the actor, the way he looks, his physical shape. Dustin Hoffman and Al Pacino are amazingly pliant actors, even though each one tends to evoke New York and there are times when all of us confuse the two.

Gene Hackman, who is a fine actor, appears to lack this pliancy. No matter what role he plays, the character seems to have some dread, Ibsen-like secret to live down from the past. His physical appearance is not pliant. This has nothing to do with his acting abilities but he seems unable to make us believe the character he's playing just happens to look like him. He overwhelms the role with a particular physical presence and brings to it a whole carload of psychological experience we've come to identify with him from his other films.

Part of this may have to do with exposure. Hackman seems to have been on our screens nonstop all year and though the movies are different (*French Connection Two, Night Moves*), Hackman isn't. Some actors cannot accommodate frequent exposure. Hackman is one of them. So is Elliott Gould.

One who apparently is able to is Jack Nicholson, an actor who has a unique ability to sneak up on roles and occupy them so completely that, while you're watching him in *One Flew Over the Cuckoo's Nest*, you're never associating him with, say, the spaced-out white-suited lawyer in *Easy Rider*.

The public personalities of actors, especially stars, are shaped as much by their high positions as by their films. Nicholson has had the good fortune to be in a variety of films that have seldom been stupid, if not always successful. His high position hasn't yet interfered with his career as it did with Marlon Brando's, once the most talented, the most pliant of them all. Paul Newman, Warren Beatty, and Robert Redford are pliant actors. Burt Reynolds may be. Steve McQueen and Charles Bronson aren't. . . .

Having gone on at this length, I should add that writing about film acting is, at best, perilous, at worst, nonsense. We can simply label performances "good," "fine," "gemlike," "lousy," or we can try to describe the performances. But describing a performance is like trying to describe the taste of broiled shad roe. You may be able to interest someone in trying it himself but until he does, the subject remains elusive.

[1975]

In the better films of the better directors—Hitchcock, Rohmer, Truffaut, Mankiewicz, Kubrick, to name just a few who come to mind for no particular reason—it's difficult to tell where the work of the director (or the screenwriter) leaves off and that of the actor begins. A good film is all of a piece. It's an entity. It has no seams. It's possible for the critic to describe such a film, to try to communicate its effect as accurately as possible, and to give some idea of what it means, but the critic can get into trouble when he tries to distribute blue ribbons. He may even feel a little silly, as I sometimes do. It's like pinning the tale on the donkey.

Not having any idea of precisely who did what, the critic can find himself paying tribute to (or blaming) someone who wasn't even on the set when a film was made.

Film acting—or as someone has called it, film behaving—is subject to so many variables, from direction, writing, lighting, and editing to the line of a jaw or of a thigh (which evoke subterranean responses probably best not analyzed) that I sometimes am reduced to calling a performance good, bad, indifferent, or excellent—but more or less blindly.

Not always, but often enough to make me realize that for film actors the reading of reviews must be about as essential as the study of calculus. The Dan Greenburg comedy, *I Could Never Have Sex with Any Man Who Has So Little Regard for My Husband*, has some funny lines in it but it is, over the long haul, a cheerful bore: a frumpy East Coast version of *Bob & Carol & Ted & Alice*. Are the four new (to me) actors in it any good? I haven't any idea. They aren't terrible, certainly, and each has his moments, but the quality of the film pretty much defines the performances.

Lots of us, I suspect, make the mistake of confusing a performance with a role, especially with the kind of small, colorful roles that were so carefully cast, mostly with nonprofessionals, in John Huston's *Fat City* last year. Were these people great actors? I doubt it. But the roles were beautifully written and someone had the great good fortune to find people to play them who, for one reason or another, were able to project the sense of the roles as written. Sometimes they did it just by looking right and by being properly photographed.

Liv Ullmann, so fascinating in Bergman's films, registers with all of the impact of boiled ham on white bread in the Hollywood-made *Lost Horizon* and *40 Carats*. Is this her fault? Does it mean she's really a lousy actress? Probably not. Yet it makes us reevaluate some of the things we've thought about her in the past. For one reason or another, Dyan Cannon seemed hopelessly ill-at-ease in Otto Preminger's *Such Good Friends*, which otherwise is one of Preminger's best films, but she is very funny, and very much at ease, in Herbert Ross's *The Last of Sheila*.

I can't quite believe that means that Miss Cannon has suddenly learned how to act. I assume that the same intelligence was at work in both films, but for reasons over which she might not have had complete control, she comes off splendidly in one film and as a kind of blank spot in the other.

There are, of course, exceptions, performers who remain somehow inviolate no matter how tawdry the circumstances in which they happen to find themselves. Mostly these are the so-called stars, people like Steve McQueen and Paul Newman and Robert Mitchum, whose professional personalities tend to distract attention from their talents as actors. When they make good films, we accept the quality of their performances as a matter of course. When they show up in junk, their reputations aren't damaged, even though their contributions may not be particularly interesting. They manage to remain aloof from the disaster around them.

All of which brings me to the point of this piece: James Neville Mason who, at sixty-four, is no longer the leading man he once was though he remains a star and one of the most consistently interesting actors in films today. I have no idea if he is actually a *better* actor now than he was in the early fifties. He was awfully good then (in *Julius Caesar*, *A Star Is Born*, *Five Fingers*), though he was known less as a good actor than as an eccentric personality. It may be that today he is wiser, more nonchalant—I have no way of knowing. What is apparent is that seeing him in two current first-run films that are not of classic caliber, *The Last of Sheila* and John Huston's *The Mackintosh Man*, is like running unexpectedly into an old friend who turns what would have been a dull dinner party into a thoroughly enjoyable evening, not by remaining aloof but by using his intelligence, wit, and experience and by allowing himself to become as completely involved as possible.

Neither role offers him the opportunities he had in *Lolita* (which was a magnificently funny portrait of seedy desperation) or even in *Child's Play* (in which he played a totally unsympathetic victim), but Mason gives the two films unexpected dimension. He does nothing so vulgar and flashy as to walk off with the films. He doesn't steal them. Rather, by creating characters that command attention, he gives the other characters in the films importance they do not deserve under the circumstances.

In *The Mackintosh Man,* which, as melodrama, ranks somewhere between Huston's *The Kremlin Letters* and *Beat the Devil* (at least it's almost as confusing as *Beat the Devil,* if not as funny), Mason has what amounts to a disposable role, that of a platitudinous Tory M.P. who is really an archtraitor to the crown. It's disposable because the character is not on the screen long enough to be identified in any way whatsoever, except as a first-class nasty. He's not a person but a plot function. Mason, however, gives the role a presence that carries over into the scenes in which he doesn't appear. We remember him, we wonder what makes him tick (even though the screenplay doesn't) and we are always aware that there is a mind at work.

In *The Last of Sheila*, Mason is cast as Philip, a once-successful film director now reduced to directing television commercials, preferably with the small, prepubescent girls with whom he is obsessed. . . . Mason invests the character with a kind of self-mocking, rueful courage (which is not in the screenplay so far as I can tell) and his technical assurance allows him effortlessly to reel off great convoluted chunks of exposition of the sort without which no whodunit can be said to have been brought to a climax.

For some time I'd been thinking that Mason was becoming a better, more interesting actor with the passage of time. Having recently reseen *Lolita, North by Northwest,* and *Georgy Girl,* it now occurs to me that he has always been superb. It's just that because so many of his recent films have been less than great, it's easier to recognize his contributions. He is, in fact, one of the very few film actors worth taking the trouble to see, even when the film that encases him is so much cement.

[1973]

Vincent Canby

TELEPERFORMING vs. SCREEN ACTING
Sally Field

People in movies are seldom convincing as packers of suitcases and in bad movies they are ridiculous: a man opens a bureau drawer, pulls out a shirt and a pair of socks that have never been worn, drops them into a Gladstone bag, and that's that. For the next few weeks or months or years, the character, looking forever spruce, changes clothes at will, coming up with variations of costume that would be beyond the capacity of a steamer trunk.

In real life the packing of a suitcase is not something one does casually. It involves a series of interlocking decisions based on itinerary, length of trip, season of the year, maximum weight allowance, reading habits and other value judgments, and, most important, the general condition of the suitcase (is this the trip on which it's going to split?). Even when the job is carefully done, is there anyone among us who hasn't at some point arrived at his destination to find that an essential prop has been left behind? Unless it's part of the plot, a man in a movie never has this problem. Also, unless the movie is a comedy, his suitcase never threatens to pull his arm from its socket, to leave him with blisters on both hands, or to throw his back out of gear.

Though I cannot substantiate the following statement with any immediate facts, I have the definite impression that suitcase-packing in movies these days has reached a new low, and I suspect that television is to blame. Have you ever seen one of Charlie's Angels pay an airline overweight? Unconvincing suitcase-packing is obviously no big deal but the way in which the manners, techniques, and personalities of television are beginning to shape theatrical motion pictures—to make them smaller, busier, and blander—must give us pause.

The first great wave of television directors who made their way to theatrical films—Arthur Penn, Sidney Lumet, George Roy Hill, Franklin Schaffner, John Frankenheimer—adapted themselves to the older medium. Even while they brought to Hollywood some of the frenetic tensions that were virtually a method of working in television when major shows were done live, these directors couldn't wait to exploit the cinema resources that then separated movies from television. The kind of imperial crane shots and deep-focus vistas that are the marks of a Franklin Schaffner film like *Patton* would have been out of the question in any live television production. For Mr. Schaffner and the others, movies were a whole new thing.

Today the exact opposite is true—possibly because these television people have grown up using film and tape. The television directors who are now switching to the big screen can't wait to reduce its dimensions, to make movies that look as much as possible like the sitcoms and so-called "television movies" that are being relentlessly ground out for the tube.

What is this "look"?

First, it is an overpowering blandness, the sort that John Denver exudes in Carl Reiner's *Oh, God!*, a sketchlike comedy about God (George Burns) and a supermarket manager (Mr. Denver). Bland has always been big in television, probably because the principal function of almost any television show is to entertain without disturbing, to occupy the eye without troubling it, to soothe without leaving a hangover. Perry Como, Dick Clark, Andy Williams, and even Dean Martin haven't endured as long as they have by sending rockets into their audiences.

Though Mr. Reiner once made a very funny theatrical film, *Where's Poppa?*, his principal experience has been in television, and television sets the style of *Oh, God!* It has the rhythm of a variety show in which the sequence of sketches is of no great importance. The colors are just a little too bright and the characters are seen in (though they don't appear to inhabit) suburban houses with kitchens in which you can't believe anyone has ever opened a can of frozen orange-juice concentrate.

There's another aspect to this "look" that's all over a frivolously rotten comedy-drama called *Heroes*, which stars Henry ("the Fonz") Winkler, as a picturesquely disturbed Vietnam veteran, and Sally ("The Flying Nun") Field as the picturesquely mixed-up young woman he meets on a transcontinental bus.

Heroes, which was directed by Jeremy Paul Kagan, who directed Mr. Winkler in the television film, *Katherine*, is an almost perfect example of what I fear may become the standard theatrical film of our television-dominated future. It's not simply that the performances of the two stars are the sort one sees in thirty-minute sitcoms where everything must be laid on the line as quickly as possible, nor that the two stars, by the frequency of their appearances on television, are now television icons of which there are maybe a half-dozen principal models (though I certainly don't agree with a friend of mine who says that Miss Field is simply a Mary Tyler Moore someone has stepped on).

I suspect both Mr. Winkler and Miss Field are not only capable but possibly talented actors when given the chance of acting instead of what might be called teleperforming. To teleperform is to use a set of simplified mannerisms that express television's five basic emotions—joy (ear-to-ear grin), anger (furrowed brow), hope (a slightly less than ear-to-ear grin), hurt/surprise (dropped jaw), ecstasy (running). (These are not the only emotions that can be expressed by teleperforming. Combining hope with hurt/surprise, for example, may approximate anxiety, and if you add these to ecstasy, you've got something very much like blind panic.) One doesn't respond to the emotion of a teleperformance as often as one reads it, as if it were a series of traffic signals.

The television roots of *Heroes* are apparent in both large and small matters. There's a brief sequence in which Miss Field calls on one of the crazy Vietnam veteran's friends and finds, instead, the friend's abandoned wife, who is black. This is fine as far as it goes, but the role has been cast and played in a manner that says less about a woman who's been abandoned by a drifting husband (also traumatized by the war?) than it says about the bland manner in which television thinks that blacks must be presented for a positive image. Olivia Cole, who plays the unhappy wife, is so stately, serene, regal and collected (and altogether unreal) that as she walks around her model home, you might think she was really the mistress of a maison of haute couture in Paris.

Heroes makes one apprehensive about the future of movies in other, more important ways, though. Television movies, because of the nature of the medium that presents them, are as carefully composed to accommodate the commercial breaks as they are to entertain, and some of the ways in which they entertain are the tricks they employ to get us across the breaks. The films are paced in bits and pieces, which is why theatrical films with fragmented narratives sometimes play even better on television than they do in theaters.

As a result of their television backgrounds, many of these new directors and writers seem incapable of putting together films that not only sustain narrative interest but build it to some kind of climax. Instead, like *Heroes* and like another new film, Michael Schultz's *Which Way Is Up?*, the new Richard Pryor comedy, the movies begin, fool around horizontally, and then end. You begin to wonder if these films would seem better, less brainless, if one could watch them in their full glory, that is, complete with commercial and station breaks.

Instead of real dramatic movement, television shows can get by—in a way theatrical films seldom can any more—by physical movement. A large part of television's police shows appears to be shots of people getting into or out of their cars, driving away from or arriving at destinations, with a bit of necessary exposition squeezed into a shot inside the car as it's en route.

Heroes opens with Henry Winkler doing a lot of busy, extremely cute things around Times Square. Not only does Henry run frequently, but when the film proper gets going, he's riding buses or automobiles. He *is* moving but the picture never gets any place until the last reel, when it must end.

Which Way Is Up?, a failed attempt to transplant *The Seduction of Mimi*, Lina Wertmuller's Italian comedy about sex, politics, and Sicily to southern California, is a lot less painless to watch than *Heroes*, but then it stars Richard Pryor, who is a very, very funny actor even though he's no Giancarlo Giannini.

Like *Heroes*, however, *Which Way Is Up?* doesn't discover its narrative and then build on it. Rather, it sort of moves through its story as if walking through someone's cluttered backyard. What happens—the events of the narrative—seem to be impediments to the real business of the film, which is to give Mr. Pryor the opportunity to perform a series of sometimes hilarious sketches, as, of course, he does on television.

The director and his writers, Carl Gottlieb and Cecil Brown, use the Wertmuller original only in the most superficial ways, and occasionally make their southern California black characters behave as if they were supposed to be Sicilian, which is very odd to watch, indeed.

The producers who make these films, of course, may well know what they're doing. It must be assumed that the people who go to see them are mostly the same people who watch television, whose attention spans are limited, and who have sensibilities attuned to movies that deal almost entirely in the kind of immediate sensation provided by the zoom lens and nonstop soundtrack music. Will these films succeed at the box office? I'm not sure. I don't know why anyone would want to pay a theater's stiff admission price to see a movie in which the characters walk around with empty suitcases. They can stay home and see the same thing free.

[1977]

There's a fine, achingly honest scene early in *Norma Rae*, Martin Ritt's new movie about the politicization of a Southern hillbilly woman, when Sally Field, in the title role, and Beau Bridges, as Sonny, whom she eventually marries, are becoming sweetly drunk in a local tavern on their first date. It is Friday night, the end of a long week at the cotton mill where they both work. They are exhausted, awash in beer, and very happy. It's at that hour in the evening when the lyrics of even the corniest laments on the jukebox speak directly to the listener.

For a moment Norma Rae is overwhelmed by her responses to the music. She furrows her brow. "... and the words are so true," she says and we laugh, not at her but in recognition of all of those times when second-rate sentiments have been musically invested with the power of ancient truths. Norma Rae goes on to remember the night her husband was killed in a fight in just such a joint as this: "He broke off the top of a beer bottle, you know? And this other guy broke off the top of a beer bottle too. . . ." The next thing Norma Rae knew, she was receiving a phone call at home telling her she'd just become a widow. For most of her life, Norma Rae has been living lyrics written in Nashville.

It's a difficult scene to describe accurately because of the contradictory emotions it evokes. Mostly, though, the effect is exhilaration, because we are witnessing one of those unusual motion-picture performances that seems to be in the process of taking off as we watch it. It's the sort of thing that happens with some frequency in the theater, where we share time and space with the actor on the stage. Movies, however, seldom allow us to feel this complicity. Though the mechanics of the screen can somehow hypnotize us into watching the most brainless claptrap from start to finish, the same mechanics have a way of laminating even great performances, not interfering with them but setting them slightly apart from us as they are being preserved forever.

Miss Field's Norma Rae represents a number of triumphs. To begin with, the role has been beautifully written by Irving Ravetch and Harriet Frank, Jr., who've created a character that embodies much of what we like to think is best about our national character, if, indeed, there is such a thing. Norma Rae is not perfect. She is a young woman of no great amount of formal education and no luck at all with men. "You got dirt under your fingernails and you pick your teeth with a matchbook," her most recent lover tells her at the start of the film, just after he's whomped her a good one and is about to dump her permanently. Yet Norma Rae is capable of learning, growing, changing. She possesses self-awareness that is rare and common sense that is not anti-intellectual but the strength of an open mind. Her awakening in the course of the film, which is about the struggle to unionize a small mill in the contemporary South, represents the continuing strength and adaptability of the pioneer stock that first settled this country. And her relationship with Reuben Marshasky (Ron Liebman), the young Jewish labor organizer from New York, represents the happiest kind of conjunction of different American cultures.

Norma Rae is—and I use the word with caution—optimistic, but it's neither foolish nor blind. It's optimistic because it exalts great possibilities, which is not the same as suggesting that no problems exist.

Though all of Mr. Ritt's films feature strong performances, none has a character to match Norma Rae, which brings us back to Miss Field who, I suppose it must be pointed out, was a nun who flew in an earlier show-biz incarnation. Her triumph in *Norma Rae* is to have shucked off at long last all need to associate her with her television beginnings, not because they are vulgar but because the performance she gives here is as big as the screen that presents it.

A small woman with a waist tinier than Scarlett O'Hara's and with a large talent controlled by intelligence, Miss Field has apparently been revving up for this performance for sometime in movies like *Sybil* (on television) and *Smokey and the Bandit* and *The End*, though we may not have known it. Her Norma Rae is the kind of complete performance one associates with theatrical films, not only because theatrical films have the time and space for details that can only be suggested on television, but because she is thoroughly committed to the role. There's nothing held back here, no reserve of the public personality into which she can take refuge if the movie itself doesn't work—one of the more common problems when television personalities switch to films.

Typical of the latter is the exuberantly cheerful, but never for a moment believable, performance given by Gabe (*Welcome Back, Kotter*) Kaplan in Jack Smight's *Fast Break*. The film is about a New York delicatessen clerk who becomes the basketball coach at a rundown college out West where blacks, Jews, and other "ethnics" are more rare than Spanish moss. Though it's a nice movie, it's as instantly disposable as junk mail. There's nothing wrong with Mr. Kaplan's performance except that it's not a performance. It's a presentation of the television personality in the frame of an extended sketch in which Mr. Kaplan speaks all the right lines, goes through all the proper motions, but remains slightly above and to the side of the character within the movie. I suppose someone can argue that this isn't necessarily less of a performance, only a different kind of performance, just as *Fast Break* is a sort of halfway house for the television personality en route to a career in films.

My fear is that this kind of uncommitted performance will become an end in itself. One of the things that makes *Moment by Moment* tolerable, at least in retrospect, is the comparison between the performances of John Travolta and Lily Tomlin, both essentially products of television comedy.

Mr. Travolta appeared to be completely committed to his rather thankless role. For better or worse he created a recognizable character and stuck with it. Miss Tomlin, on the other hand, appeared to be thinking about a character, quite seriously, but not acting it yet. Admittedly, no real character seems to have existed in Jane Wagner's screenplay, but what Miss Tomlin gave us was less an attempt at characterization than a demonstration of Miss Tomlin's thinking about it, which is the way stand-up comedians work.

This helps to explain why Sally Field's Norma Rae comes as such a grand surprise. Watching this actress give life to a woman of grit and guts, of humor and compassion, without worrying about the consequences, is the kind of marvelous experience we don't often see in movies. In *Norma Rae*, Sally Field can be identified as a major Hollywood resource.

[1979]

II.
THE
STARS

Jack Kroll

WOODY ALLEN

You sympathize with Woody's desire to erase confusion between his real and performing selves.

Woody Allen became a national hero when his movie *Annie Hall* won four Academy Awards—for best picture, for Allen as best director, for Allen and Marshall Brickman as best original screenwriters, for Diane Keaton as best actress. At the moment of his apotheosis, Allen was three thousand miles away, sound asleep in his New York penthouse. He had eased himself into slumber with his current reading, *Conversations With Carl Jung.* And before that, he had been doing what he does every Monday night—playing the clarinet with a semi-pro jazz band at a New York bistro called Michael's Pub. He had also turned off his phone, so it wasn't until he picked up his *New York Times* the next morning that he found out his fame had spread overnight around the world. "I was very surprised," says Woody. "I felt good for Diane, because she wanted to go and wanted to win. My friend Marshall had a very nice time and my producers Jack Rollins and Charles Joffe had a very nice time. But I'm anhedonic."

Being anhedonic does not mean that Woody has to wear a little bell around his neck. Anhedonia is a melancholy but noncontagious psychological condition that prevents its victim from enjoying himself. It was also the original title of *Annie Hall,* until United Artists begged Woody to change it just before the film's release. Anhedonia (the opposite of hedonism) is one of the many syndromes that have kept Woody Allen in analysis for twenty-two of his forty-two years. It's therefore one of the things that make Woody Woody—a frail-looking man (with a face that convinces you that God is a cartoonist), a brilliant comedian, a natural writer, an appealing actor, a gifted and maturing film director, and a personality beloved in the anxiety-ridden arrondissements of our urban centers.

Woody is also a man at a crossroads—if you can find a crossroads in the maze that passes for his psyche. Call it rather a turning point. Woody Allen, the funniest neurotic of our time, is about to switch his comic mask for the stern visage of serious drama. His new movie, *Interiors,* is a brooding, Bergmanesque affair without a single laugh in it. "At least with no intentional ones," says the anhedonic Allen.

Those among Woody's fans—and critics—who have not realized what a complex figure he is are apparently about to find out with a vengeance. It's as if the manic Mel Brooks were to appear before us as Oedipus, putting out his eyes instead of putting on his audience. But last week, the people who jammed Michael's Pub, eager for the first opportunity to salute Woody since his Oscar sweep, saw only the Woody they think they know and know they love.

Dressed in his customary plaid shirt and Army fatigue jacket, Woody played three sets with the informal group that's been together for eight years. Appropriately, Woody's group must be the cleanest jazz band in a notoriously raffish art form—one of the players is a narcotics agent. The band plays New Orleans jazz standards with an engaging, unpretentious affection. Woody plays the clarinet sitting down ("That's the way they play at Preservation Hall in New Orleans," he says), his casually crossed legs belying the intensity with which he gets into the stomps and blues of the music. On "Milenberg Joys," he played two straight choruses, with a driving force that reddened his face and uncrossed his legs.

Between sets Woody showed that his anhedonia extended to food (he ate and drank nothing), but he appeared somewhat more hedonic about girls. One young strawberry blonde with eyes like candle flames passed him a gift. "It's a brass heart," she said. "So's mine," replied Woody affably. "Can we go out?" begged the girl, eyes guttering. "I'm living with someone," said Woody. "She's not much, but she's all I have." Meekly the girl retreated, sighing, "I love you a lot." An older woman gave Woody a copy of a paperback she had written called *Naked Nun.* "It's my memoirs," she told him. "It's a clean book. You can read it in one setting." "You mean sitting," said Woody distantly. He grew less distant when a dark-haired angel appeared to ask for his autograph. She was very young and Woody looked after her with a complex appreciation as she went back to a nearby table. He mused: "If my moral sense ever sinks as low as my other senses . . . but it wouldn't look good for me to hang around the Dalton School with my coat collar turned up."

The room vibrates with affection for this quiet, somber-faced man who seems more focused, more himself than any other person in it. Almost stealthily, Allen has updated the old symbol of the "little man" at bay in a complex, threatening world. Woody is little, all right; "at bay" could certainly be embossed on his business cards, and God knows the world is complex and threatening. But through the eleven films that he's been connected with in one way or several others as writer, actor, or director (not to mention two plays, two books, and his record albums), Woody Allen has finally come to represent not the schlemiel he's so often called, but an almost romantic figure. The Woody we have come to know is nothing more eccentric than a chap of yearningly normal desires and high accomplishment who can't get things together because together isn't where things are heading now.

To finally become this character—the Alvy Singer of *Annie Hall*—Allen had to pull his creative skills together. The movies he's directed have always oscillated between an inspired anarchy, as in the best parts of *Bananas* and *Everything You Always Wanted to Know About Sex But Were Afraid to Ask*, and a more conventional humor, as in *Take the Money and Run* and *Sleeper*. The point about Woody's comic persona is its intense sanity, but the sanity must *be* intense—it's sanity under the severest pressure. *Sleeper* is a gemlike movie: it has a visual sense somewhere between Buster Keaton and *Star Wars* as time-traveling Woody disguises himself as an effete robot or wrestles with monstrously unappetizing fruits and vegetables.

Sex is perhaps Woody's most scathingly funny film; there his sanity is so icily sane that it smokes with Swiftian disdain of our sexual fatuities. Who can forget Woody as Sperm No. 2, pale with fear as he's about to join his mates in an ejaculation? *Love and Death* is closer to the spirit of the witty *New Yorker* magazine pieces in which Woody satirizes highbrow things he loves, in this case Russian novels such as *War and Peace*. In *Annie Hall*, Woody's beleaguered, panicky sanity nestles beautifully in a darling orchestration of tenderly failed relationships. The success of *Annie Hall*, which also won the National Society of Film Critics and the New York Film Critics Circle awards for best movie of 1977, is a recognition of the big leap forward that film represents for him.

What this means is simply that Woody has graduated from nebbish to enigma. "The schlemiel image never did describe me," he insists. "I've never been that. It's an appellation for the unimaginative to hang on me. The things I did on nightclub stages were fantasies or exaggerations from my own life—school, women, parents—which I set out in an amusing way. But you look up after a year and the press has created you: 'Well, he's a small man at odds with mechanical objects who can't cope with his relationships with women.' But all I was doing was what was funny; there's no conscious design to anything." This kind of overinterpretation, Allen believes, is what one of his heroes, Groucho, used to describe. "Groucho would be in a hotel room in Des Moines. He'd read in a paper that the Marx Brothers are surrealists and he'd think, Chico's out chasing girls, I'm trying to get a couple of jokes, and we're just trying to survive and get out of this town."

You sympathize with Woody's desire to erase confusion between his real and performing selves. But for him to protest his proud schlemiel pedigree is like W. C. Fields objecting to being dubbed a lush or Chaplin scorning the status of tramp. The delicately hilarious tension between self-deprecation and self-inflation is the trigger that explodes a comedian into a comic archetype. Woody Allen, whoever he is, was born out of such fruitful ambivalence. Woody the woman conqueror: "On my wedding night my wife stopped in the middle of everything to give me a standing ovation." Woody the woman conqueree: "Someday they're gonna give me a birthday party and wheel out a tremendous birthday cake, and a giant naked woman will leap out of the cake and hurt me and leap back in."

The fact is that Woody Allen, like many great comics, is a saintly schizophrenic, a man at odds with himself. Inside this clown there's a tragedian who's not only struggling to get out but who's just about made it. The split goes back to Woody's beginnings as Allen Stewart Konigsberg, a child of the Flatbush streets. Young Allen was a morosely vigorous semiliterate who seemed like a whirlwind visitor in the house of his parents, Martin and Nettie. "I was out in the streets from eight o'clock in the morning," says Woody; "playing baseball and basketball. At lunchtime I'd race into the house, eat a tuna-fish sandwich by myself and read a comic book—*Superman*, *Batman* or *Mickey Mouse*. I'd run back out on the street and play ball. Then I'd run back in for dinner, read another comic book, run back out again for two hours, come in, and watch the St. Louis Cardinals beat the Dodgers on television."

Young Konigsberg's instinctive moves were all against the grain. "I was a rabid New York Giants fan from 1946 on," Woody says. "It played into my fantasy of alienation because I was in the heart of Flatbush surrounded by hostile Dodger fans." Thomas Wolfe said that only the dead know Brooklyn, but young Woody proved that the dying do, too. "Even as a pre-teen," he says, "I was aware of the fact I was going to die and I couldn't figure out why I'm here or what it's all about. As soon as I became aware of the conditions of life, I've never been able to accommodate them. At the core, life is a concentration camp."

This was a feeling that didn't come out of books. "For the first fifteen years of my life I never read," says Woody. "I was just interested in going out in the street and playing ball. It was only when I started going out with women who were more cultured and made greater demands on me that I started to feel I had to read to keep my end of the conversation up." The strange thing was that Woody could write before he could read. "Even while I was reading nothing but *Donald Duck* and *Batman* I could write real prose in school compositions. There was never a week when the composition I wrote was not the one that was read to the class."

Nonreader, natural writer Allen was getting his real education from show business. "The Flatbush Theater had vaudeville and movies and I saw every comic, every tap dancer, every magician, every kind of singer. I heard 'Sorrento' sung more times than anyone. I could do everybody's act. I used to tear up the Raisinets boxes and write jokes down." By this time, in high school, Allen had become an odd kind of loner. More and more, he kept to himself. He had discovered jazz and taught himself to play the clarinet and soprano saxophone by playing along with records. "I never ate with my family," recalls Woody. "I'd eat in the cellar or my bedroom, read my comic books, lock myself in my room, and practice the clarinet and my card and coin tricks. It would drive my mother crazy—she'd hear things dropping for hours in the room."

Out of this crazy urban stew of movies, vaudeville, sports, jazz, and jokes, he finally found that he could obey the mysteriously divine message: "Be funny and multiply." "I'd write jokes and mail them to the newspapers and a week later there was my name. I couldn't believe it." It was like Dylan Thomas waking up to see his poetry printed in the local paper. Only this was nutty New York poetry, pushy one-liners printed by columnists like Earl Wilson and attributed to celebrities like Guy Lombardo and various restaurateurs.

Soon Allen was turning out such quips for press agents at twenty-five dollars a week. "It was marvelous," he says. "At that time the minimum wage you got working for a tailor or something was seventy-five cents an hour. I'd give them fifty jokes a day. There was nothing to it. I'd get out of school, get on the BMT subway, and start listing jokes. Always five to a page, ten pages." Allen quickly ascended this ladder of one-liners, writing material for performers like Herb Shriner and Peter Lind Hayes, until he arrived at the Olympus of gags, the Sid Caesar television show.

Here the prodigy, just out of his teens, at last met like-minded madmen, older writers such as Danny Simon (Neil's brother), Larry Gelbart, and Mel Brooks, people whose funniness was in direct proportion to their anxieties and depressions. "I was much less extroverted than they were," says Allen, "and the emotional adjustment was very hard for me. The atmosphere was one in which guys were shouting over one another, fighting to get their lines heard."

These true manic-depressives were very friendly and helpful to the young Allen. "There was a high suffering quotient," says Woody. "I met Mel just a month ago and we took a walk on Madison Avenue. Is it any better now? I asked him. Does he suffer less? We talked about the same things we talked about twenty years ago—aging, women, death." In those days, Allen recalls, "Brooks wanted to be Dostoevski and I wanted to be Ibsen. I had started to read when I was eighteen. The first thing I read was 'The Killers' by Hemingway, the second was 'The Bear' by Faulkner. Then I was reading everything—plays, novels, short stories, the comic writers like S. J. Perelman, Robert Benchley, Max Schulman."

Only one area remained to fill out the comic personality—live performance. Encouraged—indeed, goaded—by his agents, Charles Joffe and Jack Rollins, Allen took this on, working up his act in a number of Greenwich Village clubs. His inspiration and his despair was Mort Sahl, who was then revolutionizing live comedy with his electrifying topical routines. "Seeing Sahl, I felt I had two options," says Woody, "to kill myself or quit the business. There was nowhere to go after that. He cut a great figure in those days. He had a canine intelligence, he was witty and attractive. He wasn't a comedian in the old mode—some cuff-shooting, tuxedoed guy who'd come out and lapse into comfy purchased material."

Although Allen's politics are roughly similar to Sahl's irreverent liberalism, he's never emphasized politics in his comedy and he sees Sahl as he sees all great comics, from Chaplin and Keaton to Groucho, Hope, Benny, and Caesar, as a great stylist. "I can make the distinction between the artist and his politics," he says. "I can see Leni Riefenstahl's Nazi propaganda film, *Triumph of the Will,* and be knocked out. The politics of that movie are disgusting but the filmic art is tremendous. For some reason Mort Sahl became less skillful at hiding his rage and anger or translating it into a palatable commodity. Now, although a lot of the brilliance is still there, the rage and anger put people off." For Woody there's a lesson in this. "The primary object of the artist is to entertain. The great thing about Mort Sahl—or Mozart or Ingmar Bergman—is that they were entertaining."

Woody sees all of his heroes, from Franz Kafka to the great New Orleans jazzman Sidney Bechet, as superb performers who bring delight and insight by virtue of their style. "Ingmar Bergman has all the natural tools of the entertainer," says Woody. "He's got a woman on the screen—and she's not doing anything but her face is great and he's close on it for a long time. The mere length of time that he's on it becomes interesting. Then you're in a room and the clock is ticking and the sound is mellifluous or engaging in some way. He never loses sight of the fact that there's an audience out there and he can't bore you." Woody can call Kafka "fun," because of the exquisite balance and rhythm with which the great writer orchestrates his luminous nightmares of guilt and paranoia.

In some strange way, Woody's own operation as a performer is Kafkaesque—he accepts the gross dangers of the world with a terrified innocence disguised as comic equanimity. One of his funniest club routines is an account of his inadvertent abduction by the Ku Klux Klan (Woody says he recognized the Grand Dragon because "he was the one wearing the contoured sheet"). As the Klansmen are about to hang this Yankee Jewish interloper, Woody's life passes before his eyes. "I saw myself as a kid again. Goin' to school. Swimmin' at the swimmin' hole. Fryin' up a mess o' catfish. Goin' down to the general store. Gettin' a piece of gingham for Emmy Lou. And I realize . . . it's not my life. They're gonna hang me in two minutes and the wrong life is passing before my eyes."

Comedy itself is Woody's real psychoanalysis. He denies that he has ever felt particularly Jewish, but his routines and writings are filled with sharp and funny references to the dislocations of being an urban Jew. Woody is greatly fond of his parents, who had to scramble in various businesses during the Depression and are now retired. "Their values," he's joked, "are God and carpeting." Woody, who hated school, was kicked out of New York University and the City College of New York and knew that hurt his parents. His way of handling this was to say, "My mother is a sensitive woman. When I was thrown out of college she locked herself in the bathroom and took an overdose of Mah-Jongg tiles." Whatever the real cause of the depression and visions of death that beset him as a kid, he can joke about the whole thing: "I was in analysis for years because of a traumatic childhood. I was breast-fed through falsies."

Woody has been in analysis for more than half his life. "I knew it was going to take some time, maybe three, four, five years," he says. "But I thought when that time was over, then I could play the piano. I had an unrealistic expectation that I would not have any real neurotic problems. Maybe I haven't been able to part with many anxieties because they are common to everybody. In a certain sense, I'm not at all neurotic." But he stays in analysis (he's with his third analyst now, a woman) for a reason. "I feel if I lost some of those anxieties I'd be able to reach more of humanity with my work. A comedian like W. C. Fields, who was an enormous comic talent, spoke to a smaller audience because there was a certain lack of personal integration, a certain neurotic quality, whereas Chaplin had a greater feeling for the human condition."

More than analysis, it's been the women in Woody's life who have helped most to form him. He married his first wife, Harlene, when both were teenagers. "She was a philosophy major at Hunter College so I had four years of philosophy with her by proxy. She got me out of my parents' house, I had to earn a living and deal with real-life problems." His second wife was actress Louise Lasser, who appeared in some Allen films and has become celebrated as "Mary Hartman." "Louise was a very sophisticated, cosmopolitan person," says Woody. "She grew up on Fifth Avenue with all the advantages of an upper-middle-class, private-school education. She knew how to live in Manhattan, she knew stores and restaurants—I grew up in Flatbush and didn't know anything. I was just starting to be a comedian and she contributed in a big way to my perspective and my confidence. She's one of the brightest, wittiest women I've ever known."

The most important of Woody's women has been Diane Keaton, his longtime chum and colleague, who came into her own this year with her charming performance based on her own character in *Annie Hall*, and her shattering one in Richard Brooks's *Looking for Mr. Goodbar*. "Diane has been my lucky charm," says Woody. "She came out of the boondocks of southern California, completely guileless. She sees directly to the reality of a thing. When I made my first movie, *Take the Money and Run*, I felt I had struck out. I didn't even know how to show a rough cut. I'd show it at eleven o'clock at night to fifteen soldiers from the USO and it had crayon marks and splice marks all over it and nobody was laughing at all. But I showed it to her and she said, 'This is funny,' and she was right. And since then she's been a consistently clear mind and clear voice on every picture I've made."

Diane has influenced Woody on a more personal level. "She has an utterly spectacular visual sense. I see many things today through her eyes, textures and forms I would never have seen without her. She showed me the beauty of the faces of old people. I'd never been sensitive to that before. And there's a certain warmth and poignance associated with young women that I never would have seen without her. She's increased my affection, feeling, and understanding for women in general."

Woody agrees with Camus that women are all we know of paradise on earth. Like most modern artists, he finds art itself an embarrassment. T. S. Eliot said that poetry is "a mug's game," and for Woody, comedy is something of a palooka's pastime. "When I was doing *Love and Death* in Paris," he says, "the art director was a veteran of World War Two who had spied, been caught, tortured, and sent to a concentration camp. It made me feel so utterly trivial. It confirmed a prejudice I've always had that, as Oscar Wilde said, art is useless. Great talent to me is an accident of birth. One gesture of real courage is worth more to me than all the work of Dickens, Aristophanes, plus Woody Allen. I don't know if I could have behaved as well as Humphrey in the face of death, and that's important to me. Or Susan Sontag, when she was so ill. It's shattering when a person of that refinement and sensibility gets that kind of news. But what happens to the person who feels all sorts of inklings and intimations about life and has no talent, no way of expressing them? That's a bad position to be in." He pauses. "That's my movie."

Woody is referring to his new, serious movie, *Interiors*. "When you do comedy," he says, "you're not sitting at the grown-ups' table, you're sitting at the children's table." Woody has had the guts—or the impertinence—to get up and move to the grown-ups' table. He won't talk about plot, but it's clear that it's about the ultimate things he's always been interested in in the work of artists like Ingmar Bergman. "It deals," says Woody, "with the spiritual turmoil, the floating unrest that can only be traceable to bad choices in life. Also the apotheosis of the artist beyond his real worth. And how a lover can possess the loved one as an object he can control." But Woody's first tragedy is inevitably still a Woody movie. "At first I thought, Well, Diane Keaton is speaking for me in this movie. Then I said, 'Oh my God, Geraldine Page is speaking for me.' Then I said, 'There's a lot of me in Maureen Stapleton.' Then I thought, you know there's something of me in Marybeth Hurt. And this went on, right through the whole cast—Sam Waterston, Richard Jordan, Kristen Griffith. There's something of me in all these people."

Woody is desperately afraid of being pretentious or banal. While making the movie, he watched a lot of soap opera on television, to make sure he wasn't doing *As the World Turns* without knowing it. The possibility that he's committing an act of self-destruction is one he's well aware of, and indeed it's come up in his analysis. "Maybe a really logical person would feel that to do this just at the moment when I've achieved a certain recognition for doing comedy is suicidal," he says. "But I felt if I didn't do it, I'd never find out anything about myself." What he's hoping is that it will be "sufficiently unembarrassing" so that he can henceforth move between comedy and serious films. He's looking forward to doing a new comedy—which he is writing with Marshall Brickman—this summer with himself and Diane Keaton. What's it about? Are you kidding? "The inability to function in contemporary society," says Woody matter-of-factly.

If Woody Allen is jumping off a cliff in search of himself, has anyone else found him? "Woody is not basically a happy person," says producer Charles Joffe. "I felt badly that after the Academy Awards he could only say he was surprised. 'No joy?' I asked. 'I don't have time for that,' he said. I thought, What a shame he won't allow himself that joy." But Diane Keaton insists, "Woody has a great capacity for joy. He's moved by things and he has a great sense of beauty. He's very sensitive and he has these feelings of guilt and anger and shame. Who's to say where it comes from, or why?" Louise Lasser thinks that "Life is difficult for Woody. He's one of the unfortunate tormented people. His mind is working all the time. So is a sweet side and a silly side and a sexual side. One night I couldn't sleep, and I thought, I am lying next to one of America's foremost humorists."

Marshall Brickman, Woody's collaborator and close friend, is impatient with the emphasis on Woody's psychic state. "The happy/unhappy axis is a fallacy in contemporary society. The point is to be awake, alert, functioning. Woody has good navigational instincts in this writhing mass of egos and good and bad advice. He's not afraid to engage, even though the world perceives him as reclusive. He's a very good friend. He's dependable, helpful, he works hard, he's ethical, he saves string." Geraldine Page, who's worked with great directors, says, "He kept telling me, 'Too hammy! No!' But I'm happy he kept badgering me. He took me past the point I thought possible. I wish I could hire him to stand by me in future movies and holler at me, 'That's too phony!' "

Woody is what you might call a public recluse, having a late dinner at Elaine's with Brickman or other friends such as actor Michael Murphy. But mostly he sits in his warm and comfortable Fifth Avenue penthouse, whose clutter, from books by Heidegger and Kierkegaard to Groucho and Perelman, from *Vogue* to *The New York Review of Books*, is an image of an American mind creating itself, with passion and irony. Behind all his hang-ups is the one terror that either humanizes or destroys everyone—the sense of mortality. "I was watching Walt Frazier one night with the Knicks," he says. "He was so beautiful and young, so dazzling, but I saw the death's head looming. I thought of the inevitable deterioration, the waning away of the adulation. I felt that anger and rage, not at anything correctable, but at the human condition that you're part of, too. I was with Keaton, and leaving the Garden I had that underground-man feeling, the decay at the core of existence. So I'm no fun to be with at parties because I'm very aware of this all the time." Woody, a mighty muser, muses. "Sometimes I think I got a good thing going. I'm in a culture where being funny is important. If I was an Apache and funny, where would I be? The Indians don't need comedians, you know."

[1978]

Stephen Harvey

FRED ASTAIRE

Astaire fulfilled the American fantasy of an aristocracy based on charm and ability rather than inbreeding.

"I don't know how it started and I don't want to know. I have no desire to prove anything by it. I have never used it as an outlet or as a means of expressing myself. I just dance." With these bland closing words from his autobiography, *Steps in Time*, Astaire betrayed one of his most endearing and yet

Fred Astaire (with Ginger Rogers): *The first to realize that dance could convey and even deepen any given emotion onscreen.* (From the MGM release *The Barkleys of Broadway.* © 1949 Loew's Inc. Copyright renewed 1976 by Metro-Goldwyn-Mayer Inc.)

exasperating quirks as a performer—his utter bewilderment that anyone should take his work seriously. Although he merely managed to raise the movie musical from the level of empty spectacle to one of the few unquestioned glories of the American film, Astaire has always been notoriously sphinxlike about the nature of his art. One might just as well expect to see Garbo regaling the addicts of late-night television talk shows with charming anecdotes of her years at M-G-M, as Astaire shedding light on the internal motivations that have guided his work. Yet to accept Astaire's self-portrait as "just a dancer" would be as absurd as describing Chaplin as just a man who made people laugh, and leaving it at that.

Of course, Astaire largely owes his unassailable place in the pantheon of unique film stars to the agility of those famous feet. Well-known for his tireless perfectionism, Astaire spent infinite hours planning, rehearsing, and reshaping each of those routines that always seemed so spontaneous and effortless onscreen. All this endless hard work gave Astaire his breathtaking craftsmanship as a dancer, and his vehement determination never to repeat himself showed off his matchless versatility. From film to film, Astaire mastered every conceivable style of dance, making them distinctively his in the process, from breathless tap solos to stately ballroom duets, from jitterbug to modern dance, even extending to classical ballet and ethnic folk motifs.

Yet mere dedication and expertise fail to explain why Astaire dominated the American film musical for a quarter of a century and remains one of the movies' few genuinely legendary figures. Talent alone has never guaranteed a sustained star career in films; numerous dancers with legs like pistons in swing time have briefly made their mark in films, only to find their fame waning as soon as the novelty of their style faded.

Ultimately they failed where Astaire succeeded because, like all Astaire's predecessors, they treated dance as a vaudeville specialty only slightly classier than the average canine balancing act, which served only as a fleeting diversion from the plots and actors that surrounded them. Astaire naturally excelled at this sort of routine, as he did at everything he attempted in the realm of musical comedy; such set pieces as the title number from *Top Hat* and "Puttin' On the Ritz" in *Blue Skies* are the most exhilarating examples imaginable of sheer joyous virtuosity on display. Yet Astaire's true achievement in movies was infinitely subtler and more revolutionary. Incredibly, he was the first to realize that dance could convey and even deepen any given emotion onscreen. When the movies evolved almost overnight from a silent to a sound medium, actors and filmmakers seemed to forget that the human voice was only one tool of their craft; consciously or not, Astaire reintroduced the heretical notion that the human body could express the deepest of feelings even without the benefit of words.

The peerless dance numbers that stud his series of films with Ginger Rogers don't just provide welcome relief from the transparent stories that surround them. Instead, Astaire's solos and his duets with Ginger give the plots resonance and feeling; they both comment on these paperweight tales and propel them forward. Astaire doesn't merely tell us of Ginger's devastating effect on him—that would be too banal and too easy. Instead he sails over sofas and transforms prosaic objects like mantelpieces and seltzer bottles into syncopated instruments of poetry. In each of these films, a skeptical Ginger perpetually scoffs at Fred's gauche verbal passes in her direction; their romantic alliance is never cemented until he stops talking and succeeds in enticing her to dance with him. The duets themselves express completely the shifting moods of their ten-film love affair—the exhilaration of finding that their bodies speak the same choreographic language in "Isn't This a Lovely Day (To Be Caught in the Rain)?"; the affectionate bickering of "I'll Be Hard to Handle"; Astaire's sensuous seduction of the reluctant Rogers with "Night and Day."

Astaire even transforms the boy-loses-girl cliché imbedded in every movie musical plot into something honestly moving, simply by choreographing it to music. In *Swing Time*, Astaire sings the chilling threat that he's "Never Gonna Dance" again if Ginger walks out of his life, after which they reenact in dance their entire courtship to that point, hauntingly capturing their shared knowledge of mutual loss. As they glide up opposite ends of the curved nightclub stairway toward their separate futures, Fred and Ginger prove that, in films at least, actions can indeed be more potent than words.

"Every once in a while I suddenly find myself dancing," Fred informs Ginger when his tapping interrupts her slumbers in the room below, early on in *Top Hat*. "It must be some sort of affliction," she retorts; fortunately incurable, it seems, as Astaire continued to find himself dancing until the demise of the big-studio musical in the mid-fifties. Dancing was never just the cleverest gimmick in Astaire's bottomless bag of cinematic tricks—it was as organic to his screen persona as walking or delivering lines. Astaire the performer was irresistibly compelled to express in dance whatever emotion was felt by Astaire the movie character. Even when his feet were rooted firmly to the sound-stage floor, every gesture or vocal inflection was orchestrated to some internal dance rhythm only he could hear.

Practically no other actor expends so much physical energy just to deliver dialogue as Astaire does—swiveling forward from the waist and leading with that overabundant chin, Astaire continually pokes holes in the air around him for emphasis, strokes his jaw reflectively at his co-star's response, and shoves his hand into a convenient pants pocket to keep it still until the verbal exchange of the moment has run its course. Every motion

Astaire makes on screen, however prosaic, seems just a beat away from becoming a dance cue, whether it's a stroll down a flight of stairs in *Funny Face* or a simple roll of dice in *Swing Time.* This is what makes the usually difficult transition from story into song look so spontaneous in Astaire's musicals. At some point the kinetic energy barely suppressed behind every Astaire gesture can no longer be contained—it has to be vented in an outburst of dance.

Astaire's prodigious footwork first attracted audiences to him in the thirties, but it was the new kind of screen hero that his dancing symbolized which really made him a star. The real world may have been torn asunder by mass unemployment, social unrest, and incipient fascism in the mid-thirties, but you'd never have known it from the likes of *Top Hat.* Even Busby Berkeley's opulent and absurd *Gold Diggers* series was populated with "forgotten men" and avaricious chorines suddenly down on their luck, but Astaire never had to grapple with such weighty economic problems. Although the Astaire/Rogers films were nominally set in locales whimsically referred to as "London," "Paris," and "New York," they really took place in the same interior decorator's *moderne* vision of Paradise. *Carefree* was the title given to Fred and Ginger's penultimate thirties romp, but it could have been applied just as easily to almost all of their team efforts.

From *Gay Divorcee* through *Shall We Dance* and the rest, Fred was eternally cast as the unflappable optimist confident that nothing important lies beyond his ample grasp. Despite his worldly manner and elegant attire, the Astaire persona is basically as innocent as Shirley Temple's. The onscreen Fred is motivated entirely by caprice, trusting everything to his own charm and the happy conjunction of fate. In a world in which the greatest obstacle to his happiness is one recalcitrant blonde, Astaire remains sunnily unreflective because such defenses are totally unnecessary. What audiences relished most about Astaire was not so much his effortless savoir-faire, but rather his savoir-vivre—the joyous gusto which permeates every appearance Astaire made on film.

This brand of naïve vitality was not in itself a new quality in screen heroes; such earlier film stars as Douglas Fairbanks and Richard Dix had possessed it in abundance. But Astaire added a novel touch of sophistication to the mold, proving that such naughty screen continentals as Adolphe Menjou and Maurice Chevalier didn't hold the exclusive patent on urbanity and poise. Astaire fulfilled the American fantasy of an aristocracy based on charm and ability rather than inbreeding. Moviegoers of the time could identify with Astaire's upper-class élan and elegance because he cannily infused it with a vigorous dose of home-grown raffishness. In whatever gilded watering spot he found himself, Astaire was very much the unpretentious American abroad—deflating European pomposity, scorning artiness in favor of swing and blues, reveling in his own slangy wisecracks. Sometimes the balance was shifted a bit too forcibly to bolster Astaire's link with the masses; Astaire practically induces lockjaw as the gum-chewing gob from *Follow the Fleet* without fooling anyone for a minute. Usually, however, Astaire realized that such sops to hoi polloi weren't necessary, and reverted to his customary finesse the next time around.

Yet for all his elegant assurance, Astaire onscreen is anything but invulnerable. From his youthful escapades at RKO onward, Astaire has one perennial Achilles heel—his inveterate romanticism. At the start of most of his early vehicles, Astaire usually has immersed himself in the lackadaisical pursuit of pleasure; he's beguiling, but also a bit callow and purposeless. Love, always both instantaneous and eternal, gives his energies a focus and direction, as well as revealing his gay-young-blade bit for the rather shallow self-delusion it is. It's been widely noted that the secret behind the Astaire-Rogers chemistry was that she gave him an aura of sexuality he otherwise lacked, but Ginger's real accomplishment is that she forces him to grow up. There's usually a faint air of the overage fraternity pledge about Fred before genuine emotion takes over and carries him to adulthood. His friendly rival for the screen's dancing crown, Gene Kelly, often seems most comfortable roistering with the other boys like Donald O'Connor or Frank Sinatra, or else grappling choreographically with his own psyche. Astaire however, is never really complete psychologically until he has been mated with the appropriate female in dance.

Of course, the benefits of romance are mutual in Astaire's musicals. Just as he gains solidity from Ginger and her successors, Astaire grants them an outlet for their hidden sensuality. Most of Astaire's heroines possess a rather forbidding streak of prudery on first acquaintance; masked by an air of brisk practicality, they're really afraid of what they'll discover in themselves should they succumb to an Astaire seduction. Inevitably, Astaire's persistence always pays off—under his spell they reveal unexpected levels of feeling to themselves and the audience, and the result is exhilarating.

It's ironic that one of the most liberatingly erotic spirits in American movies should have been encased in such an unprepossessing form as Astaire's. Despite that ingratiatingly crinkly smile, Astaire would hardly seem the stuff that erotic dreams were made of. His hollow-chested frame looks oddly frail for a dancer, and apart from his trademarked, snugly tailored evening dress, clothes just hang limply from his narrow shoulders. Astaire's head looms hugely out of proportion to his narrow torso, and his features are really a cartoonist's inspiration—the bulbous domed forehead, those slightly protruding poached eyes, and a craggy nose veering downward towards his jutting, peninsular jaw.

Even on the stage, where conventional good looks aren't essential for romantic roles, Astaire's unusual physiognomy had proved something of a handicap; usually he found himself cast as sister Adele Astaire's platonic playmate while she blithely romanced some strapping young juvenile. Remarkably, Astaire turned this apparent liability into an asset once he exchanged Adele and the stage for Ginger et al. and the movies. For one thing, the erotic tension he created with his dancing partners came as an unexpected and delightful fringe benefit from a performer who otherwise seemed so asexual onscreen. For another, Astaire was so much the urbane charmer that handsomeness of the usual sort would really have been redundant. In fact, his looks gave Astaire a touch of fallibility his film personality desperately needed. Audiences might have resented his air of impeccable finesse if Astaire had possessed enormous physical magnetism to boot.

As it happened, the emotional chemistry that simmered between Astaire and Rogers proved so overpowering that it gravely threatened his screen future once their partnership came to its inevitable end. Obviously Ginger was fetching enough to be romanced convincingly by any of a host of regulation leading men, but many believed that Rogers alone held the elusive clue to Astaire's latent virility as a figure of romantic movie fantasy. This wasn't the only dilemma confronting Astaire as the forties succeeded the thirties, bringing with them a whole new set of values and priorities. Black dinner jackets were exchanged for navy blues, and the airy sophistication that Astaire symbolized began to seem irrevocably anachronistic.

That likable proletarian Bing Crosby had been a popular movie crooner in the thirties while Astaire dominated the musical field; in the more homespun forties, their positions reversed, and twice Astaire found himelf billed under Crosby while playing slightly effete capons whose restless feet posed no threat to Bing's vocalizing when it came to romance or show biz. During this uncertain period in Astaire's career, he seemed destined to travel an endless odyssey from studio to studio and ingenue to ingenue in search of the old magic and a new, more modish identity. No one was more conscious of this dilemma than Astaire himself; determined to relinquish the spotlight before public indifference forced him to do so, he opted for retirement in 1946. Ironically, it took Gene Kelly's broken ankle two years later to bring Astaire back.

The Astaire that emerged in the late forties at first glance seemed identical to the old one, but the passage of time and musical custom had brought some subtle changes. Astaire was fortunate enough to spend most of this period at M-G-M, where an accomplished team of directors, writers, choreographers, and technicians forged a new and exciting renaissance of the movie musical under the guardianship of producer Arthur Freed. This new era owed a good deal to the Astaire legacy of the thirties, but was guided by much more grandiose ambitions. Astaire's films of the previous decade had been intended as unpretentious, almost interchangeable diversions, whose slender strands of plot only served as groundwork for the musical interludes. The Freed unit at Metro conceived each effort as more of a distinctive event, combining conscious innovation with enormous technical expertise. The stories they contained, however frivolous, carried nearly equal weight as the songs and dances, and both elements were more closely interwoven; no longer was the hoofer-meets-loses-and-wins/decides-to-mount-show-with-pert-chorine considered sufficiently weighty a premise to sustain a musical.

Moreover, Astaire in the forties loomed less obviously as the *auteur* of the films he appeared in than had previously been the case. Such earlier Astaire directors as Mark Sandrich and George Stevens merely allowed Astaire to devise his own routines and photographed them as unobtrusively as possible. In contrast, directors like Vincente Minnelli, Stanley Donen, and Charles Walters had had extensive experience with musicals in both the theater and the movies, and accordingly exercised their right to shape the material with their own imprint as well. Lost was the sense of impromptu spontaneity that had been one of the most delightful qualities of Astaire's earlier work. Nor could clever scenarios, lively pacing, and technicolored visual dazzle quite compensate for the fact that the demise of composers like Kern and Gershwin and the relative decline of Porter and Berlin had left a vacuum that wasn't being filled by any of their successors. Yet at their considerable best, films like *The Band Wagon* and *Funny Face* combined the old effervescence with a new and exciting blend of opulence and inventiveness.

Astaire adapted most gracefully to the new regime. The later Astaire was more likely to be found in sport clothes than white tie and tails, his hyperkinetic boyishness easing into a kind of avuncular geniality. Middle age failed to dim the quick precision of his footwork, but it did tend to dilute his once-irrepressible amorousness on screen. Never really comfortable with the role of the casual womanizer, Astaire now usually played the pursued rather than the pursuer, generally in the guise of a myopic professional so immersed in his métier of the moment that two-thirds of the film elapsed before he could acknowledge the mutual attraction between himself and his co-star.

Complicating matters was the curious fact that although Astaire was allowed to age gradually but distinctly as his career evolved, his feminine counterparts remained perpetually twenty-five. This was hardly noticeable when Astaire frolicked with the decade-younger Ginger Rogers, but the chronological gap widened to twenty years with the likes of Garland and Charisse, and even thirty by the time he partnered such gamines as Audrey Hepburn and Leslie Caron. Astaire diluted the slight perversity of this by playing these roles as surrogate fathers turned reluctant lovers, but at any rate only the most literal-minded viewers really objected to these April–December casting ploys once the dialogue dissolved into the inevitable cue for an Astaire song and dance.

As Astaire neared the twentieth anniversary of his debut in pictures, he found himself in the odd position of being a certifiable screen legend who still participated as vigorously as ever in the field. His response was to become his own movie biographer; increasingly, his vehicles were not just tailored around his talents but retold his past history as well. Critics and audiences had long since mentally cast Astaire as top-hatted Pygmalion to Ginger Rogers' satin-gowned Galatea; in *The Barkleys of Broadway* they reenacted precisely that process, down to Rogers' rebellious urge to hang up her dancing pumps and go legit. The dogged quest for perfection in his work behind the scenes emerged full-blown on screen as a dour Astaire trained Judy Garland for the big time in *Easter Parade*. *Royal Wedding* evokes the years of on- and offstage partnership with sister Adele; *The Band Wagon* purports to relate the theatrical comeback of one Tony Hunter, middle-aged movie hoofer *extraordinaire,* whose past hits included an epic entitled *Swinging Down to Panama*. Moreover, both *Funny Face* and *The Band Wagon* are loose pastiches of two of Astaire's greatest pre-Hollywood triumphs.

Astaire had endlessly proclaimed his refusal to find himself one day pirouetting across the screen arrayed with top hat, white hair, and crutches. Yet it was not Astaire's own decrepitude that prevented him from fulfilling this vision, but the death of the genre itself of which he was master. The disintegration of the big studios, the encroachment of television, and the advent of Elvis Presley and his ilk conspired to doom the large-scale movie musical to the purgatory of television reruns and chink-in-the-wall revival houses. Astaire's usual outward composure was barely ruffled by this calamitous turn of events. Just as he had conquered radio in the thirties, he calmly shifted his efforts to the television studio, and his brilliant series of hour-long specials with new partner Barrie Chase bore him a number of Emmy awards and added new millions to the legions of admirers he already had.

Nor did the demise of the musical sound the death knell for Astaire's quarter-century-long film career; since 1959 he has from time to time returned to the screen to demonstrate that he had more to offer audiences than just a gracefully executed buck-and-wing. The nondancing Astaire affected a considerable range of screen guises, from the rueful intellectual of *On the Beach* to the gadabout socialite in *The Pleasure of His Company*, among others. By the sixties it seemed improbable that anyone as suave as Astaire could actually be just another Yank; the culture that had spawned his type seemed extinct, at least on this side of the Atlantic. Thus Astaire came to alternate playing dapper Englishmen and ingratiatingly corrupt smoothies, sometimes even incorporating the two. Many expressed surprise at Astaire's dramatic aptitude, but it had really always been there, overshadowed like his superb way with a song by his incomparable dancing.

When the sixties spawned a new cycle of musicals in the form of bloated superspectaculars based on outmoded stage properties, logic dictated that at least one of them would call for a revival of his still formidable musical talents. The subsequent years have brought unabated activity to the now septuagenarian Astaire. Occasional movie character parts have been augmented by a steady parade of dramatic guest appearances on television. And 1974 found the latter-day Astaire equally confronting his scintillating past in M-G-M's epitaph to itself, *That's Entertainment!*, as well as providing a rare human note amidst the cardboard chaos of *The Towering Inferno*. After a seventy-year career in show business, Astaire seems to defy human mortality with the same carefree ease with which his feet have always thwarted the pull of gravity. From exuberant juvenile to affable codger, Astaire's appeal has been timeless, but more than that, his legacy of musical achievements remains ageless.

[1975]

Bruce Williamson

BRIGITTE BARDOT

She has always been the right girl in the wrong picture.

Come to dinner and meet Brigitte Bardot. The glint of a golden opportunity doesn't register at first, as it might if you were back in the real New York world of hangovers, head colds, and work schedules. But this invitation arrives at the Cannes Film Festival in springtime. The rain has stopped, the

Croisette is crawling with little-girls-lost on platform heels, the Hotel Carlton is a hive of celebrities, and the PR people are peddling press lunches with names on the menu like Moreau and Cardinale—or maybe Sylvia Miles in *Heat*. To have dinner in Ramatuelle, a country mile from Saint-Tropez, means a two-hour, forty-dollar haul by car, and who is Brigitte Bardot anyway? A sex symbol. Perhaps the greatest living sex symbol of the twentieth century. Ask any Frenchman. All right, but an *aging* sex symbol—and when was the last time you saw her in a movie? *Shalako*, 1968. With Sean Connery. That Western nobody can remember, except for the scene in which the Apaches make Honor Blackman swallow her jewels. Terrible. Oh, since then there have been other Bardot films made in France, for France, but even the French ignore them.

In the end, of course, it's off to Ramatuelle. Vadim will be there. Roger Vadim. Remember? He practically invented Bardot in *And God Created Woman* back in 1956. He was also her first husband—her first anything, the way Vadim tells it—and he gave her Jean-Louis Trintignant for a leading man, and she grew to like Jean-Louis. A lot. She and Vadim were finally divorced, but that didn't matter because they both became reasonably rich and fantastically famous and free to marry a half dozen other beautiful people. Now Bardot and Vadim want to make another movie together. A modern, feminized *Don Juan*, with BB in the title role as a hard-core sexual predator. Publicly, they call it a professional reunion, privately—but not where Brigitte can hear him—Vadim says *Don Juan* will be a kind of comeback for Bardot as an actress.

Actually meeting her for the first time is a mild shock. You expect a remote and pampered sex kitten, a petulant Circe, and into the room strides this terrific chick. An incredible walk, purposeful, with everything out front in a language of movement instantly understandable from Katmandu to Peoria. She will be thirty-eight in September, but looks ten years younger. Natural dark-blond hair rather than the platinum mane she has tossed from pillow to pillow in several dozen movies. Her mouth is made for sweet nothings or more unspeakable pleasures, her voice has a timbre seldom caught by sound engineers, and when she murmurs *bonjour* through a handshake her eyes come into focus like klieg beams, as if to ask, "Who are you, and what are you doing here?" She is wary of strangers, particularly if they write.

That crisis weathered in a blaze of conviviality, Bardot flings off her fringed leather topper. Underneath she wears a skinny-knit thing that laces up when a girl has time to dress and isn't an hour late already, and she eases her boyish blue-jeaned bottom onto a floor cushion next to Christian Kalt. In discreet asides, everyone identifies Christian as Brigitte's lover. He's an actor or something, at least several years younger than BB, and beautiful. All her lovers are younger and beautiful. She just likes it that way.

Dinner is served buffet-style from a huge round white-plastic coffee table. There are a dozen floor-sitters present in the modest stucco cottage owned by a slim blonde named Catherine, an interior decorator who operates Le Tournesol, a famous gift shop. Catherine decorated La Madrague, Brigitte's beachfront home near Saint-Trop, which she continually threatens to sell because she has built a wall and a swimming pool, and still can't guarantee her privacy against bands of dedicated Bardot-watchers who stand ankle-deep in the Mediterranean hoping to be cursed out by a love goddess.

You learn a lot from Bardot's dinner companions. One friendly neighbor confides that there is a local joke about house guests at La Madrague, who customarily stop off at Le Tournesol to buy a little bauble for Brigitte. She adores gifts, and smuggles them back to Catherine for a refund the minute her guests have gone. She is said to be a mite close about money, and the bill of fare at La Madrague can no way be called lavish. Her followers say it's because Brigitte is afraid of being used, having her fame or fortune exploited. Another of the games she plays is to settle down at Saint-Trop every season near the time of the annual film festival at Cannes, which Bardot has conscientiously snubbed for years—and especially since 1967, when she went to Cannes to promote *Batouk*, a documentary about big-game animals, made by her third husband, German millionaire Gunther Sachs. Movies about animals are *not* selected for the closing program at Cannes without summit conferences to guarantee the appearance of someone like Brigitte Bardot. So Brigitte attended, was nearly crushed by the crowds—she detests crowds—and cried herself sick, according to eyewitnesses. Though she regained composure, she did not forget. Which marked the beginning of the end for Gunther.

Brigitte's table talk includes only casual inquiries about the business afoot at Cannes because she couldn't care less. She jokes a lot in rapid French, and you have to be rapid or French to keep up with her bons mots. The company pays close, appreciative attention to everything she says—superstardom has its advantages, after all—though a typical Bardot contribution is apt to offer meager intellectual challenge. "What do you do," she asks brightly, "if you are making passionate love when the telephone rings?" An extended forefinger warns her listeners that she expects some thoughtful replies. . . .

You ignore the phone.

It depends on whether you know who's calling.

It depends on the skill of your lover. . . .

Six months later *Don Juan* is nearly finished, and Vadim issues an all clear from Paris to come on over. The French press has carried regular bulletins about celestial storm signals during the making of *Don Juan*—Bardot allegedly threatening everything from strikes to retirement to suicide. Meanwhile, women's magazines on several continents have observed her thirty-eighth birthday with breezy malice aforethought. She's pushing forty, and everyone wants to know where will she go from here. If Brigitte shares their concern, say my informed sources, she has ducked the question on a holiday in Reykjavík with someone named Laurent (offscreen, there have been minor cast changes since spring, Laurent subbing for Christian). However, she will return to Paris to post-synch *Don Juan*.

Bardot as a working professional behaves pretty well for a girl with no appetite for tedium. She arrives late at a sound room in the drafty Studio de Billancourt—a cinematic sausage factory set in a dreary quarter of Paris—looking radiant in a snug beige sweater, brown jeans, and the shaggy coat she quickly throws over a chair. Vadim, the script girl, the technician, Vadim's editor, and other authorized personnel have worked on other scenes while they waited, so there's no scolding through the kisses and *bonjours* and acknowledgments of prior acquaintance in Ramatuelle.

The day's work is simple but slow. Soundless snippets from *Don Juan,* in black and white, are projected on a screen while dialogue for the sequence—in someone's hand-written scrawl—appears on a running strip below for the benefit of Brigitte and the actor who is dubbing the actor you see.

Between takes, she complains about delays, smokes cigarettes, relates an amusing anecdote about a fat man with a cigar in his mouth, and says she has decided not to grant any interviews. Vadim looks nonplussed. Vadim movies, especially in recent years, need all the publicity they can get. *"Mais je n'ai rien à dire à personne,"* Brigitte repeats stubbornly.

When she isn't saying *non,* she is absolutely agreeable, even friendly. Easy enough, because Bardot knows that Bardot does more or less as she pleases. No offense. At the end of the second day, she even offers you a ride home in her car if you promise to shut up and avoid putting anything in the form of a straight question. "As a matter of fact," she adds, smiling, "you may speak all you wish. Only I will not answer." There's been an interview in *Vogue* recently, with quotes from Bardot calling herself "the greatest sex symbol of all time." Brigitte hoots loudly, as if such idiocy were beyond comprehension. Yes, she admits she has seen the piece, that's why she's no longer speaking to the author. Anyway, it's old stuff. God, she has met so many journalists saying this time we tell the truth. Sorry about that. She gives you a last neon flash along with a friendly pat on the head, and disappears into her new Paris headquarters on boulevard Lannes, in an apartment house that looks like an airline terminal for international departures.

Messages don't move her. Two dozen peach-pink roses disappear without a trace into Bardot's long gray roster of guys asking special consideration in exchange for an armful of flowers. (Long ago, Gunther Sachs sent her one hundred red roses, but they didn't last.) Vadim's well-known powers of persuasion are reduced to impotence. Brigitte is tired, everyone tells you. She's bored, she wants to quit making movies. She isn't happy right now, the press has been hard on her. Frustration breeds crazy thoughts. The way to ensure Bardot, you suspect, is to be a tawny twenty-four-year-old Adonis with rippling loins. Too late for that, though her colleagues contemplate the proposition with those Gallic shrugs designed to handle any and all of life's little surprises. Clearly, the people closest to Brigitte have learned to walk on eggs.

Don Juan itself consumes one entire afternoon of watching and listening while Vadim checks the musical track. He is worried about the title ballad, which is sung in English. Wherever you go in Paris, you hear a lot of English sung, and the *Don Juan* lyrics convince you that slight attention is paid to the words. . . . If this is meant to be a new, mature Bardot, only her best friends will know the difference. Before she beds a reluctant priest, Brigitte lures a stolid married man off to orgies in Scandinavia, drives a moody guitar player (Robert Walker) to suicide, and evens her score with a wealthy libertine (Robert Hossein) by inviting his lovely young wife (played by lovely young Jane Birkin) to a lesbian romp. Though Vadim has mentioned doing his homework on *Don Juan in Hell,* Molière, Mozart, and the original Spanish sourceworks, for a man with his reputation he finds the wages of sin sky-high in France today—his Don Jeanne is lured to a final fatal rendezvous by the married square whose life she has left a shambles, and is burned alive. Pretty rough justice for a girl who only slept around a bit.

Idle speculation that *Don Juan* might turn out to be a thinly veiled bio of Bardot seems to end right there. "There is no evidence in the plot of Brigitte's own life, but there *is* an analogy with certain aspects of her personality." Vadim speaking. Of course, he made the movie. Vadim scoffs at the reports of attempted suicide and tantrums during the shooting. To his knowledge, Brigitte has tried suicide only twice—first in her teens, when she opened the gas jets because her scandalized bourgeois parents refused to let her marry him, then in 1960 (slit wrists and sleeping pills) after the breakup of her second marriage to actor Jacques Charrier. "Brigitte is lazy, like a child at school. She never cared to be an actress, and this time she may be serious about not doing more films. I don't think she will continue into her old age, like Bette Davis or Katharine Hepburn. The danger with her is her private life. She is a very vulnerable person. Working with her, the difficulty comes when she is in love with one man, and has to leave the man she is living with—or when someone leaves her. . . ." Vadim even risks comparing Brigitte to his last Frau, Jane Fonda. "Both are women who decided to be free on a social and moral level. Such people imagine themselves free, but Jane is enslaved—she is a political addict, whereas Brigitte's addiction is the need to have a man around her at all times. Thus she is totally dependent on something that one cannot control: Love. Brigitte should have remained a dancer. She was a ballet student when we met, and dancing was what she loved. She could have been a great dancer."

Olga Horstig-Primuz, a brusque grand dame full of show-biz savvy and pride in the fact that she has been Bardot's agent since the beginning of time, agrees to talk about Brigitte over lunch. Beforehand, she digs through the files of her cluttered office on the Champs-Elysées, and produces a couple of rare photographs—one a souvenir of Bardot's first and only appearance in the theater, at age eighteen—a minor role on the Paris stage in Jean Anouilh's *Ring Around the Moon.* Anouilh was enchanted with her, and so were the critics. The other picture shows Brigitte in a rowboat with her son Nicolas Charrier, who is now twelve and lives with his father. They are almost never photographed together. Bardot has declared for publication that she wasn't cut out to be a mother, but reporters clamoring for an audience are clued to stifle their curiosity about Nicolas. According to Madame Horstig-Primuz, Bardot is simply trying to protect the boy, who once saw a newspaper headlining a false report of his mother's suicide, and was understandably upset.

"From this particular epoch in France," Madame resumes with emphasis, "only two names will remain, and be known everywhere . . . the names of de Gaulle and Bardot." You can practically hear at a distance the swelling strains of "La Marseillaise," yet the lady means what she says. She also seconds the notion that Bardot lacks ambition, and believes she might have been happier as an interior decorator. Lost somewhere in Madame's office there's a recent issue of *Maison et Jardin,* with a picture layout of the new flat on boulevard Lannes, decorated in stark-modern style by Brigitte herself. Difficult as it is to imagine Bardot choosing upholstery fabric for a foreign minister's wife, even an agent sounds credible when she asserts that, one way or another, this girl was destined to Make It and make it Big. "You could see she was going to be famous. Before anyone knew the name Bardot, if you merely walked into a restaurant with her the whole room turned to stare."

On the subject of Bardot's love life, Madame unveils a favorite anecdote. Seems she tried at least once to persuade her illustrious client that it might be more appropriate, however lightly she trods over the hill into her forties, to develop an interest in . . . well, somewhat older men. "Why should I?" Brigitte replied with beautiful logic. "My taste hasn't changed."

Start to look, and you find Bardot stories fluttering around Paris like autumn leaves. She is an expert gin-rummy player and penny-ante gambler, who tests her skills at ten centimes a point, demands instant payment when she wins, but becomes so despondent when she loses that she has been known to stalk off to her room for a long sulk. She appears in a more favorable light in *l'affaire Schneider*, a high-comedy feud that kept *le tout* Paris amused a couple of years ago—when *Jours de France* gossip columnist Edgar Schneider hinted that Brigitte's famous face and bust had been given a lift by means of plastic surgery. Ultimately it was Schneider who got busted. Bardot sued and won after submitting to an examination by medical experts, and still has her legal hounds howling for libel damages of four thousand dollars. Lacking a single intimate friend whom she can fully trust, Brigitte looks out for herself. Call her vindictive if you will, but there is admirable determination and pluck behind that million-dollar certified-authentic façade.

Filmmaker Louis Malle directed Bardot in *Viva Maria!* and *Vie Privée*, the latter rated one of her better films, and a role made to order—as a tarnished, golden film star who finally takes a death leap from a rooftop to escape the glare of publicity. Says Malle: "It was not exactly Bardot's own life, but I never fully appreciated what the film was about until we began shooting in Geneva. A street scene, and there were housewives shopping nearby who became furious when they recognized Brigitte. Women actually spat in her face and called her a whore. This was 1960, and she was hated because she was so incredibly free and spoke the truth and did as she wanted to do—and all of it was thought scandalous at the time, though not anymore. Bardot opened the way in that sense, even more than Elizabeth Taylor or Ingrid Bergman. She was a pioneer, with *And God Created Woman* for her manifesto. She's *really* the grandmother of *la libération sexuelle,* and everyone should be grateful to her."

Malle has another theory about Bardot. "She will have a tremendous comeback, but not right away. They keep using her as what she was—playing a young woman with a child's mind. It's laughable, and also very sad, to insist she remain a sex symbol. I think Brigitte should go on the stage, which would be extremely daring and courageous, because they would all be waiting for her with guns. But as a director, I have been deeply impressed by her at times. She's very nice, kind of touching, marvelously bright. She's got enormous talent, and there are many good roles in the theater for women of forty. Cinema is a medium for the very young. When *Viva Maria!* premiered in New York, everyone rushed to get a look at Bardot, and she was brilliant at the press conference—but next day the theaters were empty. She's not so important just now here in France, either, but she'll be triumphant in the end. In the thirties, Danielle Darrieux was an even bigger sex symbol than Bardot, and faded out for a while, but now she is on top again. Time works for Brigitte the same way, she's going to be a fantastic and beautiful older woman. Great bones. There is nothing more one can say about her at the moment. We have to wait for her third period. . . ."

Writer Henri Chapier, a filmmaker as well as erstwhile critic of the leftist *Le Combat,* shares some of Malle's optimism about BB. "She is always screwed by the movies she makes, but she remains a myth because of the way the French relate to their idols. Once established, fame can last forever in Paris. Look at Françoise Rosay, Edwige Feuillère, Signoret, Darrieux, there are so many examples. Every year the public votes its choice for the most popular actress, and last year's favorite was Michele Morgan, who hasn't made a film in seven years. I believe in America they say you are only as good as your last picture, but the rule doesn't apply here. Bardot's problem is that she surrounds herself with a very bad *milieu.* She dislikes any kind of criticism, and wants to be the leader of a very small, special group, so she socializes with people considerably beneath her, friends of her hairdresser and that sort of thing. I think her deep conviction is that pleasure comes first, and her notions of pleasure are on a very primary level. Among intellectuals, she feels like a stranger . . . among her men, she encounters other complications because *she's* the man."

Finally, bits and pieces of the Bardot mosaic begin to assume a grand design, or at least a bébé-grand design, and the emerging shape is anything but that of a conventional pin-up. She has always been the right girl in the wrong picture, and will probably never change unless sheer boredom overtakes her. The years alone are unlikely to deprive her of beautiful men, for Bardot is a legend certain to attract youthful adventurers ad infinitum. Besides which, Brigitte enjoys a breed of rogue-male easily had by women twice her age, with half her income. And to date, who can match her list of conquests? Trintignant, Vadim, Charrier, Sachs—along with Sacha Distel, Sami Frey, Sean Connery, Bob Zaguri, Michael Sarne, Serge Gainsbourg, Warren Beatty, Stephen Boyd, Alain Delon, Serge Bourguignon, and Lucky Pierres too numerous to mention. Forty million Frenchman can't be wrong. Don Juan *lives,* bold and braless.

[1973]

Richard Schickel

JOHN BARRYMORE

He acted out before the motion-picture audience the final scenes in the drama of his self-destruction.

In 1926, shortly after he came to Hollywood, John Barrymore wrote to a friend in New York, "The most wonderful accident that ever happened to me was my coming out to this God-given, vital, youthful, sunny place." Barrymore was, at the time, forty-four—rather elderly to be casting his lot definitively with the movies. Already lapses of memory, perhaps the result of drinking, had begun to plague him, and there is no doubt that his taking up residence in Hollywood was mostly motivated by negative reasons—the desire to escape New York, scene of his recent divorce from Michael Strange, and the need, always chronic with him, for more money. His greatest triumph, his *Hamlet* of 1922–1923, was only three years behind him, but it had drained him (he never again undertook a part of comparable difficulty), and he regarded the Hollywood trip as both an adventure and a restorative—which for a time it was.

He was a veteran of some fifteen films when he came to the Coast. None of them, with the exception of *Dr. Jekyll and Mr. Hyde*, had been particularly notable; and the silents he made after 1925—*The Sea Beast*, *Don Juan*, *When a Man Loves*, *The Magnificent Rogue*—added little to his luster. His style, however, was eminently suitable to the romantic dramas of the time, grand without being overbearing, intelligent but not lacking in a certain dash, vigor, and humor. Heywood Broun noted that he entered a movie scene "like an exquisite paper knife"; and it was an apt description. There was an intelligence and control in his work as a leading man generally lacking in that of his contemporaries.

There is evidence, too, that he was temporarily happy. His love for young Dolores Costello had a revitalizing effect on him, as did the possession of a new yacht, *The Mariner*, which he seemed to regard as an expression of his true self in the midst of Hollywood's phoniness. His presence in pictures lent a cachet to the entire industry, and he was well worth the $76,250 he received for each of them.

Still, John Barrymore's career as a film actor would have been no more than a footnote in either his own record of achievement or Hollywood's history, had it not been for the fact that he acted out before the motion-picture audience the final scenes in the drama of his self-destruction. By 1930, as he approached fifty and as Hollywood went into its sound-inspired panic, the Great Profile began to soften and blur; his cheeks became slightly puffy, the clean line of his jaw began to sag, and a small but obvious dewlap developed beneath his chin. By the middle of the decade his marriage to Miss Costello was at an end, his earning capacity was severely impaired, and both his drinking and his lapses of memory had become chronic.

A Barrymore film now also offered a kind of horrified fascination—had the star slipped another notch, was he holding his own in his battle with this lingering illness of the spirit or was he, as sometimes happened (mostly notably in *Grand Hotel* and *Bill of Divorcement*), actually rallying? More and more, during the thirties, he played a parody of himself—an aging ham actor, a posturing drunk. Nowhere was this more bitterly revealed than in *Dinner at Eight*, an all-star production of 1933. His performance was not really good, but rarely has there been a more interesting one in the movies. Barrymore knew full well that he was playing his latter-day self, yet, throughout, he attempted to keep his distance from that self—in effect, to play another actor engaged to play John Barrymore. The attempt was brave and the younger Barrymore might have succeeded in this Pirandellian trick. Here it was quite beyond him, although he did create a kind of pathetic dignity as an actor who, in a single day, loses all self-illusions and, in a drunken attempt at a brilliant exit, commits suicide, carefully arranging the lighting of the scene before turning on the gas.

Within a few years, and despite the best efforts of friends to find him work, Barrymore, who by this time had to have his lines written out on slates and held before him out of camera range, could find no work but as this parody person. The most notable thing about his screen presence at the time was the distance in his eyes, which seemed never to be quite focused on anything. They seemed veiled, as if to protect the actor from knowledge of what he was doing, and to be looking far beyond the work at hand, perhaps back into the triumphant and profligate past, perhaps searching for a clue to this wretched present—or maybe they were merely trying to read the cue cards held up in the glare of the set. One thing is certain: never has our insistence on seizing hold of one aspect of a man's character and creating from it an immutable screen personality had more tragic results. Barrymore died May 29, 1942, of a complex of illnesses, a talented man forced into one of the most devastating self-exposures in the history of an art based on the display of the self.

[1962]

Frank Rich

WARREN BEATTY

"The relationship between theater and politics fascinates me.
They communicate ideas and involve persuasion and compromise."

He is a millionaire many times over but lives in two small, slovenly kept
hotel rooms. He travels with the fastest crowd in the country but rarely
drinks and never snorts or smokes. He is offered the best jobs in his profession but turns most of them down. His idea of sin is to eat ice cream. His
idea of a great time is to talk on the phone. His idea of heaven is to spend
hours debating the pros and cons of Proposition 13. He wears dirty jeans
three days in a row, chews vitamin pills, and remembers everything. He
makes coast-to-coast plane reservations for six consecutive flights, then
misses all of them. Almost the only appurtenance consonant with his celebrity is an address book Don Juan would envy. As one of his best friends puts
it, "He can be an idiot, and he can be brilliant. The thing is, whatever he
does, he does it bigger than the others do it. It's his appetite. His appetite is
epic. He looks at the world, and there are things in it he wants. There are
things he must do. There are people he must have. His appetite is enormous,
and he has a wonderful time getting what he wants."

The life-style may be odd, the methods unorthodox, but Warren Beatty
gets what he wants. And it almost invariably works—and sells. No actor of
his generation, not Redford or Nicholson, has been a star half as long as
Beatty has. Few in the film industry make as much money. No one can do so
many of the jobs required to create a successful film as he. In the most visible function, acting, Beatty, unlike Travolta or De Niro, began at the top.
He has been a sensation ever since he first appeared on the screen, in *Splendor
in the Grass*, seventeen years ago.

He also revels in his life. Having no strong family ties, he goes wherever
he wants whenever he wants. Having no strong compulsion to work, he
takes off months to hop around the world, read, dabble in politics, and con-
sort with beautiful and interesting women. (He has made only fifteen
movies in eighteen years.) While other stars hang out with one another in
Malibu, Beatty moves and mingles with the "right" people. He has had
breakfast with Henry Kissinger in San Clemente and dined back in town

with Vladimir Horowitz. He has numbered among his friends the likes of Lillian Hellman, Robert F. Kennedy, Hubert Humphrey, George McGovern, and Jerry Brown. The countless women in his life have included Natalie Wood, Julie Christie, and his current flame, Diane Keaton.

With all this going on, he might well show signs of wear, but at forty-one, Beatty has the looks of a crown prince. He carries his six-feet two-inch frame like a youth of twenty. Maybe there are a few crows'-feet around Beatty's bedroom eyes and a small bald spot, but these are minor imperfections. When people lead charmed lives, they age remarkably well. Explains Beatty's friend, screenwriter Robert Towne (*Shampoo*): "People say you don't learn from success but from your failures. Warren learns from success."

This week fortune is ready to smile on Beatty yet another time. *Heaven Can Wait*, his new film, opens at 625 theaters nationwide and is almost sure to be the most popular entertainment of the summer. . . .

The old-fashioned appeal of *Heaven Can Wait* gives the film some of its glow. It is easy to imagine Beatty spending his boyhood watching double features at the neighborhood movie palace. That was not the case. Growing up in Richmond and later Arlington, Virginia, Beatty (then spelled with one *t*) was a bookworm. His father, a high-school principal, taught him to read at the age of four. He had a formidable sister, Shirley MacLaine (MacLean is Mrs. Beaty's maiden name). Three years older than Warren, she was the tomboy. Today she feels that both children were greatly influenced by the powerful personalities of their parents: "Dad had this Southern talent of commanding attention in any room with his storytelling; Mom would react to him in an intense way. Though not social or gregarious, they were like a vaudeville team at home, and Warren and I would sit there and watch. It made both of us rather shy, and one of our quests in life has been to overcome that shyness with self-expression."

As a teenager, Warren threw away the books. He was only a fair student but was captain of his high-school football team and president of his class. He quit Northwestern University after his freshman year and moved to New York to study acting. Then as now, Beatty kept professional distance between himself and his sister. He told interviewers that "nobody likes to be in somebody else's shadow." He was also far from certain that he wanted the flashy career she already had.

"I wanted to be a stage director—that was legitimate!" says Beatty, "and I wanted to write for the theater. I sort of backed into acting as a way of learning the theater." In New York in the late fifties, he worked at odd jobs, such as playing "bad cocktail piano" at a dim midtown club. After appearing in a few stock and live television productions, he got a screen test with director Joshua Logan; another novice movie actor, Jane Fonda, auditioned with Beatty. Nothing came of it, but three months later M-G-M offered Beatty a five-year contract at four hundred dollars a week. He moved to Hollywood and, at twenty-two, sized up the pitfalls of the studio system in record time. Without ever unpacking his bags, he borrowed money to buy his way out of M-G-M. Back in New York, he landed a supporting role in a William Inge play, *A Loss of Roses*. Though the show flopped on Broadway, Elia Kazan happened to see it. "I liked Warren right away," the director recalls now. "He was awkward in a way that was attractive. He was very, very ambitious. He had a lot of hunger, as all the stars do when they are young." Kazan signed Beatty immediately for *Splendor in the Grass;* to this day, Kazan remains Warren's favorite director.

Even before movie audiences got their first glimpse of Beatty, he was starring in Hollywood gossip columns. Nominally engaged to actress Joan Collins, Beatty carried on a public affair with *Splendor* co-star Natalie Wood. It broke up her marriage to actor Robert Wagner, though they later remarried. (A few years later director Peter Hall named Beatty the corespondent in a divorce suit against Leslie Caron.) Beatty was notorious as a rake, and not of the garden variety, by the time his first film opened. At the time, his feelings about his profession were mixed. "When I would fly in from Europe," he recalls, "it was embarrassing for me to put 'actor' on my landing card."

Beatty followed *Splendor* with a string of movies—*The Roman Spring of Mrs. Stone, All Fall Down, Lilith*—that turned out to be disappointments, but enlarged Beatty's image. Along the way, he earned a reputation for being hard on directors. "If the director was indecisive, Warren would absolutely destroy him," says Robert Towne. "He'd ask so many questions—and he can ask more questions than any three-year-old—that the director didn't know whether he was coming or going. I think Warren's drive to be a producer was that he feared he would get into more films where the person in authority didn't quite know what he was doing." Beatty agrees: "Once I became interested in stories and getting stories told, I realized I had to be a producer to get them told in the right way."

With *Bonnie and Clyde*, Beatty's chance to tell a story in his own way arrived. He didn't fool around. "He found the script and brought it to me," says director Arthur Penn. "He put together the financing and did the casting jointly with me. Warren is a great fighter. Warner Brothers didn't like *Bonnie and Clyde* and released it poorly. Warren got in there and reorganized the advertising and the release pattern. He made himself a real pain in the

(RIGHT) Brigitte Bardot:
Forty million Frenchmen can't be wrong.
(*A Ravishing Idiot.* © Warner Bros. Inc.
All rights reserved. Used by permission.)

(BELOW) Jean-Paul Belmondo:
*Gusty irreverence for all the cobwebs of
culture and convention.*
(*Stavisky.* Courtesy of Cinema 5.)

(LEFT) Warren Beatty:
He gets what he wants.
(*Heaven Can Wait*. Copyright © MCMLXXVIII
by Shelburne Associates. All rights reserved.)

(ABOVE) John Barrymore:
*Eminently suitable to the romantic dramas
of the time.* (*The Sea Beast.*)

ass to the people at Warner's. 'Why do we have to deal with this good-looking actor?' was their attitude. People didn't recognize him as the superior businessman he is. They do now. The results of his efforts were absolutely electrifying."

To say the least, *Bonnie and Clyde* became a classic of the sixties pop culture and the year's highest grossing film. Beatty became an international culture hero. Visiting France after the movie opened there, he found that "people everywhere were dressed like Bonnie and Clyde; it was the pervasive theme." And Beatty was celebrated as its prophet. At *haut monde* parties in Paris, he recalls, "you would be seated at a table with Maurice Chevalier on one side, Arthur Rubinstein on the other, and Mr. and Mrs. Pompidou across the candlesticks. There were old men with beautiful young girls—not one but clusters of them. There were women dripping jewels, and somehow you felt, this will never come again." He had just turned thirty.

After the *Bonnie and Clyde* hysteria died down, Beatty acted only occasionally. His single memorable performance was in Robert Altman's *McCabe and Mrs. Miller* (1971); it was also his first appearance opposite Julie Christie, who had been the most important woman in his life since 1965.

Beatty was drawn into politics by Vietnam and Bobby Kennedy in 1968. He took a year and a half off to work for the 1972 Democratic ticket. George McGovern was impressed by his newfound fund raiser's seriousness: "Warren not only cares about issues, but his judgment is very perceptive." Mostly to be available for McGovern, Beatty rejected a number of major films: *The Godfather*, *The Way We Were*, *The Great Gatsby*, and *The Sting*. Once the campaign was over, Beatty got to work producing and starring in *Shampoo*, a trenchant social comedy about a randy Beverly Hills hairdresser. Its sexual frankness was almost as hotly debated as the violence in *Bonnie and Clyde*, but it was enormously successful.

These days Beatty continues to pursue his three obsessions—movies, politics, and women—in about equal measure. His base for the past dozen years has been his apartment high in the Beverly Wilshire Hotel. The suite, aptly named "El Escondido" (The Hideaway), is a mess. Half-eaten room-service sandwiches, old magazines, scripts, books, and political journals lie in heaps throughout the living room; the place looks more like the office of the editor of a liberal weekly than the salon of a movie star. Beatty, who likes to wear old jeans and open shirts, slips in and out of the Wilshire through the garage.

Two and a half years ago, Beatty began building a mansion near his pal Jack Nicholson's spread on Mulholland Drive; there isn't a soul in Hollywood who believes that Beatty will ever move into it. "There's no anchor in

Warren's life," observes one friend. "Warren is always on the go," says Arthur Penn. "He travels light and takes one small suitcase from coast to coast. I guess you'd call him a very rich migrant worker." Last week Beatty arrived in New York to organize the advance screenings of *Heaven Can Wait* and harass the Paramount sales force with endless queries. It took the elegant Carlyle Hotel two days to determine whether or not he had actually checked into his suite. At one point a maid burst into his room, found Beatty on the telephone and complained: "Nobody has slept in the bed again. I want to know—are you going to stay here tonight?" Finally Beatty sheepishly threw up his hands and announced, "Well, it looks like this hotel has blown my cover."

Such tales about Beatty are legion. He rarely, if ever, is on time for any kind of appointment: agent Sue Mengers, a friend inured to his late arrivals, says she now "plans buffet entertaining if Warren is coming to one of my parties." Wealth makes him uncomfortable. He would rather hear Mabel Mercer sing in a quiet club than boogie at Régine's; he owns a Cartier watch, but prefers to wear a Timex. An articulate man who refuses to use either Hollywood lingo or the latest L.A. hip-speak, Beatty likes to take long pauses in the middle of sentences to make sure that he doesn't say more than he intends. In action, he is fast and effective. Lillian Hellman describes Beatty as a "foul-weather friend," the first person to call in a crisis. Says Mike Nichols: "He can make sixty-five calls in three hours and plan anything." Beatty is also a health-food enthusiast and, as Nichols notes, "a postgraduate hypochondriac." He tells of the time that Beatty crossed wires making a call and overheard two strangers discussing the symptoms of a friend who was about to have her gallbladder removed. Beatty listened and then broke in: "Hey, she doesn't have gallbladder problems; she should be tested for hypoglycemia." Sure enough, he proved to be right.

In business, Beatty is a tough operator. He will collect industry gossip without offering his sources any information in return. Says Beatty: "You never really know whether you are being perceived as a monster if you are a star." A few of his colleagues do see him that way. Says one highly respected studio head: "Warren won't make commitments and negotiates forever, trying to get his fees up. I wouldn't wish a negotiation with him on anyone." Buck Henry takes a more benevolent view: "Beatty is psychotic about the possibility of overlooking anything. If he could, he would be up in the projection booth of the theater showing his movie, pushing the projectionist aside, still trying to cut or add frames, humming music he might have forgotten to include in the sound track. 'Easygoing' is not a quality he has. You know how presidents age in office? If Beatty were president, either he would be dead after the first year or the country would be dead, because his attention to detail is maniacal."

His romantic commitments are, as ever, ephemeral. Says his sister: "Neither of us would have a conventional marriage because of the intensity of the marriage we witnessed every day as children. We need more breathing room in our lives. I can't imagine Warren with children. When he first met my daughter, he examined her quietly as though she were just a specimen of human life instead of his niece."

Some friends find their relationships with Beatty one-sided. But women who have had flings with Beatty speak of him more often with amusement than rancor. One survivor of a brief affair recalls: "He doesn't just want to seduce you but to quite literally charm the pants off you. He tells you you're fabulous and laughs at all your jokes. When we first met, we spent six hours talking about politics and articles in *The Atlantic* and sex and show business and Julie Christie. He's so in love with himself that it's contagious. He's very funny. I certainly don't regret knowing him." Actress Lee Grant, a longtime Beatty watcher, feels that "Warren's conquests of women are not totally successful. His percentage is about fifty-fifty. Those he can't conquer don't want to be part of a crowd—one of Warren's girls. But the Peter Pan quality in Warren is very attractive to some. He teaches them to fly, and they have extraordinary experiences with him. Then they grow up and go on, and he keeps flying. Like Peter Pan, he always comes back to another little girl who's ready to fly off with him to never-never land."

By now Beatty is used to having others theorize about him, though press accounts still test his not inconsiderable sense of humor. "I have never talked about my personal relationships—with women, my sister, my parents—because these are important people to me. I don't want to hurt them by discussing them in public. As for my love life, I can't control what others say about it; it is what it is. I know that movie actors are overrewarded in our society, and that the press has to cut people like me down to size. So they come up with all sorts of wild things. They make me into an insane eccentric with an incredible fear of losing my youth, who lives in a bomb shelter, who contemplates or is going through plastic surgery, who has devastating relationships with women. It goes through cycles. First they say that women like me too much; then that women don't like me at all; then that they like me too much again. Somewhere along the way they say that I secretly like men—but then that men don't like me! I'm old, I'm young, I'm intelligent, I'm stupid. My tide goes in and out."

Beatty is not contemplating any changes in his ways. If he has any personal complaints, they are only about the drudgery of producing. "I enjoyed it the first time, on *Bonnie and Clyde*," he says, "because I wanted to see if I could play with the big boys. But, you know, they don't look that big after you've been playing with them." The prospect of running for public office also has lost some appeal for him, though he doesn't rule it out altogether. "The relationship between theater and politics fascinates me," he says. "They both communicate ideas and both involve persuasion and compromise." More than ever, though, Beatty loves acting; he looks forward to playing many more roles after John Reed and Howard Hughes. This is good news, for Beatty has evolved into an exceptional movie star. Once a moody, latter-day James Dean, he is now the wittiest of leading men. He brings eroticism to the screen, but not at the expense of sensitivity and self-effacing charm. At his best—especially in *McCabe* and *Heaven Can Wait*—his acting belies his looks; he makes the audience feel protective of him.

Actually Beatty thrives on taking care of himself. He likes to be alone and sometimes dreams of the day when even his work will be solitary. "My idea of freedom and independence," he says, "is to live on top of a hill with clean air—no smog—and some good food vaguely in the area. The window is ajar, and there's a breeze that smells of geraniums or honeysuckle. And there's a room with a typewriter, where you go in for a few hours a day and tell your version of things. And you get a call from someone in a distant, dirty city who tells you that you can have more money and more time to write because people are so eager to read what you have to say. That's the fantasy of quitting. The other day I was thinking about quitting, and it was really attractive to me—for fifteen or twenty minutes."

He pauses and goes on: "But then you go out to a movie theater and get this thrill when something good goes on the screen. And you want to raise your hand and say, *'Wait a minute, wait a minute, I want to make one of those!'*"

[1978]

Andrew Sarris

JEAN-PAUL BELMONDO

The first film actor to combine the intelligence and athleticism of America with the intellectuality and aestheticism of Europe.

There are times when Jean-Paul Belmondo seems almost too good to be true. His public personality has not altered appreciably since 1959, when he electrified Parisian audiences as a hard-boiled Humphrey Bogart worshipper in that tribute to American gangster movies, Jean-Luc Godard's *Breathless*. Now, seven years and more than thirty movies later, enough of his easygoing unpretentious, Rabelaisian personality has seeped across the Atlantic to appeal to those of his campus admirers who are tired of Daddy's heroic declamations on the Great Depression and the Great War. At the advanced age of thirty-three Belmondo is still one of the New People. In a Times Square shopwindow that serves as a fever chart of adolescent addictions a gigantic poster of Belmondo shares space with such other luminaries as David McCallum, Robert Vaughn, and the Beatles. Yet, unlike these unlikely companions, Belmondo has not benefited from the promotions of the mass media in the United States. His English, minuscule as it is, is execrable, and few of his movies have had wide international distribution. Despite his press clippings, Belmondo doesn't even have a press agent. In short, his career seems to have more Zen than zing.

In *Breathless*, Belmondo was cast as a cop killer, washroom mugger, purse pilferer, and taxi jumper, just to mention some of his nonsexual outrages. "Belmondoism" was consequently regarded as a new style of affluent amorality, and Belmondo himself was identified invidiously with everything from foppery to fascism. Yet four years after *Breathless* Belmondo starred in a real-life drama with the Paris police. While arguing the right of an injured motorcyclist to speedier service from the policemen on an ambulance crew, the actor was clobbered from behind by a cop and rendered *hors de combat*. Belmondo sued, and the police brought countercharges. Though Belmondo was fined for "insulting language," the impulsive gendarme was given one month's suspended sentence for "unnecessary violence." The latter penalty was virtually a milestone of human rights in a city where the lawmen make Okefenokee sheriffs look like charter members of the American Civil Liberties Union.

At the time I read of the incident I was reminded of an infantry officer in basic training instructing us in the submachine gun with the comment that its kick "would knock a runt like Humphrey Bogart flat on his ass." Undoubtedly there is something in Belmondo, as in Bogart, that deeply disturbs a certain type of authoritarian personality. This something may be largely a myth, but not entirely. In two very different generations a genuinely independent spirit flows out of an actor's apparently casual onscreen gestures. The surface arrogance of both Bogie and Belmondo conceals a tough-guy gallantry underneath.

It is no accident that the rediscovery of the forties Bogart has enhanced the reputation of the sixties Belmondo, and vice versa. Nevertheless, there is much, much more to Belmondo than the Bogey bit. Much more and much else. If at times Belmondo seems like the last of the real movie stars, it is because his extraordinary range encompasses so many different functions and traditions. Who among contemporary actors can simultaneously evoke Douglas Fairbanks and James Dean, Marlon Brando and Marcello Mastroianni, Errol Flynn and John Garfield? Only Belmondo, the first actor in film history to combine the intelligence and athleticism of America with the intellectuality and aestheticism of Europe.

Part of Belmondo's image in France as a modern Fairbanks is based on his doing his own stuntwork in films. Nowadays no Hollywood studio would permit its star to dangle from a skyscraper in Brasilia or from a helicopter over the Amazon. It would certainly never allow him to hurtle over a cliff on a motorcycle going eighty miles an hour. Belmondo's stunting is the ultimate demonstration of the nonsissiness of his métier. But in his homage to the American action movie, Belmondo has become more royalist than the king, since few, if any, of the Hollywood heroes Belmondo admires so much have ever done their own stuntwork. Which only goes to prove that Americans, being more attuned to action and violence, are also more practical about it. With the French intellectual, action and violence have become articles of faith. Belmondo, sensitive to the tastes of the French public, seems to have decided, perhaps instinctively, that there is no substitute for the real thing in a country starved for authentic heroes.

Belmondo is also addicted to speeding in sports cars, much like his ill-fated predecessor the late James Dean. Unlike Dean, however, Belmondo does not seem afflicted by a death wish arising out of a lonely morbidity. Belmondo still shudders at the memory of a reckless drive that nearly cost the life of Jeanne Moreau's young son, who was riding in the "death seat." The speed generated by his many sports cars is merely an expression of Belmondo's essentially extroverted zest for physical sensations. Driving is also an expression of the actor's oft-quoted attitude of taking life as it comes.

Even in the limited context of the French cinema, however, Belmondo is hardly the first actor to project virility on an international scale. Jean Gabin was the proletarian prototype of the thirties, full of grand illusions and earthy nobility. The late Gérard Philipe embodied the Existential Pilgrim of the late forties and fifties, the anguished age of Camus and Sartre. Philipe was beautiful, austere, puritanical, and cerebral. His was a sensibility of memory and regret in a world that had witnessed the obliteration of the values Gabin incarnated. (Gabin, incidentally, has called Belmondo his logical successor.)

Jean-Paul Belmondo was born in Neuilly-sur-Seine on April 9, 1933, the year after Jean Gabin made his screen debut. Belmondo was only seven when Paris fell, and only eleven when Paris was liberated, an event he is helping commemorate this season in the Paramount superproduction *Is Paris Burning?* There is no reason to believe that Belmondo was particularly scarred by memories of World War II, and consequently his personality is reasonably free of the tics and angsts of the thirties and forties. His father, a noted academic sculptor, provided an atmosphere of taste and elegance against which the young Belmondo rebelled in the recognizable style of the ruling classes. He was expelled from some of the best schools of France, and took up a boxing career so seriously (twenty-three amateur bouts as a lightweight) that his parents were relieved when he went into acting. His boxing bequeathed him part of the squash in his nose, that noble emblem of his Experience, and more important, the kinetic frenzy of movement and gesture, such as we have not seen since Cagney jabbed his way across the early talkies. Belmondo is six feet tall and weighs only 143 pounds, a compact combination of sinewy muscles that makes him a heavyweight in his chosen medium. Since highbrow culture seldom exploits the expressive potentialities of the human body, Belmondo would never have made it as a big star without an accompanying revolution in the cinema.

Belmondo made three films in 1959, but only *Breathless* managed to give birth to Belmondoism. Jean-Luc Godard had worked with him previously in a short film entitled *Charlotte et son Jules*, a directorial conceit consisting of a Belmondo monologue to his departing mistress, who limits herself to a wide range of gestures and grimaces pantomiming female perversity. Godard's flair for improvising bits of business for his players found its fullest expression in *Breathless*, where a universe of meanings could be contained in the way a character lit a cigarette or opened the door to a car. Godard and Belmondo thus anticipated many of Marshall McLuhan's media probes; the characters in *Breathless* became the instruments of the gadgets they manipulated. Furthermore, the key objects in Belmondo's world are luxuries, whereas the key objects in Gabin's world were necessities, and in Philipe's world there were no objects, only moral situations. By contrast, Belmondo functions and even flourishes in a world of machines and gadgets, to the neurotic point of experiencing more and enjoying less.

Belmondo fits into a time when the need for a personal style is predicated on a loss of faith in the larger configurations of religion and history. The importance of the Now, the temporal constituent of style, is related to the decline of the hereafters of heaven and utopia. Not that Belmondo has rationalized his own role to this extent. Far from it. He has merely followed his instincts to a more vigorous response toward the world around him than custom dictates. From his first days at the Conservatory of Dramatic Art, Belmondo felt compelled to pump life, however vulgar and bawdy, into the most revered classics. (Anna Karina, Jean-Luc Godard's Galatea and ex-wife, was later to sum up Belmondo's appeal in the wisecrack, "He's not handsome, but at least he's vulgar.")

There was no Actors Studio in Paris to channel these impulses; Belmondo had to swim alone against the current of convention. Gradually he acquired a coterie of lesser-known admirers, Jean-Pierre Marielle, Jean Rochefort, Michel Beaune, Pierre Vernier, and Guy Bedos. Belmondo has retained these friendships long after the big payoff of *Breathless*; and friendship, more than coincidentally, is one of the recurring themes in his movies.

One of the forgotten films of 1959 is Claude Sautet's *Classe Tous les Risques*, a gangster saga of the devotion of a young man (Belmondo) to an aging mobster (Lino Ventura). The French cult of Howard Hawks movies is derived largely from this kind of idealization of male *amitié*. Ironically, Leslie Fiedler finds this theme in American literature a symptom of the suppressed and not-so-suppressed homosexuality in American culture. Belmondo has reenacted this Hawksian relationship in two striking films of Jean-Pierre Melville, *Magnet of Doom* and *Doulos—the Finger Man*. Only Belmondo's unquestioned virility makes the treatment of this theme feasible even in France, where homosexuality is not nearly as scandalous as it is in the more susceptible States. For his part, Belmondo prefers the relative stoicism of American *amitié* movies, in which the characters never talk about their fraternal feelings, to the gushing lyricism of François Truffaut's *Jules and Jim*, in which Jules and Jim are always reassuring each other about how much they like each other.

Nevertheless, Belmondo does not deserve special credit for his virility. Such matters are not subject to choice. Nor is it particularly significant that virile actors are always in short supply and great demand. The trouble with acting, generally and universally, is the predominance of delicate, sensitive, effeminate types far beyond the correct casting percentages. The necessary narcissism is lacking in too many of the stronger personalities who would make more interesting actors. Consequently a diamond in the rough like the late John Garfield will always be a rarity and an irreplaceable treasure.

Yet Belmondo, in real life as well as in reel life, seems to have developed few of the complexes of the big movie star. Not only has he remained loyal to his old friends and reserved toward the most prominent of his new ones, he has kept the same wife (Élodie, a former dancer), whom he married on the way up, through three children and a score of curvaceous co-stars without seeming sanctimonious about home and hearth. His name has been linked romantically to many of his leading ladies, most recently to the frequently undressed Ursula Andress, his tantalizing trial in United Artists' *Up to His Ears*. Such gossip, however, is standard publicity procedure for actors far less virile than Belmondo, though admittedly some of the choicer Belmondo-Andress gossip items seem to be getting out of hand, almost like a B-picture remake of the Burton-Taylor tryst on the Tiber.

There is no strong evidence, fortunately, that Belmondo has lost the sense of proportion that goes with a sense of humor. The prevailing pattern of Belmondo's personality is still a gusty irreverence for all the cobwebs of culture and convention, but he is hardly lacking in the finer feelings. Qualities like loyalty and fidelity are rare enough these days, but there is also in Belmondo a restless search for new standards of taste. He takes on a great many assignments a canny careerist like Alain Delon would scorn as beneath contempt. Yet for all of Delon's calculations, he is merely another pretty boy in a sea of smooth-faced anonymity, another stereotyped French lover in the Hollywood tradition that has wasted such formidable talents as Charles Boyer and Louis Jourdan. Belmondo, by contrast, has gone international by staying national, become universal by being French. He has become that biggest kind of star, the kind whose sparkle is enhanced even by his bad movies.

Belmondo's instincts are probably sounder than some of his carping critics imagine. The job of a movie star is to keep making movies. It's all very well to say that one must pick only the best projects, but even the best projects have been known to go bad. What Belmondo's critics really object to is the actor's tendency to go for "movie-movies" rather than serious cinema. Belmondo apparently passed up opportunities to work with Truffaut and Visconti in order to romp around Brazil and Hong Kong in simpleminded adventure spoofs. On the other hand, Belmondo has never priced himself out of the way-out projects of Jean-Luc Godard, and has undoubtedly brought many movies the financing they needed to see the light of day. Many of the movies were bad, granted, but they were all worth trying, and Belmondo's reputation did not suffer in the process of trial and error. Who knows which of his thirty-odd movies will next catch fire in some lonely moviegoer's soul? As it is, Belmondo has more than held his own with such international luminaries as Gabin (*Monkey in Winter*), Moreau (*Banana Peel* and *Moderato Cantabile*), Loren (*Two Women*), and Jean Seberg (*Breathless* and *Backfire*), of whom he has said, "She is what every American girl should be." His roles have ranged from a priest (*León Morin, Prêtre*) to a peasant (*La Viaccia*) and from a vulgar intellectual (*A Woman Is a Woman*) to a vulgar idealist (*Leda*). *Leda*, in fact, was his third film in 1959, the film in which he most closely resembled Brando, particularly at the dinner table, but with none of Brando's anguished *Streetcar Named Desire* sensitivity.

The point is that Belmondo is ultimately an original. Despite his ·fracas with the police, Belmondo is not a cop hater like Sinatra, or a hardheaded nonconformist like Mitchum, or an amateur agitator like Brando. Belmondo is a performer, hoping to perform as well as he can, and, up to now at least, as often as he can.

[1966]

Stephen Harvey

INGRID BERGMAN

There's always been a contradiction between her air of self-sufficient composure and her warm simplicity.

Having already unraveled the knots that bind sisters (*Cries and Whispers*), fathers and sons (*Through a Glass Darkly*), lovers (*The Passion of Anna*), and spouses (*Scenes from a Marriage*), Ingmar Bergman eventually had to get around to dissecting the mother-daughter relationship. It was just as inevitable, and even more to be hoped for, that he should finally join forces with that other Bergman, namely Ingrid, Sweden's most durable gift to film acting. The collaboration between the two Bergmans has benefited both of them; he's provided her with the most demanding and meatiest role she's had in what is far too long a time, while her radiance and brio spark even

THE MOVIE STAR | 133

the film's most inert moments. Considering her own nomadic career (Bergman hasn't made a feature film in her native language in forty years), it was an inspiration to cast her as Charlotte, the cosmopolitan pianist come home for a brief sojourn. She understands the local ground rules, but can never be entirely at home within them, a circumstance that Bergman the actress effortlessly conveys.

Of all the film actresses of her generation, Bergman is the only one who continues to grow and to stretch her talents, who still has the capacity to surprise us. There's always been a contradiction in her screen presence between her air of self-sufficient composure and her warm simplicity, and throughout her career she's usually handled it by alternating between playing worldly sophisticates and big-spirited mothers (Superior or not)-of-us-all. Here the two aspects are fused into one complex characterization, and the film's greatest pleasure consists in watching her do it with such success.

During her reunion with her daughter, Eva, a rural parson's wife (Liv Ullmann, of course), as withdrawn as Charlotte is extroverted, Bergman is required to pass through an astonishing variety of moods within one brief scene—vanity and fatigue, solicitude and egotism, grief over the loss of her late lover, guilt at her neglect of her family, and fury that her laxness should be called to her attention. With subtlety and economy, she lights briefly on one emotion and then imperceptibly shifts to the next, her face hardening and dissolving to meet the requirements of the moment. As she has managed to do from the start of her international career, Bergman has once more made the near-impossible seem easy and spontaneous.

The irony is that her skill and the goodwill we bring to her as a performer eventually subvert all of Ingmar Bergman's intentions. With her simultaneous entrance into the closed world of the film and the house of her daughter, the brisk air of reality following in her wake only shows up her director's overfamiliar contrivances. Her co-star has perhaps lived too long within the confines of this world; while Liv Ullmann's performance is technically impressive, we've seen her fumble toward a martyred state of grace at least once too often.

Once more Ullmann has been handed the obligatory monologue in which, glowing and aching, she expostulates on the grandeur of God's unfathomable scheme for mankind. Once more she valiantly shatters the shell of her passive compliance to rage out at her tormentor, gaining the upper hand before extending it in reconciliation. Neither she nor Bergman seems to notice what a drag this character has become, nor does the director seem to realize how appealing, in comparison, is Ingrid Bergman's sturdy self-assurance. At least in the past the Ullmann roles were granted a kind of sympathetic objectivity by their creator, but in *An Autumn Sonata,* Eva is practically canonized before the film comes to a close.

Intimidated by the mother whose love she never won, Eva is intended as the homespun counterpoint to the blithe and worldly Charlotte, but Ullmann makes her a case of arrested development if there ever was one. Encased in brown woolen jumpers with Peter Pan collars, her hair in a coiled braid, her eyes hidden behind a pair of granny glasses, and her mouth drooping wanly at Mommy's mastery of a Chopin prelude, Ullmann projects a frumpiness that's practically a television-sketch travesty of itself. Yet this character is not only meant seriously, she is positively exalted. Everyone loves her except for Mother, who is too self-centered to perceive what an unpolished gem she is. The husband who abjectly depends on her, the palsy-afflicted sister whom she uncomplainingly nurses, even, presumably, her dead infant son, whose memory she alone is committed to perpetuating. One waits in vain for Bergman (Ingmar, that is) to give a sign that he sees through her smug torpor. But the film's frenzied climax, when Ullmann spews out her stored litany of resentment against her mother's misdeeds, tips Bergman's hand completely.

It's Mother, it turns out, who's responsible for all that's gone awry in her daughter's life, as well as the physical afflictions of the invalid upstairs, who, at this very moment, is crawling downstairs, crying for solace from Mother. Now as ever, Mother ignores her. One would have thought that this attitude of lifelong reproach would be confined to self-pitying adolescents and, lately, the grown children of movie stars no longer around to defend themselves, but it's clear throughout that Bergman identifies completely with this point of view. In the queasiest way imaginable, *An Autumn Sonata* turns out to be the wish fulfillment of any child who feels his parents once wronged him unforgivably and has cherished his rancor ever since.

Finally the tables are turned; Mommy is forced to confront her sins and at long last to plead penitently for the chance to redeem herself. Never mind any nagging notions you might have that the offspring's pious candor resembles nothing so much as the flip side of masochism, or that at a certain point men and women should take on responsibility for their own lives and mistakes. (I won't dwell on Bergman's increasingly offensive use of illness as a metaphor for emotional neglect. There's something exceedingly distasteful about using an offspring's grave physical condition as a weapon to flay a mother for not having loved her children enough.)

The denouement is even more odiously self-righteous. After musing on the fact that she would gladly kill herself if she weren't sure that God still needed her to carry out His tasks on earth, Eva decides to make her peace

(RIGHT) Ingrid Bergman:
Radiance and depth of feeling.
(*Gaslight.* © 1944 Loew's Inc. Copyright
renewed 1971 by Metro-Goldwyn-Mayer Inc.)

(ABOVE) Humphrey Bogart:
His own very personal gravity.

with her mother—not because the mother deserves it, mind you, but as yet another demonstration of the daughter's sublime goodness of heart.

Noxious as all this is, however, Bergman has so consummately crafted the whole that *An Autumn Sonata* is almost persuasive in spite of itself. Alternating harsh, tight close-ups of Ullmann's thrusts and Bergman's parries, the director generates real fire and tension in the culminating scenes, as much through the rhythms of his editing as the virtuosity of the two performers. The main prerequisite of all the actresses in Bergman's circle is the ability to open up to the emotional rigors of his gaze as it relentlessly closes in on them. Ingrid Bergman is the perfect subject for such scrutiny, as this has always been her most potent talent. Movies far slighter than this one have been made unforgettable because of a glimpse of her radiance and depth of feeling expressed in close-up.

However irritating the film's viewpoint becomes, *An Autumn Sonata* is never less than engrossing. But the achievement, finally, is Ingrid's; when last seen, the character she plays is on a train leaving her homeland, this chapter of her life closed, and she's nattering on to her agent about past triumphs and future challenges. Ingrid Bergman has likewise persevered, from Sweden to Hollywood to Rome and back, vitalizing her gifts every so often by linking forces with the most exacting film artists on both continents. Doubtless she'll continue to do the same whenever the opportunity arises. The challenge is hers, but the pleasure is all ours.

[1978]

Andrew Sarris

HUMPHREY BOGART

An undertone of irony in even his most conventional assignments.

A television network recently phoned *The Voice* to inquire if any special revival programs were planned anywhere to commemorate the twentieth anniversary of Humphrey Bogart's death, which occurred on January 14, 1957. Twenty years! It hardly seems possible. But then the peculiar agelessness of movie stars throws off all our calendar calculations.

In Bogart's case he seems to pertain less to the fifties than to the forties (when he hit his peak) and the sixties (when he was rediscovered on college campuses). The question now is whether he has been overdiscovered. To my knowledge there have been no Humphrey Bogart retrospectives around town in recent months. Does this mean anything? Is it possible that Bogie has become a cliché? We have come a long way since the *hommage à Bogie* of Jean-Luc Godard and Jean-Paul Belmondo in *Breathless*. That was 1960. The Bogart still in *Breathless* comes from his last picture, *The Harder They Fall* (1956), one that has been seldom, if ever, revived on the campuses. But the French worship a myth all the way to the bitter end. Hence, Bazin's eloquent eulogy to Bogart as an actor followed throughout his career by the angel of death. The French critics were painfully aware through the fifties that Bogie was literally dying of cancer, whiskey, and cigarettes right before their eyes. This gallant process of endurance lent poignancy and stature to his famous *films noirs* of the forties.

By contrast, Woody Allen's *Play It Again, Sam* (1972) exploits a more cheerful image of Bogart as a cool womanizer made to order for Allen's adolescent fantasies of getting laid. From Woody Allen it is only a short step to the ironic television commercials in which the Bogart imitators poke fun at a familiar voice afflicted by a frozen upper lip. Perhaps the time has come to liberate Bogart from his legend by reexamining his career in some detail. In that way we may even recall how the legend got started in the first place.

Bogart started very slowly in the thirties, so slowly, in fact, that he had to go back to Broadway to recharge his movie career. His first nine roles led him into virtual oblivion in Hollywood, and it would take a real trivia expert to evaluate his work in *Up the River* and *A Devil with Women* (1930), *Body and Soul, Bad Sister, Women of All Nations*, and *A Holy Terror* (1931), *Love Affair* and *Three on a Match* (1932), and *Midnight* (1934). In this period he played both nice guys and bad guys, but he had not yet established himself as a tough guy. Today, of course, his image jumps out at you no matter what he is doing. In the mid-thirties, however, he drifted from studio to studio as a nondescript leading-man type. Since he was already past thirty when he made his first movie, he could not linger long in the juvenile range.

His big break came on the stage as the fugitive gangster Duke Mantee in Robert Sherwood's *The Petrified Forest*. Even so, it was only the intervention of the play's star, Leslie Howard, that enabled Bogart to return triumphantly to the screen in 1936 with a made-to-order tough-guy persona. (In gratitude, Bogart later named one of his children Leslie.) The second phase of his movie career then began as a struggle, mostly at Warners, to attain full-fledged stardom. Unfortunately, Warners was one studio that was overloaded with tough guys to whom Bogart played a perennial second fiddle. Edward G. Robinson called the tune in *Bullet or Ballots* (1936), *Kid Galahad* (1937), *The Amazing Dr. Clitterhouse* (1938), and *Brother Orchid* (1940). James Cagney did the same in *Angels With Dirty Faces* (1938), *The Oklahoma Kid*, and *The Roaring Twenties* (1939), and even George Raft was top dog in *Invisible Stripes* (1939) and *They Drive by Night* (1940). More often than not, the supporting characters Bogart played were dead of gunshot wounds before the last reel. Bogart himself is said to have observed that his frequent death scenes kept his career alive into the forties. Robinson and Cagney were not averse to getting knocked off spectacularly either, but they had made their dead-end presence felt back in the early thirties (in *Little Caesar* and *The Public Enemy*), when Bogart was struggling to find an identity on screen.

Discerning critics like Otis Ferguson had already begun to appreciate the subtle villainies of Bogart, who somehow never drifted into the Warners stock company of second-string mobsters. Bogart could be mean in *Bullets or Ballots* and *Kid Galahad*, cowardly in *Angels with Dirty Faces* and *The Roaring Twenties*, or cheerfully fatalistic in *Invisible Stripes*. Yet somehow there was always an undertone of irony in even his most conventional assignments. It is almost as if he were quietly amused at the low-life spectacle he was making of himself. Bogart, unlike Cagney, was never directly wired to the streets; he was more the loner, the aloof nonconformist.

My own most vivid early impression of Bogart came from his oily, pain-ridden, baby-faced gangster portrayal in *Dead End*. I was only about nine at the time, but I found something so sneaky and malignant in Bogart's personality that I was not able to respond to him for years after. Hence, I missed most of his great forties performances, and when a girl on whom I had a crush in high school declared her own crush for Bogart I was frankly mystified. How could anyone love a man who had been so scarred by suffering that he became inordinately bitter and suspicious? I was brought up on the traditional view that the most beautiful people were those who had been unmarked by life. Obviously, I had a lot to learn and unlearn. Still, I have put it to my students on more than one occasion that there would never have been a Bogart cult if he had made his last film in 1940, for though his talent was impressive through the thirties, his type remained disquieting.

For one thing, he never got the girl in any way that counted mythically. In addition to *Bad Sister* in 1931, four 1930s films featured both Bogart and Bette Davis: *The Petrified Forest, Marked Woman, Kid Galahad,* and *Dark Victory.* However, they never really appeared opposite each other. Perhaps the chemistry would not have been there if they had. Their careers were to blossom separately in any event as they eventually became too big for each other. What they *did* have in common along with Cagney was a rebellious attitude toward Warners, certainly one of the least refined of all the studios, and one of the most raucous. One can make a case for both sides in the dispute.

If Warners provided opportunities for Bogart's career in *Black Legion, San Quentin, Marked Woman, Kid Galahad, The Amazing Dr. Clitterhouse, Angels with Dirty Faces, The Roaring Twenties,* and *They Drive by Night,* the studio provided only obstacles with such clinkers as *China Clipper, The Great O'Malley, Swing Your Lady, Men Are Such Fools, King of the Underworld, The Oklahoma Kid,* and *The Return of Dr. X.* Even his two loan-out films to United Artists in this period split down the middle, with *Dead End* giving him a lift, and *Stand In* proving to be a dead end. Indeed, Bogart's role in *Stand In* as a neurotic film director with a pet Pekingese always in his arms competes for camp honors with his Western badman in *Oklahoma Kid,* his imitation-Karloff ghoul in *The Return of Dr. X,* and his D. H. Lawrence, Irish-brogued horse trainer in *Dark Victory.*

Then, in 1941, Bogart vaulted into movie mythology with two great incarnations, one outdoors as Roy Earle in Raoul Walsh's *High Sierra,* and one indoors in John Huston's *The Maltese Falcon. High Sierra* gave Bogart more emotional depth and scope than he had ever been able to display before, and *The Maltese Falcon* provided him with a wit and an irony that had previously been more implied than expressed. Most important of all, Roy Earle and Sam Spade placed Bogart at the vital center of first-rate scenarios. No longer was he the peripheral punk, albeit with a touch of class. Nor was he the second-string lead. Suddenly he was the big noise, the brooding, sardonic protagonist. When he talked, people listened. When he listened, people chose their words with care. And through all the violent action Bogart emerged as a curiously mature star. Now past forty, his face seemed to have weathered all his career nonhappenings in the thirties. But from the audience's historical perspective it was a face that had survived the Great Depression with enough strength to meet the challenge of World War II.

High Sierra and *The Maltese Falcon* had made him a star; it remained for *Casablanca* to make him a myth. All three projects had started out as relatively routine projects, and all three ended up as classics. Yet for Bogart the role of Rick in *Casablanca* was the one indispensable catalyst in his career. Roy Earle, for all his vulnerability, was basically a hoodlum, and Sam Spade, for all his sophistication, was a jaundiced private eye. These characterizations, however romanticized, were still bounded by genre conventions from the thirties. Variants of Roy Earle had been done to death by Cagney,

Robinson, and Muni, and *The Maltese Falcon* itself had been made into movies twice before. *Casablanca* launched Bogart into the forties, a period in which all his aggressions could be harnessed for the Allied Cause.

And then there was the matter of sexual chemistry. Ida Lupino, the gang groupie in *High Sierra*, was clearly a diamond in the rough, but Roy Earle preferred to waste his emotional energy on Joan Leslie's dull, selfish waif with a Chaplinesque limp. As for Mary Astor's demimondaine in *The Maltese Falcon*, she was everything a grown-up man would desire, but Sam Spade invoked his code of honor to make her take the fall. In both films the women were too much on the shady side of the street ever to share a sunset with the man they loved. Lupino and Astor were classy dames, all right in their place, but not really the stuff that dreams were made on. Bogart had not yet met his here's-looking-at-you-kid sweetheart, who would break his heart and change his type irrevocably from tough guy to great lover. *Casablanca* changed all that with a meeting made in Hollywood heaven: Humphrey Bogart and Ingrid Bergman, neither of whom had yet hit their stride, neither of whom ever took this ridiculously romantic melodrama seriously while they were making it. Indeed, much of the charm of *Casablanca* can be attributed to the intuitive grace of its throwaway performances.

Bogart had already joined the war effort in *Across the Pacific*, John Huston's spin-off from *The Maltese Falcon*. *Casablanca* then completed the process of transforming cynicism into idealism as Rick stopped drowning his sorrows in drink long enough to join the Resistance. From 1942 through 1944 he kept up the struggle in *Action in the North Atlantic*, *Sahara*, *To Have and Have Not*, and *Passage to Marseilles*. Bogart became the thinking man's patriot; liberal, skeptical, sardonic, suspicious at first, but eventually heroic in the service of one unfashionable underdog or another—black, Russian, refugee, colonial. The war had become Bogart's Petrified Forest, the hard edge from which he could not flinch on the screen.

Howard Hawk's *To Have and Have Not* introduced a somewhat lighter note to the solemn proceedings by introducing Lauren Bacall with her growling sexual challenge to Bogart to whistle for her, a whistle that was heard around the world. Bogart and Bacall then perfected their mutual myth in Hawks's *The Big Sleep*, Delmer Daves's *Dark Passage*, and John Huston's *Key Largo*. For a time Bacall rejuvenated Bogart as a romantic lead. He was nearing fifty, a far more dangerous age for a star in that era than now. Huston helped deglamorize and demystify him as a grizzled runt of a man in *The Treasure of the Sierra Madre* and *The African Queen*, two showy performances for the actor, two costly self-revelations for the star.

In the fifties Bogart's most notable roles alternated between romantic despair (*In a Lonely Place*, *The Barefoot Contessa*) and scene-chewing villainy from Duke Mantee days (*The Caine Mutiny*, *The Desperate Hours*). Yet, he could hold a good movie like *The Enforcer* together simply by playing a subdued straight man to a gallery of gangster grotesques. He even tried sixties camp at least a decade before its time in John Huston's and Truman Capote's *Beat the Devil*. And he was making his share of bad movies all the way to the end. On balance, however, he managed to leave us a legacy of the spiritual ferment through which he and we lived.

If I had to choose one image by which to remember Bogart, it would be of that one mysterious moment in *The Big Sleep* when Bogart finds himself alone in a sinister room. The atmosphere drips with evil; the camera pauses at a contemplative distance. Bogart seems lost in thought as he looks for some invisible clue. But he is no merely deductive detective; he has staked his whole life on the solution to the mystery. He has thus brought to the screen his own very personal gravity. That is why he has proven to be irreplaceable in the past twenty years.

[1977]

Pauline Kael

MARLON BRANDO AND JAMES DEAN

The delinquent becomes the hero because the image of instinctive rebellion expresses something in many people that they don't dare express.

A "regular" movie says yes to the whole world or it says not much of anything. What is there in *The Long Gray Line*, *A Man Called Peter*, *The Prodigal*, or *Not as a Stranger* that can stir an audience out of its apathy—an exposed beating heart, a man fighting a vulture—and who cares? And who really cares about the bland prosperity that produces these entertainments? The United States has now achieved what critics of socialism have always posited as the end result of a socialist state: a prosperous, empty, uninspiring uniformity. (If we do not have exactly what Marx meant by a classless society, we do have something so close to it that the term is certainly no longer an alluring goal.) What promises does maturity hold for a teenager: a dull job, a dull life, television, freezers, babies and baby-sitters, a guaranteed annual wage, taxes, social security, hospitalization insurance, and death. Patriotism becomes a series of platitudes; even statements that are true seem hypocritical when no longer informed with fire and idealism. It may be because this culture offers nothing that stirs youthful enthusiasm that it has spewed up a negative reaction: for the first time in American history we have a widespread nihilistic movement, so nihilistic it doesn't even have a program, and, ironically, its only leader is a movie star: Marlon Brando.

Our mass culture has always been responsive to the instincts and needs of the public. Though it exploits those needs without satisfying them, it does nonetheless throw up images that indicate social tensions and undercurrents. Without this responsiveness, mass culture would sink of its own weight. But it doesn't sink—there *is* a kind of vitality in it. Even the most routine adventure pictures, with Jeff Chandler or Rory Calhoun or Randolph Scott or John Wayne, empty and meaningless as they are, cater to unsatisfied appetites for action and color and daring—ingredients that are absent from the daily lives of patrons. But if films and other areas of mass culture did not produce anything that moved us more directly, they would become as rigid and formalized as ballet—a series of repeated gestures for a limited audience of connoisseurs (the Western has reached this point). When more ambitious filmmakers want to make a film with dramatic conflict, they draw upon the hostility to conformity embodied in the crazy, mixed-up kid.

The phenomenon of films touching a social nerve is not new. The gangster films in the thirties expressed a fundamental hostility to society and authority; the gangsters made their own way, even if they paid for it by prison or death. But in the thirties the gangsters were not the only rebels, there was a large active body of political rebellion, given partial expression in films by the dispossessed heroes who asked for a job, a home and a life. In the fifties, there is no American political rebellion, there is not even enough political theory to give us a feasible explanation of delinquency itself—the new dissidents who say that a job, a home, and the life that goes with them aren't worth the trouble. One thing seems evident: when the delinquent becomes the hero in our films, it is because the image of instinctive rebellion expresses something in many people that they don't dare express. These kids seem to be the only ones who are angry about apathy: they seem to be the only ones with guts enough, or perhaps they are the only ones irresponsible enough, to act out a *no* to the whole system of authority, morality and prosperity.

The depth of Brando's contact with some sections of the public may be gauged by the extraordinary resentment expressed toward James Dean for what was considered an imitation of Brando in *East of Eden* (though Dean's acting suggests Montgomery Clift as much as it does Brando, while his facial qualities suggest Gregory Peck); and the jeers and walkouts on *Blackboard Jungle* because Vic Morrow employed a Brando style. The reaction is quite archaic—as if Brando fans feared that other actors were trying to take some power away from their god, that the public might worship graven images instead of the true god.

Alienation, the central theme of modern literature, has, like everything else, entered mass culture. Films borrow the artist-hero of literature only to turn him into the boob of *A Song to Remember*, *Rhapsody in Blue*, *Moulin Rouge*, *Limelight*; the alienation of a Stephen Dedalus or a Marcel, the heroic expense of extending consciousness, becomes inexplicable, but glamorous, misery. (The artist suffers because he can't get the girl; she, lacking the audience's hindsight, doesn't know that he's so good a catch that one day a movie will solemnize his life. The irony of the artist's suffering is his inability to guess that Hollywood will make him immortal.) Those at work in films have, however, to one degree or another, projected alienated nonartist heroes and heroines in some of the best, though not always commercially successful, films of recent years: *The Stars Look Down*, *Odd Man Out*, *An Outcast of the Islands*, *The Men*, *The Member of the Wedding*, *A Streetcar Named Desire*, *From Here to Eternity*. In these films, alienation is not merely the illusion of cynicism or cowardice which is dispelled in the rousing finish of a *Casablanca* or a *Stalag 17*.

The subject matter of *On the Waterfront* is alienation at the lowest social level. In *From Here to Eternity* Prewitt had formulated his position ("If a man don't go his own way, he's nothin' ") and was willing to take the risks. Terry Malloy, the hero of *On the Waterfront*, is alienated at the instinctive level of the adolescent and the bum, and the drama, as those who made the film see it, is in his development of consciousness and responsibility, his taking his place as a man.

The attempt to create a hero for the mass audience is a challenge and a great big trap. *On the Waterfront* meets the challenge, falls into the trap. The creation of a simple hero is a problem that doesn't come up often in European films, where the effort is to create characters who move us by their humanity—their weaknesses, their wisdom, their complexity—rather than by their heroic dimensions. Our films, however, deny the human weaknesses and complexities that Europeans insist upon. It's as if we refused to accept the human condition: we don't want to see the image of ourselves in those cheats and cuckolds and cowards. We want heroes, and Hollywood produces them by simple fiat. Robert Taylor or John Wayne is cast as the hero and that's that; any effort to relate the hero's actions to his character is minimal or routine. Real heroism is too dangerous a subject for Hollywood—for there is no heroism without failure risked or faced, and failure, which is at the heart of drama, is an unpopular subject in America.

On the Waterfront succeeds brilliantly in creating a figure out of the American lower depths, a figure simple in reasoning power but complicated in motivation and meaning; it fails to win complete assent when it attempts to make this figure into a social and symbolic hero—by fiat. But how should we interpret the view of *Harper's* magazine that, "if the makers of *On the Waterfront* had chosen to have it merely a decadently sophisticated underworld travelogue, a kind of American *Quai des Brumes*, they would have been truer to themselves, their subject and their art. Still better, they could of stood in bed." If I read this right, the implication is that if the film dealt with defeat, it would be more honest, but it would be decadent. This is a view which quite possibly *has* affected those who made the film, and *Harper's*, inadvertently and revealingly, justified the artists' fear of "decadence" by its contempt for "decadence."

It's likely that those who made the film—Kazan, Schulberg, Spiegel, Brando, Bernstein—share in the American fantasy of success, a fantasy which they spectacularly act out in their own careers, and want to believe that their material fits into a drama of man's triumph. A drama of man's defeat would seem somehow antisocial, un-American, "arty," and even decadent. It's quite likely also that art to them is a call to action as much as a reach into consciousness, so that they feel bound to demonstrate a victory of good over evil; they want the film to "come out right" politically, though this demonstration probably moves the audience much less than if it had to take home an unresolved, disturbed recognition of social difficulties. (The motive power behind much of our commercial entertainment is: give the public a happy ending so they won't have to think about it afterward.) Perhaps the artists of *On the Waterfront* feared the reality of failure not only for their hero but for themselves. If the film did not resolve its drama in triumph, it might not reach the mass audience, and if it reached a smaller audience, that—in America—would be failure.

From Here to Eternity did not convert its hero into a socially accepted leader, did not reduce issues to black and white, and it was a huge popular success. But a curious displacement occurred in the course of the film: Prewitt's fate as hero got buried in the commotion of the attack on Pearl Harbor, and it was easy to get the impression that it didn't really matter what happened to him as he would probably have gotten killed anyway.

And, as a related phenomenon, Montgomery Clift's fine performance as Prewitt was buried in the public praise for Frank Sinatra and Burt Lancaster. It was almost as if Prewitt wasn't there at all, as if the public wanted to forget his troublesome presence. Lancaster, an amazingly kinesthetic actor, has built-in heroism; his Sergeant Warden was closer to the conventional hero stereotype, and he had managed to stay alive. Or perhaps Prewitt wasn't troublesome enough: there was no mystery or confusion about why he behaved as he did. He had his own value system, and perhaps his clarity prevented him from stirring the audience. *Formulated* alienation seems already part of the past; Prewitt is the last Hollywood representative of Depression-style alienation.

On the Waterfront is a more ambitious film, though its moral scheme is that battle of good versus evil which is a film commonplace. No doubt those who made the film, and many of those who see it, view the conflict in the film not as a commonplace but as a rendering of the "supreme" theme. Yet this "supreme" theme has never been the theme of great drama because it tends to diminish man's humanity, rather than to illuminate it. Working with this theme, it is natural for the artists to take the next step and to employ the most easily accessible symbols that are ready-to-hand to the artists and perfectly familiar to the widest audience. The priest stands for conscience and humanity; the pure, selfless girl is the hero's reward; the union boss represents brutal avarice. And crucifixion is used in the broadest sense as an equivalent for suffering. . . .

The advantages of Kazan's direction are in his fine eye for living detail (for example, in Terry's first interchange with the men from the crime commission); the disadvantages are that the best things are often overpowered by the emphasis given to the worst. Rod Steiger's fine performance as the brother stays within its own framework, while Malden's priest is so overburdened with reference and effect that it disintegrates. Though this priest is not cut from the same cloth as Paramount's priests, at times (and he has his coy moments) he adopts a similar protective coloration. The musical score is excellent; then at a crucial moment it stops, and the silence compels awareness of the music. There are a few places where Kazan's dexterity fails completely: moving the union men around as a herd is too "staged" to be convincing. And even "good theater" doesn't allow for elements that are tossed in without being thought out (the shipowner, an oddly ambiguous abstraction, possibly cartooned in obeisance to the labor-union audience) or tossed in without being felt (the complacent, smiling faces of the priest and the girl at the end—converted, by a deficiency of artistic sensibility, into pure plaster). Many weaknesses go back to the script, of course (for example, the failure to show the reasons for the union men's loyalty to the boss), but Kazan, by trying to make assets out of liabilities, forces consideration of his responsibility.

If one feels bound to examine the flaws and facilities of *On the Waterfront* it is because, intermittently, and especially in Brando's scenes with the girl in the saloon and with his brother in the cab, the film is great. Brando's performance is the finest we have had in American films since Vivien Leigh's Blanche DuBois. Marlon Brando has that ability shared by most great actors: he can convey the multiple and paradoxical meanings in a character.

Brando makes contact with previously untapped areas in American social and psychological experience. If one had doubts about the authenticity of Terry's character, audience manifestations would confirm its truth. Brando's inarticulate wise guy attracts a startling number of its kind; there they are in the theater, gratified by their image, shouting at the screen and guffawing at Brando. Their derision is just like Terry's derisive compliments to the girl; they, too, are afraid to expose their vulnerability. They are exhibitionistic in their excitement when Terry gestures and voices disbelief in social values: it is not Terry as a candidate for redemption who excites them but Terry the tough. They have a truer sense of Terry and themselves than those who conceived the film.

The writer and director placed this imaginatively compelling figure in a structure which, while theatrically fairly sound, is not the dramatic complement the figure deserves. Terry has his own kind of consciousness; he is *too* compelling to act out *their* consciousness and to fit the social role they assign him. Terry is credible until he becomes a social hero. Does moral awakening for a Terry mean that he acquires the ability to change the external situation, or does it mean simply an intensification and a broadening of his alienation? We know that movie heroes can always conquer evil, but in the early sequences we didn't know that Terry was going to be turned into this kind of "regular" hero. The other protagonists have been oversimplified until they seem to be more symbols rather than human beings who might have some symbolic meaning. As dramatic characters they lack dimensions, as symbolic representations of the waterfront struggle they are inadequate. Our social problems are much too complex to be dramatically rendered in a Christian parable. The artists who made the film have a remarkable negative similarity; they do not risk alienation from the mass audience. And they do not face up to the imaginative task—nor to the social risk—of creating fresh symbols. Have they earned the right to show their hero risking his life in order to save his soul?

The myth of the creation of a saint (or, indeed, a multiplicity of saints) which cripples the dramatic development of Terry's character, does an even more obvious disservice to the social questions the film raises. The myth structure forces a superficial answer to questions for which no one has a satisfactory answer. The honest union posited at the end is an abstraction, which could not even be dramatically posited if the film had not already abstracted the longshore local it treats from the total picture of waterfront unionism and American business. An item in *Time* for September 27, 1954, is to the point:

> John Dwyer, a brawny hiring boss on the brawling New York City docks (and a prototype of Marlon Brando's movie role in *On the Waterfront*), quit his $10,000-a-year job last year to fight the racket-ridden International Longshoremen's Association. As vice president of the A.F.L.'s new rival dock union, he won thousands of dock-wallopers away from the I.L.A. But last month the I.L.A. won a Labor Relations Board election (by a scant 263 votes out of 18,551), and thereby held on to control of waterfront jobs.
>
> The A.F.L. brasshats, retreating from their attempt to reform the docks, cut their organizing losses (about $1,000,000), ended their all-out campaign and fired John Dwyer. When Dwyer protested, they ignored his letters and hung up on phone calls. Last week Dwyer bitterly told his men to "forget about the A.F.L. and go back to the I.L.A." Brusquely, the I.L.A. snubbed Dwyer and said A.F.L. rank-and-filers could come back only if they paid up back dues. For a happy ending dockers could go to the movies.

This kind of data suggests why alienation is such a powerful theme in our art: if, for the individual, efforts to alter a situation end in defeat, and adjustment (with decency) is impossible, alienation may be all that's left. Would Terry seem so compelling if his behavior and attitudes did not express a profound mass cynicism and a social truth? More goes into his alienation than the activities of a John Friendly, and his character is powerful because it suggests much more—the desire of adolescents to find an acceptable ethic, quasi-homosexual elements in this ethic, adolescent hostility toward adult compromises, the identification with an antisocial code, the intensity of aspirations. Terry's scene with his brother in the cab is drama because these accumulated elements explode. These elements and many more derive, not merely from a corrupt union but from the dislocation of youth in our society, and ultimately, if one takes a pessimistic view, they derive from the human condition. The betrayal experienced by the boy who kills the pigeons is not altogether mistaken. With *On the Waterfront* alienation reaches the widest audience at the level of the raw unconscious hero who suggests the unconscious alienation experienced at all social levels. The artists who wanted to affect everybody just about did.

Artists who aim at nobility may achieve something pretentious and over-scaled, but their aim tells us something about the feeling and tone of American life that is not wholly to be deprecated. Abroad, it *is* deprecated, and the excesses of *On the Waterfront* gave European critics a gloating edge of triumph. Is it perhaps evidence of cultural condescension that the festival committees which had passed over *From Here to Eternity* and *On the Waterfront* honored *Marty*, a thin, mechanical piece of sentimental realism—as if to say, "Stick to little things, you Americans, when you try to do something bigger, you expose your dreadful vulgarity"?

On the Waterfront came as a public shock in 1954 because Hollywood films have stayed away from the real America, just as, while feeding Christians to the lions, they have stayed away from the real Rome. According to *Harper's,* "The things movies 'say' are so much better stated through indirect sugges-tion, and Hollywood has developed so many techniques of skillful evasion, that the burden of censorship and the pressure groups has always been more apparent than real. Art thrives on limitations." One wonders if *Harper's* goes to movies often enough to see Hollywood's "techniques of skillful evasion" in operation. If there is anything "skillful" in our films, it is merely in prod-uct differentiation—in making each new film just like the others that have sold, yet with some little difference in casting or locale or extra costliness that can give it special appeal. Within the temples of *The Egyptian* you can see the shape of the lowest theater, moldy in motive and manner. When you hear the whore of Babylon ask the hero for "the greatest gift any man can give a woman—his innocence—that he can give only once" you know that those responsible for the film have long since surrendered their greatest gift. A bad film can be a good joke, as *Duel in the Sun* once so delightfully demon-strated; but *Valley of the Kings, Garden of Evil, The High and the Mighty* are not even very good jokes. Despite its defects, and they are major, *On the Water-front* provides an imaginative experience. If one regrets that the artists, hav-ing created an authentic image of alienation, failed to take that image seriously enough, one remembers also that most films provide no experience at all.

The alienated hero acquires a new dimension in *East of Eden:* James Dean's Cal, even more inarticulate and animalistic than Terry, is a roman-tic figure, decorated with all sorts of charming gaucheries, and set, anachro-nistically, in a violent reverie of pre–World War I youth. At one level he's the All-American boy (and the reverse of the usual image of the artist as a youth): he's not too good at school, he's sexually active, he's not interested in politics but has a childlike responsiveness to parades, he doesn't care about words or ideas. Yet this lack of intellectual tendencies is projected as evidence of sensitivity and purity of feeling; the strangled speech, the confused efforts at gesture, as poetry. This is a new image in American films: the young boy as beautiful, disturbed animal, so full of love he's defenseless. Maybe his father doesn't love him, but the camera does, and we're supposed to; we're thrust into upsetting angles, caught in infatuated close-ups, and prodded, "Look at all that beautiful desperation."

The film is overpowering: it's like seeing a series of teasers—violent moments and highly charged scenes without structural coherence (one begins to wonder if the teaser is Kazan's special genre?). When Cain strikes Abel, the sound track amplifies the blow as if worlds were colliding; a short heavy dose of expressionism may be followed by a pastoral romp or an elaborate bit of Americana; an actor may suddenly assume a psychotic stance, another actor shatter a train window with his head. With so much going on, one might forget to ask why. The explanation provided (Cal wants his father to love him) is small reason for the grotesque melodramatic flux. But from a director's point of view, success can be seen as effectiveness, failure as dullness—and *East of Eden* isn't dull.

If, after the film, the air outside the theater seems especially clean and fresh, it is not only from relief at escaping the cracker-barrel humanism, it's the restorative power of normal, uncoerced perspective: it's a little like coming out of a loony bin. A boy's agonies should not be dwelt on so lovingly: being misunderstood may easily become the new and glamorous lyricism. With *East of Eden,* Hollywood has caught up with the main line of American avant-garde cinema—those embarrassingly autoerotic twelve-minute masterpieces in which rejected, inexplicable, and ambiguous figures are photographed in tortured chiaroscuro, films which exude symbolism as if modern man were going to find himself by chasing the shadow of an alter ego in a dark alley. When alienation is exploited for erotic gratification, film catches up with the cult realities of city parks and Turkish baths; clear meanings or definite values would be too grossly explicit—a vulgar intrusion on the Technicolor night of the soul.

The romance of human desperation is ravishing for those who wish to identify with the hero's amoral victory: everything he does is forgivable, his crimes are not crimes at all, because he was so terribly *misunderstood.* (And who in the audience, what creature that ever lived, felt he was loved enough?) This is the victory that we used to think of as a child's fantasy: now it is morality for nursery school and theater alike. The concept of Terry was a little behind the times: he was posited as heroic because he acted for the social good. Cal is the hero simply and completely because of his *need,* and his frenzied behavior, the "bad" things that he does, establish him as a

(CLOCKWISE FROM ABOVE LEFT)

James Dean. (*Rebel Without a Cause.*
© Warner Bros. Inc. All rights
reserved. Used by permission.)

Marlon Brando:
(*A Streetcar Named Desire.*
Copyright © 1951 Charles Feldman Group Production.
All rights reserved. Released through
United Artists Corporation.)

The young boy as beautiful, disturbed animal.

James Cagney (with Pat O'Brien):
A spring-wound bantam.
(*Angels with Dirty Faces.* © 1938
Warner Brothers. Renewed 1965 by
United Artists Television. All rights reserved.)

hero by demonstrating his need. (When Peter Lorre as M said he couldn't help what he did, who would have thought him heroic? We have come a slippery distance.) This is a complete negation of previous conceptions of heroism: the hero is not responsible for his actions—the crazy mixed-up kid becomes a romantic hero by being treated on an infantile level. And the climax of the film is not the boy's growing up beyond this need or transferring it to more suitable objects, but simply the satisfaction of an infantile fantasy: he displaces his brother and is at last accepted by his father.

In theater and film, the mixed-up kid has evolved from the Depression hero, but the explanation from the thirties (poverty did this) no longer works, and the refinement of it in *On the Waterfront* (corruption did this) didn't work. It gives way in *East of Eden* to something even more facile and fashionable: the psychiatric explanation (lack of love did this). Although it's rather bizarre to place this hyped-up modern type in the setting of a historical novel, the reminiscent haze has some advantages: the basic incoherence of motive would probably be even more apparent in a modern setting. Cal's poetry of movement would be odd indeed if he were leaping and careening in the streets of 1955.

The type of heroism entrenched in most older and routine films is based on the obscenity: "right makes might and might makes right." (The hero can back up his moral and ethical edge on the villain with stronger fists.) And an absurd corollary is attached: the girl loves the man who fights for the right. *East of Eden* introduces a rather dismaying new formula: need for love makes right, and the girl loves the boy who most needs to be loved.

Films can, and most of them do, reduce all the deprivations and coercions, desires and hopes of social and individual experience, to the simple formula of needing love. In *The Young at Heart*, the bitter Depression hero once played by John Garfield is brought up-to-date: the young composer (Frank Sinatra) is simply an oddball, bitter because he is an orphan and the world has never made a place for him. But Doris Day accepts him and when he feels all warm and cozy in her middle-class family, his bitterness melts. (Most artists are, of course, bitter against precisely the middle-class coziness that Doris Day and her family represent.) In a more sophisticated version, we get Gloria Grahame in *The Cobweb*: she is all fixed up and able to save her marriage (and square the Production Code) once she knows her husband really needs her. (Lauren Bacall gives her no real competition: she has been analyzed—she is mature and doesn't need anybody.) The convenient Hollywood explanation for alienation—for failure to integrate in the economy, for hostility to authority and society—is, then, lack of love and acceptance. You're bland and happy when you're loved, and if you're unhappy, it's not really your fault, you just haven't been loved. This is the language of the jukebox, and when Freud is reduced to this level, psychoanalysis becomes the language of idiocy. (In a few years, films will probably reflect the next national swing: so I got love, now what?). . . .

[1955]

Jack Kroll

JAMES CAGNEY

Eroticism and even tenderness in all his violence.

In the brilliant coda of *Last Tango in Paris,* Brando, like any forty-five-year-old adolescent, is trying to charm back the girl he has alienated with a running routine of gagging, mugging, and dancing. Suddenly, out of this fateful vaudeville come the unmistakable tones of James Cagney—soft, regretful, menacing: "You dirty rat." Brando's quick, offhand tribute to Cagney here is one of those moments that confirm the movies as our most complicated folk art. It is a salute from one folk hero to another. And it may have signaled the arrival of full cult-status for Cagney, who, great star that he is, has not become the cult figure that Bogart has for our nostalgia-hunting time.

The current festival of twenty-two Cagney films at the New York Cultural Center is not only a feast of pure movie pleasures; it reminds us that Cagney is one of the great primal figures of movie history. Cagney belongs to the second great primal period of the movies, the early-sound period, and as such he was one of those who maintained the continuity of the movies' basic plastic power from the great silent figures such as Garbo and Chaplin. And, indeed, watching these Cagney films of the early thirties you realize he belongs with Chaplin, Keaton, Douglas Fairbanks, Sr., and Fred Astaire—the movies' greatest movers, the magical human dolls who created a kind of supermime, an electrified behavioral field that, more than the roles they played, was the source of the special thrill they gave to audiences.

In the classic Cagney pose he is a spring-wound bantam, back straight, arms hanging close to his sides, leaning forward perilously on the balls of his feet, his alert body covered by the gangster's tight-fitting suit, the boxer's trunks, the sailor's bell bottoms, the soldier's khakis, the convict's stripes, even the cowboy's leather. From this stance he is ready with lightning speed to throw a right to the jaw, a finger to the chest, a bullet to the gut, a wise-crack to the face, or a sneer to the world. Like a great dancer, Cagney turns every impulse into the spontaneous combustion of pure action. Not one of the screen's great lovers, there is an astonishing tinge of eroticism and even tenderness in all his violence, as in his legendary grapefruit-to-the-face of Mae Clarke in *The Public Enemy*.

In those lightning-fast Warner Bros. studio movies of the thirties, such as *The Public Enemy*, *Jimmy the Gent*, *Taxi!*, *Blonde Crazy*, *Angels with Dirty Faces*, Cagney took that American type—the mug—and gave it great complexity. As the killer in *The Public Enemy*, he wakes up after an all-night bash and slowly realizes that a floozy who has been after him has managed to sleep with him while he was drunk. The disgust, revulsion, and anger that seeps into his face is as sensationally powerful as one of his explosive rages.

In *Blonde Crazy*, as the bellhop who wants to be a con man, he picks up a copy of Browning's poems that a rich guy has given to his buddy Joan Blondell, laughs scornfully at the highbrow gift, and proceeds to read out one of the poems in a masterly blend of sarcasm and rhetorical accuracy. When Warners filmed Max Reinhardt's production of *A Midsummer Night's Dream*, Cagney's performance as Bottom the weaver turned all his lancing delicacy of gesture and speech into a marvel of Shakespearean comedy—the best Bottom I have ever seen.

Why then hasn't Cagney become the great cult figure that Bogart became in the sixties? For one thing, Cagney is still alive, and death is a strong mythmaking force. Also, Cagney has always been the pure professional performer; married to one woman for fifty-one years, he has had no juicy sex life, no private glamour, no scandal (again like Astaire). Offscreen, Bogart used to say such raffish things as: "The trouble with the world is that it's always one drink behind." The characteristic Cagney quote is: "My philosophy has always been to do anything that comes my way. . . . Because where I come from if there's a buck to be made, you don't ask questions; you go ahead and make it."

This is the Irish Cagney born on New York's Lower East Side, the son of a bartender, the street fighter, the self-taught hoofer, born to play George M. Cohan in *Yankee Doodle Dandy*, the actor trapped in the assembly line of the studio system and brilliantly turning adversity into advantage. In one of the few pieces to deal in depth with Cagney, Kenneth Tynan assimilates him to the Hemingway hero. But it is Bogart who is the Hemingway hero—the man, like Jake Barnes and Harry Morgan, who acts only after he has found profound reasons for not acting, the man who makes "a separate peace." Cagney is closer to the American marrow—he is an explosive inversion of the Horatio Alger hero, the bellboy, the shipping clerk, the poor kid in knickers and cap who can make it only by pure, unremitting action. In the spontaneity and unself-consciousness of his kinetic force, Cagney represents a lost innocence, a lost confidence in some primal vigor of the American character that may never be restored.

[1973]

Penelope Gilliatt

CHARLES CHAPLIN

Chaplin directs Brando and Loren.

Buster Keaton once told me that when he and Chaplin first used the new sound cameras what they most missed in them was the noise. The old silent-picture cameras made a rhythmic racket that both of them had unconsciously taken for a beat when they were acting. Perhaps this is why Chaplin now writes his own film music; knowing that he is going to be the composer, he can direct a scene with a tempo going on in his head.

To see him work on a scene in *A Countess from Hong Kong* is rather like watching a classical ballet master teaching behind glass. The beat that he can hear is out of one's own earshot, but it is holding the work together. Comedy for Chaplin is choreography: placing, movement, the intricate classical disciplining of vulgar energy. His urge to make his teaching concrete and physical is like the nostalgia of a great old dancer taking his thousandth *Swan Lake* class from a chair, unconsciously mimicking a pas de deux in a sort of muscular mumble, and exploding onto the set to dance the corps de ballet steps himself when some wretched cygnet misses a cue. The dancers in the pas de deux, whom he obviously greatly admires, are Sophia Loren and Marlon Brando. The cygnet one day was a ship's steward in the film who had to make an entrance during a scene with Brando and offer a double brandy. With so little to do he fluffed it altogether; Chaplin catapulted onto the set and mimed it himself, and it was like Pavlova with a napkin over her arm.

A Countess from Hong Kong was made at Pinewood Studios, which in their time have produced some of the most deathly conventional films ever made. To Chaplin, then seventy-seven, who had made eighty-one films, this isn't of the faintest consequence. As with most of the great classicists of comedy, conventionalism is really just what his work springs from. Rules, propriety, order, loyalty, romanticism, and a sweet decorum are the elements of his style; anarchy suggests nothing to him. A studio that had been the home of other people's technical revolts would have little to offer Chaplin. His needs are simple, oddly formal, and entirely his own.

Buster Keaton told me that to his mind the most enviable place to work was a broom cupboard. Chaplin's broom cupboard is obviously a studio. I think he would be happy enough in any studio at all, provided it was professionally competent to do what he wanted, and if it weren't he could undoubtedly teach it to be, because he knows every trade of his craft backward. The freedom that other directors find in working on location means nothing to him. The intrusions of commonplace life are not an inspiration to him but a distraction. If he works outside a studio he finds his ideas and concentration "blowing away on the wind."

The conditions at Pinewood are what he needs. They are a familiar focus for work, and everything extraneous to that seems to be invisible to him. The mock-Tudor front offices obviously don't jar on him, the crew has learned how to do what he wants, and the huge sound stages scattered with sets of a liner are a convention that only make him imagine the reality of his film more fiercely, like the genteel flower-curtained caravan on the set that is Brando's dressing room, and the tea stall where the technicians stand in line for current buns and a black brew of tea that lays a coating of tannin inside the mouth like an animal's pelt.

Chaplin in his old age seems to feel physically forty-five. Anyone watching him at first is bound to have an undercurrent of worry at the sight of a man, nearing eighty, who not only keeps the ruthless hours of filmmaking but also demonstrates practically every take himself; but after a while any concern seems a patronage. The outstripped crew have given it up long since. The only thing that bothers some of them is that they can't quite recognize him as he is now. I saw one of them holding up a finger against the sight of his distant face to blot out his upper lip and try to imagine him with the old Hitler mustache. With his present white hair he looks almost like the negative of his silent-film self. The wide mouth, stretched like a child's eating a slice of watermelon, isn't quite as one remembers it; perhaps it was always changed by the mustache.

He seems to feel the cold, but then he has lived out of England long enough to grow unused to the conditions that the locals dourly call livable. The studio is what fellow citizens think of as living-room temperature, which is like March out-of-doors. He wears a thick sweater under a thicker jacket. Usually he has a hat on against the glare of the lights. When he feels debonair he tips the hat over his eyes; when he is growling at the stupidity of his extras, or at the unwieldiness of conventional modern film lighting, he pushes it impatiently to the back of his head. During holdups he will often suddenly wheel away from the stage to find his wife, Oona, a shy, beautiful woman who generally effaces herself behind a pillar. He seems to look to her not so much for advice as for some sort of confirmation. When he speaks to her about a scene between takes, he does it almost as if he were talking to himself. Her constant presence on the set, even and affectionate, seems to have some trick of pulling the knot of his mood.

He keeps the technicians at a distance. They call him "sir," and if he jokes with them they watch carefully to make sure that they are right to joke back. "OK, print that," he says once at the end of a take, and then he hears an airplane overhead that will probably have wrecked it. "Dammit," he says; not his furious version of the oath, which is an American-accented "Goddammit," but an atavistic curse out of his English youth which is practically a pleasantry. The crew notices the inflection and deduce from it that they can freewheel with him for a minute. "There's a humming. Why didn't you tell me?" he goes on to the sound technician with the head- phones, giving the start of his wide grin. "Because you were talking, sir," says the soundman daringly, because he is suddenly licensed to. The atmo- sphere in the set is at its warmest, sunny and trustful. But one take later Chaplin says, "Oko" instead of "OK": he often pronounces words wrongly when he is in a hurry, sometimes even trying to force them into other meanings—and when the crew tentatively kid him about it he ignores them, with an implied rebuke for diverting his attention.

The immediately endearing thing about watching Chaplin work on this picture is the way he goes on laughing at it. He doesn't laugh at the lines in themselves; he laughs at the way they are executed. One has the feeling that when he wrote them he probably wasn't even yet amused. The chuckles must have come later, when the actors had gone through the lines mechani- cally, overemoted, lost their confidence, learned their moves backward, bro- ken through some sort of actor's sound barrier, and eventually found the work as easy as breathing.

It is ease that always makes him laugh. He keeps saying that this is a *ro- mantic* film, not a comedy. He wants to make a film about love that simply happens to be funny, without anyone in the picture knowing it. "Play for absolute realism, not for comedy," he says again and again. One can see the details of Brando's performance becoming daily smaller and more meticulous, like the movement of a watch. His attention to Chaplin is total. I found it technically enthralling, and often moving.

Brando plays a stuffy American ambassador to Saudi Arabia, traveling from Hong Kong with Sophia Loren embarrassingly stowed away in his stateroom as a dispossessed Russian countess. The ambassador's wife, played by Tippi Hedren, is an amused lounger who has been separated from him for two years. She discovers Sophia Loren's bra in his cabin with nothing more than elegant glee that he should have so undiplomatically been an ass. His Excellency is traveling with his valet, Hudson, played by a stone-faced English actor called Patrick Cargill; the valet has to be induced to marry Sophia Loren in order to give her his nationality as a way of getting her through American Immigration. The valet's resistance to marrying the most nubile woman imaginable is very funny on the set. When the subject is broached, he behaves as though he has been offered the wrong wine with the fish.

Most of the action happens on the ship. The sniffy valet is given his orders in the sundeck lounge. Before shooting, Chaplin sits on the edge of one of the chairs in the set and listens to Brando and Cargill running through their lines. He mouths most of the dialogue with them unconsciously and makes tiny replicas of their movements. When he is rehearsing actors his muscles often seem to twitch like a dog having a dream.

"You are an American citizen, aren't you?" says the ambassador to his valet.

"I've been an American citizen for the last sixteen years," says the valet, stiffly, in the most English voice possible. Chaplin laughs at the way he does it. Then the valet is told that he must marry Sophia Loren.

"I'd like you to marry her," says Brando so disarmingly that Cargill laughs, but also so lightly that he makes it seem like kidding.

"Don't denote anything on your face. Keep your voice up. Insist on the action."

The ambassador does the line again, bland and clear.

The valet pauses and then replies, "If I may say so, sir, this is rather sudden."

Chaplin: "More polite. You're disguising your feelings by being very polite."

Cargill says it again.

"But before you close up, just a shade of shock on that line of Marlon's. 'I'd like you to marry her.' It lays an egg a little bit." He laughs. "So long as you're not suave. A suavity here would kill the whole scene." This is real comic shrewdness; most people directing these lines would have thought that unruffled suavity was their basis. Chaplin turns out to be quite right, of course. It is like the funniness of P. G. Wodehouse's Jeeves. The comic point about the godly servant isn't that he is totally impassive but that across the immortal calm there is an intermittent flicker of ordinary humanity. The crack in the Olympian surface has to be microscopic, but it can be gigantically expressive. It is a difficult thing for an actor to do without oversignaling. Lazy American comedians now would tend to make the crack a large crevasse; lazy English comedians would leave it out and settle for unbroken haughtiness. Chaplin is patiently insistent about the point. Finally the lines make him laugh.

The extras have to walk across in the background. They have been told exactly where to go and how fast, but everything is fumbled and Chaplin watches in agony. Some of the extras are old trouts who habitually go to sleep in the armchairs on the set, although one of the masters of the cinema is working under their noses. Some of them are bored young hacks who aren't even alert enough to be nervous. They import an atmosphere of crassness and laziness that is sniffed by the members of the crew with instant dislike. The fact that they have turned up in the wrong clothes is one of the common absurdities of big-budget filmmaking, but it is enough to upset a perfectionist like Chaplin for the morning. "They should be in lovely summery clothes—lovely pale shoes . . ." I hear him saying to himself unhappily between takes. "They look as if they've just got off the eight-seventeen at Victoria Station," says the amiable cameraman with an edge of irritability.

"Remember your tempos," Chaplin calls out to the extras, who do their jobs again. One group has to saunter, the other to scurry. They manage it eventually, looking as awkward and unreal as any extras in any big studio in the world, which is one of the penalties that Chaplin pays for working under conventional conditions. The rehearsals for this scene take a long time. Chaplin himself demonstrates a steward's entrance twice, arriving and pivoting exactly on cue, saying "So-so-so-so; so-so-so-so-so-so," as dummy dialogue. It is rather like Toscanini giving an entrance to the triangle player after a hundred and fifty bars of silence.

Eventually the moves harden and become mechanical, which is what he wants. Once the routine is fixed and has started to bore the actors, the comedy begins to emerge. He works from the outside inward: first the mechanics, then familiarity and physical skill, and after that the right emotions will come. It is the diametric opposite of the Stanislavskian style that has become accepted modern dogma.

"Do that line again, Marlon. 'Oh, in about ten minutes.' Quickly. Take off the fat." The working atmosphere between them is relaxed and easy. Brando is one of the greatest screen actors in the world and he has been trained in exactly the opposite tradition, but he listens and absorbs with an attention that seems unflawed.

He is doing a close-up shot of the scene now, with the cues given to him by the producer, Jerry Epstein. Brando fluffs twice, says "husband" instead of "Hudson," and the producer starts to get the giggles. He finds himself infected and starts saying words upside down. At the end of the final take Brando squints at Chaplin, laughs, and says to the producer, "Do you want to get some Scotch tape and sew yourself together?"

Epstein is an old associate of Chaplin, and an obvious contributor to the mood of fun that Brando and Loren both sense on the set. His way of giving Chaplin a prompt when the director is signaling for it looks like the result of years, rather like an operating-theater sister shoving the right instrument into a surgeon's hand. To an outsider Chaplin's "So-so-so" and grabbing fingers aren't at all explicit, but Epstein obviously feels that he should know by instinct the line that he wants, and when his concentration is absorbed enough he does.

The attention that Chaplin demands, and gets, is fierce and total. Where other directors become most inventive by allowing energy to fly outward, with Chaplin the pull is always toward the center. He knows exactly what he is doing. When he is shooting a scene he seems to be gently chivvying the actors toward something that is already complete in his head. Like a tug edging a liner away from a quay, he has coaxed the incomparable Brando into a manner that is just faintly at odds with the one he is known by. The sumptuous, time-taking style, spaciously intelligent behind an opiate gaze, has become smaller, quicker, and sometimes comically testy, just as the histrionics of Sophia Loren's abundant comic temperament have been converted into a very funny stoicism.

In her work before *A Countess from Hong Kong*, she made people laugh by Latin fluster; in the scenes that I saw, she does it by phlegm. "He had made me quite different," she says. "When I see rushes I don't recognize myself. He doesn't like me to use my hands much, especially near my face. We're trying to do everything as naturally as possible. . . ."

Directors and actors always say now that they are working for realism, of course; it is one of the modern pieties of the profession, but in Chaplin's case it is precisely true. Again and again when he is directing a scene he will cut out some gesture or response that reveals itself the moment it has gone as a hamstrung comic mannerism. His laughs in this picture nearly always come from doing apparently as little as possible very fast. "Lots of lift, lots of tempo," he often says. The takes that he decides to print are always the ones with the most dash and lightness; sometimes when he is talking under pressure he makes a bouncing movement upward with his hand as though he were keeping a ball in the air.

"It wants a beat," he says to Tippi Hedren, after she has been working on a scene where she enters with the identifiably outsize bra that she has discovered in her husband's cabin. "This is all a great comedy to you. No malice. You haven't lived with your husband for two years. You come in with great gusto. You're kidding him." Through the next take he looks worried. "There was no tempo." He gets up from his chair by the camera, wrinkles his nose, and prances through the moves himself, saying "So-so-so," like a groom sedating a horse. "So-so-so, *Your Excellency,*" he says, pivoting on the words. "You're mocking him. You're glib. That's it. Can we come in with a bigger spread? I would burst in here. It's sort of breezy. One—two—" He gives her the time, and catches his breath on the upbeat as she enters. "Can we keep that lovely movement?" In a previous take she had turned on one of her lines and practically flowed onto a sofa; he does it himself to fix the move in his mind, looking comically grand in an imaginary tea gown, and makes sure that the camera movement fits it.

For Chaplin, the pacing of a camera articulates a scene. On the whole he doesn't seem to like camera-movement very much. ("The actors should be the performers, not the lens.") He doesn't care for trick angles and he hates the laziness of cryptically significant shots that show nothing but door-opening. "Orientation" is an important idea to him. He believes that an audience must always know where they are in a room, and that actors must know exactly where to stop, where to turn, where to stand, whether to talk directly or indirectly.

I had expected his physical business to be graphic and hilarious, but I hadn't been quite prepared for the precision of his sense of words. To talk about Chaplin's mime is rather like praising the height of Everest; it is his pin-fall ear for dialogue that is technically so absorbing to anyone fortunate enough to see him working. "There's something woolly in that word, Sophia," he says; the fuzz is there, an emphasis that is faintly implausible and faltering, but a lot of good directors would have let it go. "Most films are just in and out," said the chippie (the film carpenter). "Not this one. He's definitely got something on his mind."

When he is coming back from the lunch break or inspecting the sets in the morning he carries his script against his chest as if it were a buckler. Like Keaton, he stands and walks with the arched back of a small boy, perhaps because of the ferocious physical training that both of them had as tiny children in vaudeville. "He's a perfectionist," says the director of photography, Arthur Ibbetson. "When he did his own bit it was rather a day." (Chaplin appears in the film in a tiny part as a steward who gets seasick.) "All he really did was sweep the deck with his head down. Other people would have made a production out of it." Ibbetson does a mime of someone milking laughs. "There's one passenger asleep on the whole deck and when he's finished he sweeps the muck very neatly behind his feet. That's all he does, see?"

[1966]

Bernard Drew

JILL CLAYBURGH

She could not stop and talk about what she was doing as an actress at the same time that she was doing it.

It was November 1977, and Steven Spielberg was talking about the younger film stars of today. "There are a number of good leading men," I said, "but outside of Diane Keaton, where are the women?" Spielberg said, "Well, there's Jill Clayburgh," and I said, "Jill *who?*" Spielberg repeated, "Jill Clayburgh. She can do anything. Just wait and see."

Four days later Michael Ritchie told me, "Jill Clayburgh is the best actress around now." But he was in New York to publicize *Semi-Tough*, in which Clayburgh stars with Burt Reynolds and Kris Kristofferson. What else was he going to say?

Two months later I saw Paul Mazursky's *An Unmarried Woman*, and I, too, came to agree that Jill Clayburgh could do anything. We met when I did a story on her, and we became friends—of sorts—and then we lost touch. She went off to Rome to begin filming Bernardo Bertolucci's *La Luna*, which concerns an opera singer who returns to Italy, where she began her career. What with singing lessons and Italian lessons, in which Clayburgh had been immersed for two months before going abroad, and then four months of filming, which had finally ended up in Brooklyn Heights, I didn't see her for nearly a year. Now, at the end of 1978, she was to begin working with Burt

Reynolds and Candice Bergen on Alan J. Pakula's *Starting Over*, a kind of *An Unmarried Man* detailing the comic angst of Reynolds, who is dumped by wife Bergen and on the rebound discovers the timorous joys of nursery schoolteacher Clayburgh.

Her two days off between films are devoted to the dentist, to searching for a new West Side apartment because she is going to have to give up the spacious one on West End Avenue she shares with David Rabe, the Pulitzer Prize–winning playwright of *The Basic Training of Pavlo Hummel, Sticks and Bones*, and *Streamers*, and to a long lunch with me. We meet and stroll over to Broadway to search for an eating place with a back room where we can sit for a few hours, eat as little as we can get away with, because we're both dieting, and be left alone.

"You're one of the few people who started life on the Upper East Side and worked her way down to the Upper West," I tell her. But then her life has been a series of contradictions and reversals ever since she was born on April 30, 1944, to Albert Henry Clayburgh, a successful WASP businessman, and Julia Door, his Jewish wife, who had been David Merrick's production secretary.

"I was violent and willful and self-destructive, and my parents had to send me to a shrink for therapy when I was still very young," Clayburgh recalls now at Teacher's, where we have finally settled down. Clayburgh does not much like interviews. She is not comfortable talking about herself, perhaps a bit fearful that questions will be asked about her long, intense relationships, five years with Al Pacino and two, so far, with Rabe. I do not bring them up.

We go on talking about her upbringing, and she speaks about her mother. "She never pushed me into anything, but she was enormously supportive of me, deeply interested in anything I did. Although she'd given up working for Merrick when she married, she never lost her passionate interest in the theater and continued to invest in plays for the rest of her life."

Clayburgh pauses, her voice changes slightly, and she goes on: "My mother never even lived to see *Gable and Lombard,* yet even then she thought I was the greatest success in the world. If only she'd lived to see all this. She probably would have become my secretary and had a full-time career keeping my scrapbooks. She even used to love to type my esoteric themes while I was at Sarah Lawrence."

She is silent for a moment. "But despite all that supportiveness I got at home, I wasn't at all sure I wanted a theatrical career. I didn't think much about it at Brearley, and at Sarah Lawrence I majored in philosophy and took only a couple of theater arts courses. What had decided me, finally, on the theater was this roommate I had at college who took me up to Williamstown, Massachusetts, during the summer vacation, and that was it. You paid five hundred dollars for the privilege of being an apprentice and being allowed to paint scenery. But it was enough to hook me. I wasn't at all very good when I started. Looking back at it now, I wonder where I ever got the fortitude to continue."

After she got her B.A., Clayburgh went to the Charles Playhouse in Boston to work in the children's theater. "I've never spent a more lonely year in my life than that one in Boston before I met Al," she recalls. Al, of course, is Al Pacino, then beginning his own career with the company. They did *America Hurrah* together. Then Clayburgh appeared in *The Balcony*, *Love for Love*, and *Dutchman*. She soon moved in with Pacino, something that did not sit well with her friends and family.

Events now picked up speed. From Boston to New York—where Pacino appeared in *The Indian Wants the Bronx* and Clayburgh in the curtain raiser *It's Called the Sugarplum*. "There were a couple more off-Broadway plays, some dinky things on television, and even a couple of movies. I'm not even sure I can get the sequence straight. I know the first movie I made was *Portnoy's Complaint*. I'd gone out to Los Angeles to play Desdemona to James Earl Jones's Othello, and I was terrible in it, absolutely awful. It was a troubled time in my life, I don't even want to think about it, but while I was out there, I made *Portnoy*."

John Lehne, who has been Clayburgh's acting teacher and coach since the beginning of her career, remembers those early years. "Jill came to me fresh out of Sarah Lawrence," Lehne tells me when I talk with him later. "She joined my class and was in and out with me for nine years. When I stopped teaching her, I became her coach as she continued to grow, and I'd work with her every time she did a show. When she did *Othello*, she and Al were breaking up, and her Desdemona was not her best work. The night before the opening the director took everything away from her and told her just to stand there and say the lines, which is something you cannot do to an actress like Jill. So she came to me in tears and said she was giving up acting. Apparently friends who were close to her and Al had told her she was a mediocre actress and the best she could do was to maybe appear in soap operas, and she felt if that's all that loomed ahead for her, she'd rather do nothing at all.

"I can't imagine what these friends had in mind," Lehne continues, "except to show Al that they were on his side. But they succeeded in completely shattering her confidence in herself. I was very firm with her and told her that the friends' advice was a crock and to stop feeling sorry for herself, to train more and work harder, which she did."

Clayburgh puts it simply: "I didn't give up. I went into two musicals on Broadway, *The Rothschilds* and *Pippin.* One didn't follow the other, but I mention them together because I don't know what I was doing in musicals. I'm not the greatest singer in the world, though not the worst, and even less of a dancer, but there I was. Somewhere in between I did another movie, *The Thief Who Came to Dinner*, and I also made *The Terminal Man*, and on the stage I played Judith in the Stratford, Connecticut, production of *The Devil's Disciple.*"

None of these sorties turned her into a living legend, but she was working steadily. "What I desperately wanted to do was *In the Boom Boom Room*, by David Rabe, which was going to be done at Lincoln Center. This is years before I got to know David. I really wanted the part—boy, did I want it. When I didn't get it, I was furious. Madeline Kahn got it. She had something of a Hollywood name, and I thought, If a Hollywood name is what they're so hot for in New York, well, then, California, here I come. So I moved to Hollywood and did a movie for television, *Hustling*, that I guess really started my career. I played a prostitute, and I was very good in it. You don't have to have it screened, it's not that good—yes, it is—"

She giggles. "That's me all right," she says. "Always sure of myself. Anyway, I *was* good in *Hustling* because I played this whore as funny, sensitive, childlike, and quite mad; a girl who just doesn't know how to make it, a state I knew something about. So after that success, what do I do next? Tom Stoppard's play *Jumpers*, which just may be the single most awful experience I've ever had in my life."

"At this point in her career," John Lehne recalls, "Jill was making some peculiar choices. She would elect to do roles that were challenging to her rather than good for her career. She'd opened in *Jumpers* in Washington, and I got this frantic call to fly right down there and see her performance because she'd got some brutal reviews from people who had seen Diana Rigg play the role to great success in London. I saw the play and told her she was all wrong for the role. It was tailor-made for a bravura actress like Tallulah Bankhead or Diana Rigg, which Jill wasn't, and for that matter, I wasn't so crazy about the play, either. But she insisted on sticking with it, even though the director didn't care for her and the rest of the cast treated her like an outsider and she was constantly criticized. I stayed with her for a week; we went over everything together, trying to salvage something for the New York opening."

"For as long as I live," Clayburgh says solemnly, "I'll never know why I didn't quit *Jumpers* when it was so clear that everyone wanted me out. It can only be my stubborn Taurus nature or total self-destructiveness. I'd come to the theater every night hoping to find that it had suddenly disappeared, but there it always was, and there also would be another actress, reading for the role, waiting in the wings. But I just refused to quit, and Actors Equity wouldn't allow them to bring over an English actress to replace me, and so I endured and suffered and allowed myself to be humiliated night after night after night. I swear to you, by whatever there is, that I will never allow anyone to do that to me again or allow me to do that to me again."

After a pause, Clayburgh continues, "I tell you that there isn't money enough in this world for me to make *Gable and Lombard* today, yet when it was offered to me, I was very grateful. After *Jumpers* I was grateful for anything. Looking back on it now, the best thing to be said for that experience as Lombard is that all of my blond hair fell out at the end of the film.

"By then," she goes on, "David and I were together, living in New Haven in Mike Nichols' house while they were preparing *Streamers* for the Long Wharf Theatre, and I was thinking, as usual, that I would never work again once *Gable and Lombard* was released. You may have some idea about my morale at that point when I tell you that two pictures I wanted very much to do were *Silver Streak* and, believe it or not, *The Other Side of Midnight*. I thought it might make a good movie, but I was either too old for it or too fat. I can't remember, mercifully. But I did get to do *Silver Streak,* which was good for me simply because it was a hit. Then, within one week, Michael Ritchie suddenly wanted me for *Semi-Tough,* which I made immediately, and simultaneously Paul Mazursky offered me *An Unmarried Woman,* which I did right after."

"Jill sent me the script of *An Unmarried Woman,* and I told her I didn't like it," John Lehne concedes today. "I felt the role was sentimentally written and condescending to women, and I felt she shouldn't do it. But she disagreed with me, fortunately for her, and I then told her that if she felt she had to do it, to at least play it contrapuntally. I said she had to develop a strong sense of humor, to make the girl tough and hard, and to go in any direction she could except in the way it was written. This is how I work with Jill. We try to give the character she's portraying a dimension of behavior that has not been written into the script. Jill is one of the few people around who has a sense of the subconscious and who can perceive the reality beyond what is surface and what is written. Brando has it. Pacino and De Niro have it, sometimes Dustin Hoffman has it, and Jill has it."

Paul Mazursky agrees. "Jill brought tons of things to the role I never put into it," he readily acknowledges in his Greenwich Village office. "I didn't see a lot of actresses, and choosing Jill was one of the easiest decisions I ever made in my life. She'd read for me twice before *An Unmarried Woman* came up—two roles she didn't get: the Marsha Mason part in *Blume in Love* and the Lois Smith one in *Next Stop, Greenwich Village*. She was marvelous for both in her readings but physically wrong. Still, I could see that if the right part ever came along, she could be a great actress. By the time I started to look around for an Erica, I had seen Jill in *Hustling*, which I liked, *Gable and Lombard*, which I didn't, but I thought Jill showed energy and colors I hadn't seen in our previous meetings and in some of *Silver Streak*."

Mazursky continues, "I was looking for three qualities: vulnerability, intelligence, and a sexuality that wasn't brazen. I wanted Erica to come across as real, to make every woman in the audience feel that 'there's a little bit of me up there.' I sent Jill the script. She told me she loved the role, and then she came in for a reading. She was exactly right, that's all I can tell you. Even to her appearance. She doesn't have a modelesque beauty. If she weren't a famous actress, you wouldn't turn around to look at her, but she exudes a sexuality, like Bette Davis in her prime, that has nothing to do with conventional movie beauty."

He adds, "Once I decided on her, we spent a lot of time talking about the lady before we started shooting. We went out shopping together for Erica's clothes; she spent a lot of time with the actresses who were going to play her friends. She became close to Mike Murphy, who was going to play her husband, and to Lisa Lucas, who would be her daughter, just so they'd feel like a family together. We'd rehearse, but never all the way. We'd always leave a little bit open. Take the scene with the psychiatrist. All I told her was, 'Tell her how it feels to be rejected, how for the first time in your life you're completely alone. You don't know where you're going.' That's all I said. If I'd told her more, I'd be telling her exactly what to do, and I wasn't about to do that. So she prepared it herself and came in and did the scene, and I was shaken, shattered really. For the first time, I began to feel that this movie was even deeper than I thought it was.

"You know," Mazursky goes on, "that the trick in movie acting is to take all the preparation and experience you have as an actor and not have it show while the cameras are turning. This is where Jill is supreme. And you never have to waste time feeding her ego just so that she'll be able to go on. There's absolutely no pretense to her. She knows when she's good, and she'll say, 'That was pretty good, I think,' or else, once in a great while, she might say, 'Let's try that again' or 'That was a waste of time, wasn't it?' She's not a closed book. She doesn't bring with her awesome fears about holding on to the image she's had in other work."

Michael Murphy, who plays the rat in *An Unmarried Woman* who unmarries Clayburgh, recalls one instance of Clayburgh's skill. "Remember the scene where I tell her I'm going to leave, where I break down on the street

Jill Clayburgh:
*She can move from one extreme
to the other in the same shot.*
(*Starting Over*. Copyright © MCMLXXIX by
Century Associates. All rights reserved.
Courtesy Paramount Pictures.)

Montgomery Clift:
He refused to accept his own limitations.
(*A Place in the Sun*. Copyright MCMLI by
Paramount Pictures Corporation.
All rights reserved.)

and cry and tell her I'm in love with somebody else? Well, there was a lot of noise about me in that scene. I'm crying, but I'm not crying—I'm manipulating her. Let me tell you that there would have been no scene if Jill hadn't carried it off. Her reaction to what I was doing—what *she* was doing to get me to do what I did—carried it off. What she does is something so rare and incredible that you can only react to her in a certain way, and that way always makes you look good."

John Lehne explains this quality as "a special ability some actors have not only to perceive what other people are but to transform themselves into those other people. They can will their bodies and minds to function as someone else. The character they portray is a dimension of them without being them. Despite all of my experience in the field, I find it as hard to describe as everyone else does, and I just have to end up saying that it's the magic of acting."

It is this transformation that Clayburgh must undergo every time she assumes a new role that may be responsible for her nervous behavior, which some falsely construe as temperament. I was originally supposed to meet her last May, about six weeks before she was due to leave for Italy to begin *La Luna.* She was taking singing lessons and Italian lessons, and she could not, she said, stop and talk about what she was doing as an actress at the same time that she was doing it. She couldn't understand how some actresses saw interviewers in their dressing rooms.

La Luna is finished now, but Clayburgh says she's not going to tell me a single thing about the film until I see it, that such discussions must always be a dialogue, and how can we have one when neither one of us has seen the film. She says, "I'll only tell you that I adore Bernardo Bertolucci and that he really taught me what a camera can do. Paul uses a steady camera. It's unobtrusive, you're not even aware of it. But Bernardo zooms and dollies and cranes and uses the camera like the audience." Her role in *La Luna* was created for Liv Ullmann, and Clayburgh says, "I don't mind accepting Liv's rejects. I think she's shown as much courage in her life as she has ability as an actress, and I'm proud to take what she doesn't want."

From Rome, where he is about to start editing *La Luna,* Bertolucci tells me, "It was wonderful to work with her because she immediately understood my way of working. I improvise a lot, keep changing the script to suit the person who is in front of the camera, and as soon as I saw Jill, I knew I had to make changes in the script. Actors are usually frightened of changes, but Jill wanted to go even further in improvisations than we eventually did go. She's so flexible and intelligent, and she has limitless energy."

He goes on: "She can move from one extreme to the other in the same shot, be funny and dramatic within the same scene. It's a very strange and mysterious quality she has. It has to do with reserves she keeps inside, as if she were saying and doing one thing and thinking of something else—a duality. This is difficult to discuss, but you can see it in the depths of her eyes, something there you don't immediately understand but will later on. How can I say this in another way: It's like a fiction that suddenly becomes a documentary halfway through."

A few days later I visit the Fox studios on Tenth Avenue and Fifty-fourth Street, where Alan J. Pakula is filming *Starting Over* and where Clayburgh has begun to shoot opposite Burt Reynolds. Pakula has closed the set, but during a break I talk to Reynolds in his camper parked on the street.

"Has Jill changed a lot from the time you made *Semi-Tough*?" I ask.

There is a second's pause. This is not going to be easy. I've heard from various sources that there were all kinds of problems on *Semi-Tough*, but Reynolds now has to work with Clayburgh for another seven weeks.

"Jill is playing Jean Arthur in this," Reynolds says, "and although she's just begun on the film, I can see it's already starting to happen. I don't think she quite made it in the first one, but she will in this. If I had to describe Jill, I'd say she has a special innocence covered up with chutzpah, which, in turn, gets covered up by simple ambition and what it takes, what is necessary, to survive in this business as a leading lady.

"Normally," he goes on, "that kind of person is not attractive to me, but then you have to realize and understand the facts that create that kind of person. If you read the book *Semi-Tough*, you'd know what a fabulous girl the character Jill played was. This was a girl who in the looks department was ten. Now Jill was a hell of an actress even then, but she never considered herself a great beauty, and you know that she never felt remotely like ten. So she was frightened and insecure, and she overcompensated for that by being aggressive."

He adds: "Also, the character she was playing was brassy, and Jill's way of working—and it's probably why she's so good—is to become the character. So, it wasn't easy, and then there were problems even after we finished the movie and went down to New Orleans and had a big press conference. Someone asked her something about *Gable and Lombard*, and Jill just burst into tears and ran out of the room, really weeping. I kid her about that now, and she can really take it, even laugh about herself. I tell her, 'My God, who had more *Gable and Lombard*s than I? But looking back later on, when you know you survived them, can even be a lot of fun.' Let's face it, there's just as much pain involved in giving birth to an ugly child as in giving birth to a beautiful one, and I've had my ugly children, as you well know. But now, fortunately, even the ugly ones are able to earn a good living.

"There's no doubt about it," Reynolds says, "success agrees with Jill. In *Semi-Tough*, though she felt secure as an actress, I don't think she did as a person, and that gave her problems. But now her great success has given her an assurance and security she didn't have before, and she's a much more attractive person than she was last time we met."

Almost on cue, Clayburgh enters the camper, embraces Reynolds, and apologizes for something that had transpired during the early morning's shooting. They briefly discuss the afternoon's scene, and then she takes me up to her dressing room. I tell her that Reynolds thinks success agrees with her. "I think so too," she says. "It isn't throwing me, I can deal with it, it's all right. I think I'm even happy these days."

"You think? Don't you know?"

She giggles. "I *know* now that I'm going to have a long career and that I'm going to act for the rest of my life. That's something I was never sure of before."

She has been bathing her eyes to clear up an infection, and now she stares at herself in her dressing-table mirror. She makes a face at herself.

"You know something?" she says, turning around. "I'm glad I didn't become well-known just for my beauty, because if that's all you've got, that and nothing else . . ." She doesn't bother to finish the sentence, but smiles and asks, "Do you know what I mean?"

[1979]

Rex Reed

MONTGOMERY CLIFT

It was part of his secret technique to always hold back important information while acting.

Some weeks ago I had the dismal task of reading and reviewing *Monty,* an alleged biography of Montgomery Clift, by a hack named Robert LaGuardia. The book was so trashy I feared its seedy and repulsive gossip would sell like space shoes. A soap opera of pills, booze, and perversion, it's an extended nightmare in which Monty passes out on every page. Predictably, it has slithered onto the best-seller list, despite a barrage of protests from friends and associates of the late Mr. Clift that the book is a fraud.

Fred Zinnemann, who directed Monty in *The Search* and *From Here to Eternity*, told me his brief interview with the author was outrageously distorted into a "pack of lies." Lorenzo James, Monty's friend and secretary who was with him until the day he died, told me LaGuardia never interviewed him at all but went ahead and shamelessly turned Monty's last days into a maelstrom of inaccuracies and salacious inventions. The fact that such a work of fiction could be a publishing success is discouraging, but to be expected, like muggings in New York and corruption in government.

To sweeten the bitter aftertaste of this bile, a copy of Patricia Bosworth's *Montgomery Clift* (to be published by Harcourt Brace Jovanovich) has just arrived on my desk. I read it with fascination, delight, and immense relief. The definitive work on Montgomery Clift, Bosworth's work is intelligent, readable, and ultimately moving. This is the distinguished book that Clift's fans deserve and will cherish.

Bosworth manages, through diligent and accurate research and through her consistent and often thrilling insight, to bring both the man and the actor to life. This is especially admirable when you consider how self-contained and introspective he was. As one director pointed out, it was part of his secret technique to always hold back important information while acting. This contributed to his mysterious screen presence, making him a more fascinating and dramatic character, but as a person he remained inscrutable. Bosworth presents a compassionate, keenly shaped portrait of a brilliant and complex personality. He was extraordinarily handsome, but his most attractive trait was an intense personal vision that drew people like magnets. His friends say they felt more alive when they were with Monty, more aware of life's magic. His gift was a unique vitality, a sensitivity that made him different and kept him dancing on the lip of a volcano.

Physically, he exuded masculinity. Pitted against John Wayne in his first film, *Red River*, he displayed a vulnerable, androgynous quality that drove bobby-soxers wild, paving the way for such other sensitive male rebels as Brando and Dean. His sexuality, which set him apart from others, worked to both his advantage and disadvantage. He was forced to lead an impossibly fragmented life; striving to maintain his screen image of male sex symbol, he kept his struggle with homosexuality from some of his closest friends. It became increasingly impossible to sustain one lasting, fulfilling relationship. Monty summed it up himself: "I don't understand it. I'm attracted to men, but I really love women." He knew the dilemma of being bisexual while simultaneously distrusting both sexes.

Bosworth has uncovered the story of Sunny Clift, Monty's driven, possessive, and domineering mother, and the reasons behind her foolish, mentally unbalanced behavior—contributing factors in Monty's own rebellious life.

The real story—not even mentioned in LaGuardia's cheap saga—is that after a childhood of torment and shame at being an orphan, Monty's mother discovered she was actually an Anderson-Blair, one of the bluest of blue-blood American families. (Anderson defended Fort Sumter in the Civil War; Blair was in Lincoln's cabinet. Ever heard of Blair House?)

Her life's quest was to regain her birthright and be acknowledged formally as the "thoroughbred" she knew she was. Sophia Anderson, her aunt, admitted Sunny's claim was true and promised to present her and the children to the rest of their aristocratic kin as soon as Monty, his twin sister, and brother, Brooks, could be polished up with enough cultural sheen. They were forced to endure private tutoring, endless trooping through galleries, and relentless drilling in foreign languages. After several trips to Europe, Aunt Sophie assessed their progress as "still rough around the edges," so they were whisked away on yet another whirlwind tour.

They never did get the acknowledgment Sunny craved, and in the process her children never got even a whiff of fun, freedom, or childhood. At the age of eighty, she was still trying unsuccessfully to get legal recognition by the *Social Register*. In piecing together the true story of how Monty came to be the insecure social misfit he was, Bosworth is the only writer who had the assistance and cooperation of the Clift family.

Without flinching from the more sensational aspects of Clift's homosexual persona, Bosworth also gives an intelligent account of his intense relationships with women: Elizabeth Taylor, Myrna Loy, Libby Holman, Mira Rostova, Nancy Walker, and Ann Lincoln.

In the final analysis, his most enduring love was his work. He wanted to be the world's greatest actor, and for a while nothing stood in his way. He gave everything to his film work, to his own roles as well as the overall concepts of the pictures themselves. Often he rewrote clumsy scripts until they worked. In *The Search*, the producer fought him all the way, until it became obvious from the rushes that Monty's improvements were saving the picture, and then two other writers walked off with Oscars for "best screenplay." He rewrote *Raintree County* at Elizabeth Taylor's insistence, cut unnecessary dialogue from *Freud*, and shaped up Irwin Shaw's *Young Lions*.

Nominated twice for Oscars (*Raintree County* and *From Here to Eternity*), he never got one because he so totally immersed himself in the characters he played nobody could see him "acting." Yet he remained an inspiration to other actors with more synthetic techniques while they stole votes from him. He taught Dean Martin and Frank Sinatra how to act. (Though poles apart in every way, he idolized Sinatra, who befriended him until one night Sinatra saw him make a drunken pass at another male at one of Sinatra's parties, whereupon the "pint-sized Crosby" instructed his bodyguards to toss Monty out on his face.) Elizabeth Taylor, whom he called "Bessie Mae," says she started acting with soul when she worked with Monty in *A Place in the Sun*. In his attention to detail, he would open a door fifty ways until he found the one that suited the moment perfectly.

When his work slipped away, Monty's life turned on itself like a cat eating its young. Enthusiasm turned to dissipation, ambition was replaced with self-hate. The famous car accident that destroyed his face threatened to put him out of business. Alcoholism made him uninsurable. Success became excess. If you've read LaGuardia's book, you know the lurid details. But if you're really interested in the man behind the mask, if you care about the human being and the artist, you must read Patricia Bosworth's masterful work. It's the difference between a file index and a complete library. Her book is the professional, analytical biography of a brilliant, gifted wunderkind who refused to accept his own limitations, whose self-delusion brought perfection within reach, with the saddest of consequences.

Reading the dossier Bosworth has compiled, it is impossible to believe Clift could have been so many things to so many people, yet be an enigma to all. There are fresh anecdotes about Marilyn Monroe, who regarded him as a fellow lost orphan in more trouble than she was; Clark Gable, who, in spite of his longevity, was reduced to being an insecure bigot in his presence; and a galaxy of supporting players who willingly formed the commedia dell'arte for his Scaramouches. The section on legendary Libby Holman is, by itself, a movie. She was the decadent Auntie Mame that his mother never was. Together, they would fly to the brothels of Cuba for a weekend; so Svengali-like was her hold over him that he turned down *Sunset Boulevard* because he felt it was too much like his own life.

As a former actress (I still remember the delicate but profound impression she made in Fred Zinnemann's *The Nun's Story*), Patricia Bosworth has the knowledge and feeling to make the life of a hero throb with realism. As a professional craftsmanlike writer, whose credentials are impeccable, she has the ability to sculpt a myriad details into a rich fabric of writing that reads more like a work of literary merit than just another typed manuscript. LaGuardia's current best-seller is recycled fan-magazine junk for beauty-parlor reading. Bosworth's biography is an inquiry into the desperate hopes that lie fallow in the hearts of great artists, without which there is no meaning in moonlight, no music in the wind.

[1977]

Richard Schickel

GARY COOPER

In his late years Cooper banned both "yup" and "nope" from his scripts.

Gary Cooper was, by common consent, the archetypal American. Just before he died he said: "Everybody asks me, how come you're around so long. Well, I always attribute it to playing the part of Mr. Average Joe American. Just an average guy from the middle of the U.S.A. And then, I guess I got to believe it . . . Gary Cooper, an Average Charlie who became a movie actor."

Cooper, as he undoubtedly knew, was oversimplifying in this summation. For instance, there was the matter of his appearance. He was, by any standard, a handsome man. Yet, by his manner, Cooper depreciated the fact. This was not because of any false modesty. It was rather an insistence on the subordination of superficials to matters of deeper import. He seemed to sense that it was essential for his audience to be comfortable in his presence. He preferred, for reasons of both art and personal taste, understatement. His way was to imply strength rather than to insist upon it.

His first important assignment was in *The Winning of Barbara Worth* (1926), and his big scene was with Ronald Colman, the actor Cooper most admired. He was to die in Colman's arms, and he received this bit of advice from the Englishman: "Easy does it, old boy. Good scenes make good actors. Actors don't make a scene. My own feeling is that all you have to do is take a nap, and every woman who sees the picture is going to cry her eyes out."

Cooper napped—and scored his first major success. Through the years he developed this technique of nonacting to its highest point. One of his last directors, Anthony Mann, said: "Something in those eyes tells you fantastic things. I've directed many stars, but never have I seen such eyes. They are at once electric, honest, devastating. And he knows how to look through them. . . . No one can so graphically reveal his thoughts by the look on his face."

The thoughts of Cooper's screen character turned often to the question of morality. He believed in the standard American variety, and he took it seriously, as a code to live by. The drama of a Cooper film arose from the conflict between a man who based his conduct on the commonly accepted code and those who claimed they did, but actually proceeded on a business-as-usual basis. From this stemmed the immutability of Cooper's appeal. He behaved as we would have liked to behave were not the world too much with us.

But there was more to the matter than this. The thing that really riled Cooper was invasion of privacy. The suspense in a classic Cooper film was generated by seeing how much abuse he would take before, at long last, and with great weariness, he would unwind his lanky frame and go after his tormentors. It was his habit to exhaust all manner of rational appeal, even exhibit a willingness to submit to unmanning abuse, before strapping on his guns. Abstract principle was all right, and he would defend it, but more often he rose to defend himself and his conception of himself.

High Noon was a perfect example of this. He stayed to fight the bandit gang not for the sake of the town, which had long since proved itself unworthy of the effort, not for any social abstraction, but because the gang posed a supreme threat not only to his health but to his personal morality. He fought to defend his right to self-determination, his right to be himself as he wanted to be.

Cooper's screen personality was the honest product of a man noted for giving fair measure in his dealings both as a professional and as an individual. The career was a masterpiece of understatement and of timing, for Cooper managed it himself, shrewdly altering the externals of setting, costume, even film genre, but always making sure he touched home base every two or three pictures. A native of the West, personally a devotee of its outdoor amusements, he made certain that the intervals between Westerns were never long. He knew as well as anyone that his roots were there. "It's always been a question," he told writer Thomas Morgan, "whether to let the public see what they expect or whether you should give them something new. It always comes up. There are things Gary Cooper shouldn't do, things that offer great opportunities actingwise. . . ."

He was rather better in comedy than one expected; he was superb as a Hemingway hero (a man, as Leslie Fiedler pointed out, with virtually the same values as the screen Westerner). In short, he extended his range more than he would have had to, and perhaps this was one of the reasons for his undiminishing popularity. More than other actors of similar limitations, he offered as many variations on his basic theme as possible. He guarded his screen self jealously, and he once declared: "An oil man is allowed to deplete twenty-seven percent annually as the oil is used up. An industrialist can depreciate his equipment as it ages. Now all I have to sell is me—this body of mine. If it's maimed or broken I can't work. And it ages just as certainly as machine tools. But do they let me depreciate it? Heck, no."

The thought is not as important as the image—that of an entrepreneur handling a difficult enterprise with all the canniness at his command. He

Gary Cooper: *His career was a masterpiece of understatement.*
(Courtesy of the Museum of Modern Art Film Stills Archive.)

did that with a curious, engaging lack of ego. He was here, as in his screen roles, the easy, confident professional, so good at what he did that the doing was the only self-assertion he needed to make. The rewards were inherent in the means, although the ends were pleasant enough—and Cooper seemed to revel in being the well-tailored, quietly cultured international celebrity at home in salons both social and artistic.

He was not, of course, a simple cowhand. His family was well-to-do, his father a justice of the Montana Supreme Court and a gentleman rancher. Cooper learned the ways of the Westerner as a boy, but he also spent three years in an English public school. He went to college for three years and thought of becoming a commercial artist. Visiting his family in Los Angeles (where his father was working on a case), he ran into old ranch friends who were working as stunt riders in silent Westerns. He joined them and, through a combination of circumstance and intelligent self-interest, won his role in *Barbara Worth*.

A starring role in a medium-budget Western, a memorable bit in *Wings* as a doomed flier, and co-starring roles with Clara Bow and Lupe Velez brought him to the sound barrier as a rising star. His first sound film, *The Virginian*, was, as he said, "the big one—you had to survive the transition to talking pictures. *The Virginian* put me over the hump and made millions." It also was a film with a great deal of "yup" and "nope" dialogue. In his late years Cooper banned both words from his scripts. There was no point in giving grist to the joke mills. Like his heroes, he took no foolish chances—only calculated risks.

[1962]

Stephen Harvey

JOAN CRAWFORD

She anticipated each new trend and adapted herself accordingly.

There are times when it becomes painfully clear how Hollywood's skill for mythmaking is even more potent and insidious than we ever realized. I had such a moment during that afternoon in May when a friend called to tell me that Joan Crawford had died. The indestructible Joan Crawford? The star who had managed to endure through more than four decades of shifting public tastes and dozens of rum movies (as well as the occasional good one), not to mention both L. B. Mayer and Jack Warner? Impossible, I thought. Of course, soon enough I realized that it was not only possible, it was downright inevitable; movie legends only *seem* more vulnerable to the rigors that plague the rest of us. Logical enough, but the death of someone who has seemed such a permanent fixture on the American screen comes nonetheless as rather a shock.

The saga of Joan Crawford's rise to fame, and of the tenacious grasp with which she held on to it for so long, was really more improbable than the flossiest of her star turns which enthralled the fans over all those years. Few actresses who subsequently attained stardom were as ill-equipped for it at the beginning as was Lucille Le Sueur from Kansas City, who arrived at M-G-M in 1925 under the standard six-month starlet contract. She had worked her way up from her mother's laundry through a series of tawdry boarding schools, stints behind shop counters, and hoofing jobs in nightclubs; the closest Crawford had come to acting before landing in Hollywood was high-kicking in the chorus of two Broadway revues. Certainly that round-faced coquette with the bee-stung lips grinning from all those early publicity photos was practically indistinguishable from dozens of other movie-struck flappers who never got anywhere, and bore only the faintest resemblance to the hollow-cheeked glamour queen that emerged with the talkies. Yet from the start Crawford was doggedly ambitious, and as even the earliest of her surviving silent films attest, she was born to be in the movies.

In 1926, a scant year after her movie debut, she displayed enough sheer animal vitality as an amoral Apache dancer in a piece of melodramatic hokum called *Paris* to steal the picture from under the nose of its nominal star, Charles Ray. Two years later, with *Our Dancing Daughters*, she successfully challenged Clara Bow for the title of the movies' leading exponent of feckless American youth. The subsequent arrival of sound derailed the careers of many of her contemporaries, but not Crawford's. In a pattern that would reemerge time and again over the next three decades Crawford anticipated each new trend and adapted herself accordingly. Her black-bottoming hoydens of the twenties were replaced by swank sophisticates and downtrodden shopgirls in the thirties, and angst-ridden grande dames and hausfraus through the forties and beyond.

Along the way Crawford stopped at nothing to prove to herself and her public that her range was limitless. At various times in her career she tap-danced, sang, ice-skated, took screwball comedy pratfalls, toted six-guns, sashayed around in crinolines, and waded into the shoals of High Drama à la Somerset Maugham. None of these new Joan Crawfords succeeded in impressing her many detractors, who had never much cared for the old one to begin with. Even forty years ago, people who considered themselves sophisticated derided her tight-lipped hauteur, her half-Mayfair, half-Culver City diction, and of course those racks of padded-shouldered Adrian creations, which were a sine qua non of every Crawford vehicle of the period. Yet, as far as her legions of fans were concerned, what those cultural snobs thought of their Joan couldn't have mattered less.

At the peak of her popularity during the mid-thirties, Crawford was idolized not so much for what she did on the screen as for what she represented. To millions of moviegoers, Crawford was the symbol of the American dream of upward social mobility. She had never tried to mask her threadbare origins from the public gaze, and the result was that those gutter-to-penthouse movie odysseys of hers came to be viewed as a kind of fictionalized autobiography of the "real" Joan Crawford. The message was clear: Here was a woman who, through sheer force of will, had managed to kick over the traces of humdrum obscurity and become more glamorous, more affluent, and certainly more beloved than any to-the-manner-born aristocrat. The loftier Crawford became, the more her audiences adored her, with the proviso that she had to suffer inordinately along the way. Even royalty had to have its sorrows.

The women Crawford generally portrayed provide a revealing reflection of the attitudes and aspirations of the female moviegoers of her day. Although Crawford created her share of harridans in the course of her career, she was usually very vulnerable to emotion; that aura of steel-tempered toughness was simply a kind of psychic armor necessary to fight her way through a world where you make your own breaks. At the outset of her more typical vehicles she usually is making out very nicely for herself in her independent, if lonely fashion, until some likely male comes along who obscures her judgment and confuses her priorities. During the thirties, the conflict was usually resolved with a close-up of Crawford crushed blissfully in the arms of Clark Gable or Robert Montgomery. But by the forties, when both Crawford and her following had become a little older and presumably more rueful, the outcome was considerably bleaker. The fade-out of *Mildred Pierce* finds her impoverished and with all her illusions shattered; in *Humoresque* she ends up a misbegotten suicide; and in *Possessed* a deranged murderess in the psycho ward. Clearly something had gone awry, even in the never-never land of what used to be termed "women's pictures." Contrary to the present-day myths about such movies, in the world of Joan Crawford romance was often more trouble than it was worth.

As with all the great personalities of the studio-system era, one was never allowed to forget that whatever the role, it was always Joan Crawford up there on the screen showing off what she could do. Yet her career really had considerably more scope to it than has generally been acknowledged. Most of her lamé-draped clotheshorse vehicles are indeed a trial to sit through nowadays, but many of her films hold quite a few surprises for the uninitiated. People are often startled to discover, for example, that while Garbo of *Grand Hotel* is faintly ponderous and overemphatic, Crawford's ambitious stenographer in the same film has remained remarkably vital and engaging. Later on she successfully tackled such disparate roles as the avaricious siren let loose among *The Women*, an embittered prostitute (*Strange Cargo*), a disfigured blackmailer (*A Woman's Face*), a faddish socialite (*Susan and God*), the anal-compulsive *Harriet Craig,* and the menaced playwright in *Sudden Fear.*

Her greatest asset as an actress was that remarkably vivid, photogenic face captured in close-up. Crawford was one of the few of her contemporaries never to attempt a stage career, and she was probably wise not to do so. Although her professionalism was legendary in the industry, Crawford's most memorable moments reflected instinct rather than craft, in the way a fleeting emotion would cross that impenetrable Crawford mask. As time went on the mask became more exaggerated—with those eyebrows, that mouth, and the defiant jawline reaching almost forbidding proportions—but at its most controlled, the Crawford face was a supreme example of Hollywood iconography.

In her later years, Crawford rode the menopausal-mayhem cycle she had initiated with *Whatever Happened to Baby Jane?* to its sanguinary end. It must have chagrined her to observe that while her erstwhile rivals Bette Davis and Katharine Hepburn had achieved the status of national monuments, Crawford was increasingly treated as a kind of living anachronism. Considerations of talent apart, I think one of the reasons for this was the fact that Davis and Hepburn's public image as the eternal rebels against the gilded servitude of Hollywood has been particularly congenial to the mood of the seventies. Crawford, on the other hand, reveled in all the supposedly phony and outmoded accouterments of stardom; she relished fan clubs, red-carpet publicity tours, and all the attendant hoopla. M-G-M had never been a luxurious penal colony so far as Crawford was concerned—it was home. Not unlike those other star dragons, Swanson and Dietrich, Crawford resolutely perpetuated the same gospel-according-to-*Photoplay* world view up until the very end; it had worked since 1928, so there was no point in trying to change now.

Predictably enough, the persona she had worked so tirelessly to create finally turned on her with a vengeance. When she found she could no longer

(RIGHT) Joan Crawford:
The mask became more exaggerated.
(*Johnny Guitar.* Courtesy of IVY Film,
New York.)

(BELOW) Bette Davis (with Henry Fonda):
*"I've never felt that actors were the
best judges of their own acting."*
(*Jezebel.* © 1938 Warner Brothers.
Renewed 1965
by United Artists Television.

maintain the guise of the eternal Dancing Daughter, the woman who had eagerly posed for the paparazzi at every premiere, charity ball, and Pepsi bottling plant on both coasts and all points in between, now withdrew once and for all into her East Side co-op, accessible only by telephone. The movies may not bear much resemblance to life most of the time, but as it turned out, Crawford's slow fade bore an eerie kinship to her own movies. While in *Baby Jane* Joan as ex-movie queen Blanche Hudson was imprisoned by Bette Davis, in truth Joan Crawford was trapped by none other than "Joan Crawford." Unfortunate as this might have been, it constituted a curious kind of integrity. A half century of practice had taught Joan Crawford that above all else it was the image that counted.

[1977]

Gary Arnold

BETTE DAVIS

"The contract system was the greatest system in the world for the movie public."

"John Wayne!" exclaimed Bette Davis, articulating each word with inimitable, exaggerated precision and lifting her eyebrows nearly under her hat. George Stevens, Jr., the director of the American Film Institute, had just mentioned that Wayne was among the stars scheduled to appear on the inauguration eve gala for President Carter at the Kennedy Center. Wayne's participation seemed to strike Miss Davis, also scheduled to appear on the show, like a thunderbolt.

"But he's always been so rabidly the other way!" she remarked.

Stevens explained that an attempt had been made to prepare everyone for the shock. "He comes out saying, 'I represent the opposition, the loyal opposition,'" Stevens revealed, attempting a Wayne vocal impression that could stand a lot more work.

Davis made a will-wonders-never-cease face and reached for a cigarette. She had driven down from Connecticut earlier in the day with her agent, John Springer, to rehearse for the Wednesday-night gala.

While in town Davis had agreed to chat with the press on behalf of two upcoming AFI events honoring her—the fifth annual Life Achievement

Award ceremony and a retrospective series of fifteen Bette Davis movies at the AFI Theater.

Asked if she had Democratic Party loyalties as strong as those Wayne appeared to feel for the Republican Party, she shook her head no. "I think that like most Americans I vote for the man," she said, "and this year I felt like the majority of voters. I think we need to make a fresh start, and I feel cautiously optimistic about the new people. Of course, I have only participated in Democratic inaugurals, so I might appear to be a loyalist. I was here in 1961 for JFK, whom I admired very much, when you had a snowstorm that threatened to paralyze the city. And I attended the first Roosevelt inaugural in 1933.

"I'm certainly considered a liberal as these things are calculated in Hollywood, and I've fought tooth and nail for the things I believe in. I was in the thick of it in Hollywood during the war when I was chairman of the Hollywood Canteen, particularly over the issue of racial discrimination. I was determined that the canteen would not exclude Negro servicemen. It wasn't integrated in the current sense either, of course, but it was a struggle to keep the admissions open, maintain equal services, even hire Negro girls as hostesses. There were vehement objections, and the presence of so many white Southerners in the service made it even touchier."

Illness prevented Davis from appearing personally at last year's Life Achievement Award ceremony for William Wyler, who directed her in three important pictures, *Jezebel*, *The Letter*, and *The Little Foxes*, and whom she appears to respect above all other collaborators. Unfortunately, *The Little Foxes* brought their association to a premature, if prestigious, end. They disagreed about the role of Regina, and although Davis played it in the severe, withheld style Wyler urged, she was never satisfied with the performance. In retrospect, it seems a shame that she didn't insist on the feisty, bravura performance she wanted to give, in the spirit of Tallulah Bankhead's fabled stage interpretation.

Jezebel, released in 1938, was Davis's consolation for twice spurning the role of Scarlett O'Hara and brought her a second Academy Award. It remains one of her most stirring and beautiful vehicles. "Anyone who doubts Wyler's genius only has to look at the ballroom sequence in *Jezebel*," Davis remarked. "What a wonderful sequence that is! And do you know what we began with? Virtually nothing. There was a single line in the script: 'Julie goes to the ball.' Wyler is responsible for all the pictorial and romantic elaboration.

"I desperately wanted Technicolor for that film," she continued. "Can you imagine how beautiful the ball scene would have been in color? At that time Warners refused to shoot more than two pictures a year in color. I would beg and plead and never get it, because they knew I was a safe moneymaker without it. They rejected it as an unnecessary expense.

"Even though *Jezebel* is in black and white, no one really questions the idea that Julie goes to the ball in a red gown. The impact is still there, thanks to Wyler and to Kelly (costume designer Orry-Kelly), who was a genius, too. He knew that that black velvet dress would have just the right 'red' effect in black and white. In all fairness, working in Technicolor had its disadvantages. The Technicolor people themselves had a rather imperious tone. I recall one run-in with Mrs. Kalmus [Natalie Kalmus, wife of the inventor of the process and a compulsory adviser on all Technicolor productions for many years]. 'My dear Miss Davis,' she said, 'you'll have to do something about that organdy dress with all the lavender.' I replied, 'My dear Mrs. Kalmus, I plan to *wear* the organdy dress with all the lavender.' "

Davis seems philosophical about losing the most coveted role in movie history. "I can't have too many regrets about Scarlett," she said, "because it was my own fault in the first place. I was too mad at Jack Warner to listen to anything he said. When he begged me not to walk out because he'd optioned some Southern novel with a marvelous role for me, I wasn't impressed. I asked him what it was, and he said the book was called *Gone With the Wind*. I said, 'I'll bet that's a pip,' and went straight to England.

"When I came back a year later, I still hadn't read the book. I'd been too absorbed in the legal battles over my contract dispute with Warners. Naturally, I wanted Scarlett—once I realized what she was all about. Selznick did make the offer, but Warner insisted on a package deal with Errol Flynn and myself, and I refused. I didn't think Errol was suitable, and I was quite right. Not that I disliked him. Errol was one of the most beautiful men who ever appeared on the screen. Lazy, of course. I don't think he ever worked at acting a day in his life, but that was part of his personal charm. He was simply wrong for Rhett Butler, so that was that.

"After *Jezebel* I couldn't feel as bad about losing out on Scarlett. The same energies went into the role of Julie, and I derived great satisfaction from it. There would have been no point in playing Scarlett after Julie. Still, if circumstances had been different, I would have relished Scarlett. It would have been the greatest challenge of my career."

Davis's movie career began at Universal in 1931 when she was twenty-three. She has appeared in over eighty features, including more than fifty made under contract at Warner Bros. between 1932 and 1949. Davis has won the Academy Award twice (for *Dangerous* in 1935, considered a belated award for her performance in *Of Human Bondage* a year earlier, and then *Jez-*

ebel) and received nominations eight other times. Despite her conflicts with Jack Warner, she looks back on her old boss and the old system with a considerable amount of affection and respect.

"I resisted certain assignments violently," she said, "but the contract system was the greatest system in the world for the movie public. We were constantly, constantly making films, and the public got to know us. It's distressing to see how little regard for their profession or careers many young performers have today. They're not required to take a long-term interest in the work; so, few of them do. Since the system doesn't require it, it's left to the actors to show enough self-respect to stay in training and choose intelligently and try to sustain their careers.

"There's only so much any one person can do. It's difficult enough fulfilling your responsibilities as an actor or actress. I can't understand how anyone can function as a producer or director or whatever at the same time. One of the great advantages of the old system was the range of support you could count on. There seemed to be so many capable and enthusiastic people working for a common goal."

Springer mentioned the number of credits attributed officially and unofficially to Barbra Streisand on her remake of *A Star Is Born*: executive producer, star, supervising editor, songwriter, "musical concepts" conceptualizer, wardrobe mistress. Davis, who claims she has grown "too lazy" to see many new films but obviously keeps up on what's being said about them, frowned at this catalogue.

"It sounds impractical," she said. "In the first place, I've never felt that actors were the best judge of their own acting. If you're working with an intelligent director, you can trust him to select the best takes. It only becomes a problem when you've got a weak or incompetent director. Then I've learned you may need to step in and choose for him. But it's not a desirable solution. Paul Muni once told me, 'You'll never need a director,' and he meant it as a compliment, but he was absolutely wrong. That sort of thinking weakened his own work."

Davis said she doubted if she would even try to begin a career if she were a young actress entering the profession right now. She feels the opportunities are simply too limited and the support too unsteady. Nevertheless, she rejects the idea that women's roles have diminished because of some deliberate neglect or hostility on the part of contemporary movie companies or producers. "It just happened," she said, "and no one has devised a system to compensate for the changes. Perhaps we shouldn't complain. We had wonderful opportunities for more than twenty years. Maybe it's just the actors' turn to dominate for a generation. The themes and problems seem so much more formidable and violent now. They overshadow the content of most of our pictures, which usually had a romantic conflict at their core and were designed to appeal to a large, faithful audience of women. Those forms don't seem adequate now, but I'm not sure what can replace them. They certainly can't have the impact of the conflicts one sees in the men's vehicles."

An AFI staffer came by with a large blow-up of a scene from *Jezebel* and asked Davis to autograph it. "Now that is a still!" she exclaimed, and while composing a message she commiserated with agents and reporters in general for now having to function in a period when movie companies no longer consider it worth their while to employ full-time still cameramen. "You know what they do?" she asked in indignation. "They hire someone for two days. Any old two days. It doesn't matter what's being shot. It could be the dullest scenes in the film for all anyone knows or cares. Even then they rarely bother to duplicate the poses in printed takes. It's disgraceful what you fellows have to put up with."

She completed the inscription and held the picture at arm's length. "Oh, Bette," she sighed. "We were all such kids then!"

[1977]

Molly Haskell

DORIS DAY

One of the few movie heroines who had to *work* for a living.

For me, a veteran of the fifties now looking back, Doris Day defined the best and worst of that decade with which her rise to stardom was contemporaneous. She was energy and optimism, the sunny-side-up of an era in which the dark side of life was ruthlessly suppressed . . . and at what price we now know. She was Eisenhower chauvinism and complacency, the parochialism of people who "know what's important in life," and need look no further. But she was also ambition and self-reliance—a heroine, striking out on her own, against and ahead of her time.

Between 1948 and 1968, Doris Day made some forty films: the first third—until roughly 1953—as a musical leading lady, and the rest as a star.

The fact that as late as 1968 she played heroines who were still "in the running" as far as men were concerned, makes hers one of the longest female careers in the business.

Certainly her method of survival was not, like Joan Crawford's, to adapt herself to changing tastes and mature with her audience. On the contrary, she represented conservative values that went defiantly against the grain of the swinging sixties. Nor did she evolve, like Bette Davis, into offbeat roles. On the contrary—again—she seems to have survived largely by *not* changing, by remaining fixed in a firmament of shooting stars. But *how* she survived and what she was fixed *as* are best explained by what she was not: by not being identified primarily as a sex object or a romantic fantasy—she played mothers, teenagers, and romantic leads in no particular logical, or chronological, order—she remained invulnerable to the mutability that such fleshy fantasies are heir to.

Like most stars (and movies) who arrive on the cusp of a decade, Day combines qualities of both eras. Her emotional intensity, just this side of hysteria, is a throwback to those tearful, heartbreaking feminine heroines played by June Allyson and Margaret Sullavan in the forties. But where they were yearning, even masochistic, Day is direct and forward-moving, constitutionally incapable of succumbing to melancholy.

From singing with big bands, she went straight to singing in the big band movies that Warner Bros. was churning out. She was the blonde in the white blouse and pleated skirt—even in *My Dream Is Yours* (1949), with a fatherless son. When paired with other females, it was always they who were tough, or sexy; Lauren Bacall in *Young Man with a Horn* (1950) and Ginger Rogers as her older sister in *Storm Warning* (1951).

Next came the tomboy phase, from 1951 (*On Moonlight Bay*) to *Calamity Jane* in 1953, the year I tuned in. I had a "secret love" and, at the age of thirteen, was strenuously resisting the pressures to stop climbing trees and convert myself into that passive figurine of womanhood, the "lady." Doris Day's freckles, the lumberjack shirt, the blue jeans, the athleticism, and the occasional shrill notes of incipient womanhood may not have struck movie critics as the last word in art or glamour, but they constituted a shrine at which my barely adolescent anxieties could find relief. If she was to be pitted against the sexually blatant Marilyn Monroe-type—as she was implicitly, and later (in *The Thrill of It All*) explicitly—then I was wholeheartedly on her side. She would not twist herself out of shape to win men's love, and find instead only lust.

Looking at her career with more detachment, it was in the mid-fifties that she played her most dramatically interesting roles: Ruth Etting in *Love Me or Leave Me*; and, in Hitchcock's *The Man Who Knew Too Much*, the hysterical

American mother abroad, overattached to her son and overdependent on pills.

One of the marks of a great director is the ability to capture the side of an actor that has remained hidden. Hitchcock was a genius at exposing the neurotic underside of his stars' image. With uncanny prescience in *The Man Who Knew Too Much*, Hitchcock painted a portrait of a woman who wouldn't be defined as a type, or analyzed as a trend, until ten years later. In Day's anxious young mother, we see the neurotic overcompensation of a woman who had given up her career (the stage) for marriage. Obsessed with her son, she has become an emotional invalid of a wife, as if to punish the man (the husband played by Jimmy Stewart) who had forced her to make such a choice. And with further insight, Hitchcock gave to Doris Day, in the song "Que Será, Será," what I was to discover was her philosophy of life.

It was in the late fifties and early sixties, when she herself was in her late thirties, that she won her reputation as the eternal virgin, a crystallization of those traits that had endeared her to masses of Americans and damned her forever with the cultural arbiters. The films in which she *did* accept her years and matronliness with wry equanimity, like *Please Don't Eat the Daisies,* were not as successful as those in which she resisted her fate. Likewise, her more subtle musicals and comedies (*The Pajama Game* and Billy Rose's *Jumbo*) were ignored by audiences and critics for the increasingly abrasive confrontations of the Fox and Universal farces (*Pillow Talk*, *Move Over, Darling*, and so on), in which Day and a lover/antagonist would enact sexual duels as horrifying, in their folksy way, as the armageddons of Strindberg.

In these films, virginity and masculinity were the citadels under siege. But for all the coy plot devices contrived by screenwriter Stanley Shapiro to keep Day from turning into Night, the lady herself was willing to surrender—as long as she could cloak her deed with the missionary purpose of reclaiming one faltering soul to manhood. If these films made us uncomfortable, surely it was partly because they touched upon anxieties we all felt, in a society and a decade in which women were little encouraged to expose themselves sexually. To lose one's virginity was to lose everything. Small wonder that Doris Day clung to hers with something akin to desperation.

But when I remember her roles in these films, it is as one of the few movie heroines (and one of the last) who had to *work* for a living. Grace Kelly and Audrey Hepburn, bless their chic souls, floated through life. Voluptuous Ava Gardner ran barefoot and bohemian through exotic places. Marilyn Monroe was the sexual totem for the various fetishes of fifties America. Kim Novak and Debbie Reynolds and Shirley MacLaine, who, like Day, were not goddesses and hence had to exert themselves, still sought a man to lean on. One never felt in them the driving, single-minded ambition one felt in Day—the very strength that was used as a weapon, in the sex comedies, to impugn her femininity.

She had excellent positions—as an interior decorator in *Pillow Talk* and an advertising executive in *Lover Come Back*—and she worked because she loved it, was good at it, and needed the money; not just to find a husband. She had come to the big city to make her way. And thus she seemed to be resisting, in a way that would find its voice in the Women's Movement, the creeping paralysis of adult womanhood as it was coming to be defined in the fifties. It is surely from this period of suburban migration and domesticity as a consuming vocation that the reductive notion of being "just a housewife" dates.

But gradually the hardening process set in. Her brisk, no-nonsense approach was institutionalized through farcical exaggeration. Her latest films—*The Ballad of Josie, Where Were You When the Lights Went Out?, With Six, You Get Eggroll*—were all "Oh, here comes the nutty lady" variety. If her natural talents never left her, neither were they permitted to develop within the coy vehicles and overproduced comedies designed to keep her afloat in the sixties. But in even the silliest roles—from damsel in distress (*Julie* and *Midnight Lace*) to feminist of the Old West (*The Ballad of Josie*)—she kept her head, and saved her face, when all around her were losing theirs. She remained true to herself: for that alone she deserves more than passing interest.

[1976]

Jack Kroll

ROBERT DE NIRO

He symbolizes the search for identity that has become pervasive and hectic in an uncertain America.

Robert De Niro is a dim-witted baseball player who's dying of Hodgkin's disease. Robert De Niro is a young Sicilian immigrant who establishes a Mafia dynasty in America. Robet De Niro is a psychopathic New York cabdriver who arms himself to the teeth and triggers a bloodbath. Robert De

Niro is the scion of an Italian landowning family who's caught in the swirling winds of revolution. Robert De Niro is a jiving, wise-cracking musician in the big-band era of the forties.

Robert De Niro *is* all of these characters—and more. It is this astonishing variety and authenticity of his characterizations that make him, at thirty-three, the most exciting young American actor on the scene, the one with the greatest potential to combine superstardom with extraordinary creative ability. More than that, De Niro is the heir apparent to the post of American Cultural Symbol once occupied by Marlon Brando and the late James Dean. As Brando and Dean did in the postwar decades, De Niro seems to embody the conflicting, questing energies of his generation, the generation coming to young maturity in the fragmented seventies.

Brando and Dean symbolized rebellion and resentment in an exhausted, uptight America; but the rebel, with or without a cause, no longer occupies the center of the American stage—or screen. De Niro symbolizes the search for identity that has become pervasive and hectic in an uncertain America. Brando and Dean had strong, sharply defined personalities that pulsated through all of their roles. De Niro seems to have no personality at all; he becomes the characters he portrays—the dying catcher in *Bang the Drum Slowly*, the paranoid cabbie *Taxi Driver*, the young Mafia boss in *The Godfather, Part II*, the Hollywood producer in *The Last Tycoon*, the demoralized landowner in Bernardo Bertolucci's *1900*, and the jazz musician in Martin Scorsese's *New York, New York*.

Elia Kazan, the one director who has worked with Brando, Dean, and De Niro, recognizes the significant shift from rebellion to role-playing. "Brando was deeply rebellious against the bourgeois spirit, the overordering of life," says Kazan. "Dean represented the release of anger against parents, resentment at the failure of parents to understand. Brando was happily arrogant, a free spirit. Dean was sad and sulky, you kept expecting him to cry. De Niro is a number of things all at once. There are lots of different people in him. He finds release and fulfillment in becoming other people. Picture after picture he gets deep into the thing. He's found his solution for living at a time like this in work."

Aside from his great talent, this protean quality is what distinguishes De Niro from other outstanding actors of his generation like Al Pacino, Jack Nicholson, and Dustin Hoffman. It's not just the plastic and personal rhythm of good acting that De Niro gives you. He gives you the shock of becoming, of a metamorphosis that can be thrilling, moving or frightening. His Oscar-winning performance as Vito Corleone in *Godfather II* projected the chilling dignity of a young man forced into crime to keep his freedom from criminals—the arm's-length gesture of his first killing had a ritual, almost noble solemnity.

It is of course a perverted nobility, and De Niro's instinctive insight into perverse behavior is one of his credentials as the most expressive actor of this moment. All great acting has an ethical dimension, and De Niro always suggests positive energy that has been perverted. Even his poor, crazy, shaven-skulled Travis Bickle, aiming his vigilante guns at pimps and politicos in *Taxi Driver*, expresses a diseased gallantry that's a tragic part of an era in which you can't always tell the saints from the swine. . . .

De Niro has become nearly legendary for the dogged determination with which he researches his roles. As Bruce Pearson, the doomed catcher in *Bang the Drum Slowly*, he went down to Georgia and tape-recorded the local people to pick up the accent. He spent weeks observing the technique of major-league catchers like Johnny Bench and more weeks batting and catching baseballs hurled at varying speeds from a pitching machine. To play Vito Corleone, many of whose scenes were shot in Sicily, he learned the Sicilian dialect with such fluency that it appeared to be his first language. For *New York, New York* he learned to play the tenor sax with amazing naturalness, so that the instrument seems a part of him just as it does with a real jazz man.

De Niro's teacher was George Auld, one of the outstanding tenor saxophonists of the swing era, who appeared with the big bands of Artie Shaw and Benny Goodman, as well as with his own groups, and is still a fine player. De Niro learned the fingering for every number in the film and played the sax to the sound track that Auld had recorded, while Auld watched him off-camera, ready to give Scorsese a slit-throat sign if De Niro took a wrong breath or pushed a false finger. Auld rarely had to slit his throat. "I can't get what has taken George so many years to develop," says De Niro. "But I can create the illusion of doing it, which is my job as an actor. The musical phrasing is a lot like an actor's rhythm and phrasing. And once in a solo I had that feeling of total control. It was complicated but I practiced it so much that I felt it, I had it down, I really got behind it."

It's doubtful that any other actor pursues what he calls "truth" with De Niro's dedication. "There's nothing more offensive to me than watching an actor act with his ego," he says. "Some of the old movie stars were terrific, but they romanticized. People chase illusions and these illusions are created by movies. I want to make things concrete and real and to break down the illusion. There's nothing more ironic or strange or contradictory than life itself. What I try to do is to make things as clear and authentic as possible." De Niro is suspicious of terms like style applied to acting. "Technique is concrete," he says. "I don't want people years from now to say: 'Remember

De Niro, he had a real style.' I want to do things that will last because they have substance and quality, not some affectation or style, because that's all bullshit."

Ironically, De Niro's pragmatism becomes almost mystical in its intensity. He's our foremost current example of the paradox of acting—to create poetry out of behaviorism. De Niro is willing to think of an actor like Brando in those terms, but not himself. "Early Brando seemed to romanticize," he says, "but it's really the poetry of his whole being. I don't know about my poetry, but you just look at Brando and you're interested. He has a sense of truth in all his instincts." When De Niro was preparing his role of Vito Corleone in *Godfather II*, he studied videotapes of Brando's performance as the old Vito in the first *Godfather*. The result was an uncanny feat. "I watched the tape and I saw if I had done the part myself I would have done it differently. But I tried to connect him with me, how I could be him only younger. So I tried to speed up where he was slower, to get the rasp in his voice, only the beginning of the rasp. It was interesting. It was like a scientific problem."

Yes, but. If that were all, Albert Einstein would be a greater actor than Laurence Olivier. De Niro, as Kazan points out, is "obsessive," and this obsessiveness can result, significantly, in some bizarre "scientific" solutions. There is a scene in *Taxi Driver* in which Travis Bickle is intimidated by a pimp, played by Harvey Keitel, and doesn't know how to react. "I got the idea of making Travis move like a crab," says De Niro. "It's a hot sunny day. He's out of his cab, which is his protective shell—he's outside his element. He's all dry and hot, finally he breaks down. I got the image of a crab, moving awkwardly, sideways and back. It's not that you imitate a crab, but the image gives you something to work with. It gives you another kind of behavior." Of course. Scientific De Niro is a poet, just like T.S. Eliot, whose demoralized Prufrock said: "I should have been a pair of ragged claws / Scuttling across the floors of silent seas."

De Niro takes acting seriously. He has none of that self-revulsion toward his profession that Brando has developed over the years. "Acting isn't really respected enough as an art," he says. "Your body is an instrument, and you have to learn how to play an instrument. It's like knowing how to play the piano. There ought to be acting schools that take you in as children, the way it's done with musicians. You don't need experience to learn technique. You'd learn your technique, and as you got older and had experience you'd apply it to what you know."

Acting is really the only formal education that De Niro has had. He grew up in the section of New York's Greenwich Village known as Little Italy.

His parents, who separated when their only child was two, are both artists. His father, also named Robert De Niro, is an extremely gifted and respected New York painter who's a sculptor, critic, and poet as well. His recent book, *A Fashionable Watering Place*, contains this inscription: "These poems are by Robert De Niro, the painter, not to be confused with Robert De Niro, the actor, his son." This apparent mixture of pride and self-assertion is certainly charming and perhaps significant. "Robert's passionate, cultivated, very complex," says a fellow artist who's known him for thirty years. "His involvement with his art is a matter of life and death."

That could be a description of the younger De Niro's attitude toward *his* art. Father and son are remarkably alike. "The physical resemblance is astonishing," says the friend. "Robert is the outline and Bobby is the part inside the lines." His sensitive drawings of his son might be self-portraits of the father's younger self—an odd and moving reflection of De Niro's handling of the Vito Corleone "problem." "In *Godfather II* Bobby was so much like his father," says the friend. "They both have a natural elegance. They project a sense of gallantry." Like so many children of that powerful postwar generation of New York artists, the younger De Niro was not coddled by his parents—who had fought hard to create their own artistic identity. "Bobby was out in the street a lot as a child," says the friend. "He wasn't being rebellious—that's just the way the cookie crumbled." After finishing *Godfather II*, De Niro gave a gift to director Francis Ford Coppola—two paintings by his father. "He knew I have a father who's in the arts," says Coppola. "So he gave me a gift that represented something important to both of us."

The streets presented a more compelling education than the various high schools that De Niro entered and exited from. He also attended various acting schools sporadically but did not stick to those, either. At one of them the director asked him why he wanted to be an actor. "I told him I didn't know," says De Niro. "He said: 'You want to be an actor to express yourself.' And later on when I got into acting seriously I remembered this and I said that *is* the reason I want to be an actor—to express myself." Stella Adler was the first teacher who gave De Niro "a total sense of theater and character" and taught him how to break down a script and analyze it.

From the beginning he had his own highly personal approach and an almost fearsome dedication. Even the young stage and film directors with whom he's always felt most congenial were often flabbergasted by what seemed pure eccentricity until it exploded into a startling creativity. Brian De Palma, for whom De Niro made three surreal independent pictures about the counter-culture in the sixties—*The Wedding Party*, *Greetings*, and *Hi, Mom!*—recalls that in *Greetings* De Niro played a militant right-winger who suddenly enlists in the Army. "He showed up to shoot the scene," says De Palma, "and I didn't recognize him. We had to hang a title card on him to remind the audience that they'd seen him earlier in the film. It was makeup and clothes, but it was more than that—he just inhabits a character and becomes different physically."

Playwright-actress Julie Bovasso, who's known De Niro since he was seven or eight, cast him in her off-off-Broadway comedy *Schubert's Last Serenade*. "For the first week or so of rehearsal I thought, Oh my poor play!" she recalls. "He arrives at his characterization by what sometimes seems like a very circuitous route. He wanted to do one scene while chewing on breadsticks. Dubiously I let him, and for three days I didn't hear a word of my play—it was all garbled up in breadsticks. But I could see something happening, he was making a connection with something, a kind of clown element. At dress rehearsal he showed up without the breadsticks. I said: 'Bobby, where are the breadsticks?' And he said simply: 'I don't need them any more.' "

Something similar happened with the brilliant Bernardo Bertolucci on the filming of *1900* near Parma in northern Italy. "The first few days were a nightmare," says Bertolucci. "But I told myself that what I had felt about Bob when I met him was so strong I couldn't have been wrong. I began to try to help him build confidence, and slowly a fantastic actor emerged. The fact is that with Bob you mustn't judge by the first few days. He's a very sensitive and probably neurotic person, so a director can be fooled. But if one has patience, well, it's worth it."

One director who didn't think it was worth it is Mike Nichols, who fired De Niro from his comedy *Bogart Slept Here*, a project that folded soon after. "Nichols claimed that Bobby was undirectable, which is completely untrue," says Shelley Winters, who first met the young De Niro when he briefly attended the Actors Studio. "He's the most pliable actor I've ever seen—he just has to find his own way to generate it."

Winters played the thirties gangster Ma Barker in *Bloody Mama* and De Niro was her junkie, sadist son Lloyd. "He drove to Arkansas in an old Volkswagen to make tapes of the speech patterns," she recalls. "He lost forty pounds in three months, he got scabs on his face and he'd scratch them. When I had a scene at his grave site he insisted on getting into the grave himself." It was in Winters' own underrated 1970 play *One Night Stands of a Noisy Passenger* that De Niro made his first big stage impression. "It was like watching sexual lightning onstage," she says. "Every night was a different performance."

Not everyone admires De Niro's demonic dedication. George Auld came away from his experience with De Niro on *New York, New York* with mixed feelings. "He has a talent for grasping things like nobody I've ever seen," says Auld. "I couldn't believe he could do that great. He must have listened to the records seven thousand times." But Auld grew to resent De Niro's "obsession" to learn the saxophone, which turned Auld into a "slave." Auld's wife, Diane, says: "We thought he was going to climb in bed with us with the horn." De Niro's unrelenting seriousness was a turnoff for the gregarious fifty-seven-year-old Auld. "He's about as much fun as the clap," says the jazzman. "I called him Mumbles. He reminded me of Benny Goodman when I worked with Benny." Auld's rating on De Niro's sax playing in the film is that "he had the externals, but not the inside stuff. That was a robot up there."

But Liza Minnelli disagrees. She remembers De Niro's constant work on the music through all twenty-two weeks of filming. "At night," she says, "I'd leave the studio at eleven or twelve, and I'd hear the wail of his saxophone. As a musician he was fabulous. The way he found the character, putting it together. I don't think Bobby will forget his musical learning, because he really likes to play the sax." As a matter of fact De Niro now plays his own saxophone. "I bought an alto—it's easier to carry around," he says. "I know the fingering and I'm learning to read a little now. But I like to improvise— I get off on it if I improvise for myself." De Niro has nothing but admiration for Auld and assigns to Liza his highest praise: "She works hard."

The next artist to feel the impact of De Niro's research is Jake LaMotta, the former middleweight champion whose autobiography, *Raging Bull*, will be filmed by Scorsese with a forty-pounds-heavier De Niro. LaMotta will start making a fighter out of De Niro this summer (during the filming of *The Deer Hunter*, the actor's next movie about Vietnam vets in a steel town). "I made him throw some punches," says the champ. "He's a natural, but he's real shy. He hates to show me how much he doesn't know. He's proud. When I get through with him, he'll be able to fight professionally." De Niro picked up LaMotta's book at a low point in the fifty-five-year-old ex-champ's fortunes. "I lived on unemployment for a while," he says. "Bobby came from heaven. He gave me a whole new lease on life. I'll always be indebted to him."

As usual, De Niro is tunneling as deeply into the subject as he can. He's taping interviews with Jake, his opponents, his family. "Fighting actually turns me off," says De Niro. "It's too primitive. But Jake is more complicated than you would think. That style of his—sticking his face out, taking punches, wearing out his opponents. There's got to be some kind of guilt involved in deliberately taking punches." LaMotta says that De Niro "is more qualified to be a psychiatrist than a psychiatrist. He goes very deep. He's telling me things about me that I never knew. I thought I was a bad guy for a while but he made me realize I'm not. I'm a pretty good guy."

There's a certain irony in De Niro's deep probes into LaMotta's psyche. Auld's beloved Mumbles is notorious for his determined protection of his privacy from everyone except his most intimate friends, such as Martin Scorsese, actors Harvey Keitel and Peter Boyle, and Shelley Winters. "There's a great sense of mystery about him on screen," says Liza Minnelli, "and in person he's like that too. There's something very dangerous about him."

"Bobby's a hider," says John Hancock, who directed De Niro in *Bang the Drum Slowly*. "Like a lot of actors, he reveals himself when he can wear a mask. Bobby is very smart but he feels he's not, and in *Bang the Drum Slowly* he tried to show what it was like to be stupid and trying to catch on to other people. To play Bruce Pearson, the catcher, he used stupid eyes. Most actors play a dumb characterization with a wide-eyed, bland look. Bobby really knew what stupid eyes are—you're watching carefully in hopes of finding out what's going on, but you don't want to get caught watching." "Every once in a while," says Jake LaMotta, "I catch him looking at me. He studies me."

"Bobby is a strange, dark figure," says Francis Ford Coppola. "I don't know from where he's looking at me. But I'm comfortable with him. He has the talent and the conceptual ability and he works hard. I would not hesitate to cast Bobby De Niro in any role whatsoever—from a little street rat to Valentino. I think he's going to be one of the major stars and give a whole string of incredible performances. Of course, he likes things I don't like. The only thing we agree on is that I like him but I'm not even sure if we agree on that. I like him but I don't know if he likes himself."

De Niro has just moved to a renovated house in the Brentwood section of Los Angeles, where he lives in forbidding seclusion with his wife, the glowing Diahnne Abbott, a young actress who has appeared in *Taxi Driver* and *Welcome to L.A.* and does a sensational number as a singer in *New York, New York*. They have an infant son, Raphael. "I love my child so much," says De Niro. "It's so great to see him laugh."

The feeling in his voice is direct, clear, strong, and beautiful. There's no mask, no hiding. At this moment De Niro is relieved of his dark mystery, the actor's obsession—to assume the shape and energy of other identities. Great actors are the strangest creations of human culture—what was the impulse that first drove a human being to put on the aspect of another human being?

Obviously such an impulse is an escape and a revelation. De Niro escapes from himself to find himself in another self. Actors who have a genius for this sleight of body are surrogates for the rest of us who are trapped in our own selves. To create a new human being is to re-create the very idea of humanity, to refresh that idea for us who grow stale in our mortality. A crazy cabbie, wanting to hurt a hurtful city; a dying ball player with stupid eyes that will be as smart as anyone's in their last moment of vision; a fighter who wants to be hit because he knows he's his own real adversary—look for Robert De Niro in those selves, and in many more to come.

[1977]

Roger Ebert

KIRK DOUGLAS

"If you become a star, *you* don't change—everybody else does."

This was a restless man. He rocked on the balls of his feet. He looked, turned, looked back to where he'd turned from. Demons were gaining. He peered out the window. Opened the door. Closed the door. Peered out the window. Evoked a pastoral image.

"There was a lovely little picket fence," Kirk Douglas said. "And a mailbox with my name on it, and a soft little carpet of green grass out there in the middle of the desert. It got to be a joke. But I've spent so much of my life on locations that after a while . . . well, we had that goddamn trailer fixed up like a garden spot. The crew members used to compete to see who could think of something new to add."

And that was on . . .

"That was on this one. *There Was a Crooked Man.* The last of my current trilogy and my fiftieth picture. *Jesus!*"

Douglas took a seat on the very edge of the sofa. He leaned forward, his elbows braced on his knees. Then he slammed his hands together, looked down at the carpet, and shook his head.

"Fifty pictures." His voice caressed the words. "That's what it all amounts to, you know. Staying power. I was a star before I even *heard* of Julie Andrews."

He smiled the Kirk Douglas smile, half nostalgic, half rueful, half ferocious.

"I remember meeting Tito once. The English ambassador had been waiting six months to present *his* credentials. Tito sent his private plane to pick me up, and we talked for three hours. Turned out he'd seen just about every one of my movies. He sees one or two movies a night. He said they take his mind off his problems.

"And that's where it's at. That's what movies do. Take *Lonely Are the Brave*. There was a movie that communicated on all levels. Maybe it was anti-Establishment, or maybe it was about a kooky cowboy. A movie like that is so much better than some foreign horseshit about an actor chewing for twenty minutes.

"But you never know. I made a movie two years ago, *A Lovely Way to Die*. They pushed me into it. Kirk, they said, you oughta make a cop picture. It was a bomb. Well, why was *Bullitt* a success? Nobody understood *Bullitt*. It had two good elements in it: the chase and the killing in the bedroom. Otherwise, it was as hard to understand as *Last Year at Marienbad*. I didn't know what *that* was about either. The foreign directors are always fumbling about in obscurity, and the critics are always writing about the juxtaposition of black and white and the existential dilemma and all that shit, to disguise the fact that *they* don't understand the first damn thing about it, either. . . ."

Douglas wore frayed denims, no shirt, boots. Hair long and combed back like Ratso in *Midnight Cowboy*. He'd just come from the set. Now he went into the bedroom of his bungalow on the Warner Brothers lot and came back wearing a blue terry-cloth robe.

"But now, yes, I've made a trilogy I'm proud of. My forty-eighth, forty-ninth, and fiftieth pictures. *The Brotherhood, The Arrangement*, and *There Was a Crooked Man*. It gives me a certain measure of pride to look back at these three pictures and realize I've come this far and remained intact."

He backed into a corner of the room, and stood looking up at the ceiling.

"The Brotherhood. I got a lot of indirect messages from the boys on that one. They wanted to meet me."

The Mafia?

Silence.

He was gently tapping his head against the wall.

You weren't . . . uneasy?

A sharp laugh. He advanced from the corner, sat in a chair. "I know Italians and I like them. A lot of my father's best friends were Italians. I responded to that in making the picture. I put a lot of warmth into that character. Those immigrants were tough, more *intensive* than people are these days. I'd love to discuss the picture with . . . the boys. I'm not interested in movies anyway; I'm interested in people. I love talking to interesting people, people like O. J. Simpson, Andretti . . . I love champions. A champion has something *special* about him."

Douglas was filled with nervous energy, raw vitality. He couldn't sit still. It was in a sense actually wearying to be caged in a room with so much restlessness. Douglas walked halfway across the room and then whirled, fixing me on the quivering tip of a rhetorical point.

"I preceded a lot of this youthful revolution," he said. "And Thoreau did too, back in 1825. Compared to Thoreau, Saint Francis of Assisi was peanuts. And don't get me wrong. There's nothing the matter with building castles in the air. It wasn't so much Thoreau as his philosophy. It's like, you ever heard that song? 'I've Gotta be Me.' "

Douglas sat again on the couch, as the last notes lingered. He was quieter now, subdued, called back to the mortal present.

"Too often," he said slowly, "I have not been what I wanted to be. I've succumbed to pressures. Yes, I have. The things I've done that I liked, I've always done against advice. The bad films everybody was high on. The good films, they advised me against. But . . . by . . . God! From now on, 'I've Gotta be Me!'

"*Champion*, for example. I had a chance to be in a picture with Gregory Peck and Ava Gardner over at Metro. I said, no. I want to make this picture *Champion*. The agents thought I was nuts. On the other hand, I let myself be pushed into *A Lovely Way to Die*, and what a load of shit that was. And *The War Wagon*. Well, *War Wagon* wasn't bad. It was entertainment. I rather enjoyed it. But that woman, Pauline Kael—did you see that piece she wrote about it, about *War Wagon*? If Pauline Kael were sitting here right now," he said, indicating an empty chair, "I'd tell her, you're a bright dame but you're full of shit."

He stood up, continuing to address Miss Kael.

"Don't crucify *me* because of what your idea of a movie star is," he said, pointing a finger at the chair. "I didn't start out to be a movie star. I started out to be an *actor*. You people out in the East have no idea what goes on out here." He punctuated his speech with short thrusts of the finger. "No awareness or knowledge whatsoever. You lose track of the human being behind the image of the movie star."

Leaving Pauline Kael speechless, Douglas turned back to me.

"You know," he said, "sometimes an interviewer will look at me and say—'You're bright!' They're actually surprised I might be bright. Well, I say, What if I wanted to be a writer? I just might be better at it than you are! Ever think of that? There are a lot of journalists who are just plain dumb.

"And I understand what's going on here, for example. The subtleties of the situation. An interview is not simply reporting what somebody said. It's a point of view toward that person. It incorporates the point of view of the interviewer."

He jerked his thumb over his shoulder toward the chair where Pauline Kael was sitting.

"I don't need a critic to tell me I'm an actor," he said. "I make my own way. Nobody's my boss. Nobody's *ever* been my boss. Your only security is in your talent. I didn't get into this business as a pretty boy. I've made good pictures, bad pictures, I've been a maverick, I've never been under contract, except for one year at Warners after *Champion*—I've made my own way!

"You know what it makes me think of sometimes? That picture, *Young Man with a Horn*. Bix Beiderbecke in his lonely personal quest to hit that one unattainable note. I like to play that role. The rebel. The guy fighting against society. The champion!"

Douglas lay down flat on the floor and braced his feet up on top of the coffee table. He rested his head on his hands, and looked up to the ceiling. He talked in a faraway, thoughtful, pensive, reflective, philosophical voice.

"In all dramatic stories," he said, "death is the inevitable end. There aren't many songs you have to sing. They're all variations on a theme. I'm attracted and fascinated by how difficult it is to be an individual. The thing of being a so-called movie star works *against* you. Sure, you can always make exciting pictures, adventure pictures, but when you try something different they dump on you because you're a star. And yet that theme of the individual, fighting against society . . . it's always obsessed me. *Lonely Are the Brave* . . . *Spartacus* . . . *Champion* . . . it doesn't matter if you're a nice guy or you're a bastard. What matters is—you won't bend!"

He swung his legs off the coffee table and rolled over onto his stomach, resting his chin on his hands, sighting along the hallway toward the kitchen, where lunch was being prepared.

"Somebody who *won't bend*. That's what *The Brotherhood* was about. But a star's image is determined by what the public wants. They want me to be tough. A loved enemy. Neither the public nor the critics want you to do something they don't want you to do."

He sat up now, cross-legged on the floor.

"That's why the perfect movie star is John Wayne. I was in a lousy picture with him once, *In Harm's Way*. I used to think about John Wayne that he brings so much authority to a role he can pronounce literally any line in a script and get away with it. But I figured *In Harm's Way* had a line even John Wayne couldn't get away with. It was: 'I need a fast ship because I want to be in harm's way.' I thought, Oh, shit, I've gotta hear him say this line. But you know what? He said it, and he got away with it. Now that's John Wayne. . . ."

Lunch was served: vegetable soup with herbs, relish plate, rolls and butter, cold cuts if you wanted some, but nobody did.

"And there's nothing wrong with a John Wayne movie," he said. "I hate arty-farty pictures. What you always hope to make is a good, honest picture with balls. We did that with *Spartacus*. That was the best big spectacle ever made. *Ben-Hur* made almost three times as much money and didn't even compare. In our spectacle, the characters dominated the setting. It was a picture about men, not production values. Well, it made money. But my best pictures have seldom been my most successful. *Lust for Life* wasn't a big money-maker. *Paths of Glory* has now finally broken even. *Lonely Are the Brave* . . . boy, the nonartists really balled *that* one up. Instead of putting it in a little theater and waiting for the reviews, they shoveled it into saturation bookings before anybody heard about it.

"That's what I mean, it's gotta be me! You got to fight!" He clenched his fist and shook it, and clenched his teeth, too. "In *The Brotherhood*, that great scene in the bedroom with Irene Papas, where I'm drunk and we both have all our clothes on and, Jesus, that scene was erotic! It could have easily fallen on its ass, and Martin Ritt wanted to cut it out of the script, but, no, you got to fight for those things.

"But then you make the money on the others. I was offered a million and a half to star in *The Fall of the Roman Empire*. And you know something? Now that I look back, I was a fool not to take it."

Douglas wasn't hungry. Too wound up. He dabbed at his soup with a roll and finally stood up and paced back and forth, chewing on celery sticks.

"I have a sixteen-millimeter print of every movie I ever made," he said. "It was a fight to get them! But I can look at those prints, fifty prints after this one, and I know there's good stuff there, great things in those pictures, and they can't take that away from me. Like in this forty-ninth picture, *The Arrangement*. A-ha!" He smacked his fist into his palm. "Working with Kazan was a real experience. An actor's director. He relates to the actors. He'll do anything short of committing a homosexual act to get the best out of his actors."

Smack! "But you got to fight for what you believe in. I remember in *The War Wagon*, I fought with them for the nude scene. Remember, where I was walking away from the camera bare-ass? I said that's the only honest way to shoot it. I'm in the sack, see, and John Wayne's knocking at the door, and we've already established that I wear a gun at all times. So we play the whole scene at the door, me with my gun on, and when I walk back to bed you see the gun is the only thing I'm wearing! Great! You put pants on the guy, the scene isn't honest anymore.

"I'm not surprised, though, they wanted to destroy the scene. Dealing with Universal is always . . . well, they are the aces who got me where I lived on *Lonely Are the Brave.* I wanted to call it *The Last Cowboy.* It had a simplicity to it. But the aces put it through a computer and came up with a nothing title. And things like that. . . . And *A Lovely Way to Die* . . . I hated that one. . . . I said, from now on I'm only doing what I want to do. And now, after fifty pictures and the last three damn good ones, it's time to take inventory."

Douglas collapsed on the couch, legs outstretched, heels digging into the carpet, arms crucified on the sofa's back. He sighed.

"I'm getting to be a tired warrior," he said. "I've killed so many Romans, and so many Vikings, and so many Indians."

He sighed again.

"The killing must stop."

A pause. A silence. It became a long silence.

"What I need," he said again, "is a pause to take inventory."

He twisted to lie flat on the sofa, head braced against one arm, feet propped up on the other. "You know what I did the other day?" he said. "I did a crazy thing. I took a walk out there on the back lot at Warners. Back there behind Stage 19. And it was like it was haunted. . . ."

Very slowly, he lifted his feet and swung them around to rest them on the carpet again. And then he rested his elbows on his knees and his chin on his hands and it was like he was looking back in time, remembering other days, other rooms. . . .

"There were staircases," he said. "Dozens of staircases. You've never *seen* so many staircases. And you could imagine ghosts on them. Cagney. Flynn." He chuckled nostalgically. "Bogie." His voice took on a wondering quality. "And you couldn't help thinking, One day these staircases were seething with activity. And as you walked among them, that line of poetry came to your mind. You know, the one about *what town or peaceful hamlet* or something or other. Well, I can't remember how it goes . . . *Ode to a Grecian Urn,* that's the one. And you can't help thinking, Jesus! The ghosts that walk here at night. Because movies are filled with the stuff of everyone's dreams, and you know what a studio is? A dream factory. Staircases . . . barrooms . . . barbershops. . . ."

Another silence. Douglas stood up, put his hands in his pockets, looked out the window. His voice came back over his shoulder.

"And then it occurred to me; hell, I'm a star, too. And the final test is staying power. After forty-seven pictures, I was still in there, still working in interesting movies. I was glad I had those sixteen-millimeter prints. It's a rough business. You lose that freshness. It's a struggle to stay alive in every picture . . . and, hell, I don't know.

"I turned down *Stalag 17*; Holden won an Oscar. I turned down *Cat Ballou*; Marvin won the Oscar. But, hell, you never know. Decision making . . . I'll tell you one thing. Five pictures in a row like *Paths of Glory*, and I'd have been out of business. And then when you *try* something ambitious, like when I went back to Broadway in Kesey's *One Flew Over the Cuckoo's Nest*. Van Heflin warned me. He said, 'They hate actors who've made it. They'll kick you in the ass if they can.' But, hell, I was just like any other regular fellow making a couple of million a year." He laughed at that. "I knew Kesey early on, and then I met him again later. I did the play because I believed in it. But, Kesey . . . Christ, I don't give a shit what anybody does. But to destroy a talent is wholly unjustified. God, Kesey looked bad when I saw him again.

"There is something sad and dramatic about the disintegration of a talent. At the start, Brando was the best. And now . . . well, it was a damn shame he had to miss with Kazan. Kazan, of course, wanted Brando to play the lead in *The Arrangement*. The two of them, together again. But after Kazan talked with Brando, he felt Brando wasn't quite with it . . . didn't have the old enthusiasm . . . but, hell, I don't want to get into that. And yet, you know something!"

Douglas turned away from the window now and sat on the floor. His knees were pulled up and he bridged them with his arms.

"Being a star doesn't really change you. If you become a star, *you* don't change—everybody else does. Personally, I keep forgetting I'm a star. And then people look at me and I'm reminded. But you just have to remember one thing: The best eventually go to the top. I think I'm in the best category, and I'll stay at the top or I'll do something else. I'm not for the bush leagues. I remember as a kid of twenty, on Broadway, I had a chance to take a good role with a road company, or stay in New York playing a walk-on and an offstage echo. I stayed. I wanted that association with champions."

Douglas looked up almost fiercely.

"Champions!"

The next morning, the door to his elaborate home was opened by a maid who hadn't been informed that anyone had an appointment with Mr. Douglas. The housekeeper also looked suspicious. They thought perhaps a mistake had been made. A misunderstanding. Perhaps if . . .

"Hi, I know who you are," Peter Douglas said. "He's okay," Peter told the servants. "Come on in here and have a seat. I knew you were coming. I like to keep in touch around here. . . ."

Peter was perhaps twelve, sandy-haired, personable, looked like his father. He wore tennis shoes and a T-shirt.

"Dad'll be down after a while," he said. "You want some pretzels? No? I'd offer you something else, but at the moment" (he sighed dramatically) "it's pretzels and that's it."

Peter shrugged his shoulders stoically. "Know the one I'd like to make a movie out of? *Fail-Safe.* I'm Peter, by the way. I'm just a slave here."

Peter headed toward the pool. The room he left was a sort of den and library, half open to the living room and the bar. There were several animal skins on the floor, and a two-year run of *Time* laid flat on a shelf with the spines overlapped. And there were a lot of books on the shelves, and a display of primitive carvings and statues, and—

"How about a cup of coffee?" Douglas said. He had entered silently on bare feet. "It'll be here in a minute." He grinned in anticipation. "That first cup . . . ah!"

He touched one of the skins with a bare toe. "How do you like that leopard skin?" he said. "Isn't it a beauty?" He sat down and his voice became serious. "What a terrible thing it is to kill. I impulsively went on one safari. I thought, Jesus, I can't shoot an animal. But once we left Nairobi, I discovered the real me. A killer. I shot about thirty animals. I was shocked and embarrassed. I was confused. I asked myself, *Do I really want to kill?* The philosophers say, know thyself. But what really counts is how honest and how brave you are. You ask of a man, where is he strong? Where is he weak? The bully with the low voice may be secretly frightened. . . ."

The coffee came, and with it a plate of chocolate-chip cookies. Douglas picked up his saucer in his hand, sipped, considered his cup. "The home of the brave," he said finally. "What a violent nation we are! A violent people. *That's* why there's so much violence in the movies. The Greeks had a word for it. It's a catharsis. Audiences love gangsters. Virtue is not photogenic. Christ, even Disney bakes people into cookies."

He paused to nibble a chocolate-chip, and then held it up. "Great? The best! They have to be. They're made by my cook. But the West . . . there was a certain simplicity and directness there."

He leaped to his feet, balanced the coffee cup in his left hand, adopted a shoot-out stance (legs wide, right hand poised) and snarled: "Smile when you say that!" Then he shook his head in resignation. "It's childlike," he said. "No one can be an artist without a childlike quality. If I were really sophisticated, how could I, a grown-up man, carry a gun in a movie?"

He put down his cup and picked up one of the primitive statues in the room. "Take this," he said. "Childlike in its innocence. Look here. On this side, you can see it's a woman. And then you turn it around and, well, on this side, it's pretty obviously a man. It has an innocent bisexuality. It comes from a society where all things mix naturally together.

"Reminds me." He sat down again, still considering the statue in his hands. "Kubrick once had this great idea. We'd make the world's greatest pornographic film. Spend millions on it. And then maybe only show it in one country, like Switzerland, and fly people in to see it. Kubrick. A great director. I thank him for so much that is good in *Paths of Glory* and *Spartacus*. You know, at one time with *Paths of Glory*, even Kubrick wanted to cop out. He wanted to rewrite the script, make it a sort of B picture, a commercial thing. But I'm glad we stood by our guns. There's a picture that will always be good, years from now. I don't have to wait fifty years to know that; I know it *now*. Certain pictures have a universality of theme. *Champion* did. Audiences are all the same. They love the guy who's up there on top. And yet, you know, in real life. . . ." He sighed and finished his coffee.

"Somebody asked me not long ago if I was going to write my autobiography. Well, I have one good enough reason. I'd write it for my four sons. But nobody else would be interested. My life's too corny and typical to make a good autobiography. I wouldn't even do it as a movie. My life's a B script. My life. The violins playing . . . the kid who didn't have enough to eat . . . the parents who were Russian immigrants. . . .

"I taught my mother to write her name. It's like my parents came out of the Middle Ages, and in one generation I jumped to here." He indicated the room with a sweep of his hand. "My parents did the one essential thing. They didn't miss the boat. I grew up in Amsterdam, New York. My parents never did understand my success. I'd say, 'Ma! I just signed a million-dollar contract!' 'But son,' she'd say, 'you look so thin. . . .' "

He leaned forward intensely. "And yet my mother was a great woman," he said. "She had little formal knowledge, but she knew much about life. They used to come to her with sores, with boils. She'd take an old, moldy loaf of bread and apply it to the sore, as a poultice. And this was years before penicillin."

He gave a wry twist to his mouth. "My life," he said, "a B picture. And yet my life is an American life. Because the real American life, the typical one, *is* a B picture. Like mine—the kid who worked up from abject poverty to become a champion. But you got to fight! Our forefathers set the bar so high we keep trying to go under it, instead of over. . . ."

He stood up again now, and looked out the window to where two of his sons were swimming in the backyard pool.

"Look at those kids," he said. "Olympic material."

He smiled, watching as Peter did a racing dive off the edge of the pool. Then he spoke again, slowly. "At this period in my life," he said, "I look at this trilogy, these last three pictures, and I must admit I feel I'm functioning well. You have to set your own standards. I was nominated for *Champion.* Broderick Crawford won that year. I was nominated for *Lust for Life*, but Yul Brynner won. You set your own standards. You have to. And then these arty-farty foreign movies come along, and—"

He whirled and strode away from the window, his fist slamming into his palm. The softness was gone from his voice; he was angry.

"You know why they criticize me?" he said. "I'm criticized because I can jump over two horses! And they sneer. *Hollywood,* they say. Hollywood. Well I for one am plenty proud of Hollywood. They go over there to Europe and they forget their roots and they lose the nourishment of Hollywood. I say if you want to grow a plant, put it where there's some good horseshit to grow it in!"

He walked rapidly toward the bookcase, and indicated a set of matched volumes. "See those?" he said. "It's a rare edition: *150 Years of Boxing.* It's all in there, and it's all the same. Acting is like prizefighting. The downtown gyms are smelly, but that's where the champions are."

[1970]

Dave Kehr

CLINT EASTWOOD

Probably the first self-conscious actor/*auteur* in the history of the American genre film.

Clint Eastwood, the actor, has achieved such a spectacular level of success that Clint Eastwood, the director, can do whatever he damn well feels like. Which is exactly what he's done with *The Gauntlet:* throwing nearly every contemporary conception of cinematic propriety to the wind, Eastwood has produced one of the most eccentric, original, and downright audacious American films in quite some time.

Eastwood is probably the only American male star who can still conjure teeming hordes at the box office by simply putting his name above the title (Barbra Streisand, alas, being his female counterpart). Unlike Charles

Bronson, who stumbled into superstardom only to lose his way in a series of poorly chosen, undemanding projects, Eastwood has lent his success to a number of artistically adventurous undertakings—films like Don Siegel's *The Beguiled,* a perversely lyrical Gothic horror story set in the Civil War South, which never would have stood a chance without Eastwood's name to give it credence. Eastwood is a star of the old school: following the Waynes and Stewarts, he has developed a mythic presence through his screen roles, graduating from the status of a mere actor to the higher plane of cultural icon. As a performer, he *means* something, standing for a particular collection of attitudes and ideals culled from the collective unconscious of the moviegoing public.

But where Wayne and Stewart were largely content to function as elements in other people's creations (most notably John Ford's), Eastwood has taken his myth into his own hands—he is probably the first self-conscious actor/*auteur* in the history of the American genre film. By making his own movies and exercising an unnatural degree of discretion in his choice of roles in other directors' projects, Eastwood obviously participates in the creation of his own screen image, but he does more than that: he examines the cultural role that has been forced upon him, looking for its implications, exposing its shortcomings, probing for its strengths. *The Gauntlet* is a movie about the classic American action hero—as embodied, in particular, by Clint Eastwood. Eastwood likes some of the things he sees, dislikes others and looks for ways to correct them. Running *The Gauntlet* along with Shockley—the down-and-out, alcoholic cop Eastwood plays in the film—are past Eastwood roles, among them Sergio Leone's Man With No Name (from *A Fistful of Dollars*, *For a Few Dollars More*, and *The Good, the Bad, and the Ugly*) and Don Siegel's *Dirty Harry* (rerun in *Magnum Force* and *The Enforcer*).

The gauntlet is a (hopefully) now archaic form of military punishment: the offender's fellow officers would form two lines, and, armed with clubs, chains, or whatever, try their best to beat the victim to a pulp as he ran between them. The title refers specifically to a sequence at the end of the film, but the image of the gauntlet—an attack directed from both sides, a punishment, and, in some sense, a ritual of purification—gives the film its structure. Eastwood's Shockley is a boozy, not too bright Phoenix cop who still clings desperately to a romantic self-image, inherited, no doubt, from Clint Eastwood movies: in his mind, he's a fiercely independent, supernaturally competent professional, whose lonely lot it is to protect society from itself. An inspector tells him, "You get the job done," and Shockley proudly parrots the phrase whenever his identity is on the line, as it is throughout most of the movie. Sent to Las Vegas to pick up "a nothing witness for a nothing trial," Shockley finds that he's been set up by a corrupt official: the witness, a young prostitute (nicely played by Sondra Locke), has information that ties the Phoenix police to the Vegas mob, and soon she and Shockley are caught in the middle, running the gauntlet from Vegas to Phoenix with the cops lined up on one side, the outfit on the other.

Caught in the middle, of course, is the classic posture of the American action hero. The tradition of the alienated hero runs back in American popular culture at least as far as James Fenimore Cooper's Leatherstocking Tales—"caught in the middle" between civilization and savagery, the action hero bridges a fundamental gap in the American character, between the comforts of conformity and the lure of anarchic freedom. It's a division so crucial that for two hundred years we've been telling the same story to explain it to ourselves—the story of the Indian scout who leads the settlers through the wilderness, but who can never belong to the group; the story of the detective who risks everything to protect his middle-class client, but who can never enter the middle-class world because he knows too much about another, darker one. The outsider exercises such a powerful sway over the national imagination because in him, the extremes are reconciled and the contradictions smoothed—he is both shopkeeper and outlaw, churchgoer and killer, the successful embodiment of two very different sets of yearnings. In his majestically aloof pose, he is responsible for protecting law and order and everything we hold dear; yet he personally is responsible for nothing—he has no wife to support, no kids to feed, and a life of perfect freedom before him.

The outsider is a useful figure, but he is also juvenile, hopelessly romantic, and completely divorced from the world as we know it. In clinical terms, he's a clear psychotic—a screaming paranoid, a raving megalomaniac. That, more or less, is the Shockley we see in Eastwood's credit sequence. In a marvelously ambiguous image, Shockley emerges from a seedy all-night bar and crosses the street to his car. It's dawn, and with the rising sun behind him, Shockley is momentarily silhouetted in a mythic pose—he could be Wyatt Earp, walking down Main Street on his way to the OK Corral. And, no doubt, that's just how Shockley sees himself at that moment. But after a long, reflective drive through the deserted city streets that Philip Marlowe would have relished, Shockley arrives at police headquarters, opens the door of his car, and watches in pain as a half-empty bottle of Jack Daniel's falls out and smashes on the pavement.

Shockley is an icon, not a human being, and consequently his redemption will be more symbolic than psychological. Following the classic model of American filmmaking, Eastwood alternates scenes of character conflict with action sequences that work out the characters' tensions. During the trip from Vegas to Phoenix, Shockley and the prostitute, Gus Mally, fall in love

(TOP LEFT) Robert De Niro: *He suggests positive energy that has been perverted.*
(*Taxi Driver.* Courtesy of Columbia Pictures.)

(BOTTOM LEFT) W. C. Fields: *Author of his own life.*

(RIGHT) Kirk Douglas: *"I like to play the guy fighting against society."*
(*Young Man with a Horn.* © Warner Bros. Inc. All rights reserved. Used by permission.)

Clint Eastwood:
The traditional alienated
hero caught in the middle.
(Escape from Alcatraz.
Copyright © MCMLXXIX by
Paramount Pictures Corporation.
All rights reserved.)

(somehow that almost goes without saying), and that relationship will give him the means to abandon the heroic pose and reenter society. But the courtship is conducted without hugs and kisses; like Bogart and Bacall in Hawks's *Big Sleep*, Shockley and Mally circle each other for a while, testing reflexes and reactions. Affection grows in the moments of physical danger, as Shockley learns to respect and depend on Mally's superior intelligence, and as she learns to respect his dogged determination.

While Shockley emerges as a more vulnerable, dependent, and—in short—believable character, the action sequences become more stylized, abstract, and—in short—unbelievable. The three central action scenes (set, with perfect structural precision, first in Las Vegas, then on the state line, and finally in Phoenix) all employ the same image: a squad of armed men blasting a target (respectively, a house, a car, and a bus) into literal smithereens. The odds become more and more outrageous, but Shockley survives by never firing a shot. His genius isn't the traditional capacity for skillful violence of, say, an Errol Flynn: it's the humbler, more prosaic one of sheer tenacity. You can kick him, you can shoot him, but you can't keep a good schmuck down. As Eastwood makes his final approach on the courthouse, driving a hijacked tour bus with his lover/witness by his side and one half of the Phoenix police force blasting away at him with rifles and machine guns, the great, dumb, lumbering bus becomes the perfect image of the Eastwood character: sublime in its stubbornness, creeping slowly toward its goal, ridiculous but somehow noble. Eastwood achieves a remarkable tone here: the climax is widly exhilarating but still gently funny, as Shockley climbs from the bus, bruised, bleeding but triumphant, followed by Mally, still proudly clutching the box of red roses that he gave her in a dimly remembered quiet moment. Dirty Harry has come through the wringer, much diminished but with a self-respect that is his own, now, and not that of a pop culture god.

Every frame of *The Gauntlet* contradicts the current prejudice toward film "realism"—Eastwood plainly enjoys style for its own sake, and his is something to be enjoyed, making use of a light, mobile camera, a dynamic montage technique (most skillfully in a helicopter chase sequence), and an appropriate respect for the integrity of the Panavision frame. The escalating outrageousness of the action is deliberate, controlled, and effective, but Eastwood has paid the usual price for daring to be different: *The Gauntlet* has received some of the worst reviews of his career. Don't believe them. *The Gauntlet* looks like a cop movie out of control, but it's really the best love story of 1977—and there's nothing more audacious than that.

[1978]

Richard Schickel

DOUGLAS FAIRBANKS

Our first urbane movie hero.

It takes an urban culture to produce a Douglas Fairbanks and, in truth, he was our first urbane movie hero. The "difficult discipline" he underwent and the "elaborate system of knowledge" he acquired to lay claim to our admiring attention, were utterly different from those of the Westerner. Fairbanks' skills were acquired not through communion with nature, but in the artificial atmosphere of the gymnasium. Similarly, his manner. Not for him the granitic countenance, the leisurely pace, the slowness of emotion which belong to the man attuned to nature's rhythm. Instead, he was quick, breezy, cheerfully optimistic, shallowly bright—a city man, a man whose business was business. He was, both onscreen and off, an indoors man at a time when America was becoming an indoors nation. On the screen he proved to his audience that there need be nothing unmanly about its new way of life, that, whatever its critics might say, decent values could continue to exist, even flourish, in the new environment. Indeed, he implied that they could be adorned with a new grace and wit and style.

"At a difficult time in American history," Alistair Cooke writes, "Douglas Fairbanks appeared to know all the answers and knew them without pretending to be anything more than 'an all around chap, just a regular American.'" How comforting this was to a nation standing on the brink of a war in which it was clear that for the first time the courage of the new America would be tested in the ancient manner—trial by combat.

We tend to remember Fairbanks in terms of the romantic costume epics he produced for himself in the twenties. In war's aftermath Fairbanks, the canny showman, was among the first to sense the shift in taste from the everyday settings and situations of the flickers' early days toward highly romanticized material. Taking advantage of this, he leaped with his customary easy grace backward in time to distant places, but however he costumed himself he remained very much the same "Doug" he had always been. This personality was created in a single year, 1916, when he made eleven films— more than a quarter of his total output—on the Triangle lot. There, Fairbanks, an irrepressible prankster, and an equally irrepressible gymnast, was encouraged to set his own pace, work out his own athletic improvisations on basically simple scripts. If, as some have suggested, the basic concern of Americans is not with end product but with process, then it was at the moment of these improvisations that Fairbanks achieved real greatness in our eyes. It was not important where or why Doug was going; what was important was *how* he went. Man is great, said Emerson, "not in his goals but in his transitions." Fairbanks, even in his late, mannered work, was the greatest maker of transitions in screen history.

[1962]

Penelope Gilliatt

W. C. FIELDS

He plays the muttering straight man to Life.

Not everyone responds to Fields, but the people who do love him recognize a blood brother. He is one of life's losers, and the hell with it. He is not in the race. Fields is truly debonair and his own man, a covert friend to mongrels and a brilliant enemy to privilege, hiding affliction under a far-off and sulfurous view all his own. He is Chaplin's diametric opposite. Chaplin's little man can seem to be on his knees and begging for sympathy with his bravely managed suffering, but Fields is on his feet and thinking. ("It is much more easy to have sympathy with suffering than it is to have sympathy with thought," wrote Oscar Wilde in an essay on Socialism.) Fields is a smoldering independent who asks no pity and who saves himself with eccentrically conceived and harmless vengeances.

In *It's a Gift*—which has been turning up regularly at the art houses, along with the other Fields works—he tries hard to run a grocery store that is eventually flooded with molasses by Baby LeRoy. Fields lets the little saboteur go unscathed. The incident merely adds a baleful new jot to his analysis of the human condition, and the notice that he hangs on the door of his wrecked shop mildly reads, Closed on Account of Molasses.

Surrounded by virago wives, soppy girls, and overblessed children, he deals unexceptionably with the immediate situations, walks away with a skeptical expression somewhere around the hips, and implies that the better part of his considerable brain is disreputably engaged with other things. His battleship wife, Mrs. Bissonette ("pronounced Bissonay," he writes loyally on a placard, obeying her haywire snob teaching), makes him halve a sandwich that he then has to eat in the middle of a storm of cushion feathers. She yells, never satisfied, that these were her *mother's* feathers. But Fields has secretly won, all the same, for even if he is getting hell for obligingly eating a stingy half sandwich full of feathers, he is also eating the half sandwich that contains the complete sandwich's ration of meat, which he has neatly swiped from his own greedy child during the forced act of partition.

Fields often has a bad time, but he is no victim. He is fortified because he always holds an opinion, even if the opinion isn't exactly communicated in speech as we know it. Fields doesn't so much speak as amuse himself with self-addressed soliloquies. The to-and-fro of less doughty men is not for him. His is only the fro. In his great films he is always the reactor. He plays the muttering straight man to Life, the counterblow to a punch in the stomach. His surreal retorts are conceived for himself alone, like his endearments and his curses.

In *Million Dollar Legs,* as the weight-lifting president of an otherwise rather weedily athletic state called Klopstokia, he tries to do something about the economy and simultaneously deals with his dopey daughter's suitors. One of them is visible out of his window. "What's his name, Angela?" he says, with native distaste for his own offspring's name, though his hungover Richard Tauber voice suggests that the seraphic fib committed at her christening is only the way of the world and scarcely worth reacting against. "I call him 'sweetheart,'" says Angela. "Hey, sweetheart!" yells Fields vaguely out the window, and thereafter he is so beguiled by the wooziness of the word that he applies it to various sports trainers and members of his Cabinet throughout the film.

No one can use endearments more dangerously than Fields. *"Please sit down, honey!"* he bawls at a blind man who is in the process of exploding a pile of electric light bulbs by feeling around him with a white stick. If this sounds a particle cruel, the next sequence shows Fields covering his eyes with terror at the sight of the same man weaving his way through traffic. Secretly alert to everything, Fields pretends to a protective callousness. His kindnesses are clandestine; his open and implacable hostility is beamed at the fortunate, the armor-plated, and the prissy. This axis includes Deanna Durbin-like stars, mayors, milk, gambling laws, literal-minded listeners, and soupy women, among whom I think he would have put the nurses who tried once, in real life, to look after his own broken neck and were waved away ("It's only a flesh wound") with stories about far worse calamities that had befallen him and that he had survived with the help of "Doctor Buck-halter's Kidney Reviver."

At the last ditch, which was where he lived from toddling age, Fields took refuge in improvisation, in wild names, in veiled ripostes to child stars whom he sensed to be looking after number one far better than he had ever managed to, and in a huge ration of carefully selected booze. When a friend of mine once met him, he was drinking three martinis for breakfast and looking at a rose garden. He preferred martinis to anything else. He told her carefully (she was about eight) that Scotch could begin to taste like medicine and that bourbon led to drunkenness. He genuinely hated drunks for their vehemence and mawkishness—two things that this calmly out-of-step and stoic man despised. As his biographer Robert Lewis Taylor has recorded, he always used to take a martini shaker to the studio. He would say that it was filled with pineapple juice. Somebody mischievously once put actual pineapple juice into it. "Somebody's been putting pineapple juice into my pineapple juice!" he yelled. But he never failed to turn up for shooting, and he generally finished days ahead of schedule. One of the many reasons he drank seems to have been that he was frightened of making the subtly understood technical miscalculation of speaking his lines too fast, which he never did when he wasn't cold sober.

He had an outlaw's gift that was matched by no other comedian. Faced by the conventional breakfast, he would suddenly ad-lib an inviting burble suggesting that ordinary food might as well go out the window. "How'd you like to hide the egg and gurgitate a few saucers of mocha-java!" he mutters convivially in one film. He liked words very much. "Sars'parilla" engaged him. So did "my little plum," and "kumquats," and a game he called "squidgalum," and an uncle called "Effingham Hoofnickel," and foggy snatches as descriptive narrative out of the blue: "She dips her mitt down into this mélange. . . ."

He can make gracious sentences to the dignitaries who are his natural enemy. "I am Dr. Eustace P. McGargle," he says, elegantly switching from gambling to preaching in the presence of a mayor. "Perhaps you've read my book on the evils of wagering. . . . I was a victim of this awful scourge. A helpless pawn in the coils of Beelzebub. Beelzebub . . . Beel-zee-bub . . . Lucifer."

His famous puffy nose was a source of distress to him. Most people believed the misshapenness to be due to drink, but it was really because of the bashing and pounding it had taken when he was a child living in ditches. He slips in a revealing line somewhere: "The man had a rather prominent proboscis, after the fashion of eminent men."

Fields allowed himself no sympathy and he joined no one. He was the author of his own life, and he behaved as though he had no kin. It isn't surprising that new generations have loved him, and that a record of clips from his sound tracks is on the hit parade. The fact that it is No. 41 on the list is something he would probably have quite relished. He never wanted anyone else's favors. He had the wiser trick of extending a license to himself, and he died an agnostic, without help, as he promised he would. "I'll go without knuckling under," he droned once, about believing in God.

[1969]

George Morris

ERROL FLYNN

Flynn was not afraid to drop the mask of the dashing rogue, allowing his fans a glimpse of vulnerability.

Errol Flynn was a true original. Douglas Fairbanks may have been the prototype for the swashbuckling roles Flynn inherited, but it is doubtful that Fairbanks could have equaled the diversity and range Flynn brought to such roles as George Custer, James Corbett, and Mike McComb. Flynn played the devil-may-care adventurer better than anyone else, but his most interesting performances revealed the dark underside of this image. In many of his roles, Flynn was not afraid to drop the mask of the dashing rogue, allowing his fans a glimpse of a vulnerability and helplessness akin to that of a small boy lost in a man's world.

The comparisons with Fairbanks are inevitable, but the differences in their respective personae are illuminating. Fairbanks was a prototype formed during the halcyon days of the silent cinema. Stars of his era seemed to be from another planet, so remote were their public images from the everyday world of most viewers. When sound revolutionized the industry, however, the distance between audiences and stars narrowed, resulting in a demand for more recognizable, lifelike idols. Thirties moviegoers wanted Joan Blondell instead of Theda Bara, James Cagney over John Gilbert, and Errol Flynn rather than Douglas Fairbanks.

Most of the time, Flynn *was* larger than life; he indisputably had that intangible element known as "star quality." But he was also human. He descended from the Mount Olympus of movie stardom often enough to be acceptable to changing mores and audience standards.

Flynn was also fortunate in his timing. People went to the movies during the Depression to forget the financial turmoil rippling through the nation. They wanted escape and adventure, and in 1935, when an incredibly attractive young man swung across the screen on the rigging of a pirate vessel for the first time, he connected with this audience. Flynn's dash and vigor inspired the young, excited the women, and rejuvenated the men. Flynn's low-key acting style made it easy for audiences to identify with him, so that the more idealistic males in the audience strutted out of movie houses, convinced that any derring-do Flynn could do, they could at least *dream* about doing better.

Flynn's immense popularity with his female audience cannot be underestimated. Flynn's appeal to women was a curious mixture of mock chivalry and sexual aggression. Extending a tradition begun by Cagney's grapefruit uppercut to Mae Clarke in 1931, there is an undercurrent of hostility and indifference in Flynn's attitude toward women running throughout his films. However, his undeniable charm and impudence mesmerized the ladies, serving as vital restraints in preventing this aggressive attitude from lapsing into overt misogyny. His ardent wooing of Olivia de Havilland often seems tongue-in-cheek, and his most passionate vows of love are always mitigated by the vanity and ego he exudes in every scene. Richard Schickel has described Flynn's onscreen technique as "using the act of love as an act of aggression," a comparison that reflected Flynn's offscreen reputation as well.

Flynn's hell-raising screen image coincided with a private life that was punctuated with peccadilloes and various scandals, all of which were juicily detailed in fan magazines and newspapers. A scandalous paternity suit brought against him in the early forties merely increased his box-office power. These offscreen escapades reinforced his fans' preconceptions and aroused the curiosity of others.

The rebel aspect was always an important part of Flynn's screen persona in any case. He played a rebel of one kind or another in almost all of his best films. There is a strong antiauthoritarian impulse hovering beneath the surface of his most interesting characterizations—an impulse that usually emerges at a crucial moment in the narrative. He rebels against the tyranny of James II in *Captain Blood*, forges orders to make the *Charge of the Light Brigade*, is an intractable recalcitrant in *The Sisters*, and burns a Union payroll in *Silver River*. Numerous Flynn vehicles find him disobeying orders from

Errol Flynn: *Robin Hood . . . the defiant, colorful antiauthoritarian figure.*
(*The Adventures of Robin Hood.* Copyright © 1938 Warner Brothers. Renewed 1965 by
United Artists Television. All rights reserved.)

those higher in authority. Who is Robin Hood anyway, but one of the most defiant, colorful antiauthoritarian folklore figures?

Flynn's personal life, before stardom as well as during it, provided a rich source of experiences for the actor to utilize in his roles. Like a great many stars, the distinction between Flynn's private and public image was often blurred. The adventurer and the lover worked both sides of the screen. The reality often reflected the illusion, and the illusion reinforced the reality in the minds of a most susceptible and willing public.

[1975]

George Morris

HENRY FONDA

The roles which adhere most closely to the public's image of Fonda are the least interesting of his career.

In Sergio Leone's *Once Upon a Time in the West*, a homesteader and his two children are spreading a picnic in their front yard. This frontier idyll is shattered by the materialization of five menacing figures, who kill the family in cold blood. The sense of violation is exacerbated by the familiar, reassuring smile on the face of the leader of these merciless specters. It's the smile of young Abe Lincoln, Tom Joad, Wyatt Earp, and Mister Roberts, a smile which for four decades in American movies has reflected the honesty, moral integrity, and egalitarian values synonymous with its owner—Henry Fonda.

By casting him as an almost abstract personification of evil in 1969, Leone dramatically reversed the prevailing image of Fonda, at once complicating and commenting on our responses to that image. But as Michael Kerbel points out in his perceptive book on the actor, Leone's choice had its precedents. Fonda had already portrayed gunslingers of questionable morality in such Westerns as *Warlock* (1959) and *Firecreek* (1968). And in one particularly inspired piece of casting, Otto Preminger chose the actor to play Robert Leffingwell, the controversial figure whose nomination by the president for secretary of state precipitates the political melodramatics in *Advise and Consent* (1962).

By the sixties, Fonda's image had become so fixed and secure that such modulations and reversals had a remarkable dramatic effect. For most moviegoers, he will always represent the highest manifestation of the rustic American. In his formative films under John Ford—*Young Mr. Lincoln* (1939), *Drums Along the Mohawk* (1939), *The Grapes of Wrath* (1940), and *My Darling Clementine* (1946)—he projects an incorruptible strength of will, a tireless dedication to the pursuit of truth, justice, and equality for all. He even has the features of a pioneer. His lean frame, the lanky walk with its awkward grace, the open, handsome face, and penetrating eyes that inspire confidence and trust—all are eloquent reminders of a rural America and the basic virtues associated, however romantically, with that heritage.

These qualities form the foundation of the Fonda persona which has evolved through nearly a hundred films since his screen debut in 1935 in *The Farmer Takes a Wife.* Like most great movie stars, he developed and sustained this image over the years, shaping it to a point where it could simultaneously accommodate the embodiment of American values Ford celebrates in *Young Mr. Lincoln* and the darker vision of a Sergio Leone. But even Ford recognized that the actor had a dark side. In *The Grapes of Wrath*, an undercurrent of violence runs through his performance as Tom Joad, periodically erupting and eventually isolating him from his family and society. As Fritz Lang did three years earlier, in *You Only Live Once,* Ford links the release of these violent impulses to Fonda's outrage and helplessness in the face of class inequities and social injustices.

It was Ford who finally provided Fonda with a role which more or less liberated the contradictions in his screen persona. In 1948 he cast him as Colonel Owen Thursday in *Fort Apache*, the first part of the director's magnificent cavalry trilogy. Loosely modeled after General George Armstrong Custer, Thursday is really the first character of Fonda's career whose actions and behavior are morally ambiguous. The actor brilliantly captures both the narrow rigidity of this martinet and his higher sense of duty and honor, and his performance is amplified throughout by Ford's own ambivalent attitude toward the man and the tragic consequences of his command.

In a way the roles which adhere most closely to the public's image of Fonda are the least interesting of his career. The 1955 movie version of *Mister Roberts*, for instance, contains one of his blander performances. The actor reportedly replaced the director, Ford, with Mervyn LeRoy, because his former mentor was drastically altering the original play (whose success on Broadway in the late forties had revitalized Fonda's career). Ironically, what one remembers from *Mister Roberts*, an inferior film by any standards, is the galvanizing trio of James Cagney, William Powell, and Jack Lemmon. Not that Fonda is bad in the movie; he has never given an unprofessional or embarrassing performance. Even when physically and temperamentally miscast, as Tolstoy's confused idealist Pierre in Vidor's *War and Peace* (1956), Fonda manages to communicate total belief and authority in what he is doing.

And he has done so much that is memorable. His laconic delivery of dialogue and wide-eyed incredulity have always made him as ideal for comedy as he is for drama. Preston Sturges certainly realized this when he cast him as the ingenuous ophiologist who succumbs to Barbara Stanwyck's charms in *The Lady Eve* (1941). Fonda makes it look so easy, too. His relaxed manner before the camera belies the intensity he brings to parts like the tormented war veteran in Preminger's *Daisy Kenyon* (1947), the all-too-vulnerable police commissioner in Don Siegel's *Madigan* (1968), and especially, the bewildered victim of a Kafkaesque nightmare in Hitchcock's *The Wrong Man* (1957). This last is one of my personal favorites among his films. Fonda's innate decency and moral rectitude have never seemed so threatened, nor his control over the darker edges of his personality more precarious. It is truly an extraordinary performance by one of the finest actors in the history of the American cinema.

[1979]

Jack Kroll

JANE FONDA

Her very behavior seems to mean something even before we connect it with the role she's playing.

"I love you, Julia." It's the ultimate movie cliché line, heard a million times with only the name changing through the alphabet from Arlene to Zenobia. And in Fred Zinnemann's new film, *Julia*, it's uttered as it so often has been on a romantic hillside, with nature beaming down on two beautiful young people in the sweetness of their bond. but in *Julia*, it is spoken by one woman to another, and that is likely to make it the most significant line of the year. The love that Lillian (Jane Fonda) is expressing for Julia (Vanessa Redgrave) is the deep friendship of one woman for another, a relationship

that films have notoriously been ignoring while finding new variations on the male buddyhood that made Redford and Newman the fun couple of the decade. *Julia* supposedly signals a new deal for women in films, in which they'll no longer be satellites to men but suns and stars in their own right. . . .

When Jane Fonda exclaims with real happiness, "Oh, just to be able to play in scenes with another woman. And that people will see a movie about women who think and who care for each other," you know she's thinking ruefully about Jane Fonda, the cute daughter of Henry Fonda, the cute ingenue of *Tall Story*, the sweet slut of *Walk on the Wild Side*, the comic-strip porno kitten of *Barbarella*. The story of Jane Fonda is almost as good as the story of Lillian and Julia. "Back in the fifties," she says, "you had to be sexy, glamorous, and if you were those things then you could become successful as an actress. Women weren't like a James Dean, a Montgomery Clift, or a Marlon Brando who said, 'Screw that stereotype, I'm going to be what I am.' Women didn't have enough power to do that. So I opted to become what they told me I should become if I was going to be a successful actress. And to my amazement it worked."

It worked, but success didn't smell so sweet. "You think, Well, I did it," says Fonda. "Then you begin to realize, so what? I'm not the actress I should have been. People whom I respect don't respect me. My father was very loyal, but he didn't approve of some of the films I did. And suddenly I'm thirty years old and what am I doing with my life anyway?" Fonda recalls when she was making *Any Wednesday* and her brother Peter was shooting a motorcycle-gang movie called *The Wild Angels*: "One night I'd come home from some idiotic scene I was doing and Peter comes rolling in on his motorcycle. He was at the beginning of his counterculture trip. He'd just finished a scene where there was this huge fight in a church and he had this guitar with him and he was writing songs. And I realized that at least he was relating to *something* that had to do with the American culture, while I was making this ridiculous movie about a young mistress of a married executive."

Marriage to the charming, faintly sinister and intelligently decadent Roger Vadim (whom she now calls the "crazy Russian") was no solution. Vadim, who had been married to Brigitte Bardot, tried to turn Jane into the American Bardot in *Barbarella*. This was the low point of Fonda's self-esteem; Vadim recalls that one day she said to him, "How can you love me and respect me? I'm nothing!" From this dangerous dejection Jane got a chance to make *They Shoot Horses, Don't They?*, a movie about the marathon-dance craze of Depression America, directed by Sydney Pollack. For Fonda, this serious film was like an oasis in the desert. Vadim remembers that "she often slept at the studios to keep her makeup on overnight. She was living her part with almost morbid intensity."

Up to then, says Fonda, "I had no political consciousness. I started talking to more and more women and reading some of the first books that were coming out. I began to understand that I myself had been conditioned a lot by images of women." The political events of 1968—the student revolt in France, the violence at the Democratic convention in America—were decisive for a changing Jane. "It was a time of really tumultuous currents in world history. So on a personal level you feel that your life is going by and you have to change at a time when history is changing." The American Bardot changed with a vengeance. Her highly visible—and audible—involvement in the antiwar movement, which included a trip to Hanoi, and her passion for the new feminism, American Indians' rights, and Puerto Rican independence made her a lot of powerful enemies. "I wouldn't mind if you cut her tongue off," said one Maryland legislator.

Attempting to integrate her new political consciousness with her acting, she filmed *Tout Va Bien* with Yves Montand for the radical director Jean-Luc Godard in France. Fonda underrates this often brilliant film about the Paris student revolts and strikes of 1968, apparently because of her aversion to Godard's political "sectarianism" and to his behavior. "To be a revolutionary you have to be a human being," she says. "You have to care about people who have no power. Godard had contempt for people, contempt for extras. I'd rather work with someone ideologically very different from me if they have concern and humanity toward their crew."

More successful as a political-artistic synthesis was *Klute*, directed by Alan Pakula, in which she gave her best performance up to that point as Bree Daniel, a prostitute who's threatened by a pathological killer. Fonda researched the part by getting to know scores of people in the New York sexual underworld. "I noticed in all of these women a terrible hardness," says Fonda. "Many of them are sleeping with senators, executives of major corporations, of television networks. They told me names, and they told me unbelievable stories about sadomasochism. You can imagine the view that it gives them of the rulers of this country."

Fonda won an Academy Award for *Klute*, a sign perhaps that the hostility generated by her political activity was beginning to fade. And more and more the contradictions—personal, political, and professional—that once gave her life an almost schizoid split have been resolved, thanks in great part to her marriage to the sixties radical Tom Hayden, for whom she worked hard (and contributed $300,000) in his losing but impressive senatorial primary campaign last year. Her eyes light up when she talks about

Hayden. "I met this guy, this brilliant person I had respected from afar. I'd read his books. It turned out he was very into films, and we'd talk about films in a way I'd never thought about. He had more respect for films than I did. So I thought, through some strange quirk in my life I've become a movie star. Now I've become a political activist. Why not try to blend the two? So I formed a movie company."

Fonda is also an important force in Hayden's small but energetic grassroots organization called the California Campaign for Economic Democracy, which currently is lobbying for legislation on behalf of solar energy, a state development bank, and housing, among other issues. The CCED recently bought a small ranch in the mountains north of Santa Barbara, and the Haydens also have a modest house in Santa Monica, where they live with their four-year-old son, Troy, and nine-year-old Vanessa (not named after Redgrave), her daughter by Vadim. Hayden says, "It's important that Jane be restored to legitimacy now, when she's active, and not in the twenty-first century, which usually happens to controversial people. Lillian Hellman is very 'in' now, but she wasn't not too long ago. I'm very impressed by how rapidly Jane's image has started to reverse itself. It's not just her doing, it's a sign that the country has been changing."

With her associate Bruce Gilbert, Fonda's company, IPC, has already made its first movie, *Coming Home*, in which she plays a Marine officer's wife who falls in love with a paraplegic veteran. Fonda, who's forsworn sex scenes since her *Barbarella* days, plays what she calls "an explicit sex scene" with the paralyzed soldier. "It's central to the theme of this movie," she says, "which is a redefinition of power and of manhood. This man, who is paralyzed from the waist down, but who can listen and feel and receive pleasure from someone, is more of a man in some ways than a man who has his whole body but who isn't responsive to someone's needs."

Fonda is now shooting *Comes a Horseman,* in which she once again is being directed by Alan Pakula. It's a contemporary Western in which Jane and James Caan join forces to prevent land baron Jason Robards from gobbling up their holdings. Fonda got the ranch hands on the Colorado location to teach her everything a real ranchwoman would have to know. She even learned how to castrate bulls. "In *Klute*," says Pakula, "I felt she could play a range of characters beyond that of any star of her generation. I feel that even more strongly today. Jane is one of those people who have a vivid, supreme star personality and also the capability of a superb character actress. That's very rare. She's so alive, so immediate, so interested, and she has genuine curiosity about other people and other ways of life."

Aliveness and immediacy are what's most important about Jane Fonda.

She's never used her acting to project any kind of ideology or dogma; it's always the electric impact of observed life that comes through sharp and clear. Fonda, who calls herself a progressive democrat, is totally at odds politically with the Trotskyite Redgrave (a situation they handle by not discussing politics), but each has a deep admiration for the other as an artist. "With Vanessa," says Fred Zinnemann, "you don't feel there's any work, any effort. Her acting just flows. With Jane, there's a lot of painstaking detail and work. Fonda has one quality she shares with Porfirio Díaz, the old Mexican dictator, and Louis B. Mayer, the old M-G-M dictator—she can cry at will and be totally convincing."

Fonda calls Redgrave "the best actress. In the good-bye scene we'd stand there and before the shooting began she'd say things to me like, 'Lilly, I want you to be brave, I don't want you to give up on your writing. . . .' I looked at her hands and I started to cry because she's got these huge hands that are very moving to me." Fonda, originally trained in "the Method" at New York's Actors Studio, is more pragmatic. Observing Lillian Hellman, she picked up certain things, like the way Hellman would cross herself and say "Oy vay" at the same time. But, adds Fonda, "Lillian is a homely woman and yet she moves as if she were Marilyn Monroe. She sits with her legs apart, with her satin underwear partly showing—she's a very sexual, sensual woman. Well, that's fine for Lillian, but it wouldn't look right if I did it. So I played her more ascetic than she really is."

The friendship of Lillian and Julia is a paradigm for the new films about women. . . . "This is the first time in years we've seen women who aren't dealing with men," says Shirley MacLaine. The danger in this, she thinks, is that women will be ghettoized in the new pictures. "I'm still not seeing scripts that deal with adult relations between men and women," she says. MacLaine is skeptical about the studios' apparent interest in women. "They couldn't keep us out forever," she says. "But the quickest way to clean out a Hollywood party is to discuss women. I don't think there will be a change unless these films make money. If they don't, we have a problem."

Jane Fonda says much the same thing. But she is likely to be the most important figure in this latest, uncertain cycle in a notoriously cycle-happy industry. In the end, a Jane Fonda is more important for the pleasure and enlightenment of audiences than the unseemly scrambling of the moneymen. Her career already has the shape, the grace, the movielike drama of the most interesting female movie careers, like Hepburn's or Lombard's. She's a fine actress whose very behavior seems to mean something to us even before we connect it with the role she's playing. And despite her sometimes strident radicalizing that angered many Americans in a divided time, she's an image in the American grain—direct, clear, appealing, with the resilience of the old American optimism, good faith, and high spirits in her movements and her voice.

In this, she's very much her father's child. It was only when she reached her own maturity that she realized that her father in his way had made some of the same kind of movies that she wants to make. It was only in the late sixties that she first saw *The Grapes of Wrath,* which Henry Fonda made with John Ford when she was just two years old. "I knew that my father made serious movies and that in his heart he is a very progressive person. But I was just blown away by *The Grapes of Wrath.* I think it's the most brilliant acting I ever saw. It's a perfect movie, the kind of thing I would like to see. All my life has been privilege. You can be a privileged movie star, or you can commit yourself to the idea that people can change their lives and can change history. I want to make films that will make people feel stronger, understand more clearly, and make them move forward—women and men. That's what I'm interested in."

[1977]

Molly Haskell

JODIE FOSTER AND TATUM O'NEAL

Perfect sex symbols for a country that has arrived at decadence without passing through maturity.

In the science-fiction book and movie *Logan's Run,* the world of the future is populated exclusively by the young. Upon reaching "a certain age"—twenty-one in the book and thirty in the film (presumably to allow Michael York to play the lead)—one's subscription to life is automatically canceled. Now, Hollywood appears to have established a similar Maximum Age Allowable, only the limit is considerably lower—somewhere in the teens—and it applies only to women.

Female kiddies, moppets, and nymphets—of course!—an ingenious solution by moviemakers to complaints about the shortage of women in films. This solution will enable them to come up with the requisite ten female performances a year (five starring, five supporting) for Academy Award nomi-

(ABOVE LEFT) Jane Fonda: *Direct, clear, appealing.*
(*Tout Va Bien.* A New Yorker Films release.
Courtesy New Yorker Films.)

(RIGHT, FROM TOP)
Tatum O'Neal. (*Paper Moon.* Copyright © MCMLXXIII by
Paramount Pictures Corporation. All rights reserved.)

Jodie Foster. (*Taxi Driver.* Courtesy of Columbia Pictures.)

The Lolita trend.

nations without having to go to the trouble of developing actual parts with dialogue for full-fledged honest-to-goodness thinking and talking grown-up women.

Heading the new line of teenybopper sex symbols are baddy-baddy Tatum O'Neal, who has just unseated Barbra Streisand as the only female on *Variety*'s annual industry list of the ten top box-office stars, and Jodie Foster, the teenage temptress of *Taxi Driver* and *Bugsy Malone*. The two, whose combined ages add up to twenty-seven, are being offered movie contracts faster than their guardians can sign them.

Then there's Linda Blair (*The Exorcist I* and *II*), Florrie Dugger (the blond ingenue in *Bugsy Malone*), Glynnis O'Connor (*Jeremy, Baby Blue Marine*), Kay Lenz, who played the teenage inamorata of William Holden in *Breezy*, Mariel Hemingway, and the cast of *Carrie* (including Sissy Spacek, an old lady of twenty-seven, who holds on to her teen status in the film), to name only the better known.

America has always had its child fetishists, and movies have as happily supplied fantasies to this market as to any other. Mary Pickford was forced by an adoring public to remain its child sweetheart even when she wanted to act her age, and Shirley Temple, the ringleted dynamo of the thirties, had a box-office stature that topped Garbo's. But both were unique phenomena, talented originals, who flourished alongside a variety of full-grown female stars playing their age, whereas the sheer number of the seventies' teen queens, and the fact that they are the only female game in town, is less a tribute to their talent than a testament to their sociological significance.

Other than quantity, what distinguishes them from their predecessors is their sexual precocity. However much Mary Pickford and Shirley Temple might attract the closet Humbert Humbert, their own approach to life was irresistibly wholesome, the sunny side of American innocence, and they appealed to children as well as to adults. But their modern counterparts, with their suggestive looks and gutter language, seem to have been there and done it all, and—ultimate irony—most of their movies are off limits for their own age group. (*Taxi Driver* was rated R, as was *The Exorcist*.) Others (*Paper Moon, The Bad News Bears, Alice Doesn't Live Here Anymore,* and *Nickelodeon*) can be seen by the little stars and their friends only with parental guidance.

Since we are meant to assume that they only half understand the words they are uttering and the roles they are playing, the kick they offer is a double one of innocence and corruption—perfect sex symbols for a country that has arrived at decadence without passing through maturity, that is disillusioned without ever having been fulfilled. *The Exorcist* offers the most explicitly grotesque example of this double titillation, the extremes of innocence and depravity represented in the spectacle of a pubescent girl spouting the obscenities that signify her "penetration" by the Devil.

Could *The Exorcist* also be read as a subliminal warning from Hollywood directed at the Women's Movement? Are they trying to tell us that the Devil has gotten into us, that we want and know too much, and if we don't behave like sweet little girls we're in for big trouble? One doesn't have to be paranoid or in the conspiracy market to see a connection between the child's affliction and her mother's status as a divorced career woman.

Just as building films around child stars is a device for filling the female quota without dealing with real women, so dressing them up in adult clothes and mannerisms is a way of referring to grown women—and to women's growing self- and sexual awareness—without having to contend with it on a realistic basis . . . and register a rebuke as well. The disturbing precocity itself is an implied warning not only to the kids but to parents as well. The good little girls who get in trouble (Mariel Hemingway in *I Want to Keep My Baby* and Linda Blair getting raped in prison in *Born Innocent*—both movies made for television) and the ambiguous ones who "turn bad" (Jodie Foster in *Taxi Driver*) do so, it goes without saying, from maternal neglect. Not only are we being told as females to stay forever young and forever virginal, but we are being told *as mothers* to stay home and mind our daughters or they will turn out like this!

In day-to-day moviemakers' terms, for the film industry the pint-size vamps and virgins are like pets or mascots—women who are not too hot to handle. Directors are more comfortable with cartoon women—models or little girls or clearcut "types," like Streisand and Minnelli. I happen to think Jodie Foster is the most exciting talent to emerge in Hollywood in the last five years, and the only female with potential star quality. I'm not sure, yet, of the reasons, but I like to think it has more to do with camera presence and a certain oblique mystery than with age or the kinky characters she's played. Her vogue is attributable to a phenomenon that she may yet transcend.

Nor is the Lolita trend restricted to Hollywood. Of all the noteworthy female athletes to have come along recently, the media selected nymphet gymnasts Nadia Comaneci and Olga Korbut (the latter having just hung up her leotard at the ripe old age of twenty-one) as the superstar darlings. And in Italy—where the radical solidarity of women in recent proabortion demonstrations must have shaken male chauvinism to its foundations—the popularity of the nubile stars of films like *Malizia* and *Bambina* suggest that men all over the world are robbing the cradle to find women soft and pliant enough to satisfy their fantasies and stimulate a potency that is based all too clearly on power rather than equality.

For the man whose ego is sustained not by inherent worth, but by a sense of superiority over the weaker sex, there is a need for constant worshipful glances from the "little woman." Since there are few grown women left who will perform the shrinking act for this purpose, he will have to resort to little women in the literal sense. Only the two-foot teen queen is willing and the appropriate height to hold up the magnifying mirror to him. Perhaps a Hollywood full of Daddy's little girls will make all those producers and directors feel like great big men again.

In the meantime, if anyone is ready for an adult woman in the movies in a real love story, there won't be one available. Although the woman's film is said to be making a comeback this year, thanks largely to Jane Fonda going back to work, it remains to be seen how many of these films will treat adult women as adults. And it will be ten years before the current crop of kiddies comes of age as women stars—if they aren't forced into mandatory retirement at twenty-one.

[1977]

Andrew Sarris

JEAN GABIN

The doomed proletarian hero.

Gabin was the Movie Star in perhaps his purest form. In the late thirties and early forties he was often described as the French Spencer Tracy, but that comparison is seldom made anymore. Gabin's magnetism was peculiarly cinematic. His brooding silences would have seemed eerie on the stage. The cinema is faces, the theater voices. Olivier is the opera singer of actors. His electrifying voice identifies his star essence even when he is buried under tons of character makeup. But until and unless he speaks he does not truly exist. Gabin fully exists every second of screen-time.

This is not to say that stage acting and screen acting are rigorously segregated disciplines. A Ralph Richardson and a Louis Jouvet can glide from one medium to another with all their magical mysteriousness intact. It is often a matter of luck and career conveniences. Richardson was blessed with a variety of obsessive, eccentric roles on both stage and screen. Even Michael Redgrave was fortunate enough to etch a bit of movie mythology in *Dead of Night*. Olivier will always be treasured for Heathcliff, Darcy, De Winter, Nelson, the Shakespearian roles, and not really too much else in the cinematic repertory, but it is more than enough to validate a theatrical legend, more, certainly, than Lunt and Fontanne have left as their cinematic legacy in *The Guardsmen*. With Jouvet a different issue was involved: the minimalism of his facial expressions. He became, in Otis Ferguson's phrase, the Buster Keaton of high culture. The cinema, so susceptible to somnambulism, embraced Jouvet almost as eagerly as it did Gabin. Still, when Gabin and Jouvet did appear together in Jean Renoir's curiously Gallic version of Maxim Gorky's *The Lower Depths*, the two actors seemed to inhabit two different realms. In one scene they are walking on the uneven terrain of a hillside. Gabin's feet grip the ground as if he were a mountain goat of movie reality. Jouvet lurches and sways as if his feet were groping for the level surfaces of the stage. It is not a matter of better or worse but of different.

Gabin's myth of the doomed proletarian hero was established in the thirties in Julien Duvivier's *Pépé Le Moko*, Carné's *Quai des brumes* and *Le Jour se lève*, and Renoir's *La Bête humaine*. No Hollywood movie star, not even Bogie or Garfield, was ever allowed a comparably tragic destiny in his films. The private lives were something else again. But on the screen Gabin has been perhaps the most ill-fated of all stars, even more than Garbo. By contrast, his famous role in Renoir's *La Grande Illusion* is relatively optimistic. And I have been told by people who have known him that the one role that captures Gabin's real-life personality is that of the bumptious bumpkin in the Madame Tellier episode in Max Ophul's *Le Plaisir*. He has left a void that will never be filled.

[1976]

Charles Champlin

CLARK GABLE

He always seemed to view Gable the Film Star with a kind of half-amused, half-chagrined detachment.

The tales they were spinning might be—often were—the silliest kind of cotton-candy nonsense. But whatever they were saying, the movies from the beginning could not help telling a good deal about all of us as well.

Their heroes and heroines reflected the real if improbable aspirations of

232 | THE MOVIE STAR

vast numbers of moviegoers, dreams of courage, wit, wealth, security, adventure, desirability, and love. And even though Hollywood's heroes and heroines might be large magnifications of reality, they also at some basic level reflected the audience's vision of itself. The stars' priorities as displayed on the screen were the audience's priorities. And this rough parallel was, as indeed it still is, a prerequisite for stardom.

Clark Gable was the greatest heroic male star of his time, and to think about him now, at the beginning of the seventies, is to realize with sorrow and a double sense of loss how much we and the world have changed and how distant and uncomplicated his time already seems.

He was unabashed virility, but the world moves toward unisex. He was an outdoorsman, but the outdoors is being macadamized in our day. He portrayed men of action and instinct, and we survivors feel paralyzed by numbers, rules, costs, and awareness. To think about Gable now is to experience an almost unutterable nostalgia, not only for the gruff and dashing figure he was but for the unsubtle and straightforward period in which he moved.

No small part of Gable's great charm and attractiveness was that he always seemed to view Gable the Film Star with a kind of half-amused, half-chagrined detachment, as if parading before cameras was not quite the sort of thing a grown man ought to be doing. In fact he worked very hard at his craft, but our impression of his bemusement made the roles somehow seem all the more virile and credible. No one after him has played the raffish, roguish male nearly as well; it is a lost art, as it is a lost breed.

Although they were contemporaries, Gable and Humphrey Bogart, for example, already seem to have arisen in different eras: Bogart anticipated the later day of the faintly or heavily neurotic sophisticate who was likely to be antiheroic if not actively villainous. Bogie was heroic, but he tended to be the abashed or reluctant hero. Gable, the unabashed hero, was reluctant to be drawn into the very modern world (witness the rebellious adman in *The Hucksters* or, far more tellingly and impressively, the cowboy born out of his time in *The Misfits*).

It is not quite right, for once, to say that an era died with Clark Gable. The truth is that an era had predeceased him. The kingdom of film over which he reigned for so long had begun to crumble and change a decade at least before his death. But more than that, the kind of hero figure Gable was has come to seem an impossible dream in our days—not undesirable but unachievable. And this, of course, is a commentary not on Gable but on all of us, tethered by the paper chains of circumstance and vibrating to the hum of computers.

Gable the King—impudent, free, rascally, courageous, resourceful, direct, uncomplicated, charming, all male but without need to overassert it, sane and self-reliant, gallant and natural—remains what we would wish to be, but what we sense we can now fully be only in spirit.

We make do with lesser and more brittle gods.

[1970]

Richard Corliss

GRETA GARBO

Once she retired, she became the chief curator of her film image by staying out of the public eye.

Edwin Booth described the professional actor as "a sculptor who carves in snow." Onstage, the actor's performance is glazed in the collective memory of those who've seen it; and it melts as the memory fades. Theater is, after all, a kind of group hallucination, and theater criticism an impressionist's report of a séance. So the least we can say for screen acting is that, forced by the properties of the medium, it dares to be seen and judged by posterity. We can talk precisely about Mary Pickford's film acting, and not about Sarah Bernhardt's stage acting, because Pickford is a tangible fact and Bernhardt an evanescent myth. The twenty-first-century student of acting won't have to rely on books like this to discover what Garbo's Camille was like (as he would to learn about Olivier's Oedipus). In a feat of true movie magic, he will simply open a tin coffin, and the dead will awake—all talking, all singing, all dancing.

He will, if he visits other crypts, find that it was Garbo, among all film performers, who provoked the most sustained and voluptuous writing on movie acting. Mention her name, and yellow journalists turn to purple prose. What was it about Garbo's persona and performances that evoked the superlatives—whether it was the European appellation "La Divina" or Alice B. Toklas's nickname for her, "Mademoiselle Hamlet"? Perhaps it was because Garbo was both the definitive movie-star actress and a practitioner of some other, unique acting style, a resident of some other world. Many critics have had their eloquent say on Garbo the legend and the star (notably Kenneth Tynan, Jack Kroll, Alexander Walker, Raymond Durgnat,

Molly Haskell). Here we shall attempt something more precise: a critical description of Garbo as a great film actress.

In the three decades between the appearance of Bram Stoker's novel and Bela Lugosi's incarnation of the demon, the male vampire was transformed into the female vamp. Theda Bara, in 1915, developed the movies' first negative image of the D. W. Griffith virgin princess. The anagrammatic Arab Death herself was in fact Theodosia Goodman, born in Pittsburgh; but the most successful vamps of the twenties were exotic foreigners—and Garbo was cast in this mold. The vamp character was simply a baroque variation on The Whore, one of the two basic female stereotypes in movies of the time. The other, of course, was The Schoolmarm. Garbo was no schoolmarm—she possessed an electrifying presence that could lend substance to roles created out of cardboard and convention. Her characters did some unbelievable things, but she was almost always believable. She was intelligent and beautiful; whatever she did, she must have had a reason.

Metro-Goldwyn-Mayer, the studio where Garbo made all twenty-four of her Hollywood films, favored adaptations of novels by the likes of Hermann Sudermann and Vicente Blasco-Ibáñez—writers who enjoyed stoking the passions of their characters (and their readers), and then throwing a bucket of natural or divine retribution on the sinners. M-G-M's motto might have been Rasputin's: Sin so ye may repent. And the more attractively ye sinned, the more spectacularly ye had to repent. Garbo, whose talent for conveying and arousing passion verged on the hypnotic, was thus forced to endure some pretty heavy climactic suffering. The finales of her early films compose a catalogue of Draconian vengefulness: she goes mad (*The Temptress*, 1926), drowns in a frozen pond (*Flesh and the Devil*, 1927), throws herself under the wheels of an onrushing train (in the original final print of *Love*, 1928), and drives smack into a tree (*A Woman of Affairs*, 1929). It's true that death was quickly followed by resurrection—in her next film. But she was like a phoenix on a treadmill: she would live again in order to die again.

So she fell in love with Count Vronsky and Lieutenant Rosanoff and Baron von Geigern and Captain Karl von Rhaden and even Napoleon. She suffered and died and was redeemed—sometimes all in the same movie. And, much of the time, she gives the impression of a Pavlova walking through her roles. She "walked" divinely—but we are saddened to know that she rarely danced. Not that Garbo was to blame that most of her scripts were typed with one finger, and in one key. It was Irving Thalberg, the production chief at M-G-M from 1923 to 1936, who chose as film properties stories that often acted as a ball and chain around our ballerina's feet.

Thalberg seemed to think that the greatest thing he could do for his star actresses was to turn them into ladies. With some of his stars—Norma Shearer, for example—it couldn't have mattered much: Shearer might have been a great lady, but she was never a really good actress. Garbo, because she had much more to give, had much more to lose by being placed in one epic of antic nobility after another. It's not that Garbo needed roles of majestic tragedy—she got enough of those!—but she showed, in films as slight as *The Mysterious Lady* (1928) and as substantial as *Ninotchka* (1939), that she could have fun without sacrificing the sense of fated seriousness that made her roles, and sometimes even her films, something special.

But before we decide to deface Thalberg's grave, we should admit that Garbo *needed* M-G-M. It offered a motherly bosom for this least secure of superstars. And though, early in her tenure there, she held out for seven months until her projects were upgraded from Sudermann to Tolstoy, she seems to have found her later pabulum congenial enough not to make a fuss over. (She even vetoed a David O. Selznick proposal to do the hit play *Dark Victory* with a screenplay by Philip Barry—a meaty contemporary role that might have helped her more in 1935 than a remake of *Anna Karenina*.)

The result of all these forces—Thalberg's protectiveness, the public's image of a star, her own complacency, the outdated conventions of her chosen genre—was that Garbo made fewer good films than any major performer, and almost no films (excepting *Ninotchka*) that would have been good without her. But if you look closely at the contours of her career, you can trace the creation of a beautiful young woman from a chubby Swedish starlet, and the flowering of a great actress in the Culver City hothouse.

Garbo made her last film in 1941, when she was thirty-five and still a matchless beauty in the twilight of her young womanhood. But great changes had taken place since she was first recorded on film. In a 1921 "commercial" for a Stockholm department store, we see a plump, giddy girl modeling three dresses; in a promotional film made the following year for a line of bakery products, this same undistinguished girl gorges on a cream puff, then greedily grabs some cookies. It's not until director Mauritz Stiller, and then the Irving Thalberg body shop, took this chunky teenager in hand that the mist of corpulence clears—teeth are capped, eyebrows plucked, hair restyled—and out walks the breathtakingly beautiful Garbo whose languid splendor will endure for the rest of her career.

On this particular pedestal, there was room for only one. In contrast to her, Garbo's leading men often seem like so many male concubines in her central-casting harem—at best, gentlemen-in-waiting to a snow queen. It's hard to say whether they, or their scripts, or their directors are to blame;

still, the general impression is that they are pleasant enough as dancing partners, but hardly the sort of man who could, with complete sexual authority, sweep Garbo off her feet and into his arms and out of a stuffy masked ball. They project domestic gentility, and a certain embarrassment in the presence of this fated force of nature. They come to her as princes and, like a beautiful wicked fairy, she turns them into frogs.

If Garbo's co-stars in her silent films come closer to holding their own, it's because the early Garbo was passionate: she had to play those perfervid love scenes with *somebody*. Often you'll find the lovers in an oddly contorted embrace that will become standard in Garbo silents: she above, he below; his head in her lap, her head on his chest—miming a movie euphemism for the love that dare not speak its number. But as her career developed, and the shadow of her mystique lengthened, she discarded the physical for the metaphysical. Many of her most memorable love scenes were played with herself, or with props: the flowers in *A Woman of Affairs*, the furniture in *Queen Christina* (1933), a handsome but wooden Robert Taylor in *Camille* (1937). She was less in need of celebrants than of altar boys. So the actors were often neutered before they ever walked on the set.

There were exceptions, of course: Melvyn Douglas in *Ninotchka*, John Barrymore in *Grand Hotel* (1932), Charles Boyer in *Conquest* (1937), Nils Asther in *The Single Standard* (1929), Clark Gable in *Susan Lenox: Her Fall and Rise* (1931), even George Brent in *The Painted Veil* (1934). But the great exception was John Gilbert, a great star and a fine actor, with whom she made four films. At his apogee in the twenties, Gilbert personified the best that America could think of the boys it had raised: dashing, generous, faithful, and incurably romantic. Their first love scene, in *Flesh and the Devil*—with Gilbert as Adam and Garbo as the most delectable fruit in a garden of heavenly delights—gives off the sparks of two novas colliding head-on, high in the night sky, celestial and spectacular. Their last love scene, in *Queen Christina* six years later (by which time Gilbert had become a casualty of the transition to sound), will be of a quieter, more melancholy combustion: a shooting star and a falling star grazing each other on the way to their separate eternities.

Is film the art of the director? Then Garbo's films are not art. Her closest professional relationship was not with an exemplary director, or even a sympathetic writer, but with cameraman William Daniels, who photographed twenty of her twenty-four Hollywood films. She also relied heavily on Cedric Gibbons, M-G-M's supervising art director, and Gilbert Adrian, who designed her costumes. Clarence Brown directed seven Garbo films, from

(RIGHT) Clark Gable: *Impudent.*

(BELOW) Jean Gabin (with Pierre Fresnay):
His magnetism was peculiarly cinematic.
(*Grand Illusion.* Courtesy
Janus Films, Inc., New York.)

Greta Garbo: *Goddess emeritus.* (From the MGM release *Camille.* © 1936 Metro-Goldwyn-Mayer Corporation. Copyright renewed 1963 by Metro-Goldwyn-Mayer Inc.)

Flesh and the Devil in 1927 to *Conquest* a decade later, and in his silent-film work surrounded her with a witty and artfully designed *mise en scène;* in the sound films, though, he receded beneath the M-G-M patina of Good Taste, and effectively surrendered the reins of visual authorship to Daniels and Gibbons. The gloss was still there, but the glow was gone.

Mauritz Stiller, the Swedish director, had discovered Garbo; had cast her in an important role in an important film (*The Saga of Gösta Berling*, 1924) when she was only eighteen; had brought her to Hollywood; and was assigned to direct her second Hollywood film, *The Temptress*. It's tempting to speculate on what kind of a star a long-term Stiller-Garbo relationship might have produced. Sternberg-Dietrich? Rossellini-Bergman? Bogdanovich-Shepherd? The speculation is idle. Ten days after shooting began on *The Temptress*, Stiller was fired. There are stories of Stiller shouting "Stop!" when he wanted his cameraman to start filming, and "Go!" when he wanted him to stop. Soon enough, Thalberg said "Stop!" and Stiller was gone. He died in Sweden two years later.

In this early film, the ecstasy Garbo projects is still a set of rigid mannerisms, and not yet the expression of an incandescent soul. You can almost hear the off-camera instructions to her in words of one syllable, and you can see Garbo reacting with gestures that are painted on, like Pinocchio's smile. The lips part slowly, in a cartoon of lust; a thousand Lilliputian stagehands raise those asbestos eyelids (and take their time about it); the eyes roll mechanically back and forth, evoking the spirit of Betty Boop. This is the vamp as camp. It's what people who don't like silent movies remember of them: unfelt intensity, glamour without craft.

And yet—when discussing even the worst Garbo film, there is always an "and yet"—it is still easy to see why she became a star in so short a time. In *The Temptress*'s first scene (masked ball), Garbo at twenty admirably suggests a sense of exhaustion—until Antonio Moreno plucks her from a maelstrom of waltzing revelers. She removes her white eye-mask, and with it the last shred of an inhibition. She surveys Moreno's face with her hands—as if she had never before experienced hunger, and now realizes she's been hungry all her life—and kisses him full on the mouth. We sometimes forget that before Garbo became the Divine Masochist, whiplashed by fate, she had been a certified Sex Goddess. After seeing Reel One of *The Temptress*, we are unlikely to forget it again.

Even with all that heavy breathing, it's hard to see why her character, Elena, is thought to be so evil—a label that stuck to the Garbo woman throughout her vamp period. As a satanic presence, Elena is rather passive, usually standing around looking gorgeous while infatuated men throw their hearts at her feet like quoits. Is she to blame for her beauty, or their foolishness? The Garbo character's real problem is that she lives by a moral standard held too high for men to reach—so they grab what they can touch: her body. When told that she has ruined the lives of half-a-dozen men who would do anything for her, she replies bitterly: "Not for me, but for my body. Not for my happiness, but theirs."

Garbo wanders through most of her early films like a world traveler without a passport, renting her body out to many men but pledging her love to only one. To her, sex is a pleasant time killer, marriage a nonbinding contract—and love a sacred vow. "I told you I *loved* you," she says to Moreno. "I have never said that to any other man." But Moreno, like so many of Garbo's movie suitors, can't accept the idea of a madonna who's not also a virgin. He wants retroactive rights to her body as well as universal rights to her soul.

By the end of *The Temptress*, Elena sits, crazed and diseased, in a Paris café, at last pursuing the trade men have been urging on her for so many years. Like Tennessee Williams' Blanche DuBois, she had got on the wrong streetcar: not ecstasy but desire. And, like Blanche, she has a devastating curtain line. When Moreno tries to remind her of their great love (which was really only hers), she replies, vaguely, "I meet so many men"—and wanders away, down another street.

Toward the end of *A Woman of Affairs*, Garbo is lying unconscious in a French hospital, the victim of a nervous collapse after learning that her late husband was an embezzler. The flowers sent her by John Gilbert, who plays her one true love, have been removed from her room. As Gilbert paces nervously in the hospital corridor, Garbo suddenly appears. She sleepwalks down the corridor and, in a single swooping gesture that is one of the great moments of silent passion, removes the flowers from their vase and clutches them to her breast. "I woke up—and you weren't there," she murmurs to her love surrogates. "I don't want much—only you."

Here we can see one of the most majestic transformations in the cinema: from acting to being, pulp to poetry. It's a minute of screen acting that by itself makes *A Woman of Affairs* one of her most imposing achievements—especially considering the idiocies of plot and supporting acting that have preceded it. (Garbo and Gilbert refuse to say "I love you" to anyone else, but marry others anyway; Garbo's unloved husband commits suicide because the police have discovered his crime—and then the police tell no one about it; Garbo endures a seven-year plague of abuse simply to keep a secret that would trouble no one except her brother.) For Garbo, after all this, to create something beautiful out of almost nothing is less a case of skating on thin ice than of walking on water.

Throughout her career, Garbo's characters struggle against all the conventions of Victorian morality—which, because Garbo was so often a great actress, seem especially unworthy as antagonizing forces. She deserved to be struck down, not by some fustian social custom but by the gods, by a fate that was inevitable rather than simply predictable. Since Garbo was finally her own, and only, ideal antagonist, the great Garbo role would have traced a descent into madness. But except for the climactic scenes in *The Temptress* (made when she was twenty) and *A Woman of Affairs* (made when she was twenty-two), Garbo was never given a "mad scene" worthy of the name. That she made, so early in her career, so much of these meager opportunities suggests what she might have done with a decent mad role ten years later, in the fullness of her beauty and art.

Garbo's beauty was always evident, but she frequently hid her art up the sleeve of her Adrian gowns. In films that couldn't engage her talent or interest, she resorted to extravagant gestures which, uninformed by any feeling, look ludicrous—the nervous biting of her lower lip, her hand running tensely through her hair. In *The Kiss* (1929), her last silent film, Garbo looks divine but distracted. She walks through the role as if her mind were on other things: the English lessons, the impending challenge of her first talking picture. The ennui she so often projected through her characters here seems to be coming directly from the actress, and it's contagious. Everyone must have realized it was time for Garbo to speak.

She slouches into a waterfront bar, falls into a chair, and says to the bartender, "Give me a whiskey, ginger ale on the side, and don't be stingy, baby." In her talking-film debut, Garbo looks just right as Anna Christie. She had obviously taken great care in altering her soignée image to fit the contours of Eugene O'Neill's washed-out prostitute. She seems to have swallowed her chin; her tongue is dry and dirty, parched with too much life; the whole cast of her face is lower-class Nordic instead of the usual, aristocratic woman of the world. Though the photographs of these first scenes suggest a beautiful actress in five-and-dime garb, in the film she looks appropriately seedy.

If you listen to the M-G-M album of highlights from Garbo talkies, you can hear a rich, lugubrious tone that breathes life into O'Neill's stammering prose. On screen, however, picture and voice don't jell. It's not the occasional mispronunciations (on the order of "The yudge told me to get a yob"); it's that Garbo's acting is pitched at the wrong level. Her Anna is a travesty of despair; the movements of our primal ballerina are often jerkily grandiose. (In her next film—*Romance*, 1930—she had even more trouble but it was M-G-M's fault: the studio cast her as an Italian diva.)

Garbo had learned her trade in the silent cinema, and she still remembered most of her lessons in the early sound period. Talkies were developing their own conventions, but Garbo films—and Garbo herself—remained anchored in the dramatic and cinematic past. Because she ignored a new style of acting, which she would anyway have been unable to master, because her films were locked in an unbreakable embrace with Ruritanian melodrama, Garbo pictures strike today's audiences as more remote—and therefore, perhaps, less dated—than the "contemporary" comedies and gangster movies of the thirties.

By 1932 Garbo was still only twenty-seven years old, and had been in Hollywood for seven years. But she had made seventeen films for M-G-M, and her identity was firmly fixed as the "older woman"—older in spirit than her middle-aged leading men, older than all the queens and courtesans she played, older than Eve. So the plots of her films had to describe the rejuvenation of an "experienced" woman at the hands and heart of a callow idealist. In *Mata Hari* (1931), Ramon Novarro, like a dozen other Garbo co-stars from John Gilbert to Robert Taylor, plays the role of man-child to Garbo's ageless Circe—the naughty boy, cute and irresistible, especially to a woman tired of men pretending to be as worldly-wise as she. Garbo's affinity for children and animals has often been noted; and we might add that many of her screen lovers fit this puppy-dog mold. They allowed the star to surrender herself but not her superiority, to treat men as love objects but not as equals. Sacrifice is much nobler when performed for the benefit of the unworthy.

The same plot strands were woven time and again into the fabric of Garbo's films until they began to resemble factory-made crazy quilts. Finally, in 1936, she made *Camille*—an anthology of these plotlets, and their apotheosis. Every hoary cliché was recast and polished until it shines like a new truth. For once, Cedric Gibbons' decor, like George Cukor's direction, splendidly served the story and its star. And Garbo responded with what Gary Carey has justly called "the single most beautiful performance in the American sound film."

As Garbo transcended the role of Marguerite Gautier, so does she transform her face into a tragic mask. It's paler and more severe than before, with new laugh and worry lines. Her hair and eyes are darker, her mouth longer and thinner—harder, if you like. Even her nose seems longer. There are other modifications: her voice is deeper and the tempo of her speech is quicker; her posture is not only heroically weary but almost frozen in a not-quite-upright position. And the famous two-syllable laugh is forever threatening to erupt into a small, ominous cough.

Some of these effects can be credited to co-cinematographer Karl Freund, who contrasts the chiaroscuro shadings in Garbo's face with bland halftones in the background, producing a kind of twilight chic. But the hint of tragic disintegration in the eyes, the intimation in her posture that she is about to collapse in a tubercular swoon, the weight of a thoughtful passion that gives substance to every word—these are Garbo's achievements alone. It's a technically audacious performance, one that weds an encyclopedic knowledge of the craft of screen-acting with an innate, acute sense of a character's behavior; and it allows Garbo to play Marguerite at high pitch and with perfect precision. You may feel that no other actress could create such a performance, or get away with it.

As she and her lover Armand (Robert Taylor) begin to make love, Garbo throws her head completely back, looking to heaven for assurance and prefiguring the exact angle to which her head will drop when she dies. She pushes Armand away and simultaneously grabs for him. She kisses him all over his face, then on his mouth, then sends him away, and—in a single movement—falls back toward her mirror in a sick swoon, clutching her precious pillbox as she falls.

Garbo's performance is studded with these desperate, contradictory gestures. As she kisses Armand, her hand both covers and claws at his face. As they talk love, she pulls frustratedly on his jacket, drops her head on his chest, and cries her anguished happiness directly into his body. Every smile, every word is painful—she sometimes sways when Armand's name is mentioned—and we realize that each time she sees him, a little life leaves her. Armand's function is not to help Marguerite live but to help her die more beautifully.

It is the nature of such fables that the lovers must separate, and that it must not be the woman's fault. Enter Armand's father (Lionel Barrymore), creaking with arthritis and homilies. Somehow he convinces Marguerite to renounce Armand. And when she realizes what she must do—"make Armand hate me"—Garbo drops suddenly to her knees, felled by the enormity of her task. As she later pushes Armand away, shamming a determination to return to her old lover, Garbo again throws her head back, and for the first time we can see the strong sinews of the actress's neck—Marguerite's selfless resolve made visible. Her hand involuntarily caresses Armand's back, for the last time in a long time, and then drops, in a lover's miniature death.

To watch Marguerite's death scene as played by Garbo is to see an actress breathe life into a character's soul, and then to see it extinguished with a final dying fall. Now all is conveyed in whispers—from the deepest gratitude for a friend's generosity (with just a wan smile and a feeble touch) to the strongest devotion for Armand. Only a little laugh and the treacherous cough are voiced. It's both a helpless child and a hoarse old woman whom Armand sweeps into his arms. As he pours his honeyed love into her ear, Garbo's eyes open for the last time, rolled up into her head, and close forever. The camera moves in on her face, the head falls back, and the light fades to the merest shadow—allowing us to retain the image of her silhouette, now a true death mask, for a last precious second.

If *Camille* is Garbo's greatest film, *Ninotchka* is surely her warmest. Her Nina Yakushova may be a less sublime creation than her Marguerite Gautier, but it's no less demanding, for it asks that Garbo express Marguerite's malaise through the guise of rigid Communist femininity. John Baxter has charged that Garbo, "in an absurd self-parody . . . plays comedy with more enthusiasm than skill." Wrong: what she did was to make no distinction between comedy and tragedy. She played them both with the same intensity, the same soaring spirit. As for grotesque self-parody, that came soon enough, with Garbo's next and last film, *Two-Faced Woman* (1941). If we want to say good-bye to the great Garbo, we should do it with *Ninotchka,* and not look ahead.

The premise for *Two-Faced Woman* must have seemed promising: send Ninotchka to an extramarital masquerade disguised as her sophisticated rival, the Duchess Swana. But instead of gracefully nudging the Garbo mystique, as *Ninotchka* had done, *Two-Faced Woman* performs a wicked, off-key burlesque. After delivering a line like "I'm a flower of the evening—a few burning, flamelike years and it will be all over," Garbo must wink to the audience and gulp down a conspiratorial smile before the other characters notice her. By treating Garbo as a joke, the film asks us to reproach ourselves for ever having taken her seriously. The actress had brought dignity and pain to her most inane melodramas; to a nasty farce such as *Two-Faced Woman,* she can bring only pain. At one point she leaves a posh Manhattan party, and says brightly, "I look forward to my return." So did her audiences, fervently—but to a different party, in another film.

Why should anyone care about an actress who retired almost forty years ago? Generally, if we're curious about a star's life offscreen, it's because we know something about it—and want (eagerly, perhaps morbidly) to know more. Monroe, Bardot, Harlow all fit this pattern. Garbo doesn't. We know little of her love life, little more than a list of names from several continents and persuasions.

That's all we know, and more than we need to know. Garbo isn't "one of us," living out our most lurid fantasies of money and sex. She is, now, something completely "other": a goddess emeritus on lifetime loan to the world—but not to touch, and for most of us not even to see. Because we have been spared the spectacle of Garbo playing in a road-company *Mame,* Garbo doing coffee commercials, Garbo as a horror-movies gargoyle, Garbo offering us a fossilized version of her legend à la Dietrich, we find it easier to retain the vision of Garbo the actress. What we do know about her private life indicates that it was largely a preparation for, or a relaxation from, her more beautiful incarnation onscreen. And once she retired, she became the chief curator of her film image by staying as completely as possible out of the public eye.

That's why those news photos of Garbo shielding her face with her hands—the gesture of a shy schoolgirl rape victim—seem obscene. It's more for us than for herself that she covers up the evidence of the disintegration of age. In her last and most lasting performance, Garbo is protecting the image we have of her. For seventeen years, in the movies, she was Garbo. Photographs before and after that period are really of a young girl—and an older woman—named Greta Gustafsson. The truer evidence is on film: the Garbo of her creation, and ours.

[1974]

Judith Crist

JUDY GARLAND

We can't give her anything but love.

The Hollywood star system, some experts hold, came a cropper when the studio publicists started turning the stars into the folks next door. But when the girl next door becomes a Hollywood star—ah, well.

For my generation, for those of us who adolesced and came of age with the movies of the thirties and the forties, Judy Garland was and will always be the girl next door who became a movie star and managed to survive the system. This wasn't a case of fan-mag mythology, of press agentry, of a manufactured studio bio; we were there, we saw it happen, we watched it all unfold step by step and we were glad for Judy and we laughed with Judy and we cried with Judy and we triumphed with her and we sorrowed and

246 | THE MOVIE STAR

Judy Garland: *A marvel of vitality and charm.*

rejoiced and suffered and to this day we know she can do no wrong because she's all pro and all heart and we've lived our lives together and we can't give her anything but love. And there never was and there never will be another film star quite like her because there will never be another Hollywood like the one that created and used and abused her or another movie audience like the one that loved her. Nor is it likely that there will be another film star who could move from screen to stage with such professional ease and capture theater audiences around the world with that same charismatic appeal to the heart that turned the mass response of thousands at a time into an individualized affection.

It isn't easy to analyze the unique qualities of Judy Garland as movie star or cult-idol, so closely are they related to her personal qualities; indeed, the tragedy of her life may well be that she was all movie star and never had a chance to be a private person. Coming from vaudeville as a "little girl with a big voice," tabbed right off the bat by Sophie Tucker herself as her probable successor as the Red Hot Mama of show biz, Judy Garland came to movies as a "natural," a song-and-dance actress who had never had formal training in singing, dancing, or acting. As a child star she was no raving beauty: Ann Rutherford and Ava Gardner were the lovelies who got Mickey Rooney in the Andy Hardy pictures. Judy, somehow biggish-bosomed and thickish-waisted, albeit with lovely slim legs, with sort of hair-hair and a pert nose and—well, Judy was *real* and a good sport and—boy, how she could sing and dance and just be—well, like a girl you knew and liked and could talk to and be real *with*.

There it was—the timeless truth at the heart of Judy Garland's appeal throughout her career: the little girl lost, the wide-eyed good sport, the believer, the vulnerable creature who had nothing to see her through except her talents and her feelings, and those were put right out for all to see. No fake, no fraud, neither a false eyelash nor a false note, just the real thing from heart to head. And how could anyone, of any age, resist the appeal or fail to respond to the fun and the frolic and the joy and—ah yes, the quaver, the fine tremulous suggestion of vulnerability, the depth of feeling glimmering through that shining but never slick surface?

There are fashions in love goddesses, in vamps and villainesses, in mother images and sex symbols. But there is no fashion in talent and professionalism, and thus, from fifteen to twenty-eight, in some thirty films for M-G-M, and on into the thirties and forties (and ours) she developed those talents and polished her professionalism and we watched her grow on the screen, on stage, on television. From the kid serenading Clark Gable to Dorothy longing for over-the-rainbow happiness, from the youngster pitching in to put on a Depression-era show in the barn and making it in the Ziegfeld Follies to the ready-for-romance St. Louis charmer, from the pal who two-a-dayed with Mickey Rooney and was dazzled by the Broadway big–time to the gal who could not only keep in step with Gene Kelly and Fred Astaire but win them in romance, from the onscreen Oscar ceremonies that spelled personal tragedy to the harrowing witness box of Nuremberg that symbolized world tragedy, Judy lived through the troubled times with us, always there, always contemporary, always on top of the material, always a reality for her public.

Bette Davis, Joan Crawford, Hedy Lamarr, even Lana Turner were all given us as grown-up ready-made stars, somehow, swathed in the ermines and diamonds of screen queens. But Judy was the girl from our block—and if we spotted her with jewels and furs we felt it was a dress-up occasion. And if, in her offscreen life, we read of a domestic problem or heard rumbles of suspensions and tensions—it was Judy in trouble because she was in thrall to a heartless studio, Judy victimized by a system, Judy fighting off the rigors of diet and overwork and nervous strain. It was Judy in top hat and mini-tux, the long lovely black-stockinged limbs never changing; it was Judy in Oz, really believing through it all that there's no place like home; it was Judy, smudge-faced and perspiring after the "Couple of Swells" tramp number, sitting on the edge of the stage at the Palace or Palladium or Metropolitan Opera House and taking us over the rainbow to the purity of heart we all once knew.

We remember Judy young and happy and a marvel of vitality and charm—and we think we all must have been that way; we see her in her latter years and we know that we've all been through a lot but not quite the way she has. And there it is—not the Red Hot Mama Miss Tucker envisioned—the girl next door who became a movie star and who never moved away, but stayed right there so we could share it all with her. And we did. All the way. Some of us wound up fans, some made a cult of Judy-worship—but all of us are marked by a singular experience, of having cared about the person as well as the personality. And the evocation thereof is uniquely Judy Garland's.

[1969]

Rex Reed

GIANCARLO GIANNINI

Giannini has come along at a time of sexual confusion, when men on the
screen are getting a fresh look at themselves and are not afraid to cry.

Giancarlo Giannini is the new noise in movies. People outside Rome and
New York have probably never heard of him. Even in New York, where his
consistently volatile performances in the cynical, comic, explosive films of
Lina Wertmuller have made him the most talked about international star
since Belmondo, there are people who have never heard of him. But the
people who mold opinions and influence the arts are talking a lot, and the
sounds they're making are loud, clear, exuberant.

They call him the new Marcello Mastroianni—dynamic, appealing, and
sexy. In person, he's more like the old James Dean—frayed, intense, arrogant, bristling with moody intelligence and energy. The bags under his eyes
challenge his youth, but there's a wild shock of Kennedy hair and a taut,
lean body to prove he's only thirty-three.

In New York to publicize the new Wertmuller film, *Seven Beauties*, he became the toast of the town. He moved from party to party in casual sweaters
and blue jeans, charmed the press with raging discussions about movies,
dined with everyone from Francis Ford Coppola and Joseph Papp to Anita
Loos and Comden and Green, danced till 5 A.M. with Marisa Berenson,
and dragged himself home to Italy in a state of exhaustion. His huge, piercing green eyes recoil in horror at the mention of stardom, but he knows what
to do to get it.

Onscreen, he's bigger than life, swaggering his way passionately through
Wertmuller's films playing lustful, raging chauvinists, virile Communist la-
borers, and assorted pimps, assassins, and murderers. ("I don't believe in
heroes," he says with authority, "especially in films!") In his suite at the
Hotel Pierre, he collapses in an overstuffed chair surrounded by his press
clippings, like a child waiting for his nurse to turn the bed down.

He is small and boyish (the camerawork carefully conceals his five-feet-
nine-inch height and adds weight to his hundred and forty-three pounds).
His eyes are bloodshot. He hasn't shaved for days. An interpreter works
hard to translate every comma while he munches a chicken sandwich. His
English is good, but he fears it. My Italian hits a red light after "Arrive-

derci!" We laugh together at the silliness of interviews, then plunge ahead with one.

In *Seven Beauties*, Giancarlo plays a Neapolitan mafioso who abuses women, murders his sister's pimp, rapes a female patient in an insane asylum, and ends up in a Nazi concentration camp, where he survives because he seduces the swinish lesbian camp commandant. Back in Naples after the war, he is a broken man, but he has lived by using and destroying others.

In Italy, the critics attacked the film because it says Italian men will always survive no matter what the cost. In America, the film has been praised because it raises the question of whether survival is worth it if the cost is greater than the humanity that is paid. There have been so many different interpretations of the film you'd think it was seven movies instead of one.

Giannini smirks contentedly at the furor *Seven Beauties* and his powerful portrayal have caused. "I learned a long time ago not to read what they write about me. Success pleases me. It's a great compliment. And it amuses me to see the film viewed in so many different ways. Each critic has a right to see a film the way he feels it to be. Even if they don't agree, they're talking. Besides, it is very difficult to be specific today because society is so complex. But if the public understands the man I play at the end, I am happy.

"He says he's alive, yet his eyes are dead. He's a dead man. It's very simple. Italian men are simpleminded. To love and eat spaghetti and live is the most important thing to Italian men. But what Lina's films say is that there is more than one way of looking at something. There are infinite ways of molding clay. If to live means to live by betraying everything you believe in, then it's better to die."

He says he plays dramatic, combustible characters because "they are much more interesting than I am." In his own life, he has gone from a degree in electronics engineering to the make-believe world of acting "to feed my fantasy." He enrolled in a three-year acting course with no experience, and halfway through he quit to play Puck in *A Midsummer Night's Dream* at the age of nineteen. A year later, he shocked the Italian critics by playing Romeo in Franco Zeffirelli's stage production of *Romeo and Juliet* by unzipping his fly onstage. Five years ago he shocked them again by playing Hamlet as a hippie who danced the boogie-woogie and played football with the skull of Yorick. The critics murdered him. "They didn't understand it," he shrugs bitterly. "American critics are much more intelligent."

By this time, he was tired of the stage anyway, and movies were calling. Although he has become famous to American filmgoers in the Wertmuller films—*The Seduction of Mimi, Love and Anarchy, Swept Away*, and now *Seven Beauties*—he has also made a series of Italian farces that never crossed the

Atlantic. In one of them, called *Mad Sex*, he played ten different characters, all totally different. He says his ambition is to play a woman.

"I never do anything easy. If I had to play characters close to me, I'd be ashamed to do it. To play characters different and weird is to act upon my fantasies. This allows me to speak in a more direct way to my audience. Each man feels a need to communicate. Acting is the way I do it. Deep in myself are facets of all the characters I play. But to bring them out is a complicated thing that causes me much agony. I can't turn it off. I go home and drink coffee and play with my kids, and my mind is still on my work. When I dragged the woman across a deserted island in *Swept Away*, I did not go home and beat my wife. But I thought about it."

He says he acts because he loves it, but the "buts" are infinite. "I take photographs, I paint, I'm a good cook. But it's better to do one thing well than many things badly. I'd rather make a big mistake at the thing I do best than have a series of small successes. When I do a film, I'm involved in the daily rushes, editing, camera angles—every aspect of filmmaking. Yet I rarely look like myself on the screen. I like to hide what I am. Actors used to wear masks. I like that even better."

And who is the real Giancarlo Giannini when the cameras are silent? "Nobody. Just an ordinary man. I have all the problems all fathers and husbands have. The difference is, I arrive home one night with red hair and curls, the next night with blond hair and a mustache. My family is used to my life. When I did *Hamlet*, my oldest son was in the wings in his playpen looking at me like I was a madman. That is a jolt for a man. But they got used to it. Now they just say, 'What is Papa playing tonight in those funny glasses?' "

His older son, Lorenzo, is eight; the baby, Adriano, is four. When he came to Lina Wertmuller's set to visit Papa on *Seven Beauties*, she had the brainstorm of casting him in the role of Giancarlo as a child in the flashbacks. The four-year-old took one look at the thirties' wigs and underwear, and said, "I will not play a *pagliaccio* [clown]—not even for Papa." Luckily, the eight-year-old was there to step into the role. "I think he liked it too much," frowns Giannini. "I don't want him to be an actor." Mrs. Giannini is an ex-actress now studying to be a child psychologist in Rome.

When he isn't acting, Giannini dubs American films into Italian. Unlike most stars, he doesn't mind the work and says it teaches him hidden aspects of his craft while he earns good money for doing it. Currently, he is the voice of Jack Nicholson in Antonioni's *The Passenger* and the voice of Al Pacino in *Dog Day Afternoon*.

"I've learned a lot from dubbing Americans into Italian. Only a genius can be a born actor. I am not a genius so I learn all the time. I love Chaplin and copy his walk all the time. I get very emotional in films. Fatally, I see actor's flaws and tricks, but if the film is good I can have just as much fun as the average person.

"I don't do it for the money. Money is only important to eat and sleep. I don't care much for material things because I wouldn't know how to use them if I had them. I could buy a motorboat, but I get seasick. I could buy a car, but then you have to have it waxed, so I ride in other people's cars. I don't have a very commercial mind, but I would like to make American films. I'd have to work very differently, learn to think differently. Anything is possible, but I have no desire to make musicals or cowboy movies. Most of the films in America are not worth making. And I might not have the control over everything I have with Lina."

After so many films with Wertmuller, he has now made a new one for Luchino Visconti. "I had to work differently. I trust Lina. I even tell her how to photograph my eyes. But I'm very stubborn with other directors in order to defend myself. The actor is always the victim. Visconti was no problem. He cares about actors and says little but listens to everything. He leaves his actors free to establish their own responsibility to the film."

The new one is called *The Innocent*. He plays a man with a wife and a mistress. When the wife has another man's baby, he murders the child, then himself. Not exactly a million laughs. "The story is very banal, but it shows how men who try to bend everything to their way of thinking end up destroying themselves. It's another antihero."

Like Jack Nicholson, Giannini has come along at a time of sexual confusion, when men on the screen are getting a fresh look at themselves and are not afraid to cry. "There are two factions to work for—the critics and the public. I work for the public. In Italy, I have the public. In America, I have the critics *and* the public. You can be a good actor, and nobody comes to see you.

"I've been lucky. If I try to analyze my success, I say Women's Lib has done it. Men are frightened; there is chaos everywhere. We wait to see what will happen. Women have always had the upper hand. Now they see what their power is doing to men in the characters I play—I knock them around, but they always do me in at the end. Men identify with the characters I play, and women feel sorry for them. This gives me power, and I love that."

The momentary elation subsides. He scratches his stubble of beard, and his voluminous eyes fill with tears of self-pity. "Power is another fantasy I live in. The truth is, I am weak. My goal is to find the strength to stop acting. It's not a profession for a real man. I find myself on top of a woman

(RIGHT) Mae Marsh:
Our dream of earthly beauty.

(BELOW) Giancarlo Giannini:
Dynamic, appealing, and sexy.
(*The Innocent.* Courtesy of
Analysis Films Releasing Corporation.)

making love, and I am really on top of a chair. The actress has gone home and the camera is shooting me making love to a chair. It's an insane profession."

But it buys a lotta pizza.

[1976]

Pauline Kael

LILLIAN GISH AND MAE MARSH

Mae Marsh is less ethereal, somehow less actressy, more solid and "normal," and yet, in her own way, as exquisite and intuitive.

One can trace almost every major tradition and most of the genres, and even many of the metaphors, in movies to their sources in Griffith. The Ku Klux Klan riders of *The Birth of a Nation* became the knights of Eisenstein's *Alexander Nevsky*; the battle scenes, derived from Mathew Brady, influenced almost all subsequent war films, and especially *Gone With the Wind*. A history of Russian movies could be based on the ice breaking up in Griffith's *Way Down East*, taking that ice through Pudovkin's epic *Mother* up to Chukhrai's *Clear Skies*, where the thaw after Stalin's death is represented literally by the breaking up of ice. One can also trace the acting styles. Mae Marsh returned to us via the young Garbo and other Scandinavian actresses, and Lillian Gish returned to us via Brigitte Helm of *Metropolis*, Dorothea Wieck of *Mädchen in Uniform*, and *most* of the European actresses of the twenties. Griffith's stylized lyric tragedy *Broken Blossoms*, though smaller in scope than *The Birth* or *Intolerance* is, I think, the third of a trio of great works. It is the source of much of the poignancy of Fellini's *La Strada*. Donald Crisp's brutal prizefighter became Anthony Quinn's Zampano, and Lillian Gish's childish waif must have strongly influenced the conception of Giulietta Masina's role as well as her performance.

Griffith used Lillian Gish and Mae Marsh contrastingly. In his films, Lillian Gish is a frail, floating heroine from romantic novels and poems—a maiden. She is the least coarse of American screen actresses; her grace is pure and fluid and lilylike. She is idealized femininity, and her purity can seem rather neurotic and frightening. Mae Marsh is less ethereal, somehow less actressy, more solid and "normal," and yet, in her own way, as exquisite and intuitive. She is our dream not of heavenly beauty, like Gish, but of earthly beauty, and sunlight makes her youth more entrancing. She looks as if she could be a happy, sensual, ordinary woman. The tragedies that befall her are accidents that could happen to any of us, for she has never wanted more than common pleasures. There is a passage in *Intolerance* in which Mae Marsh, as a young mother who has had her baby taken away from her, grows so distraught that she becomes a voyeur, peeping in at windows to simper and smile at other people's babies. It's horrible to watch, because she has always seemed such a sane sort of girl. When Lillian Gish, trapped in the closet in *Broken Blossoms,* spins around in terror, we feel terror for all helpless, delicate beauty; but when Mae Marsh is buffeted by fate, every ordinary person is in danger. Mae Marsh died at seventy-two, but the girl who twists her hands in the courtroom scene of *Intolerance* is the image of youth-in-trouble forever.

[1968]

Charles Champlin

CARY GRANT

It is a demeaning myth that superstars are bad actors who get by simply by playing themselves.

The commissary at Shepperton Studios on the fringe of London. A raw and wind-whipped day outside. A pleased and excited burble of lunchtime conversations inside. An Academy Award-winning actress lunches with her director and with her young co-star, who would soon have an Academy nomination of her own. Nearby sits the male star of a phenomenally successful American television series.

Shepperton is in full swing—the storm before the lull of the late sixties—and in the commissary is an almanac's worth of the famous and near-famous from both sides of the camera.

Suddenly a wave of silence, as tangible as a draft, moves forward from the door. The Oscar-holding actress stops in midsentence. The debonair television star stares at the visitor like a bleacherite at a Hollywood premiere.

Cary Grant, the well-silvered hair tousled by the wind, collar up against the chill, an untidy folder of business papers under his arm, a secretary scurrying to keep up, has popped in to see an associate.

He strides through the room, trying to be unaware of the paralyzing effect he has had on all other activity, giving half-embarrassed smiles and nods to familiar faces, looking for all the world like a Hitchcock hero on the lam and bluffing his way through a party he's crashed in hopes of eluding pursuers. He joins his friends, and the lunchtime murmurations resume. But he doesn't stay long, and another watchful hush follows him to the door and out into the gray English winter afternoon.

The memory is indelible, because no other actor could have had so stunning an effect on an audience of fellow professionals, who had, after all, watched many a star rise and wane and many a talent blossom and fade.

There is another memory. A warm summer night at Malibu. The designer Jean Louis and his wife, Maggie, are giving a party for their house guests, Rudolf Nureyev and Dame Margot Fonteyn. The guest list ranges from Anouk Aimée to Loretta Young. The Rolls-Royces if laid end to end would have stretched halfway to Santa Barbara, and, as I remember, they did.

Toward three in the morning, Shirley MacLaine is frugging with Nureyev to the four-piece rock group. Cary Grant and Dyan Cannon wander in from a stroll on the beach (they plunged into matrimony a few days later) and pass through the rooms amidst a cone of awed silence and turned heads. They watch the dancing.

"I don't know," says Grant, grinning. "When I dance with a girl, I like to hold her. I mean, that's the pleasure of it." He gazes at the floor space between the dancers and lifts his eyebrows in the look of startled, innocent disbelief which generations of light comic actors have tried hard to duplicate.

"Uhn-uhn. Don't like it," Grant was saying. "And another thing. Bucket seats are an abomination." His hands measure the vast, incommunicable gulf between bucket seats. "I don't know what the world is coming to." He grins again, wraps his arm around Miss Cannon and they move off to say good night to their hostess.

It is a Philip Barry moment—an urbane, amusing, romantic encounter in the world of the rich and beautiful.

That memory is indelible, as well, because you sensed that Cary Grant was himself aware that art and nature had in that brief instant come close together, and that he was being the figure he has so often played. The grin was gently self-mocking, not displeased.

Every actor who becomes a star and then a superstar endures because he embodies better than anyone else a particular life-style. He is a charismatic individual, vivid and unforgettable, and his is also a more general figure—a type—embodying a set of attributes and qualities which are the projections of the audience's wishes and dreams.

Cary Grant, more than any other actor, has perfectly and totally embodied the idea of the debonair romantic hero, moving with ease, assurance, and charm, with quick wit and swift resourcefulness, through a world which has most often and most successfully been urban and contemporary, moneyed and literate.

He can be a dramatic actor of very great power, as he proved so eloquently in *None But the Lonely Heart* in 1944, when he was a poor young man inspired by Ethel Barrymore to escape the blighting darkness of a life of crime. It is in fact probably our loss and his that he has not been asked more often to stretch himself with more urgent and compelling dramatic material.

He has also acted the traditional robust action hero, as in *Gunga Din* and *Destination Tokyo*, and in so thickset an enterprise as *The Pride and the Passion*, which created little of either.

But neither he nor Hollywood have had any doubts about where his real strength lies. For what distinguishes Grant from such fellow superstars as Gable and Cooper, Stewart and Wayne, and Bogart and Fonda, is his special mid-Atlantic (really almost stateless), classless, romantic, articulate, freewheeling, free-spirited, worldly yet oddly naïve and idealistic charm.

There used to be an Ivy League joke to the effect that a Yale man walked into a good saloon as if he owned it, a Princeton man as if he knew the owner, and a Harvard man as if he didn't give a damn who owned it. Grant in his most memorable moments has projected a kind of rakish insouciance which embraces all three attitudes.

The Grant character owes much of its appeal to the several paradoxes it incorporates. That matchless accent, for example, is English but it owes a good deal more to Bristol (or Bow Bells) than to the BBC and Oxford. It is cosmopolitan and capable of great elegance but it is not stuffy, Tory, or harmfully upperclass. It is smart, engaging, and mobile.

Mobility looms large in the Grant persona. Thinking back over all the bright roles, you somehow remember him as footloose but, paradoxically, not irresponsible—a swinging bachelor who, however, would never let a lady down and who has clearly only been waiting for the right girl to come along. He is agile, not Alfie.

Grant, like his accent, has seemed essentially classless: comfortable and

Jean Harlow:
Many mirrors, much white satin.

Cary Grant:
Footloose but not irresponsible.

welcome among the working stiffs, yet not nervous or out of place in the marble halls of the superwealthy (unless, as in *Holiday*, the script asked him to be). He has also worked the neat trick, like such rougher-cut diamonds as Steve McQueen, of exerting a massive romantic appeal on women without rousing men to anger or contempt, and indeed while keeping their respect and admiration.

The other paradoxes which have surfaced in the Grant characterizations over the years include his special blend of worldliness and naïveté and his ability to mix polish and pratfalls in successive scenes. Grant is also, refreshingly, able to play the near-fool, the fey idiot, without compromising his masculinity or surrendering to camp for its own sake. His ability to play off against his own image as the strong and handsome romantic hero figure is, as a matter of fact, probably unique among the superstars. No one else comes to mind who could similarly toy with his own dignity without losing it.

It seems very likely that there is a kind of hierarchical ranking even among our dream figures and our fantasies. Dreams of athletic glory are one thing, dreams of swashbuckling heroics are another and probably even more wistful thing. But very possibly the most potent dreams of all—because they are both the nearest to hand but also the most maddeningly elusive—are the dreams of social grace. To be the man who knows what to say and do and be in any social situation, and most particularly to be able to move with assurance through the world of the successful, is enviable beyond price, and the charm of a figure who can do it is immense.

And what may well, therefore, give Cary Grant his special place among superstars, his ability to roll a ripple of appreciative silence across a crowded commissary, is that what he is and does excites the envy of us all (man and woman alike) so powerfully. He is, perhaps, the man more of us would be in dreams than any other, the man more women would have had their lover be than any other. And not least, he shows an almost miraculous ability to defeat time, and thus enacts the most powerful dream of all for us.

It is one of the demeaning myths which have grown up around the movies that superstars are bad actors or worse, who get by simply by playing themselves. The truth is that being natural in front of a camera does not survive the first two takes, and the performer who is merely trying to play himself is, by the twentieth reading of a line, a sweat-eyed wreck with his stomach knotted like a gourd.

Superstars may or may not have begun with the element of stagecraft in hand (Grant did), but if they survive and prosper they become very gifted actors indeed—or they are crafty enough to work with directors who have enormous patience and cunning.

Grant had obviously learned a lot about presence during the days of his music hall apprenticeship, and it's been his good fortune to work with some of the most perceptive directors in the business, most notably George Cukor, who extracted the first screen performance (in *Sylvia Scarlett*) with which Grant was fully happy and who, in *Holiday* and *The Philadelphia Story*, helped Grant add further luster to the high-polish romantic comedy style he had developed while working with Howard Hawks and Leo McCarey.

Unfortunately, even Hollywood itself (as reflected in its Academy Award choices) is less impressed by the difficulties of doing comedy than of chewing the scenery in dramatic roles. But the truth is that Grant quickly became and has remained one of the ablest actors in the movies. The further truth is that light comedy is actually the heaviest and most difficult discipline of them all (as anyone painfully knows who has watched a comedy fail to work). Grant's glossary of grins and grimaces, the lifting eyebrows, the earnest bafflement, the dawning awareness that something has gone terribly, terribly wrong, the panicky suspicion that the lady's intentions are dishonorable and perhaps even carnivorous, the double takes for openers, the falls and cowerings and the blithe assurance which precedes the fall, are all the hallmarks of an extremely skilled actor who has never stopped learning.

But if Grant is an uncommonly fine comic actor, he is also, of course, an incomparable romantic actor, and it is hard to say whether history will more honor the bright comedy or the idealized romance (or feel it necessary to isolate the two).

By now, more than four decades after his astonishing career in the movies began, Cary Grant has peopled the dreams of uncounted millions of us everywhere in the world. He has helped define the aspirations and shaped the dialogue and the deportment of many of us in ways that neither he nor we recognize. He is, in fact, one of the last of the great consciousness prototypes who arose in the golden age of the movies and who are unlikely to arise there again—certainly not with the positive attributes of wit, charm, and romantic idealism which belong, incomparably, to Cary Grant.

[1973]

Richard Schickel

JEAN HARLOW

The sex queen always ends up playing a parody of herself.

Jean Harlow provided the feminine counterpoint to the staccato chatter of the machine gun. Her face was as hard as that of a porcelain doll. Her settings were always high-key, brilliant. There were many mirrors, much white satin, both on her person and in her bedroom, to which the camera quickly repaired and where it lingered long. Her principal occupation was the painstaking application of makeup—a makeup of such high gloss that one could almost catch a reflection in it. The platinum in her hair seemed the result of electroplating, not dye. In her way, she was as frank about sex as Mae West, but with considerable difference—symbolized by their figures. West seemed soft and yielding, a kind of painted earth mother for whom pleasure was everything. Miss Harlow's body was trim and efficient; no doubt she would prove highly efficient in her lovemaking, but there was no promise of a comforting and comfortable afterglow with her. Instead, the implication was that the final act of love's drama would be the exchange of money.

In the movies, the sex queen, the Theda Bara, the Mae West, the Harlow, the Marilyn Monroe—even the Garbo—always ends up playing a parody of herself. It is as if the audience cannot stand for long this physical manifestation of its dream life. It must at a certain point relieve the inner tension engendered by such stars through laughter. With considerable relief, the critics burst into print with the information that the Symbol has become an extremely talented comedienne. Harlow was such when she died in 1937, having refused, because of her Christian Science faith, medical aid for complications following uremic poisoning.

It is also true that stars who symbolize an era's sexual longings rarely find sexual happiness themselves. Harlow's only marriage ended in a month, with her husband's suicide. He, it developed, had been unable physically to satisfy any woman. Only William Powell brought her any happiness. For many years after she died he saw to it that fresh flowers were always present at her grave.

[1962]

Judith Crist

KATHARINE HEPBURN

Onstage, onscreen, and in person, she has brought the singularity of her person and personality directly to the audience, always generous in giving of herself.

"I'm a personality as well as an actress. Show me an actress who isn't a personality and you'll show me a woman who isn't a star. A star's personality has to shine through."

The quote is Katharine Hepburn's—and no truer words have been spoken about this woman who has been one of the outstanding personalities, actresses, and stars of the American stage and screen for nigh onto half a century.

Determined, from her graduation from Bryn Mawr in 1928, to be a great actress, she fulfilled that ambition in both stage and screen, through popular success and failure that would have damaged and/or daunted a lesser personality. And she fulfilled herself as a woman with courage and integrity that put her far beyond the females of her generation—and succeeding ones.

I can think of few actresses who served, as Hepburn has, as inspirational "role model" for so many of us. For my generation the initial impact came with her portrait of Jo in *Little Women*, her fourth movie, made in 1933 and a classic for young people thereafter. To me she has always been Jo, part tomboy, part romantic, part poet, her beauty so ingrained that it has always gone against the fashion, her spirit so valiant that it has always implied defiance of convention, her courage so much the moral effort of a sensitive and vulnerable personality, her independence an inspiration for us all.

Certainly, she has proved herself as achiever, from the time of her arrival in Hollywood after four years of success-and-failure-and-success on and off Broadway. Since her smashing film debut in 1932, *A Bill of Divorcement*, opposite John Barrymore, she has made only thirty-eight theatrical films (in contrast to the more than eighty by Bette Davis, say, or the late Joan Crawford). But in the course of them—and despite being labeled "box-office poison" during the forties and fifties, when some of her best work was done—she became the unofficial Oscar champion. She is the only star to have won three best actress (or actor) Oscars, her first for her third film,

Morning Glory, in 1933, and the third star to have won it two years in a row, for *Guess Who's Coming to Dinner* in 1967 and *The Lion in Winter* in 1968. And she is the only star to have won eleven nominations in the course of her career.

Elegance—that innate breeding that provides both the comedy to the pratfall and the drama to the heartbreak moment—and intelligence have been the hallmarks of Hepburn's work. Skinny, seemingly gawky, red-headed and high-cheekboned, her Bryn Mawr accent and rapid-fire delivery a boon to impersonators as her lean features and build have been to caricaturists, Hepburn sustained both her radiant beauty and her individualism throughout the years. She was as much the lovely capricious flirt in 1975's *Love Among the Ruins* (for television) as she had been in 1938's *Bringing Up Baby*; she was as feisty a character in 1975's *Rooster Cogburn* as she had been in 1952's *The African Queen*; she set the Broadway theater aglow with *Coco* in 1969 as she had in *The Warrior's Husband* in 1932.

Offscreen, Hepburn, daughter of a crusading physician and an ardent feminist, practiced the independence so many of her film roles preached. But let's digress for a moment and realize that contemporary mores forced many of those preachments to be a lot more limited than, I suspect, Hepburn herself would have wanted. In such films as *Woman of the Year* and *Adam's Rib*, for example, the final moral always turned out to be that the man, after all, did know best.

But in her own life, Hepburn proved herself a completely independent person, one who eschewed ersatz glamour, spoke out politically, and associated as she wished. Her pre-Hollywood marriage, to a Philadelphia socialite in 1928, ended in divorce in 1934. Then came the years of her pursuit by Howard Hughes (a one-fourth backer of her major stage triumph in *The Philadelphia Story* in 1939). And after her encounter with Spencer Tracy in 1941 as they prepared to co-star for the first time with *Woman of the Year* (when, legend has it, Hepburn, five-feet-seven, said, "I'm afraid I'm a little tall for you, Mr. Tracy," and he replied, "Don't worry, Miss Hepburn, I'll cut you down to my size"), their offscreen friendship dominated her personal life until his death in 1967.

The Tracy-Hepburn teaming, in eight films, bore its special magic: Hepburn seemed to assume a softened glow, a sexiness tempered by an undertone of feminine submissiveness. In retrospect my favorite is 1952's *Pat and Mike*, where the easy give-and-take of their performances seems so much a duet by intimates. But there is far more fire and ice to her teaming with Cary Grant, with whom she co-starred in four films, setting with him, after *Sylvia Scarlett* in 1936, a new high for sophisticated comedy in *Bringing Up Baby*, *Holiday*, and *The Philadelphia Story*. And somehow the qualities of both relationships spilled over into her co-starring with Peter O'Toole in *The Lion in Winter*, as the complex love-hate contest between king and queen results in brilliant performances by both actors.

Onstage, onscreen, and in person Hepburn has brought the singularity of her person and personality directly to the audience, always her public's partisan, always generous in giving of herself, intense about her work and interests. And in this video age, she carved herself still another niche in the hall of fame, let alone in our hearts, by keeping Dick Cavett's inane interruptions to a minimum and his awe inarticulate during their hour-long interview. It takes a great woman, actress, star and personality to accomplish that, of course.

[1978]

George Morris

CHARLTON HESTON

Intractability is the source of much of his appeal.

If he didn't always seem to take himself so seriously, Charlton Heston would probably have fared much better with critics than he has. He is an adequate actor with an imposing physical presence, but somewhat like Burt Lancaster, he has frequently tried to stretch his talent without considering its inelasticity. He has seldom been relaxed before the camera. His earnestness and probity may never be in doubt, but because he is essentially humorless, his attempts to behave nobly and selflessly have a touch of the sanctimonious about them. Heston is agonizingly aware of the purity of his intentions, and he never tires of externalizing this agony on the screen. His body is always coiled and ready for some kind of combat. Even his features look as though they might have been carved with great difficulty out of some particularly intractable rock.

And yet, paradoxically, it is this intractability which is the source of much of Heston's appeal, and perhaps the main reason he has been a major movie star for thirty years now. Even at his most pious, or during his most anguished efforts to be stoic and just, he's always so damned likable. When Heston sets the firm line of his jaw, or fixes those penetrating eyes with determination, you know that nothing short of death will stand in his way of landing that airplane, mobilizing a city against an earthquake, or halting the invasion of an army of Maribunta ants.

THE MOVIE STAR | 265

It was 1954 when he held those ants at bay in *The Naked Jungle*, and looking back over his career, it now seems inevitable that he should have survived into the seventies as the definitive hero of such disposable, interchangeable disaster epics of the decade as *Skyjacked*, *The Omega Man*, *Soylent Green*, *Earthquake*, and *Airport 1975*. In one form or other, Heston has always been defending civilization from the forces of chaos and barbarism. Cecil B. De Mille irrevocably charted the direction of his career when, in 1956, he cast the actor as Moses in *The Ten Commandments*. Heston has never really been able to cast off this image. He even perpetuated it by continuing to appear in such epics as *Ben-Hur* (1959), *El Cid* (1961), *55 Days at Peking* (1963), *The Greatest Story Ever Told* (1965), and *The Agony and the Ecstasy* (1965).

But like many popular stars whose careers fall into stereotyped patterns, Heston occasionally broke the mold with the help of an especially gifted director. For example, Anthony Mann's *El Cid* and Nicholas Ray's *55 Days at Peking* are memorable exceptions to the rule. In the former, Heston truly achieves the stature of a tragic hero; while in the latter, he eloquently embodies the last of Ray's tormented rebels. Heston does some of his finest, least affected acting in this film, particularly in his scenes with the Chinese orphan, whose dependence and trust eventually link them in a bond of mutual emotional commitment.

But the two directors who have used Heston's persona most expressively—and most daringly—are Orson Welles and King Vidor. In *Touch of Evil* (1958), Welles exposes the limitations of his star's inflexible image by plunging him into a nightmarish world from which all traces of order and moral rigor have disappeared. Welles systematically undercuts Heston's high-minded efforts to control the progress of the criminal investigation in the story, strongly implicating him in the fates of several characters (including Janet Leigh, who plays his wife). And in Vidor's *Ruby Gentry* (1952), Heston plays a man whose rigid adherence to duty and honor destroys both the land he has worked to develop and the woman he has always loved. Vidor typically links Heston's repression of natural passion and sexual desire with a denial of life itself. The actor is unequivocally superb in *Ruby Gentry*; he responds beautifully to the melodramatic requirements of the story and Vidor's intensely physical direction. Since it is one of his earliest films, it is tempting to speculate the direction Heston's career might have taken if, instead of falling in with De Mille and Wyler, he had continued to work with directors like Vidor.

[1979]

Joy Gould Boyum

DUSTIN HOFFMAN

The biggest star of the new starless system.

Some actors are chameleons. They are the ones like Laurence Olivier and Alec Guinness (perhaps not so strangely, both British) who can totally transform themselves on the screen. From part to part, their faces change, their voices, their gestures, their strides—and frequently, with minimal help from the makeup man. And partly because of their talent and partly because it is change itself that we associate with them, a distinctive and distracting persona doesn't hover over their various and varied characterizations. Does Olivier seem more temperamentally suited to play the lowly and demonic Heathcliff than the regal and courageous warrior, Henry V? Does Alec Guinness look more like the reserved and meek bank clerk he played in *The Lavender Hill Mob* than like the martinet he incarnated in *The Bridge on the River Kwai?*

Other actors are clearly less versatile. They are the ones like Marlon Brando and Paul Newman (perhaps not so strangely, both American) who are sharply defined by their faces, physiques, voices, mannerisms, and the personality that total presence suggests. Their roles are frequently variations on a theme and when they wander from type—as Brando especially has done from time to time—their screen personalities tend to shadow them closely. To watch Brando, for example, play Napoleon in *Desirée* or Sakini in *Teahouse of the August Moon* is never to lose sight in the artifice of a hairdo or altered eyes of the sometime brutal, immensely sensual tough with the touch of the poet about him that is the Brando persona.

Brando and Newman are, of course, American actors who developed in the forties and fifties. And the star system and the cult of personality it encouraged has presumably since that time weakened in American film. The new breed of performer who came along in the sixties seems to resist the idea of personality in his attempts to project through his unglamorous, even homely appearance not only a high level of reality but also an expansive range. He aspires, in other words, to versatility.

Take, for example, the chameleonlike screen roles of the biggest star of all of this new starless system: Dustin Hoffman. There is the champion debater and track star of *The Graduate*; the crippled, consumptive con man Ratso

Katharine Hepburn (with Spencer Tracy): *Elegance and intelligence.* (From the MGM release *Keeper of the Flame.* © 1942 Loew's Inc. Copyright renewed 1969 by Metro-Goldwyn-Mayer Inc.)

(LEFT) Charlton Heston:
A touch of the sanctimonious.
(From the MGM release *Ben Hur*.
© 1959 Loew's Inc.)

(ABOVE) Glenda Jackson:
One of the most brilliant actresses.
(From the motion picture *Hopscotch*.
Courtesy of Avco Embassy Pictures Corp.
Copyright © 1980 by Edie and
Ely Landau, Inc.)

Rizzo in *Midnight Cowboy*; the wise one-hundred-year-old Indian of *Little Big Man*; the successful but miserable rock musician of *Who Is Harry Kellerman and Why Is He Saying Those Terrible Things About Me?*; the unmanly intellectual of *Straw Dogs*; and currently, the brilliant counterfeiter Louis Vega, victimized by the French penal system together with his friend, Papillon; and the shy and inhibited Italian husband of *Alfredo Alfredo*.

The range is clearly a wide one, with each role sharply differentiated from the other. Nevertheless, and despite the apparent aim of Hoffman to avoid it, an identifiable and in fact unmistakable Hoffman persona has developed. And it's all the more curious that it has, since it's not until *Alfredo Alfredo* that Hoffman has had a role which clearly articulated it. Two related questions follow: How then has this persona been created? And what does its presence reveal about the nature of Hoffman's acting?

The answers are to be found, of course, in all of Hoffman's films, but are most conspicuous in his two latest ones. And probably because both manage to isolate Hoffman's performance though in very different ways. On the one hand, Franklin J. Schaffner's *Papillon* allows us to focus on Hoffman by offering us 150 minutes where there is little else to interest us. The film is adapted by Dalton Trumbo and Lorenzo Semple, Jr., from ex-convict Henri Charrière's memoirs concerning his experiences in and various escapes from the penal colony of French Guiana. And on film even more than in print, Charrière's life emerges an unlikely melodrama in the tradition of Dumas père that has forgotten to borrow, along with the heroics and striking improbabilities, the vigor and tension that provides the master's flamboyant narratives with most of their interest. Steve McQueen plays the innocent, butterfly-tattooed superman who races unharmed through jungles, leaps safely from the cliffs of Devil's Island, spends a sun-bathed interlude with a silent, gorgeous, topless native girl, and charts rough seas with his fellow prisoner and pal, Louis Vega. Since Hollywood, like Charrière, owes a huge debt to the Dumas tradition, we have seen such romantic adventures many times before, but never realized so dully and at such a slow pace. Even more distended, though, are the years in between these exploits, a good many of which Papillon spends in solitude. There, especially, we have lots of time for contemplation, and we can drift off to thought of Louis Vega and the actor, Dustin Hoffman, who plays him.

On the other hand, Pietro Germi's *Alfredo Alfredo* spotlights Hoffman's acting by separating him from his voice. A dumb spoof on that well-worn subject of Italian marriage before the institution of divorce which moves fast enough and wildly enough to make you laugh in spite of yourself, the film has an Italian-language sound track and the voice attributed to Hoffman is clearly not his own. The effect of this is that we tend to see his performance as if we were watching it on television and had turned off the sound. Every gesture is emphasized; every expression is enlarged.

What emerges from these two films is the image of an actor tailoring a role to his own personality, while at the same time differentiating characters out of a comedian's grab bag of surface effects. Hoffman's Louis Vega declares his cleverness with bifocals, his age with a bald spot, his physical cowardice and weakness with a nasal voice, a duck walk and abrupt angular movements, and his goodness and love with tears in his comically split eyes and a toothy, sincere grin that is released only at the point that Hoffman allows his upper lip to relax its tight grasp on his lower one. Could this be "the biggest crook in France"? The bartender, counterfeiter, and millionaire who pulled off jobs that could be solved by only "France's smartest cops"? Of course not. It is instead the amusing, antiheroic loser, the loner alienated by his sensitivity and shyness that is the Hoffman persona.

And it is really little more than another version of this very same character whom we encounter with a good deal less interference from the makeup man in *Alfredo Alfredo*. Here, Hoffman's props to turn him into an Italian are merely slicked-down, thick black hair and a pair of dark glasses. But he is once again, the awkward, inhibited and feeling good soul. Only this time, the character is written into the role. And put upon by a devouring female—the beauty played by Stefania Sandrelli who manipulates him into marriage, who sends him telegrams containing thirteen "Forgive me's" and twenty-five "I love you's," and who exhausts him with her physical passion—he is indeed a Latinate version of Benjamin Braddock in *The Graduate*. (And not, I should add, the conventional and athletic and articulate WASP the screenplay called for, but the lovable, suffering schlemiel that Hoffman played.)

And despite lip service to the contrary, I suspect this is precisely the person Hoffman's fans want him to be in each of his films. It is, after all, the Hoffman they fell in love with and turned into a generational hero; and because they kept wanting to revisit this persona, they accept instead of the kind of deeply felt characterizations that would obscure it, those cleverly mannered caricatures that manage to allow it to surface. What Hoffman and his popularity suggest to us, then, is that the concept of screen acting in America hasn't really changed, that it is still committed to the strong screen personality who retains from film to film a consistent set of qualities. What has changed, instead, is our taste in types.

[1973]

Richard Schickel

BOB HOPE

A man without roots or human ties.

Bob Hope is the man who adapted the principles of the assembly line to the production of humor. He turns out a standardized product—topical wise-cracks—in a rapid-fire stream. There is nothing very elegant about the product; it lacks the intricate charm of humor that is carefully handcrafted to express a highly individual point of view. But it is a miracle of sheer volume, and in each string of gags there is usually at least one that has a seemingly accidental perfection.

Like a machine, Hope maintains a perfectly neutral relationship with his environment. It exists only to provide him with "material" which he efficiently and unemotionally processes. It is impossible to tell from his jokes what—if anything—he really values or really loathes. He lays about him with a fine impartiality. His sallies are completely without passion. Ironically, he is therefore able to get away with more cruelty in his wit than a comedian who invests his humor with a more personal feeling.

So far as his public is concerned, Hope is a man without roots or human ties. No major celebrity of our time has more successfully separated his public existence from his private life. His sketchy biography tells us he was born in England, grew up in Cleveland, entered show business as a dancer, spent long, lean years in the lower levels of vaudeville, switched to comedy somewhere along the line, and achieved his first success in Broadway musicals. Radio—a medium that was made for his style—was next; then movies, starting with *The Big Broadcast of 1938*.

Undoubtedly his finest hour occurred during World War II, and it is possible that when the definitive social history of that war is written, Hope will be recognized as representative of what was best in America's response to crisis. With no thought of a cost-plus contract, he put his joke factory to work for the government, providing his special brand of civilian-type humor for men who were suddenly, shockingly not civilians anymore but who welcomed a reminder that they had been and wanted to be again. Hope has never explained why he undertook his program of good work. Like his humor, it simply came to exist, a surprising *beau geste* from a man who has managed the remarkable trick of being funny without ever revealing his true self. [1962]

Bernard Drew

GLENDA JACKSON

"I cannot sit in a room for the rest of my life and make one perfect picture."

Glenda Jackson is one of the most brilliant actresses on stage, screen, and television anywhere in the world today and when she made her sensational Broadway debut as Charlotte Corday, a decade ago, in the Peter Brook–Royal Shakespeare Co. production of *Marat/Sade*, she seemed on the threshold of the most successful career an actress could possibly have in our time.

And that is precisely what happened. Over the next few years, she was seen in the film version of *Marat/Sade*, and then *Women in Love*, which won for her the New York Film Critics award as Best Actress and the first of her Academy Award Oscars, then she received further laurels for her *Elizabeth I* series on television, more international awards for her work in the film *Sunday, Bloody Sunday*, and her second Oscar for *A Touch of Class*.

No actress over the past decade had enjoyed such continuous triumph. Then came such movies as *Triple Echo, Mary, Queen of Scots, The Nelson Affair, The Devil Is a Woman*, and *The Romantic Englishwoman*, all films which had begun with high minded purpose, but which had come to very little.

Glenda's admirers, which include most of the New York critics, began asking, "What's wrong, why is she doing these things? She's so good, so intelligent, what's happening?"

Then came her controversial *Hedda,* based on the Royal Shakespeare production, *Hedda Gabler,* with which she toured the world, and most recently she has delineated Sarah Bernhardt in the Readers Digest production *The Incredible Sarah.*

Glenda and I are, as this business goes, old friends, and when we meet now in her suite at the Sherry-Netherland, we recall an afternoon spent at her home in Black Heath, outside of London, four years ago, and then I ask my nasty question, "Why is Glenda doing all these things?"

She snaps angrily, "Because Glenda wants to do them, that's why. Some of them haven't turned out as well as hoped but that's too bad, it can't be helped. I like to work and I cannot sit in a room for the rest of my life and make one perfect picture, I can't wait around for that. If you felt that way, you'd never go outside and cross a street for fear of being knocked down by a car."

When I point out that *The Devil Is a Woman*, which was filmed in Italy, was edited and dubbed badly after she had left the country, Glenda shrugs and says, "I never saw that film. But that doesn't matter either. You commit yourself to a project, you do the best work in it you can, and then you go on to something else. What they do with it afterward is their problem. I can't spend the rest of my life in editing rooms either, closely watching what they do to me."

She breaks into a smile again and says, in a milder voice, "I guess I just like to work and I can't sit around waiting for perfection."

She is highly enthusiastic about her next film, *Nasty Habits*, based on Muriel Spark's novel *The Abbess of Crewe*, which is about a group of nuns in a situation closely paralleling the Watergate affair. . . .

I recall, during our visit at Black Heath, Glenda's saying she was sick and tired of theater and had no plans ever to do anything more on the stage, but now she appears to be spending about half of her time in the theater. What changed her mind?

"When I said that to you, I had just completed three full years with one company, the Royal Shakespeare," she says. "I was sick and tired of it, they were so self-satisfied. I don't like to knock subsidized theater, but I'm afraid it makes for subsidized audiences. In England, they only want to see what they've seen before, only want to hear what they've heard before, and they don't want to be shocked ever and they're always comparing you with some perfect performance they saw fifty years ago.

"We have a basic problem in England at this moment. There are no new playwrights saying anything new, demanding changes. And if we don't have the writers, we don't have the plays and films and we don't have the audiences alive to them.

"That's one reason I prefer playing in America and Australia. Their audiences are unfiltered and give it to you straight. Besides, England loves losers. What John Schlesinger told you is absolutely correct. The English simply worship failure.

"Still as soon as I return there, I go into rehearsal in a play based on the life, letters, and poetry of Stevie Smith, who died two years ago, a very fascinating lady and a fine poet. No, it won't be a one-woman show. There'll be another actress in it and one man playing all the male roles. We should open in London February or March."

Glenda suddenly looks at me accusingly and demands, "Why don't you write a play or a movie? You know you're dying to, why don't you? And make it good. Everybody's feverishly looking for scripts. So write. Maybe it'll keep you so busy you won't have time to tell me how lousy my pictures are."

And then she laughs.

[1976]

Gary Arnold

BUSTER KEATON

The pathos that once seemed to set Chaplin apart hasn't worn as well as Keaton's ironic deadpan.

The Buster Keaton Film Festival offers moviegoers the rare, exhilarating opportunity to enjoy the best work of one of our greatest popular artists. Organized by film archivist and distributor Raymond Rohauer, this collection of Keaton is at once comprehensive and abundantly entertaining, a revelation as well as a delight.

The series lasts twenty days and consists of the ten feature-length comedies Keaton made as an independent producer-director-star between 1923 and 1928 plus twenty-one two- and three-reel comedy shorts made between 1917 and 1922. . . .

Although the shorts are not placed in strict chronological order, the first film Keaton ever appeared in—*The Butcher Boy*, a two-reel comedy starring Roscoe "Fatty" Arbuckle—is on the same bill with *The Three Ages*, along with the first two-reeler Keaton himself starred in, a high-speed dazzler called *The High Sign* (made in 1920 rather than 1917, as listed in the theater program). Of the twenty-one short films, half a dozen are Arbuckle vehicles in which Keaton was a supporting comic. In addition to *The Butcher Boy*, audiences may find special historical interest in *Fatty at Coney Island* (billed with *Our Hospitality*), evidently the only film in which Keaton smiles, and *Out West,* the first two-reeler the Arbuckle company made after migrating from New York to southern California.

When Arbuckle left his old company to begin making films for Adolph Zukor in 1920, producer Joseph M. Schenck proposed that Keaton take over the unit and Keaton agreed. In the next three years Keaton produced nineteen two- and three-reel comedies, and fifteen of these are in the Rohauer package.

The series does not include a feature Keaton made for Metro in 1920—

The Saphead, an adaptation of a vehicle that Douglas Fairbanks had done on the stage and screen—or his last two silent features, *The Cameraman* and *Spite Marriage*, made under the aegis of M-G-M. Although perfectly decent pictures, *The Cameraman* and *Spite Marriage*, which have been revived occasionally at the American Film Institute, mark the beginning of the end for Keaton as an independent and fully creative comic artist. As Keaton put it in his autobiography, "In 1928 I made the worst mistake of my career. Against my better judgment I let Joe Shenck talk me into giving up my own studio to make pictures at the booming M-G-M lot in Culver City."

Both Charlie Chaplin and Harold Lloyd had warned Keaton against the move to Culver City, and the process that Chaplin warned him would happen did happen. As Keaton recalled, Chaplin told him, "They'll ruin you helping you. They'll warp your judgment. You'll get tired of arguing for things you know are right." Keaton approached Zukor, who demurred on the grounds that he had just signed Lloyd and couldn't use two great comedians. Ultimately, Keaton acquiesced in Schenck's plan to shift the Keaton company to M-G-M and perhaps it was an unavoidable mistake: Joe Schenck was Keaton's brother-in-law as well as his business adviser, and his brother, Nicholas Schenck, was running M-G-M.

At Culver City Keaton's own unit disappeared into the corporate factory, and Keaton was assigned directors and new stables of gag writers. Keaton always insisted that the best sequences in *The Cameraman* and *Spite Marriage* were achieved *despite* M-G-M's interfering solicitude.

The present series is about as complete, as "definitive," as one could hope for: a third of the comedies from the period of Keaton's apprenticeship with Arbuckle; most of the independent two- and three-reelers; and most of the silent features, including the indispensable ones like *Sherlock, Jr.* and *The Navigator* and *Seven Chances* and *Steamboat Bill, Jr.* and *The General*, perhaps the single most beautiful and satisfying motion-picture comedy ever made, the classics' classic.

Buster Keaton, born Joseph Frank Keaton in 1895, was only twenty-two when he inadvertently entered the movie business, after accompanying a friend to Arbuckle's New York studio and being invited to join in the planned mayhem later released as *The Butcher Boy*. However, Keaton and his parents, Joe and Myra, had been vaudeville stars since the turn of the century, and their act, "The Three Keatons," had established certain aspects of Buster's personality, particularly the deadpan expression and the acrobatic skill.

"The Three Keatons" was essentially a roughhouse act between father and son. Buster, the mischievous little kid, would pester Joe, and Joe would pursue and toss Buster all across the stage. Myra Keaton, relieved of knockabout duties after Buster became a permanent fixture of the act at the age of five, would punctuate the slapstick with songs and solos on the alto saxophone, then a brand-new instrument. Indeed, Mrs. Keaton was known as "America's first lady saxophonist."

In his biography *Keaton*, Rudi Blesh attempts to re-create the freewheeling quality of the Keatons' act:

> Monday might be twenty minutes of up-tempo mayhem relieved by "My Gal Sal" on alto sax—practical joke and counterjoke, slips, tumbles, trips, slides, and the unbelievable comic falls. Tuesday might develop into one long comic-story routine all in off-the-cuff pantomime and not a word spoken. Wednesday would perhaps unfold as recitation time, with merciless parodies of Bernhardt, Eva Tanguay, or Sothern and Marlowe's Romeo and Juliet, with the balcony and Buster falling on Joe.
>
> Thursday might be devoted to one long outrageous burlesque of some popular melodrama. Or all these things and more might be cross-stitched into a Keaton sampler of the modes of madness. Not only was it Keystone Comedy long before Mack Sennett met movie camera, it was surrealism before Salvador Dali was even born and pop art before the first Campbell's Soup can sat for Andy Warhol.

One can see all of these elements in Keaton's films, synthesized in a different way for the new medium, which encourages even more fantastic feats of slapstick and parody and spectacle. The movies offered Keaton's fertile, restless comic imagination a spacious, timeless field of play. Pursued by a wrathful Joe on the vaudeville stage, Buster expanded the chase to epic dimensions on the screen, where he could be pursued by legions of policemen (in *Cops*) or fortune-hunting women (in *Seven Chances*). Obstacles that can't be contained on stage become astonishingly possible on film—an avalanche, a cyclone, stubborn ships and locomotives.

In Keaton's greatest films, one is simultaneously impressed by the spectacular nature of the slapstick situations and the heroic resilience, resourcefulness, and perseverance of Keaton's comic persona. Misfortune and misunderstanding assail him in frequently staggering forms, but Keaton always copes. One remembers him in certain characteristic postures—taking flight or skidding to a stop or solemnly scanning the horizon—but perhaps the most revealing and touching moment occurs in *Steamboat Bill, Jr.*, when he's slanted forty-five degrees to the perpendicular, bravely attempting to make some headway against a cyclone. Keaton draws up all his strength and tries to make progress by jumping into the wind, which knocks him back. In an instant he's back up, trying another tack.

At one time it might have seemed unthinkable to rank Keaton or Lloyd on a par with Chaplin, but now one often hears people say that they prefer Keaton or Lloyd. The pathos that once seemed to set Chaplin apart, to make him the most beloved and "poetic" of the great silent-film clowns, hasn't worn as well as Keaton's ironic deadpan or Lloyd's cheerfulness. Chaplin's work still seems wonderful when the comedy and pathos are balanced—as they are in *The Gold Rush*—but when the pathos is in overpowering, self-pitying ascendance—as it is in *City Lights*—Chaplin gets a bit thick.

While the Keaton and Lloyd characters may now seem more attractive because of their emotional reserve and modesty, one doesn't need to choose between these artists at their distinctive, idiosyncratic best. At the level of *The Gold Rush*, *The General*, and *Safety Last* it makes more sense to count your blessings than play favorites.

The Keaton series is a long-overdue treat. It was set for the Key two years ago and then withdrawn when, according to Rohauer, the theater got a new booker who couldn't understand why anyone would want to see something like *that*.

Maybe now he'll know. The movies have never offered a sight more edifying or entertaining than Buster Keaton coping with adversity and calamity.

[1973]

Rex Reed

DIANE KEATON

Beneath the wafting tones of disorganized speech, I sense a genuine fear of the naked exposure that accompanies stardom.

Who is this Chaplinesque creature schlepping down First Avenue in the rain? Baggy pants, well-cut hacking jacket, and bowler hat. Coming through the door. It's Keaton! No, not Buster, dummy. Diane! A movie star. See, she looks just the way she does in Woody Allen's colossal blockbuster, *Annie Hall*. She's wearing the same sunglasses even though it's pouring rain. If the street-smart waitress in Diane's neighborhood greasy-spoon coffee shop thought I was meeting a movie star, she never blinked. Glazed, she plunked down the ubiquitous plastic glass of New York ice water and stared at Keaton as though she was a teenage runaway.

In days before movies, the warmly shy and gently reticent actress might've been a beloved, reclusive poetess like Emily Dickinson, or a repressed but daring novelist like Katherine Mansfield, whose artistic talent might have led more to the shallows of obscure eccentricity than the peaks of fame and fortune. Today, however, there's no doubt that Miss Keaton is standing in the shadow of stardom as surely as *Annie Hall* is cleaning up at the box office. Word is already out that she is merely magnificent in Richard Brooks's screen version of the best-selling shocker *Looking for Mr. Goodbar.*

Safely tucked on the edge of a leather booth Diane observes the world through rose-colored glasses and removes her hat, releasing a fall of fine, shiny ginger-colored hair instantly tamed by being tucked into her jacket collar. Black coffee is all she wants. Amid the clatter of chipped cups and saucers, her laughter is quiet but infectious. "I don't understand stardom very much, you know. One should have the responsibility to do worthwhile projects and not be forced to make decisions about money."

Understand? It's important to her, and she tries to get it out before the sun goes down. "If you have the opportunity . . . you know? I mean, to do meaningful work . . . well, that's the thing to do. And that's the thing that scares me . . . if I have to stand up . . . make decisions about the right thing to do at the right moment . . . to maintain stardom . . . or what's good for me. . . . Wow! When you get successful, you have to pay so much more attention, and think things out a lot more clearly . . . just because you want to work. I'm just a bit frightened by all that's happened to me since *Annie Hall* opened. . . ."

By now, you understand that darling Diane clutters her conversation in a confusion of interrupted thoughts that make perfect sense when you're looking into her downy soft eyes, but leave me puzzled when trying to punctuate her babble. Beneath the wafting tones of disorganized speech, I sense a genuine fear of the naked exposure that accompanies stardom.

"I've never been hampered by a high public profile," she continues. "I could walk down any street and do anything, and maybe somebody would say, Hey, you were okay in *The Godfather*, and that was fine. But to be roughed up and pushed around by fans would be a nightmare. What has that got to do with real life? It's crazy. I don't think that will ever happen to me, because I'm not, after all" (sneaking a giggle) "Farrah Fawcett-Majors. I don't think I'll ever have her public image. I'm an actress, not a fad. I don't think I stand out in a crowd. I don't have a prominent face or all that

(ABOVE LEFT) Diane Keaton: *"Emotional embarrassment is a condition of acting."*
(On the set of *Annie Hall*. Copyright © 1977 United Artists Corporation. All rights reserved.)

(ABOVE RIGHT) Buster Keaton: *Resilience, resourcefulness, and perseverance.* (*The Navigator*.)

(BELOW) Gene Kelly: *Exuberant, muscular, comic-strip-hero handsome.* (From the MGM release *An American in Paris*. © 1951 Loew's Inc. Copyright renewed 1979 by Metro-Goldwyn-Mayer Inc.)

hair or all those teeth. I mean, I've got hair and teeth but—" Keaton's giggle has turned into a full-bodied, vitamin-soaked laugh, and at that minute, I'm thinking I could really spend the rest of my life with her never finishing a sentence.

Diane auditioned for roles—until she met Woody Allen, and things got easier. Every actress in Hollywood read for *Looking for Mr. Goodbar,* but Richard Brooks saw something vulnerable in her comedy films and grabbed her to everyone's amazement without an audition. "The script is wonderful, but tough. It's a very masochistic part. I had a hard time doing it because I kept wanting the character to change and not go back into another singles bar to pick up another man. This woman is an emotional cripple, incapable of having a relationship with anyone. I think it's going to be a strong, powerful film, and I learned so much from Richard Brooks. He's crazy as a loon—but very affectionate, hilarious, dear, and wonderful. No, Woody never came near the set. Richard Brooks closes his sets, and he means everybody keep out, including Woody."

She says after the emotionally draining experience of *Looking for Mr. Goodbar* she was "glad to get home to my own dishes again. Boy, I hope life never gets so complicated that I don't do my own dishes. Having maids and help around makes me very uncomfortable. I always have to get up early when the maid comes. So I'd rather be alone and get up early, do everything fast, then get back into bed for the day, guiltless. Isn't that silly? I live with two cats, lots of plants, and my darkroom. I love photography and working with my hands. Photography is better than acting because I can do it alone. I have a great feeling for the visual arts. I don't have the talent to be a painter, but I make great collages. All I need is a glue pot."

A sudden idea hits her. "I should sign up for a course in something visual. . . . I enrolled in a printmaking course last summer in Greenwich Village, but when I got there I was so threatened by it I couldn't go into the classroom. . . . All of my psychological problems got in the way. . . . Too bad. . . . I would like to know how that stuff is done. . . . Maybe one day—" She's being wistful. No one is more charming and vulnerable when wistful than this spacey wisp of a WASP who has been co-star, friend, and constant companion to Woody Allen until recently. *Annie Hall* is clearly an autobiographical outcome of their intimate relationship—and its unhappy-happy-unresolved ending.

Whatever you call life's liaisons—affairs, marriages, relationships—when they end, they are simply, sadly over. But Keaton and Allen have had a rare opportunity to live theirs once, go back, rewrite it, film it, and live it again—on the screen. I'm reminded of a dear friend who, heartbroken at the end of a long love affair, cried: "What will I do with seven years of home movies?" "Why," answered her shrink, "don't you run them through again and see where you make your mistakes?"

I wondered aloud if *Annie Hall* wasn't a bit like taking that advice. Was making it ever emotionally embarrassing for her and Woody? Diane's answer was short and immediate: *"Yes!"* Then silence. Her decision (do I go on with this line of thought?) was forming. I could almost hear the thoughts, like tiny ice crystals, tinkling in her mind. "It is always embarrassing to reveal my personal life ... but emotional embarrassment is a condition of acting ... revealing yourself even when you're not playing your own life ... the biggest worry I had making *Annie Hall* was whether or not I would get in my own way. I was afraid that unconsciously I might stop myself from showing the truth because it made me uncomfortable. But" (she shrugs) "the whole process of acting is uncomfortable anyway."

She worries too much about what "they" will say—audiences, critics, unknown phantoms. "All of this is a great time waster that gets in the way of a performance. I wanted to do *Annie Hall* fully, without worrying what I did wrong in real life. Understand? I had to stop fantasizing about what kind of person I am. Am I bad? Was I wrong in that situation? Did I hurt Woody too much? Was I selfish? There were so many conflicts. But in the final analysis, working out my relationship with Woody was, and still is, great fun, and always a surprise and a revelation to me."

Is it over? "Look ... Woody and I ... we're beyond getting involved again with each other ... and beyond really hurting each other, which is a wonderful place to get with someone you love ... there's humor, affection, and a certain dependency between us. He's my closest and dearest friend. The only other situation I know like ours—where a movie was made of the actor's offscreen affair—was *Made for Each Other* with Renée Taylor and Joe Bologna. That was a comedy, too, but with sharp edges."

She obviously has a neurotic love-hate relationship with acting, but says forlornly, "I don't know what I'd do without it. I'd be in a pickle." She's kinky but proper, a well-bred all-American girl hiding behind funky shades, just like Annie Hall. "My real name is Hall, but when I registered with Actors Equity, they made me change it because there already was a Diane Hall. I took my mother's maiden name, Keaton. In the beginning—and this is interesting, psychologically—I took my sister's name, Dorrie. After six months it dawned on me how terrible I was ... after all, Dorrie was *her* name ... she *is* Dorrie Hall. ... I think I did it because I like her, and thought her good qualities would rub off on me, but if I was a flop as an actress, all the bad reviews would be going to *her*. ..."

Keaton also has a granny, just like the one in the film, "with the greatest sense of humor . . . I love her so. . . . I was raised in Santa Ana . . . John Birch country . . . California. . . . I'm still smitten with the horizontal view. . . . I have such wonderful memories of my childhood in the desert. . . . Woody hates California and is unrelenting about how much he despises it, but to me Hollywood is not California. I couldn't take Hollywood any more than Woody could. . . . Joan Didion also hates California. . . . God, how I wish I could work with her someday! . . . Remember *Play It as It Lays* with Tuesday Weld? Isn't Tuesday great? She plays my sister in *Looking for Mr. Goodbar,* and she's great . . . I love Tuesday. . . ."

The bowler hat appears once more and she slowly tucks the straggling hair under its crown. "Nothing is happening next . . . I have no films lined up. . . . Maybe I'll get to take that visual arts class . . . that would be nice. . . ." A tiny wave of the hand sends Keaton off into the rain. Nobody notices as she passes through the crowded luncheonette. Only the waitress comments: "That crazy kid gonna get drenched without an umbrella."

[1977]

Richard Corliss

GENE KELLY

The avatar of the go-get-'em young American male embodied in the teens and twenties by Douglas Fairbanks.

Grace vs. energy. Elegance vs. sex appeal. Class vs. mass. The Continental vs. the all-American. Fred Astaire vs. Gene Kelly. They were the most engaging of polar opposites, who shared nothing but a scratchy tenor voice and the responsibility for turning dance-on-film into one of the signal contributions of American movies to twentieth-century art.

Think of the characteristic poses of the two men. Astaire is a scarecrow, in top hat and tails, his arms languidly bent starboard, his fingers playing delicate Kabuki charades, his thin body buffeted a half step backward by the wind, or a *faux pas.* Kelly is a halfback (from one of the lesser Ivy League colleges) meeting alumni after the big game, his body extended almost horizontally as if he's still hurtling over a phalanx of blockers toward the goal line, his strong arms reaching out and the glorious megawatt smile flashing and the go-getter voice shouting, "Glaaaad ta see ya!" Astaire seems to recede from medium shot into the solitary space of his uniqueness; Kelly looks to smile, dance, and positive-think his way right through the movie screen.

Kelly first attracted notice on Broadway as the happy hoofer—"I'm a natural-born dancer and comedian"—in Saroyan's *The Time of Your Life* (1939), achieved stardom as the charming heel Pal Joey (1940), and made his film debut, at age thirty, co-starred with Judy Garland in *For Me and My Gal* (1942). Over the next fifteen years, Kelly turned the ghetto of the dance film into a neighborhood as vital and glamorous as Old Broadway. This is not to say that Astaire, after splitting with Ginger Rogers, soft-shoed his way into early retirement. On the contrary, Astaire was never so formally inventive as when dancing up and down walls, or in slow motion, or just by himself; and he and Kelly engaged in a kind of friendly competition through the forties and fifties to see who could more dazzlingly exploit the special properties of film and feet. But Astaire was aging, and without Rogers he worked best in solo, while Kelly—exuberant, muscular, comic-strip-hero handsome—had a vitality expansive enough to include in its embrace the likes of Rita Hayworth (*Cover Girl*), Vera-Ellen (*On the Town*), Leslie Caron (*An American in Paris*), Debbie Reynolds (*Singin' in the Rain*), and even Mitzi Gaynor (*Les Girls*). It took all his physical skills, but Kelly managed to make eye and body contact with both his harem of leading ladies and the audience in the movie house.

Kelly is unlikely ever to have made it as a straight dramatic actor: in *Cross of Lorraine* or *Black Hand* or *Marjorie Morningstar* his big lungs fill up with a big heavy thought when they should be storing up air for a more profound musical statement—like *"Got*-ta dance!" But he was adroit and winning during the dialogue sections of his musicals. He could be brash and too full of himself in *The Pirate;* or quick and smart with the punchline (the deathless "Hey, Joe, get me a tarantula!" from *Singin' in the Rain*); or effectively winsome with a girl, plucking imaginary daisy petals and describing an invisible semicircle with his toe. He was, in short, the avatar of the go-get-'em young American male embodied in the teens and twenties by Douglas Fairbanks—and the lineal ancestor of the wisecracking but vulnerable hunk that Burt Reynolds now plays. (And Kelly had sturdier, better-looking thighs than either of them.) The Kelly character was always spunky and impulsive enough to shout, "Let's put the show on right here!" knowing full well that the other Kelly—actor-dancer, director-choreographer—would put on one heck of a show.

[1979]

Bernard Drew

BURT LANCASTER

That cold fury at a rotten world he never made seems to have dissipated.

Just enumerate some of Burt Lancaster's films over the past twenty-seven years and you have a roster of some of the most thoughtful and courageous movies of the period—indeed some of the best—*The Killers* (his debut), *Come Back, Little Sheba, From Here to Eternity, Sweet Smell of Success, Elmer Gantry, Birdman of Alcatraz, Seven Days in May, The Professionals*, and many others.

Along the way, he has picked up an Oscar and won three awards from the New York Film Critics and though he may loathe the word, he was a superstar before the term was even invented.

He has made a long journey from Harlem, where he was born in 1913 and grew up in its streets and back lots and then went to DeWitt Clinton High School, from which he graduated into the Depression and a WPA circus, where he performed his trapeze acts up until World War II.

It was after that he made his Broadway debut in Harry Brown's *A Sound of Hunting*. He was over thirty, not young to be only starting in the theater. The play lasted three weeks but he gave a memorable performance in it, much better than anything he would do in the first seven years of his movie career.

He became a star and potent box office almost as soon as he arrived in Hollywood, and once he formed his own production company with Harold Hecht and could make the films he wanted and could take some chances, he became an actor as well, something not every star has to do.

Now here he is in Washington, playing an aging CIA agent suspected of selling out to the Russians, in a film called *Scorpio*. He is being pursued by an assassin played by Alain Delon and later the action will move to London, Paris, and Vienna, where Paul Scofield, as a Russian agent, is waiting to join the cast.

I arrive at the location late in the afternoon and observe Burt spend the rest of the day emerging from a neat white house on a shaded street in Georgetown, then stare thoughtfully at an automobile filled with CIA agents parked across the street, get into his own car and drive off, pursued by the CIA. And that is all.

The next morning as he is finishing breakfast in his suite at the Watergate, I make some mention of his work the afternoon before and he laughs and says, "No, it isn't very interesting, is it? We're just shooting exteriors here, out of context, and it's hard to keep the continuity in your mind. You have to keep doing little things inside in order to keep going."

Burt looks older than he did in *A Sound of Hunting*, though he does not look like a man who will reach sixty before the year is over. But there is something different about him. That anger, that cold fury at a rotten world he never made and didn't want, seems to have dissipated. He always was thoughtful, but now he seems gentle too, even wistful. He has a look now which seems to say, "What's the big rush? Life moves fast enough and it's over too soon. Suppose you do, suppose you don't, does it really matter?"

Maybe I'm reading it wrong, maybe he doesn't feel that way at all, so I turn the conversation to the formation of his own company in the forties. I know he is proud of that, not only of his own films, but those he didn't act in, like *Marty* and *The Bachelor Party*.

"Yes." He smiles. "We started with *Kiss the Blood Off My Hands*, which nobody remembers, but then we made two pictures that still hold up—*The Crimson Pirate* and *The Flame and the Arrow*. They were the first camp before anyone knew what camp was. People went in to sneer but they remained to laugh. The pirates were the honest folk, and the establishment were the crooks, and we played it absolutely straight.

"Waldo Salt wrote the scripts," he recalls, "so it had a poetic quality, as well as being highly satirical.

"I've always respected the work of writers because everything starts there," he says. "We were the first to insist that the writers be on the set while we made the picture. We couldn't afford to pay them their full salary but they went along with it because nobody had ever given them the chance before to be there and to see that nobody hacked up their scripts.

"And we used Broadway actors in the secondary roles. The typical thing in those days was to use Beautiful People only. Of course, if you were making romantic fluff by let's say, Kathleen Norris, naturally the characters would be papier mâché, but if you were doing something about real people we figured, why not use real people?

"Yes, I would like to find a good new play for Broadway now," he says in answer to a question. "But where are they? It's never been easy. In twenty-seven years in movies, only twice have I picked up a script that I wanted to do as it was—*Birdman of Alcatraz* and one I recently finished, *Ulzana's Raid*. The rest had to be worked on and worked on. It's never been easy and it gets harder as you get older.

"Everything gets harder as you get older." He smiles. "It's a problem and one that we all have to face. In movies, in the theater, in life. You want to make a good picture with something to say, but people are going to have to want to see it or it's no good."

"So you have to make an *Airport* in order to be able to make another picture that says something," I murmur.

He laughs. "You have to make popular pictures sometimes so that you can sometimes make those that aren't. You have to keep looking for new ideas and new concepts because, you see, as you get older, you tend to ossify somewhat. You have to watch that. You can't throw everything that went before, out, of course, but you still have to keep the door open for something new."

We speak of current films and directors—Fellini, Visconti, Kubrick and *Clockwork Orange*, which is called Fascist in some quarters.

Burt laughs again. "I thought it was brilliant. No, Kubrick doesn't show people to be angels, and why should he? We have every reason to believe that man is a beast and a predator, but we always have to keep in mind the dream of man. What is it that he wanted? What would he, given the chance, rather be? Can't we believe he'd rather be good if he could?

"You think that the revolution is over?" he says doubtfully. "I don't. How can it be? There's still so much wrong. In the deepest sense of maturity, we learn with time that consideration of others—a lover or just others—is the hallmark of that maturity. What is growing up anyway? Not so much to be a better person, though that may be the end result. But having a sense of security and well-being and some self-respect.

"I think you have to get to love yourself a little and then consequently, you can love other people. You can't go through life being a warrior. Somewhere it has to stop."

We speak now of our mutual alma mater DeWitt Clinton and the old days of growing up in New York.

"That was the place and that was the time," Burt says warmly. "I can remember seeing Lillian Hellman's *The Children's Hour* in 1935. The whole audience stood up to hiss that little girl at the end of the second act. A year later I saw John Gielgud's *Hamlet*. It was the first Shakespeare I'd ever seen. I had a friend who worked in the box office and he gave us tickets in the second balcony. I was with a WPA circus then, Orson Welles was with the Federal Theater. There was the Group, the Civic Repertory and Boleslavsky's American Lab Theater.

"Years before," he says quietly, "When I was a kid on 106th Street between Second and Third avenues, two blocks from the Union Settlement House, I went to the theater constantly. I was doing this school play, Booth

Tarkington's *Three Pills in a Bottle*, I was the little boy in a wheelchair who taught everyone the meaning of love. Boleslavsky saw me and came to our house. My mother looked at me and I said, 'Naah, that's sissy stuff. I'm going out to play stickball.' Now who knows what I would have become if I'd gone with them?"

"Truman Capote, maybe?" I wonder.

He laughs and says, "Now wouldn't that have been something if I'd have become Truman Capote."

[1973]

Judith Crist

JACK LEMMON

White-collar everyman for the mid-twentieth century.

There are stars—and there are stars beyond stars in the Hollywood heavens, for those of us who are the astronomers of the region, movie nuts who have devoted their years, for pleasure and/or profession, to studying that factory town's galaxies. There are the flashers, the durables, the professionals who are stars—and beyond them are the flashing durable professional stars who edge their way onto the screen and glow and grow in ever-increasing, always-more-dazzling intensity, ever beyond the magnitude we once assigned them.

Small doubt that Jack Lemmon is in the forefront of that all-inclusive star category, the actor whose professionalism is his hallmark, whose versatility is his crown and whose persona is the key to the affections of his audience. For much as Chaplin's clown in his time embodied the commonality of the common man, so Lemmon's white-collar everyman has provided the empathetic symbol for the mid-twentieth-century man in his uphill struggle against the bogies of the affluent fifties, the sour sixties, and the uncertain seventies. Whether he's the smooth operator or the schnook, the crafty conniver or the victim thereof; whether he's out for the laughter or tearing at the heart—he's one of us, the all too human people in the middle who get it from top and bottom alike.

Lemmon is, above all, a craftsman, devoted to his acting art, and that, I

(LEFT) Jack Lemmon:
Professionalism is his hallmark.
(*Save the Tiger*. Copyright © MCMLXXII
by Paramount Pictures Corporation,
Filmways, Inc., Jalem Productions, Inc.
and Cirandinha Productions,
Inc. All rights reserved.)

(BELOW) Burt Lancaster:
"You have to get to love yourself a little."
(*The Young Savages*. Copyright © 1960 by
Contemporary Productions, Inc.
All rights reserved. Released through
United Artists Corporation.)

suspect, explains the surprise with which even Lemmon devotees look back at the varieties of his performances, the risks taken in the course of a career that spans more than two decades. Symbolically, consider the range in his two Oscar-winning roles, eighteen years apart. His 1955 Ensign Pulver, which won him the Motion Picture Academy's Best Supporting Actor prize, combined all the brash, braggingly lecherous sass of young manhood with the laziness, the timidity, the callowness, and the essential decency that are equally the characteristics of youth. At the other end of the scale, his 1973 Harry Stoner, which won him the Best Actor Oscar, was the desperate middle-aged spokesman for Pulver's generation, the ensign grown up and ground down, a decent man whose decency can't survive in a world without rules, without a memory of the past, with a reverence only for the material present and no hope or dream beyond another season of economic survival.

And fore and aft and in between Lemmon gave us a constant variety, initially as pure nice-guy in a spate of fifties fun, with time out to portray a warlock or prove that he could be hilarious in girls' gladrags while proving irresistible to men and women alike. Proof of his triumph over sleaziness lies not only in that *Some Like It Hot* role but also in his portrait of a cog in the big-wheel success struggle in *The Apartment*, making a quasi-pimp not merely palatable but actually appealing and proving himself not only an actor of sensitivity but a master of taste. And barely had one classified him as serious master of comedy than along came *Days of Wine and Roses* to prove him a dramatic actor of the first rank in a performance that grows in intensity with each re-viewing, one that starts with the familiar glossy man we expect and recognize and carries him to the very depths of physical horror and spiritual torment. And then back to the flip and the hip and the glossy.

The mark of the man is, perhaps, that he has worked with a number of directors a number of times, consistent in that mutual professional admiration, or admirable professionalism, that distinguishes Lemmon's career on- and offstage. Just as friendships from 'way back are honored, so are associations—a rare quality in a star whose "clout" has been acknowledged for more than a decade. There have been ups and downs with Billy Wilder, from *Some Like It Hot* to *The Apartment* to *Irma La Douce* to *The Fortune Cookie* to *Avanti!* to *The Front Page*; win some, lose some, but it's the collaboration that counts. The partnership with Walter Matthau, with its particular chemistry under Wilder's directorial hand in *The Fortune Cookie* and *The Front Page* and still another under Gene Saks's in *The Odd Couple*, led to further creativity, with Matthau starring in *Kotch* in 1971 under Lemmon's direction; Matthau's portrait of the seventy-two-year-old widower was perfection but it was Lemmon's sure directorial touch that made the charm outweigh the sentiment in this touching and meaningful consideration of old age. And in turn, Lemmon is willing not only to perform for aspiring student directors but sponsors showings of their works to help their careers. He is not one to leave behind the days of his own struggles and aspirations: an added zest to his finally appearing on stage with Maureen Stapleton (and Matthau) in a Los Angeles production of *Juno and the Paycock* early in 1975 was the shared memory of back when—when he was the piano-playing MC and Ms. Stapleton a song-and-dance girl in a barnlike nightclub that was going broke while they were both hoping for that big break onto Broadway.

While the Lemmon "character"—the harassed man, outflanked, out-ranked, and outmaneuvered, slipping on the invisible banana peels that beset the paths of us all—has its mannerisms, it's the particular Lemmon touch that individualizes each performance. The best example, perhaps, is in his Felix Unger, the role in *The Odd Couple* that for me will always be par-ticularly his. Lemmon made Felix a revolting mass of tics and twitches and fussbudgetry but—and this is the triumph of craftsmanship—with all the priggishness and domesticity, his Felix is all male, without even the sugges-tion of camp or hint of a limp wrist. It's that fine precision of stopping—not on anything as gross as a dime—on the thin rim of the dime. It is, I suppose, what we call good taste.

One wouldn't, presumably, expect less of a Harvard man. Lemmon's of the gentleman breed of actors, the college graduates with a serious interest in acting—as opposed to the truckers and cowboys and drifters who became manufactured glamour boys in the days when movie stars could be stamped out on the assembly line of the Hollywood factories. It is that seriousness that has provided the flash of inspired performance, the infinite variety of accomplishment, the steady growth. Only a serious performer, after all, could provide us with the joyous laughter of Lemmon's comedy—and only an actor of many humors touches our emotions so deeply in his dramatic moments. How fortunate for us all that some twenty years and more than thirty films seem to mark only the beginning of a career!

[1977]

Charles Champlin

CAROLE LOMBARD

Well ahead of her time, she was all Woman and all Liberated.

The trickeries of time and film seem never so haunting to me as in the interrupted life of Carole Lombard. She would have been sixty-one as I write this, and would I daresay have been a remarkably alluring adornment of our day. It was clear that her lithe figure and the superb face with those unforgettable sculpted cheekbones would have lent themselves to maturity with matchless grace. And it takes no great stretch to imagine for her an age-defying, soul-deep romantic élan, infused now as then with a kind of intelligent sensuality.

It is true to say that she died at the peak of her beauty, powers, and fame, I suppose, yet it may be even truer to say that the greatest achievements were still to come. I say this not out of easy sentiment but from a feeling that, as prototypical of her time as she was, she was also well ahead of her time. She was all Woman and all Liberated, a third of a century before the ladies laid aside their brassieres in a symbolic rejection of all their hang-ups.

In the beginning Miss Lombard was the perfect embodiment of the star myths of early Hollywood. Her life helped to define them: the tomboyish, star-struck, fiercely energetic and ambitious kid from the Midwest (Fort Wayne) come to Hollywood as a moppet, opting for dance lessons and acting classes above all other forms of improvement, playing extra bits at nine and, thanks to a kindly neighbor's assist, joining the Mack Sennett custard pie company.

Within a decade of her first regular movie job, she had become the highest-paid female star in Hollywood, earning just under $500,000 a year—an astonishing sum in a day when a dollar meant three to five times what it means today. Sifting through the yellowed clippings about her, as I did not long ago, you feel you are reading footnotes for a myth: the breathlessly reported marriage to co-star William Powell, the honeymoon cruise to Honolulu, her illnesses, her jewels stolen, her arm mauled by a chimpanzee, rumors of divorce, divorce, Gable, a war-bond tour to Indianapolis.

But from all the glamour-queen trappings emerged something and someone rather different and quite unexpected: the sophisticated comedienne, witty and self-reliant, a man's woman who not only went hunting and fishing with Gable but seems to have adored it; a lady who (one suspected) achieved independence without toughness, romance without self-indulgence, and fulfillment in marriage without the loss of her own identity and sense of achievement.

She was breathtakingly beautiful in a day which began by demanding plastic beauty of its heroes and heroines, but what would, I think, have led her on to still greater stardom were the interior qualities, of wit and unaffected worldly wisdom, untrammelled spirits, honesty, directness, and what seems to have been her awareness that being free is not necessarily the same thing as being alone and that the truest freedom is within a secure love.

From the slapstick beginnings, Carole Lombard had been evolving in a more interesting and exciting way—so it seems now—than almost any other actress of her day. Like films themselves, she appeared to be moving into new and uncommon ground of sensibility and intelligence, and toward the highest comedy, which arises from the truest contemplation of the world's ways.

It becomes almost impossible to judge old movies with any detachment, because we seem to see them through a scrim of our private accretions of memory, association, and our sense of our own frail transience. But the existing achievements of Carole Lombard look stunning to our most ruthless and unsentimental eye. And that we cannot know what her ultimate triumphs might have been is not least of the sorrows of that January night above the Nevada desert.

[1970]

Vincent Canby

SOPHIA LOREN AND MARCELLO MASTROIANNI

Great performers present the surface characteristics of a role while somehow making a comment on those characteristics.

Very early in Ettore Scola's *A Special Day,* you feel that things are going to be all right, that the director and his actors know what they're up to. The time is the day in 1938 when Mussolini threw a gigantic rally to honor Hitler on his visit to Rome in celebration of their historic axis. The setting of the film, though, is confined entirely to a modern working-class apartment block of terrifying drabness. The moment I'm thinking of occurs just after

Antonietta (Sophia Loren), the barely literate mother of six and prematurely exhausted, has just packed her children and her husband off to the rally. She slops the coffee remains from several cups into one, sits at the littered table and sips the coffee while surveying the incredible kitchen mess. She doesn't anticipate the morning's chores with any pleasure, but she still can enjoy the momentary peace. Suddenly this peace is broken by the cry of the family's pet mynah bird who, though it can talk, always gets her name wrong. There's something very funny and touching and revealing about Antonietta's reaction. She's both annoyed with the bird and aware that to be furious with a bird is a waste of her energies.

Exactly how Miss Loren manages to suggest this so easily I've no idea, but it's just one of the dozens of sequences in the film that are simultaneously mysterious and brilliantly revealing—mysterious because we aren't sure how certain emotional effects are obtained and revealing because of what those effects say about the characters. It's movie acting at its best, though I'm not at all sure anyone can accurately define, in general terms, what great movie acting consists of.

A Special Day is a very good, though something less than great, film that is an acting tour de force for Miss Loren and Marcello Mastroianni, who plays the unlikely role of a suicidal homosexual, just fired from his announcing job on the state-sponsored radio station. Gabriele (Mastroianni) is an intelligent, literate fellow who responds to Antonietta's no-nonsense approach to everyday matters and to her natural warmth, though he's appalled by her hero worship of Mussolini (she keeps a scrapbook on the dictator's life) and by the way she parrots the wisdom of Mussolini without question ("Genius is strictly masculine. . . .").

A Special Day is essentially a two-character film in which, in the space of a few hours, Antonietta and Gabriele meet, become friends, fight, reconcile, and, toward the end, make love in a gesture that will not change either of their lives outwardly (Gabriele is not thus "saved" from his homosexuality) but will profoundly alter their view of life and themselves.

Scola, who collaborated on the screenplay as well as directed the film, has provided the stars with an intelligent script but I can't imagine any other two players who could have turned this essentially somber tale into an experience of such good humor. When I say good humor, I don't refer to what goes on within the film, but to the effect of seeing Miss Loren and Mastroianni take off with their material in ways that not only illuminate the characters but also give us a chance to marvel at what they are doing as actors, something more often experienced in the theater or at the opera, where performers are in repertory, than in the movie house.

Oddly, I think, this is something that happened much more often in the era of mass-produced movies. When the same stars appeared in three or four films a year we came to understand them so well that we could read the variations in their performances to a degree that was impossible with unknown actors. Some of the extraordinary responses that Katharine Hepburn and Spencer Tracy were able to achieve were the result of our having come to know how they played together. It was our familiarity with them in various earlier roles that gave later performances a resonance that was special to them.

This is partially responsible for the fun of watching Miss Loren and Mastroianni in *A Special Day*, no matter how sad the tale. They've made eight films together and though only two of those—*Marriage, Italian-Style* and *Yesterday, Today and Tomorrow*—are memorable, they have been able to create special moments even in a turkey like *Sunflower*. They work together with a self-assurance that allows each to take risks, which, in *A Special Day*, includes a scene in which Miss Loren seduces Mastroianni, something that, I'm sure, could have been unintentionally hilarious had the seducer been anyone of less style and experience than Miss Loren. One watches this sequence breathlessly, much as one waits to hear whether a singer is going to be able to hit the high note, or falter and fake it.

One of the qualities that both Miss Loren and Mastroianni have as performers—and something that, perhaps, all great performers share—is a way of presenting the surface characteristics of a role (the gestures, expressions, language) while also somehow making a comment on those characteristics. It's a dividend. It's why we watch Laurence Olivier doing outrageous things as the sadistic dentist in *Marathon Man* and yet come out of the theater buoyed up and maybe even smiling, not because of what the character did in the film but for the way Olivier set the character off by, in the case of *Marathon Man*, sheer technical effrontery.

I've a suspicion—still somewhat dim in my mind and incapable of ever being proved—that all great actors, if not essentially comic, are gifted with an appreciation for paradox that is one of the roots of comedy. Olivier has this. So do Ralph Richardson, Marlon Brando, Dustin Hoffman, and, I suspect, Robert De Niro. At the peak of her form in a film like *The Little Foxes*, Bette Davis was funny—dishonest and stingy and mean, but also funny. One doesn't necessarily laugh, but the awareness of the wit within a performance is one of the pleasures of both the cinema and theater.

Jane Fonda has it, though it's not always apparent in the high melodrama of *Julia*, directed by Fred Zinnemann, the film adaptation of the Lillian Hellman story from *Pentimento*. It's not obvious in the film's scenes of intrigue, but it is apparent in her scenes with Vanessa Redgrave and especially in her scenes with Jason Robards, who plays Dashiell Hammett to Miss Fonda's Lillian Hellman.

This is definitely what Miss Loren and Mastroianni have, but it's a quality that often takes a bit of time, a familiarity with the way an actor acts, before one can identify it. Not always. There are debut performances—offhand I think of Audrey Hepburn's in *Roman Holiday*—that are so complete that the performer, sprung on us brand-new, seems to have arrived with the kind of presence and associations it takes other performers years to acquire.

Miss Loren was one of those who had to work long and hard, mostly in a lot of rather ordinary Hollywood films, before she emerged as one of the best actresses and comediennes we have. Vittorio De Sica's *Two Women* is the film that forever separated her from the mob, and so opened our eyes that never again did we look upon her work, even in bad films, as perfunctory.

One of the few fond memories I have of any Cannes Film Festival (where it's an achievement just to get from one screening to another on time) is of the festival of 1961 when *Two Women* was screened in competition.

In the rarefied atmosphere of the festival *Two Women* was a revelation of truth, but more than that, Miss Loren's performance was astounding. The audience watched the neorealistic movie with the sort of pleasurable excitement that might have been thought unseemly when connected with the tragic events on the screen. The excitement, though, had to do with what the actress was accomplishing on the screen. Success *is* fun.

When the film was over, a spotlight was thrown onto the box where the actress was sitting. She stood up, wearing a smashing white evening dress and what looked to be the complete stock of Van Cleef and Arpels. The contrast to the drab but heroic peasant woman we'd been watching on the screen was obvious and intentional and, in the fashion of her best performances, exhilaratingly funny. She brought down the house then, and is still doing it.

[1977]

ROBERT MITCHUM

"Are all the rumors about you true?"
"Oh, sure, every one."

"I never did see *Secret Ceremony*, to tell you the truth," Robert Mitchum said. "Did Mia call Elizabeth her daddy? They did some weird things with that script because contractually they had me for ten days only. They were in trouble when I got there and I don't think I improved the situation any.

"Apparently after my ten days were finished they took two scenes that I was in and recast them with Elizabeth. You know that bathtub scene? In the script, I was in the bathtub with Mia." Mitchum's eyes narrowed. "The scene where she was rubbing Elizabeth's back. In the script that was my back."

A slow grin. "I was scheduled for milk and cookies," Mitchum said. He spun the ice in his glass. "What's this? Scotch? No cookies? We were shooting in that hideous house the whole time. Joe Losey has an architectural fetish. Sometimes you think he'd be happy to clear the actors out altogether and just photograph the rooms. He never says a word. Not one word. He walks into a room and engineers and choreographs and then the actors go through it. Then he prints it, and that's that.

"All the same, I guess *Secret Ceremony* was good at the box office. Just after we made it, lesbianism came in. Maybe that's why they reshot the bathtub scene. I'm no damn good as a lesbian. Play anything else, but not that. Of course lesbianism has been around for a long time. But Losey's heart must be gladdened by the success of *Secret Ceremony*. Maybe not. I doubt if anything really gladdens old Joe's heart. I think he has dyspepsia."

Mitchum stretched his legs out long under the coffee table. Whirled the ice in his glass. Whistled: "My heart goes where the wild goose goes." Across the room his man, Harold ("Harold? He's my man"), mixed fresh drinks. It is Mitchum's day off from shooting David Lean's new movie, *Ryan's Daughter*. The afternoon runs down into evening as well in Dingle [Ireland] as anywhere, inspiring nostalgia, deep thoughts, philosophical questions. How long you figure you got to live?

"About . . . oh, about three weeks. I have this rash that grows on my back every twenty-eight days. I was bitten by a rowboat when I was thirteen, in a park in Cleveland, Ohio, and every twenty-eight days a rash appears on my back. I've offered my body for science."

My heart flies where the wild goose flies. "Meanwhile, I sit here in Dingle and vegetate. I was a young man of twenty-six when I arrived here last month. The days are punctuated by the sighs of Harold as he waits for the pubs to open. But don't get me wrong. Usually I'm gay with laughter, fairy-footed, dancing about, and rejoicing. But this afternoon . . . well, I just woke up. So I sit here and weep. Finally everyone staggers into town to Tom Ashe's pub and leaves me here alone weeping. That's my day."

Mitchum whirled the ice in his glass. "Thanks, Harold." Harold poured Chivas Regal into the glass. "Harold stands in for me."

He doesn't look like you.

"Doesn't have to. He's an object on which to focus. Been with me for years. Lost without him."

Mitchum sits in Dingle in a cottage by the bridge over the river, waiting to do his stint in *Ryan's Daughter.*

"At least *Ryan's Daughter* is the latest thing they're calling it," he said. "First it was going to be 'Coming of Age,' then it was going to be 'Michael's Day,' or some goddamn thing. Then for a long time it didn't have a title at all. It was called the David Lean Project. It was during that period that Trevor Howard and John Mills nearly got killed when their boat overturned in the surf. That was on every front page in the world, and the movie didn't have a title. So they blew millions of dollars of publicity. Now it's *Ryan's Daughter.* They're having a hell of a time matching shots. We had one perfect day on the beach, and then the rain closed in. Ireland makes the rain a national monument, so the tourist season lasts twelve months a year. After the first ten days of shooting, we were already seven days behind. So here I sit, practicing my accent.

"With *Secret Ceremony,* they sat around discussing who they could get with the right accent. Finally Elizabeth suggested me. They didn't want an actor whose accent was so English it would bring Elizabeth's into relief. So Losey called me in Mexico and asked if I could do an English accent. Hell, yes, I could. What do you want? North Country? Lancashire? Cockney? He asked for an indifferent accent, so that's what I gave him. Then I read a review asking what in hell Mitchum was trying to do if he thought that was an English accent. They should write the director's instructions on the edge of the screen.

"But I don't give a damn. I must be good at my job; they wouldn't haul me around the world at these prices if I weren't. I remember one picture—*Wonderful Country,* I think it was—where the character comes across the border from Mexico. Bob Parrish was the director and he wanted me to gradually lose my Mexican accent and then pick it up again when I went back to Mexico."

Mitchum spreads his hands, palms up, and shrugged. "Parrish is essentially a cutter, not a director. There are several of those. Bobby Wise, for example, couldn't find his way out of a field without a choreographer."

"Bobby even times a kiss with a stopwatch. He marks out the floor at seven o'clock in the morning, before anybody gets there. Lays it all out with a tape measure. True. It's very difficult to work that way. I worked with him and Shirley MacLaine and Shirley said, 'Why doesn't he go home? He's just in the way. . . .' "

Mitchum's attention drifted. Outside the window, children played in the road. They called to each other in Gaelic; in places on the Dingle Peninsula, Gaelic is still spoken. The Lean film is set there during the Easter Uprising of 1916. Mitchum plays a schoolteacher. He marries Sarah Miles, but she falls in love with Christopher Jones, a British officer. . . .

Mitchum rubbed his eyes and yawned. Then he laughed again. "Bobby Wise," he said. "I never saw *The Sand Pebbles*. Of course, that was a problem picture out in front, with Steve McQueen in it. You've got to realize that a Steve McQueen performance just naturally lends itself to monotony." A melancholy shake of the head. "Steve doesn't bring too much to the party."

A silence fell. Mitchum yawned, and let his head drop back. He stared up at the ceiling. "No way," he said. "There's just no way." Drawing out the no. "Noooo way. No way." He took his glasses out of his shirt pocket and put them on. Then he swung around again and dropped his feet to the floor.

"I've got two astigmatisms from boxing," he said. "I had the conjunctive nerve cut here, and the eye injured up here, and this one was knocked out once. The last time, I got hit with the sight of a rifle, about sixteen months ago in Spain when we were making *Villa Rides*.

"But who gives a damn? I've gotten grooved into making movies, so why not? It's too late for anything else. Before that, I used to be a writer. I wrote movies, radio continuity—I was a junior writer at a studio. I've only written one of my own pictures, though: *Thunder Road*. Right into that big transformer. What a way to go. Well, I can think of twelve different ways to go. But I was a writer."

Mitchum put his glasses back in his pocket. He emptied his glass. "I've put away more goddamn Scotch since I got to Dingle than I've put away in my whole goddamn life," he said. "No, there was Vietnam. . . . One day we were out there in the boondocks and I must have had fourteen, no, sixteen cans of beer and the greater part of a bottle of whiskey. And that was at lunch. Then they took me back to base in a helicopter and all the clubs—

(RIGHT) Carole Lombard:
Sophisticated and self-reliant.

(BELOW) Sophia Loren
(with Marcello Mastroianni):
Wit within a performance.
(From the motion picture
Yesterday, Today and Tomorrow.
Courtesy Avco Embassy Pictures Corp.
Copyright © 1964 by Embassy Pictures Corp.)

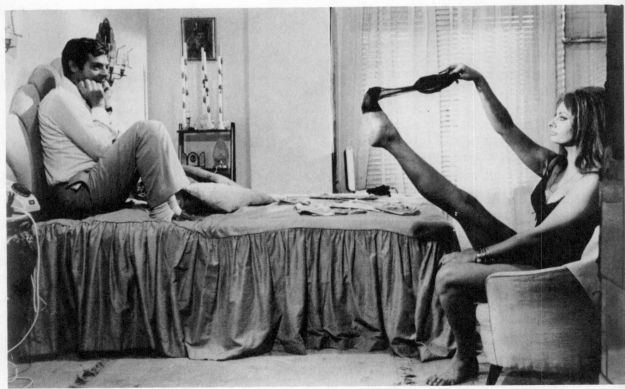

(ABOVE) Marilyn Monroe:
*A tragicomic blend of sumptuous courtesan
and stammering small girl.* (*Some Like It Hot*.
Copyright © 1959 Ashton Productions, Inc.
All rights reserved. Released
through United Artists Corporation.)

(LEFT) Robert Mitchum:
*"I must be good at my job;
they wouldn't haul me around the world
at these prices if I weren't."*
(From the MGM release *Home from the Hill*.
© 1959 Loew's Inc. and Sol C. Siegel Productions, Inc.
Copyright renewed 1960 by Loew's Inc.)

the officers' club, the noncom's club, the enlisted men's club—they all said, come on, Bob, have a drink. No way, I said. No way. I'm a Mormon bishop. Sure, Bob, we know. . . .

"That goddamn place. You know what the gooks do? They bomb the outhouses. They know how to get the Yankee dog where he lives. The Yanks are always building outhouses and the Cong is always shooting them down."

Mitchum took a fresh glass from Harold. "No way," he sighed. "I've looked into it, and there's just no way."

How'd you get started?

"Well, my father was killed when I was three, so I was principally shipped around to relatives. I finally left when I was fourteen. Jumped on a train, came back, left again when I was fifteen, wound up on a chain gang in Savannah, came back, went to California. My first break was working for Hopalong Cassidy, falling off horses.

"So now I support my favorite charity: Myself. That's where the money goes. My wife, my kids. I have a brother, weighs about 280 pounds. Two sisters, a mother, a stepfather. I think my sisters are religious mystics. They belong to that Baha'i faith.

"Somebody asked my wife once, What's your idea of your husband? And she answered: 'He's a masturbation image.' Well, that's what we all are. Up there on the screen, our goddamn eyeball is six feet high, the poor bastards who buy tickets think you really amount to something."

Mitchum stood up and walked over to the window. "Let's take a walk around the house," he said.

It was nearly dark outside, cold and damp, the lights of Dingle on the hill across the river. "It's going to be a good picture," he said. "I trust Lean. He's a good director. He'd better be. This is eight goddamn months out of my life. I'll be here until the last dog dies." He kicked at the grass, his hand in his pockets, his face neutral.

"Any more questions?" he said.

Are all the rumors about you true?

"Oh, sure, every one. Where there's smoke, there's fire. Make up some more if you want to. They're all true. Booze, broads, all true."

Pot?

"I don't have any," he said. "I sit and weep and wait for the weather to change, waiting for my crop to grow." He leaned over and picked up a flowerpot that was leaning against the side of his cottage. A sickly spindle of twig grew in it. "My crop," he said. "I'm waiting for my crop to grow. In my hands I hold the hopes of the Dingle Botanical Society."

[1969]

Penelope Gilliatt

MARILYN MONROE

Her sheer gift of poignant physical presence is an essence of film acting.

After she had been working with her on *The Prince and the Showgirl*, Sybil Thorndike said about Marilyn Monroe:

> On the set, I thought, surely she won't come over, she's so small-scale, but when I saw her on the screen, my goodness, how it came over. She was a revelation. We theater people tend to be so outgoing. She was the reverse. The perfect film actress, I thought. . . .

O wise and piercing sibyl. The long to-and-fro about whether or not Marilyn Monroe is an actress is really a question of semantics. If acting means the ability to project the idea of a big role through a proscenium arch, the answer is obviously no: on a stage, I doubt whether she would have a fraction of the extraordinary sweet power that she has on the screen. But then nor would Garbo, with whom she has, in fact, a good deal else in common: the same curious phosphorescence on film, the same hint of sympathy for the men who fall in love with her, and the same mixture of omniscience and immaturity, though where Garbo is half ice goddess and half a surprisingly athletic boy, Marilyn is a tragicomic blend of a sumptuous courtesan and a stammering small girl. In a way, her sheer gift of poignant physical presence is an essence of film acting, for the weight that cinema gives to sensuous detail is one of its great potencies, distinguishing it sharply from the theater. When this characteristic fuses with an actor who has as much physical magnetism as James Dean, or Marlon Brando, or Marilyn Monroe, the effect is transfixing. It is also much more than simply sexual. Apart from the "flesh-impact" (Billy Wilder) and the "tortile, wambling walk" (*Time*), Marilyn Monroe's abundant physique has the most subtle and perfected comic implications.

[1961]

Penelope Gilliatt

JEANNE MOREAU

Something about her transmits a concept of eternity and of a
better world elsewhere.

After Jeanne Moreau was in Louis Malle's *The Lovers* (1959), film fans in
France began calling her Jeanne d'Arc du Boudoir. People in the profession
who knew her better countered with Jeanne la Sage. We were recently in
the country in France, together in the beautiful place she has made of a
century-old farmhouse above Saint-Tropez. We went for a walk and saw a
child watching some piglets. "I like children. I also like the children of pigs,"
she said solemnly. "Pigs are innocent and honorable." Of this woman,
François Truffaut, who directed her in *Jules and Jim* (1962) and *The Bride
Wore Black* (1968), said to me, "She has all the attributes of a woman, together with all the qualities one expects in a man, with none of the incon-
veniences of either." Peter Brook, who directed her in *Moderato Cantabile*
(1964), said, "She is one of the most remarkable actresses I have ever worked
with. She has a somnambulistic quality." Orson Welles, who directed her in
The Trial (1963), *Falstaff* (1967), and *The Immortal Story* (1968), said, "She
has the sense of drama and the sense of dream." Tony Richardson, who
directed her in *Mademoiselle* (1966) and *The Sailor from Gibraltar* (1967), said,
"She is more informed, committed, and passionate than any other actress I
know."

Yet Jeanne Moreau herself says, "Being another character is an absurd
ambition. I hated acting the novelist's wife in Antonioni's *La Notte*, in 1960.
There are people like that poor woman, of course, but not for me. That is
not what love is like." There is despair in the beautiful downturned mouth
but also ready blitheness. "I hate people who say, 'You're a real pro,' " she
says. Her word for what they are trying to get at is *"précise."* "Acting isn't a
profession, it's a way of living, and it's one that I may—I don't know—leave
behind. I would like to be a good director. I would like to die a good writer."
In New York, she had laughed and also said, "I would love to be an archi-
tect. How many of these buildings are scaled to the human size? And how
many were built by a woman?" In the South of France, where she seems
most at home, she spoke less harshly of herself as an actress: "When you
work with a new director, you open the door. *C'est le début, l'initiation.* I think

that's why I'm related so deeply to the countryside. Everything begins here. There's nothing in it to disturb the consciousness." She traced the indented date—1860—on a stone fountain outside her house. "In a city, I would never be able to create a place like this. In the country, you watch a river. In the country, a house is built for the flow of the family. The fireplace is not a sign of the power of the head of the household. It's connected to family organization. In a plane, I have the impression that I'm going to be intimate with whatever city we're all traveling to in this great ship that used to express aspiration, but it doesn't happen. I like small harbors for the same reason. Everything there is connected to the convenience of the people who live around them."

We went inside, out of the light, and up to her bedroom, where there is a Picasso drawing of a woman and a little boy. "In fact, why are we connected to artists?" she said, with her legs tucked under her on the bed. "The Picassos I love most are the early ones. But his passion to paint, that's the thing. In Avignon, he was like a man losing his blood. He painted and painted, and sometimes it was magnificent, always something you are linked to. He understood that art is not autobiographical. I suspect autobiographical art. Perhaps having such a relationship with the facts and the self is dangerous." She went out of the bedroom into a gallery that overhangs the drawing room, and put on a record of Billie Holiday. We listened for a while, and then she began to talk vigorously of Truffaut, who is her great friend. "People have accused him of being 'too sweet.' What is too sweet about affection? About kindness? The thing that is too sweet is what is vulgar and simply fishy—a fish going bad. . . .

"Some of the best directors I have ever watched value chance, know how to use it. I don't believe it's a good thing to be extremely clever. A director like Jean-Pierre Melville wants so badly to be brilliant, to startle with clever cutting. It seems cold. Sometimes I think how few men there are who love the camera now. They are not astonished to have it in their hands, like Lumière or Keaton, or like women directors, who I believe will keep that innocence. Clever men often use the camera to prod you into excitement, not to find out what is in the script and the actors. But Orson, now, with *Citizen Kane*, he was so young he was in love with the camera. He didn't manipulate it; he was saying, 'Let's see what we can make together.' Of course, with women's films there *will* be dross. There will be a poor commercial cinema of women's films, but one hopes not too much." . . .

Playing a recording of Prokofiev's "Classical Symphony" in the gallery, she spoke about England. Her mother is English. "Now that everyone is poor in England, that's liberty. That's why you say it is such an invigorating country to be in just at the moment, though its friends are sorrowing for it. The thing is, outsiders see only the loss of empire and the economic crisis. That will pass. In the Industrial Revolution, England was forty years ahead of everyone else. The present money trouble has come about because the English are inventors, not businessmen." Moreau has a sense of national differences. Her books tell one something about the spread and exactitude of her tastes. She has many art books, D. H. Lawrence, Balzac, Jack London, Giraudoux, Malraux, Proust, a volume on Joan Crawford. She loves books of reference, and her questions are as eager for information as her talk is to provide it. Her country house is a place for thinking. It is full of corners where her friends can be alone and read. She must be one of the best-mannered actresses in the profession.

"When I'm acting, I feel I have no family—only the director," she said. "It's a dialogue, not a monologue. Luis Buñuel is one of the men I have most loved working with. It's not for any applause. That's wanting response, not reward—it's dying of lack of company, not of thirst. I have made a lot of box-office duds." She has always been profoundly dedicated to directors, and has a private and lasting affinity with the ones she admires. "Some actors are creative without wanting to take over the film. A director can give you a good part, but you can give him back just as much if you're rich enough to suggest to him the thousands of doors to open. One discovers the character during shooting. It's an encounter." She has acute stagefright. "But what is good about stagefright is that it's transformed into concentration as soon as you're working."

Louis Malle, who directed her not only in *The Lovers* but in *The Fire Within* (1964) and *Viva Maria!* (1965), says that she is one of the actresses who must build up into a scene. "She is not at her best in the early takes. She has to construct a contact."

"Making a film is like life aboard ship, except that every day is an emergency," she said in the South of France. "And then there is the aloneness afterward. Of course, there is loneliness and being alone. Being alone is an opportunity, yes? Except, perhaps, the tragic aloneness when you are physically ill. Emotional loneliness has a cure."

On another day, she said, "Actors shouldn't ask questions, they should do things. That's what Peter Brook thinks. I was impressed by the way he worked. When we'd made *Moderato Cantabile*, he was asked how I did it. He said it was sometimes an actor's desperation to be able to give anything that is needed. To me, the Method preparation for concentration is some actors' way of doing what I try to do in a different way. I can't use thought and intelligence while I'm shooting. If you think too much about the character— Well, intellect has nothing to do with acting. Thought can go on before. Then you just have to be here, present. Suppose the director says that pages twenty-two and twenty-three are cut, and he says that instead of showing you standing in front of Claridge's and buying Dunhills we'll show you down at the swimming pool. Well, you just do it, because you are the character. You have to live up to the character. I think that this passion for nakedness in films above love is often beside the point and won't last. It's an exaggeration of the time. When you want to do something, you overemphasize. Mystery is a taste that we have lost, but it will come back. Maybe the longing to see the naked body is a longing to know everything about someone. But you find then that the body itself is a cover. That's the reason the way one is dressed has meaning." Moreau is one of the best-dressed women in the theater, with natural style and a nearly bygone feeling for prettiness. Not for her the overalls and Earth shoes and stamped T-shirts of film stars just as beautiful.

"A director's instinct and an actor's instinct will coincide if they're attached to the idea of making the character distinct, and not debasing it," she said. "There are never ten ways to do something. Only one. That is a question of morality. You have to be true to yourself and to others. The plot—that is, the character narrative—takes you with it. Virginia Woolf once said that the plot is like a river: it carries you along and it shows you the countryside around the people." She changed a record, and then said, "For some reason, I was thinking of Buñuel's 1972 film *The Discreet Charm of the Bourgeoisie*. About that film I felt like a child. With Buñuel, one feels that anything can happen. For instance, a dog can speak. I always had that dream in childhood."

Moments of her own performances came to mind: the unforgettable half smile of triumph at the success of a dark compact just before she kills herself, near the end of *Jules and Jim*; her self-mocking suggestion of conquest in love in Roger Vadim's *Les Liaisons Dangereuses* (1961); the moment in Buñuel's *Diary of a Chambermaid* (1965) in which she bends herself to her master's fetishes, looks resigned, but shows her heart to be scornful and chilled. She is a woman of invention beyond the scope of most actresses. In Jean-Louis Richard's *Mata Hari* (1965), besides acting magnificently, she pulled most of the dialogue together, with the help of Truffaut. "You don't have to do anything in front of a camera," she said. "You just have to be concerned." About an actor trained in the Method, when he was wondering what his motivation was for picking up an ashtray, she said, "You want to say to him, 'Just pick up the ashtray and shut up.' " She has a capacity for transmitting extraordinary intensity of understanding between her and other characters, which is one of the reasons she enjoyed making *Viva Maria!* with Brigitte Bardot. "Films tend to say that women can never be in rapport with each other": a thought that obviously prompted much of her own film, *Lumière* (1976), written and directed by her, and with her playing a part in which she is intimately concerned with several other women. One has the feeling that, unlike many actresses in the English-speaking commercial cinema, she could never fall into reposing a character on being hagridden or having a fishwife's emotional range. There is something about her, clear to all the great directors she has worked with but hard to pin down, that always transmits a concept of eternity and of a better world elsewhere.

In Paris, last year, when I was seeing her before she married the American director William Friedkin, we spent time in her beautiful apartment in the rue du Cirque. It had a main room with pale-orange muslin curtains and an orange carpet. Jeanne Moreau talked, over lunch, about other people's films. "The best period in the American cinema was the thirties and forties, when actors and actresses were under contract, and not maneuvering on slippery ground from one film to the next. People were craftsmen then. They didn't think of themselves as being artists. A film took ninety minutes, no more, and each frame had to be full. What strikes me now when I look at those older films is that they are so packed with energy. It grows in one's mind: the music, the editing—everything. If one wants to learn what to do, one not only watches Fellini, one also watches Howard Hawks." When she was casting *Lumière*, she chose Keith Carradine because she found herself dreaming over an early photograph of Gary Cooper. "I wanted a man who had those purely American qualities—the simplicity and integrity and innocence."

She keeps small notebooks with her for writing down details of characters in a new film she is working on: their roots, their originality. The story is set in France between Bastille Day of 1939 and September 1, 1939, the day World War II began. One character used to live in Poland: Jewish, a doctor. She had read endless newspapers of the day. "I want to make a film that says something about the older men, their relationship with the land. Their anguish over the 1914–18 war—that they had fought in it and won it and then lost all the same. Now there was this new war, which was to produce Vichy: another defeat, and this one full of remorse. After Munich, men in the French countryside lived their lives in a spasm of false shame. They thought, This happened twenty years ago—how can it happen again? They felt that it was their fault. Their feeling for the land is important, and the memory of their past, when the men were called on to fight again and then to have their country occupied. The connection between God and farming and the Church was still the same as ever; it created a powerful feeling about Good and Bad. These men felt that everything had become Bad, and couldn't believe that it could be so. Even if people are well-informed, they have very little of what one can truly call information. People who work the land say 'That can't be' about a drought. 'There hasn't been one for twenty years.' Young men who lived in the country had heard of America as the land of gold, India as the land of jewels. They had heard their fathers talk of the Great War. They couldn't imagine their own Europe and themselves involved in its private bloodshed again. It was a legend. In 1940, the women were already talking very independently about this men's war. The Women's Lib movement started after the war, when some of the men came back. I'm so deep in this film already that I hardly notice Paris. In making a film, one is making a complete world, but it relates to. . . ." She traced a shape with her finger on the table meaning "nowhere." "There is total intimacy among the people working on the film, and no resentment about the loss of it afterward."

Another time in Paris, when Jeanne Moreau had had to put thoughts of her film aside, because she was working on *Lulu,* we met at a bistro and she again drew with her finger on a table. "I have been thinking about the Berlin Wall. The situation would be this. Two figures, a man and a woman, start off walking quite normally. They break into a run. They reach *here.* The woman trips. Maybe they don't know each other. They are killed." She ate for a minute and then said, "When *Lulu* is finished, I shall go back to the country. Though sometimes I have a sense of nonsense in the country. Not a thought but a feeling. It is because the country is so strong. There is this feeling of nonsense even in Paris about such a situation as we have in the German capital. As I began to say, the French countrywomen after the last war understood what was happening much better than the men who survived. The deeper you go into life, the more you have to forget everything."

Jeanne Moreau was born in 1928. Her father, who died three years ago, was Anatole-Désiré Moreau, the owner of a Montmartre restaurant called La Cloche d'Or. Her mother is an English former dancer, Kathleen Buckley, who danced with the Tiller Girls at the Folies-Bergère. The Moreau family is descended from farmers. Born in Paris, Jeanne, as a child, used to spend her holidays at Mazirat, a village of about thirty houses in the Allier Département, between the Loire and the Cher. Her best friend, who lived in Vichy, where Jeanne and she were both at school, died of croup when Jeanne and she were eight. After the outbreak of war, Jeanne and her mother and sister were obliged to stay in Paris, because her mother was an alien. (Her father was cut off from them in the South of France, in Vichy. He was a soldier there. They struggled to join him, and finally succeeded, but it took fourteen months.) "I read many books far too soon. They make me sick even now, some of them, with terror and fascination. I read Zola when I was thirteen. My father often sent me to carry a bowl of soup to the film ticket-seller, and the man would say, 'Wouldn't you like to go in?' Once—I must have been sixteen—my father took me to see *La Bête humaine.* He fell asleep, but I was carried away. I was a good student until I was sixteen. Then I went to see Anouilh's *Antigone.* I heard my mother say to a neighbor who would be sympathetic to my longings, 'I have a daughter who wants to be an actress.' I went to the Conservatoire National d'Art Dramatique. My parents were separated when I was at the Conservatoire. Then I joined the Comédie-Française. Some things about it were disgusting. The big stars would take parts just to stop others from having them. After that, there was the Théâtre National Populaire."

She has a natural feeling for the theatrical. She said to me in New York about *A Chorus Line,* "It's real because it's fake. When mirrors on the stage are turned onto the audience, that is extraordinary. People in the audience are forced to look at themselves in a mirror. It is a great moment. The reflection of those pale faces of the audience, as if they were the ones who were auditioning! When I was young, I couldn't dream of that sort of poetic device. Soon after the Théâtre National Populaire, I was in a Paris *Pygmalion* for two years. One of the wittiest plays, whichever language it's performed in. I was often sad then. I was shy, totally diffident, at the end of the war. I felt as if I had started talking only a short while earlier. Before that, it was an epoch of silence. Perhaps my silence made me feel unusually close to my sister, Michelle Cavanaugh, whom I could always talk to. I was married to the director Jean-Louis Richard when I was twenty-one. Our marriage was dissolved shortly afterward, but he is still a great friend. We had one child. A son."

When I was in London last year, the telephone rang and Jeanne Moreau asked me from Paris if I would go to see her sister in a hospital in Fulham, because she was concerned about her and couldn't leave Paris herself. Jeanne has powerful family feelings. She telephones her son, who is now nearing thirty and lives elsewhere in France, practically every day. His name is Jérôme. Jeanne is nine years older than Michelle. She seems to have been a very motherly sister.

Michelle Cavanaugh is much like Jeanne in the legs—she sits like her, with fine calves tucked under her—but quite unlike her facially. She was reading Bertrand Russell when I went to see her. Jeanne had asked me to take her a particular scent, and a nightdress, as a relief from hospital clothes. The requests were very precise. The nightdress should be white cotton and simple, with no sleeves. Michelle laughed about her love for Jeanne and said, "We have an overdeveloped independence, both of us, like an overdeveloped muscle. I live mostly in Ibiza. My therapist thinks I shouldn't, but he's never set foot there. He thinks that because he's very possessive. Not like Jeanne." Michelle Cavanaugh apologized for having a therapist. "Once, Jeanne said if she hadn't been an actress she was afraid she might have been a neurotic. Later, she told me that her real reason for being an actress was to fight self-deception, to find the truth in the characters' predicaments. She has been through much more than I have."

Jeanne Moreau said to me in Paris one day, talking about her family and the planning of her next film, "My mother's father—English, of course— was responsible at the outbreak of war for the protection of the people of Littlehampton. My mother and my sister and I were in England, and with the first of September, 1939, my mother wanted to go back immediately to France. We took the boat from Newhaven just after New Year's Eve and arrived back in Paris at the end of February. Mazirat, where we had spent so much of our lives, was the root of many things I want to think about that have to do with the war. The institutions were always run by the left. But people were still related to the Church and sent their children to the Church school. It was an accommodation. And it was very healthy for the balance of life in the village. There were internal fights, it's true, but it's also true that fights—not wars—are good."

This was when she was rehearsing *Lulu* in Paris. As with many French rehearsals, work started after lunch and went on until the small hours. She was wearing a short fox coat that looked fake because it was dyed pale blue: appealing, on this beautifully dressed actress, who is an old friend of Pierre Cardin. She would concentrate totally on what the director was saying, repeat the same movement or fragment of a scene again and again—one of the movements being a climb up a ladder, which resulted in the fall that injured her knee—and in a break she would come downstage to kiss an inexperienced young actor, run over to a box in the darkened auditorium to ask if I was interested. *Lulu* is a difficult piece, and she did it superbly. She has always been remarkable for choosing worthwhile, hard things to do, and rejecting the commonplace. "People don't seek power, I think," she said to me once. "They seek the possibilities for doing things."

(ABOVE) Jeanne Moreau:
A natural feeling for the theatrical.
(*The Bride Wore Black.* Copyright 1968
Les Films Ducarosse. All rights reserved.
Released through United Artists Corporation.)

(RIGHT) Paul Newman:
*He has nothing in common with
earnest, romantic heroes.*

Another day in Paris, she said, in English, "Men can scream, women can whimp"—meaning "whimper." It was one of her few mistakes in the language. About women's liberation, she said, "I am not a feminist, but I can understand that people who are discontented cannot hide it. That the rich are powerful is a fable. It is not the rich who are powerful, it is the people who feel themselves free. The women's movement is about the fact that men have imposed on women emotionally. I myself think it's more that they have deterred us intellectually, robbed us of the faculty of invention. But one is not given such things—one has to take. It's easier to live by blaming convention, but nobody insists on its rule, apart from oneself. I've noticed that the women who are most resentful about conventions are often the ones who most want them. That year called the International Women's Year—it sounded fine but it wasn't very serious. Every year is the year of men and women."

When she went to Washington to introduce *Lumière* there, she made this speech, in English: "Thank you for coming to my first film. There's no time for long speeches. Thank you. Good-bye." This first film is imperfect, but it is full of interest: it has common sense, and is not a whit autobiographical—which it has sometimes been taken to be, simply because it is about an actress played by Jeanne Moreau. The director was involved to the fullest when she was making it, in her usual, unique way of seeming to be a little underwater while she is working. The film is about a woman who, though she has a genius for friendship, commits follies of egomania and thoughtlessness, especially toward a dying doctor, wonderfully played by François Simon. The director edited some of the film by cable from Hollywood to her editor in Paris, and told me that she hadn't realized until she saw the final cut that the last words in the film were "Forgive me."

[1978]

Stephen Farber

PAUL NEWMAN

His salient quality is supreme bitterness.

Paul Newman is probably the most important American film actor since Brando and James Dean, which is not the same as saying that he is the best (though it would be difficult to think of anyone who has given as many compelling performances over as many years). Certain actors, almost without seeming to act, in their sheer physical presence—voice, body movements, facial mannerisms—project a quality that seems recognizable, important to millions of people. They play themselves, with only occasional variations, in every performance, and they keep us interested. Newman's salient quality is supreme bitterness. In his early movies, when his face was softer, he seemed more innocent, more sensitive, which was why he played so many Brandoesque imitations in those years. As he has matured, though, the vulnerability has disappeared. He has nothing in common with earnest romantic heroes, the ones played by Rock Hudson or Robert Redford, and he is pathetically uncomfortable in straight parts—*Torn Curtain*, for example, or several of his romantic comedies. Newman's image is tough, sarcastic, cynical. In *Hud*, *The Prize*, *Harper*, and *Hombre*, he mocks and scorns sentimental pieties; he goes his own way, and he has nothing but contempt for respectable poses.

But he is unlike Brando's alienated hero of the early fifties, for he is witty and articulate in his rejection of society, while Brando's alienation, in *On the Waterfront*, is awkward, imperfectly understood, inexpressible, yet profound. Even when cast as a less sensitive hero—in *A Streetcar Named Desire*, for example—Brando's rebellion was more primitive, more volatile, less literate than Newman's. The image has changed with the audience's education. Newman is also different from Bogart, another great American cynic, for Bogart's cynicism, as articulate as Newman's, is much calmer; it has reached a state of philosophic tranquillity and vision. Bogart's appeal to so many college students must be just this unstated assurance that he has understood all of life's tricks and can no longer be hurt. He has mastered life—his cynicism and his detachment are highly intellectual and virtually complete. Bogart does not get angry in *The Maltese Falcon* or *The Big Sleep*; when he does seem to lose control of himself, at one moment of *The Maltese Falcon*, it is only a ruse, and it certainly hasn't convinced us. Newman's bitterness, by contrast, always feels more personal, more urgent. This is why the traces of his boyish vulnerability that we still catch at rare moments are important, suggesting that his cynicism is the result not of philosophical reflection but of a powerful emotional wound. We can never know how the Bogart character in *The Maltese Falcon* became so sour, and we cannot be concerned; as far as we know, he has always been that way and always will be. Newman's cynicism in *Hud* and *Hombre*, on the other hand, has specific antecedents— we must know how these characters have been hurt and humiliated, because Newman cannot present bitterness without suggesting a deep, still explosive involvement that the Bogart character never admits. And to many people this compelling image of a man chiselling detachment out of intense pain is at least as attractive as a clean nihilistic stance, studied instead of suffered.

[1967]

Bernard Drew

LAURENCE OLIVIER

"Willie Wyler was the man who altered my feelings toward films. He saw that I felt superior to films. He took me in hand and altered my entire career."

Lord Laurence Olivier, considered by many to be the world's greatest actor, is on the floor of the stage at the Wien Studios in Vienna, struggling with Gregory Peck for possession of an automatic gun. Peck is straddling Olivier, seemingly sitting on him, but, in fact, he is carefully avoiding putting the brunt of his weight on him. As a hand-held camera hovers over them, they fiercely grapple for the gun, their faces straining.

There's a break. Peck murmurs to Olivier, "Nice faking." Olivier, still flat on the floor, looks up at Peck, bats his eyes flirtatiously, and says, "Just like Tristan and Isolde."

The scene, which is supposed to be taking place in Erie, Pennsylvania, is the climactic confrontation between Olivier as a Jewish Nazi hunter and Peck as a diabolic Nazi physician in *The Boys from Brazil*. Franklin J. Schaffner is directing.

THE MOVIE STAR | 315

Both Olivier and Peck have thrown themselves into their roles with relish, carefully acquiring the appropriate accents. Peck has a perfect Katzenjammer accent after months of study for his first totally unsympathetic role in his thirty-four-year career. He says with a laugh, "I raped, robbed, and killed in *Duel in the Sun*, but I was only Lionel Barrymore's spoiled son, not really evil." In *The Boys from Brazil*, he plays Dr. Josef Mengele, the real Nazi physician who helped send millions to their deaths in the gas chambers of Auschwitz-Birkenau and who murdered thousands more in genetic experiments. It was a role that Laurence Olivier more or less played in the recent *Marathon Man*. But now Olivier has switched sides. In *The Boys from Brazil*, he portrays Ezra Lieberman, a cinematic version of Simon Wiesenthal, the celebrated Nazi hunter who has been stalking Mengele for more than twenty years. He has been stalemated by Mengele's reported asylum in a remote area of Paraguay, something the country vigorously denies.

So much for facts. On to best-selling fiction. In the novel *The Boys from Brazil*, on which the movie is based, the novelist Ira Levin had the fanciful conceit that not only is Mengele alive and well and living in Paraguay but that in 1943 Hitler permitted Mengele to take blood and skin cuttings from his ribs so that the good doctor might later clone any number of Hitlers if the need arose. Some years later, Mengele did exactly that, injecting more than ninety Nordic women with sperm created in the laboratory from Hitler's cells. Around the world dozens of fourteen-year-old boys are found to look exactly alike. Ezra Lieberman learns of the plot and pursues Mengele. In Erie, Pennsylvania, the two archenemies finally confront each other.

"Welcome to Erie, Pennsylvania," says cinematographer Henri Decaë, greeting me with an ironic smile and a shrug. It's a small signal acknowledging the external craziness of movie people who decide that the interior of a Pennsylvania house should be shot in a small studio in Vienna built in 1912 for silent movies. In fact, there's a wild rumor about that *Ecstasy*, with a nude Hedy Lamarr, was shot here. It's so poorly soundproofed that Gregory Peck's twenty-year-old son, Anthony, who is the third assistant director on the film, must constantly run outside and plead with everybody to please keep quiet while the cameras are rolling.

I never did find out why the company chose Vienna. Two weeks, though, were spent in Erie to shoot exteriors, followed by a break, and now, on a freezing Monday morning, I'm here waiting to be allowed a few minutes—no more—with Olivier. I have been told that he is not feeling well, that he is seeing no press at all, that each day he is simply driven from the Hotel Sacher to the studio and after his scenes are completed, from the studio to the Hotel Sacher, and that's that. Indeed, Olivier looks very frail. But the executive producer, Robert Fryer, has told me I will see Olivier. He has exacted a promise from Olivier, and Olivier always keeps his word, and so I wait. . . .

Now on the studio floor, Olivier holds a whispered conference with director Schaffner and producer Fryer about his dialogue next week, then is helped to his feet and walks slowly to his camper on the set, where his dialogue coach Marcella Markham, awaits.

"Have I got that line right, Marcella?" he asks, and when she corrects one word, he says, "Damn!" furiously to himself. "It's a tricky line," he mutters. "I was afraid I'd forget it completely."

"It was almost perfect," she reassures him. He seems to require reassurance now, and she quietly suggests, "At the end of the scene, why don't you emit an 'oich—ch—ch,' like the cry you gave at the end of *Oedipus*, only smaller."

"Do you think so?" he asks, and she nods.

That cry he gave in *Oedipus* still lives in my mind, and I will hear it for the rest of my life. He played the role during the visit of the Old Vic Theatre company to New York in 1946, when on successive evenings, he portrayed Hotspur in *Henry IV, Part I*, Justice Shallow in *Henry IV, Part II*, Astrov in *Uncle Vanya*, and finally *Oedipus*. His Oedipus moved critic John Mason Brown to observe that "Olivier shakes out thunder from the skies." Usherettes were armed with smelling salts for that moment when Olivier shrieked and then gouged out his eyes. On the night I saw the play, the final evening of the company's six-week engagement, Lynn Fontanne and Alfred Lunt, sitting directly in front of me, asked Olivier's wife, Vivien Leigh, "Exactly how does he do that, Vivien?" in one of their celebrated stage whispers which reverberated throughout the house. The following evening, the film *Henry V*, which Olivier had produced, directed, and starred in, opened, and the reviews acknowledged it to be the finest Shakespearean film ever made.

Now, as I finally meet Olivier, I am filled with a deep sadness that this frail man, whose performances have been filled with astonishing physical movement, can extend his hand to me only gingerly because a disease known as dermatomyositis has affected his nerve endings so grievously that even a handshake is agony for him. "My father was a priest," Olivier used to be fond of chortling. "A priest," he would repeat, enjoying his listener's discomfort. His father was actually an Anglican curate in a long line of clergymen going as far back as the chaplain to William the Conqueror. (Before that, the ancestry is French Huguenot.)

Olivier often says that it was while observing his father in the pulpit that he first learned the difference between acting and being. It was his father who encouraged him to enter the Central School of Speech Training and Dramatic Art on a scholarship. Elsie Fogerty, his teacher, was not overly impressed with him. She thought him bumptious, disliked the position of his hairline and eyebrows, and endured him only because there were fewer than ten boys to the sixty girls in the school and she needed him to fill in the theatrical exercises. By 1926, after playing in touring companies and provincial repertory, he settled down for two years at Sir Barry Jackson's famed Birmingham Repertory Company. Ralph Richardson was part of the company. Olivier's film debut came in the completely forgotten *Too Many Crooks*, and during the run of Noel Coward's *Private Lives* in New York in 1930, he signed a contract with RKO. Movies, at that point in his career, offered a quick and financially attractive way of being known, perhaps of even becoming a box-office name and thus in line for more exciting roles on the stages of London and Broadway.

Sitting now and sipping coffee in his camper, Olivier recalls those days. "I was supposed to be a threat to Ronnie Colman, you see," he smiles. Photographs from that period reveal Olivier's pencil-stripe mustache, marcelled hair, and rather insipid smile. "It was all so bloody awful," Olivier says with a laugh. In one of his early Hollywood films, a steaming melodrama called *Friends and Lovers*, he and Adolphe Menjou vied for the favors of Lili Damita, while Erich von Stroheim scowled at everybody. Then on loan to Fox, he portrayed in *The Yellow Ticket* a British journalist who saves Elissa Landi from the clutches of secret police chief Lionel Barrymore.

Raoul Walsh, who directed this old-fashioned but oddly fascinating thriller, likes to take credit for discovering Olivier and giving him his first break. Olivier smiles, and says, "If it makes him happy to let Raoul feel he discovered me, let him. In a way, perhaps he did."

When his contract ended, he returned to England. "In 1933," he recalls, "I was rehearsing a play when Metro offered me a long-term contract at a thousand dollars a week. I wasn't interested in long terms, but I thought I might consider one film, and they offered the lead opposite Greta Garbo in *Queen Christina*. That I accepted." Olivier tested with the Divine One, but she had already decided that her old friend John Gilbert was more in need of the shot in the arm that this movie would give him than this unimportant Englishman was. She was remote with Olivier, and before walking off the set observed, "Life is a pain."

Olivier could only agree with her. His firing was a blow to his pride. To recover, he took the lead in *The Green Bay Tree*, one of the first Broadway plays to deal with the verboten subject of homosexuality. The play was a sensation. "It enabled me," Olivier remembers, "to take a bloody vow to let the dust of Hollywood blow off me forever." Not that he abandoned movies. He subsidized himself with potboilers like *No Funny Business*, *Moscow Nights*, and *As You Like It*, a movie which convinced Olivier that Shakespeare could not be done on the screen.

But in the theater, Olivier was finally stretching: *Hamlet*, *Macbeth*, *Coriolanus*, Sir Toby Belch in *Twelfth Night*, Iago in *Othello*, all for the Old Vic. It was during this time—in the fall of 1938—that Olivier was offered the role of Heathcliff in *Wuthering Heights*. Producer Samuel Goldwyn, who knew of Olivier's distrust of Hollywood, assured him that the Emily Brontë novel would make a movie "which could only do your career good." Olivier, deep in his Shakespearean abundance at the Old Vic, was in no hurry to accept the role. It was only after a meeting with director William Wyler that he was finally persuaded that a splashy role in a successful movie could only be an asset to his theatrical ambitions.

It went very badly at the beginning. He fought Wyler's direction, and early rushes indicated that he was not giving the kind of performance everyone had expected of him. There was a worried conference, and Goldwyn threatened to close down the production unless Olivier came to heel.

"Willie Wyler was the man who altered my feelings toward films," Olivier now concedes. "He saw that I felt superior to films, that I was condescending, slumming. He took me in hand and not only saved my performance as Heathcliff but altered my entire career. He taught me that while working in film one had to make oneself believe that it was the greatest medium even if one really didn't. I'd argue with him. I'd say, 'But you can't do Shakespeare on film.' He'd say, 'Yes, you can. You just have to find the way of doing it. Of course, you can't do it as you would onstage. That's the mistake of all the Shakespearean films so far, but that doesn't mean that it can't be done.'

"That's what Willie said to me, and it was a revelation," Olivier says. "Nobody in films had ever taken me aside before and said, 'Look, this is what we are and this is how it is done.' Later, when the War Office asked me to do *Henry V*, which would be good wartime propaganda for the British in 1943, and no director that I wanted was free to accept, I had to assume that duty myself. Though I had never attempted it before, I had to find a way to do it."

I recall now, for Olivier, the excitement I felt as a thirteen-year-old, looking down from my balcony seat, with my parents' opera glasses, at him and Vivien Leigh in his New York production of *Romeo and Juliet*. Olivier, fresh from *Wuthering Heights*, and Leigh, fresh from *Gone With the Wind*, would find hundreds of young admirers outside the stage door, but the critics demolished the production. "You know," Olivier tells me, "I never thought it was as bad as they said it was."

I had been told by the film's publicist to ask Olivier no personal questions and, above all, not to mention Vivien Leigh. The publicist looks at Olivier nervously and says, "Larry is tired, and he has to work soon. Two more questions." Olivier says, "Three more questions. I would like to finish my coffee, please. Four questions. Maybe five."

We talk about *Henry V*, which Olivier made a year before the Allied invasion of France. By opening and closing the film on the stage of the Globe Theatre (supposedly during an actual performance of the play in 1600) his camera moving "once more unto the breach" to accompany the dialogue, the use of the Bayeux Tapestry and Books of Hours as art motifs, his inspired casting—all prove that in every area Olivier had indeed "found the way to do it." He has said that as an actor he had moments in the theater which gave him a deeper satisfaction, but that as a person he never enjoyed an experience more or felt a greater sense of power than he did while directing *Henry V*.

In the following years—then at his height—came the film versions of *Hamlet*, which he modestly labels "an introduction to *Hamlet*," and *Richard III*, with the extraordinary support of Ralph Richardson, John Gielgud, and Cedric Hardwicke. His attempts to film *Macbeth* failed; he could not raise the money. He grew discouraged, perhaps even bitter. There were still great moments on film: His electrifying performance as the broken-down vaudevillian in *The Entertainer*; his *Othello*; *Three Sisters*, in which he plays the old doctor to the Masha of Joan Plowright, his present wife.

But his attention turned more to theater, particularly England's National Theatre, which he helped found. There he was an administrator, director, actor, still finding time for small forays into film—everything from *Spartacus* to *Bunny Lake Is Missing*.

He has done cameos in films like *Oh! What a Lovely War*, *Nicholas and Alexandra*, *The Seven–Per-Cent Solution*, and *A Bridge Too Far*. Occasionally these bits reveal Olivier's still glittering artistry as he fleshes out an indifferent role, but they remain hardly worth his efforts.

Plagued by ill health, he nonetheless goes on, filled with the desire, it is said, to leave money to his three young children by Plowright. His performances in *Sleuth*, in the television film *Love Among the Ruins*, and in *Marathon Man* were more than respectable, even if his appearances in *The Betsy* and in the television versions of *Cat on a Hot Tin Roof* and *Come Back, Little Sheba* were severe tests of his most ardent admirers' loyalty. But then Bette Davis is in *Return from Witch Mountain*, and Katharine Hepburn plays a ragwoman in a movie made a year and a half ago which still has not been released. Great stars of seventy may still be great stars, but the times are not good to them.

Now I stand on a corner of the set at the Wien Studios as Olivier and Peck prepare to roll on the floor again. Fryer tells me, "Olivier is incredible. Did you know that when I came out of the Army in 1946, the first job I had was as an assistant in Theatre Incorporated which brought the Old Vic to the Century that year? My job was to be Olivier's coffee boy—this was my Broadway debut—and to bring him coffee, to coach him in his lines, to do whatever was needed to make him happy. Olivier was always grateful and considerate, always a little embarrassed to be fussed over, and he still is."

I know that at one point Walter Matthau thought he was going to play Ezra Lieberman, Fryer says. "Several important stars wanted the role, but Frank Schaffner and I always insisted on Olivier, and Lew Grade supported us. Olivier is getting the same amount of money as Peck is for this. I can't tell you how much it is, but it's a lot. And I'll tell you something else I couldn't say for too many people—he's worth it. We talked about it before he even made *The Betsy*, and we waited around for him to finish it. That's how much we wanted him.

"There was a scene last week Olivier had with Bruno Ganz," Fryer goes on. "It called for him to walk down a flight of steep stairs. Now frankly, when I saw those steps and I knew how much pain he's in, I didn't see how he could possibly do it. He must have been in holy agony, but he walked down those stairs without even holding on to the banister and never once complained. Another thing. At first, he didn't want anyone to act as dialogue director for him. But when he saw that Marcella Markham could help him in his Viennese-Jewish accent—it's different from any other because it's a little singsongy and he's such a perfectionist—he changed his mind, and now they're inseparable. He told her, 'Don't ever be intimidated by me. Don't let me get away with anything.'"

Olivier is again on the floor, Peck straddling him as they grapple for the gun. It is obvious that Peck is faking the scene as best he can, carrying the burden of his own weight. Still, the scene must look believable to an audience, and with all of Peck's assistance, there is still a great physical strain on Olivier. Schaffner, Decaë, and his associate, bearing a hand-held camera to catch close-ups of the actors' strained faces, hover above.

There's a break, and Schaffner says, "We'll shoot this scene in sections, just like paella. And that's as far as we go for the moment."

"Ah!" Olivier sighs in mock disappointment. "This is only as far as we go?" Peck laughs and goes to makeup to have his villainy refurbished a bit, and Schaffner lies down beside Olivier.

"Nice and relaxing," Schaffner says. "Do you do yoga?"

"Yes," Olivier says. "It's marvelous, very refreshing, but the physical exercises are all I do. I just never could do the meditation, to concentrate on that shiny place in the middle of your forehead. I never could find that bloody shining place. I guess I'm too earthbound."

Peck returns from makeup, resumes his position atop Olivier, and for the rest of the afternoon, they continue to fight for the revolver.

The next morning begins another physically arduous day before the cameras. Schaffner calls for action, and Olivier walks onto the set and sits on a couch opposite Peck, who is leveling the gun at Olivier's head while he delivers a tirade.

"Oh, yes," villain Peck hisses in his German accent. "I'm going to kill you. And I want you to go to your death with the knowledge that your efforts have gone for nothing. I want you to know what is coming in twenty years or so. . . ."

"The Fourth Reich?" Olivier asks fearfully, and Peck recounts the cloning plot and how more than ninety Hitlers are growing up around the world. Olivier has risen and attempts to move toward the door. As he is about to open it, Peck shoots him several times. Olivier is supposed to turn, stagger, and fall near a couch.

"You can drop here, Larry," Schaffner says.

Olivier concentrates for a moment, looking around the room, then says, "It would be better, wouldn't it, if when I'm shot, I wheel around and then fall against the couch, perhaps on the armrest, and then fall off the couch onto the floor."

"That isn't really necessary, Larry," Schaffner says softly.

"It would be better, Frank," Olivier says. "I can do it. Don't worry, Frank, I can do it." Schaffner starts to say something, stops, then simply smiles.

They do the scene as a rehearsal without cameras. It looks perfect. The expressions of fear, contempt, and hatred which rapidly replace each other across Olivier's face as he listens to Peck's *Götterdämmerung* are something to behold. You can read not only into Lieberman's mind but into his soul. And then when Peck shoots him, he turns around in wonder, his face expressing confusion as to why he's lived, why he's dying. At that point, he falls atop the armrest of the couch, slides onto the couch and then off the couch onto the floor, and emits a low "oich—ch—ch!"

We all stand on the side, watching him incredulously. Anthony Peck asks me what the cry indicates, and I tell him that it's a smaller version of the one he emitted in *Oedipus*, which might be the apotheosis of his career. "The things I saw him do," I tell Anthony, "I didn't think I ever would again. But there it is."

Olivier is still not quite satisfied with the effect. Magnificent as it is, it still does not quite live up to his vision of what he feels he can do. He confers with Marcella as the makeup man paints more blood on him. He stands by the door, gathering all of his strength together, then, noticing the concerned, respectful, affectionate faces all looking at him, he smiles reassuringly. It is a dazzling smile. It is the smile, if only for a flash, of Heathcliff and Darcy and Henry V. I see the space between his teeth he never filled in because he never needed to.

His makeup man comes over to where Anthony Peck and I are standing and says, "I've been with him, on and off, for forty years now, ever since *Fire Over England.* We've been through a lot together. No matter what he and everybody says, I don't think it's for the money. When I first saw this script and read about all these physical scenes, I asked him how he could do them, and he said, 'I can't. How can I? I can't raise my arm to shake someone's hand. They'll have to use stuntmen. I can't do it.' But there he is. Just look at him."

[1978]

Bruce Williamson

AL PACINO

"You have to dare to fail at something."

Al Pacino, in his second film role as Number One son of *The Godfather*, won a National Society of Film Critics' citation as top actor of 1972, edging out Laurence Olivier and Godfather Brando himself. While he was at work on his third film, *Scarecrow* (co-starred with Gene Hackman), there were rumors in the trade that Pacino was becoming a bit touchy and inaccessible. Star temperament, the Brando bit, maybe. Forget it. Next thing you know he's in New York with a soaring temperature, saying come join him for breakfast at his hotel, then a flight to Boston, where he's due to read with some actors for a Theater Company of Boston production of *Richard III.*

The moment he appeared in pajamas in his Manhattan hotel suite, the

Al Pacino: *"I guess I'm not a real movie star, in the sense of being a personality."* (*. . . And Justice for All.* Courtesy of Columbia Pictures.)

idea of Pacino playing Shakespeare's Richard was no longer so strange as it had sounded. He even looked the part—long shaggy hair, enormous expressive eyes, a fine-timbred voice, and slightly stunted in stature, with a head almost too big for his body. But an actor's head, inside and out. Amiable as hell with a temperature of 102, Pacino said he got his reputation for surliness by going on television talk shows. "I'm no good at it up to now, but those people have no idea how to talk to a young actor. On the Merv Griffin show, I was a disaster. Right away, Griffin says to me: 'So how'd you get from the Bronx to Broadway?' Wow, man, that is some question. So I say, 'I walked—I didn't have the carfare.' Zonk. From the audience—nothing. So then Griffin comes back with: '*The Indian Wants the Bronx* and *Does a Tiger Wear a Necktie?*—aren't those funny names for a show?' So how the fuck do you answer that? I thought to myself, No, *Merv Griffin* is a funny name for a show . . . the interview was downhill from there on."

En route to La Guardia and during a half-hour wait in the airport bar, Pacino seldom stopped talking. He ordered his favorite drink, Wild Turkey bourbon ("I'd like to do a commercial for them. . . . *I've had a hundred Wild Turkeys today, and I feel GREAT*"), and talked about plays, films, fame, and fortune. "I'm sure the reason I've got this flu or whatever is because of going up to work onstage in Boston. I have to, yet I resist it. I guess it's something to do with being . . . well, an artist." Whenever he feels himself coming on too seriously, Pacino becomes wry or diffident. Nevertheless, he hopes to avoid the rap he thinks was unfairly laid on Brando by meeting the challenge of stage roles periodically. If it worked out well, he thought he might do *Richard III* in New York. In the future he also wants to play Brecht's *Arturo Ui* and Chekhov. "I don't get it off making movies the way I do in theater. I wasn't getting it off on *Scarecrow* while we were shooting out in Denver, so I started performing in a nightclub. A place called Kit's Club. My name was never announced, but I'd drop by there and play conga drums, or jump up and dance . . . sometimes solo, or with the singer there, or customers. I'm a pretty good dancer."

Pacino acknowledged that his impromptu musical performances had made him quite a local attraction—SOP for a bright Bronx kid who started out mugging through softball games in grade school. "The kids used to call me *the actor,* because I'd go for a ground ball and fall down twice. Drama." From these humble beginnings, his path naturally led to a professional children's school, repertory theater, off-Broadway and the two plays (*Indian* and *Tiger*) for which he won Obie and Tony awards, and got Hollywood knocking at his door.

"Before I went into *Panic in Needle Park*, I turned down seventeen movies," he said, whistling as if still amazed at himself. "But I knew I had hold of something when I first played *Indian* up in Waterford and Provincetown. I had this rhythm going, I knew it would all happen. You just *know*. I knew I would get *The Godfather* when everyone said I wouldn't. . . ." Pacino's next role will be *Serpico*, probably followed by *The Godfather, Part II.* "I don't like to repeat myself. When they first showed me the second *Godfather* script, I said no. They hit me with another offer, I said no. They came back again, and wham . . . now I'm getting so *much* fucking money! Money doesn't mean anything anymore, I'll be taking percentages. The rest becomes an artistic struggle." He said he wished someone would ask him to play the homosexual bank bandit who made news when he held hostages to spring his lover from a hospital for a sex operation.* "—A really complex, fascinating character. Make a wonderful movie." He paused and hunched forward to look left and right down the bar. "People hardly ever recognize me in public. Maybe because I'm not very tall, or it's the way I dress. . . ." True. In high leather work shoes, crumpled bell jeans, and red wool lumber jacket, with a dark-green knit hat pulled down square over his forehead, he looked more like the hitchhiking vagrant of *Scarecrow* than a fast-rising film star.

In midflight, he discussed his work methods, which are not those of your average budding superstar. "I'm crazy about music, for example. I'm always reading biographies of Beethoven, Bach . . . and I use music when I work. In *Tiger*, I'd listen to Bob Dylan as preparation before I went onstage at every performance. Then in *The Godfather*, I knew nothing about Harvard Law or those specific inner things that set my character apart from his family—that make him kind of quiet and remote—so I just listened to a lot of Mozart and hoped something would rub off. I'm going to work with music in *Richard III*, too."

Home for the Theater Company of Boston is a squat, four-story brick tenement not far from downtown. Pacino got his professional start there—after a fallow period of delivering handbills, or ushering at Manhattan's Cinema I—and the Theater Company's dingy office displays evidence of his loyalty in posters advertising Pacino in *The Basic Training of Pavlo Hummel* and *Sticks and Bones*, which he played in Boston after finishing *The Godfather*. "I *draw* in Boston, they know me up here," he said, as if to explain his return to the large barren rehearsal hall where a band of local actors sat in a semicircle of folding chairs, waiting, none visibly impressed by Pacino's arrival. "These are mostly local or college kids," he murmured aside. "I sit in and read with them a little—and it doesn't intimidate anybody because I read

* Someone did, and the result was *Dog Day Afternoon*, for which he deserved an Oscar.

so badly." He read flatly, as a matter of fact, as if searching the language and himself—though now and then he would latch onto a line, or hear the music, and lift his voice to send a shiver of excitement through the room.

Late that day, Pacino went to pull himself together in a suite at the Ritz-Carlton overlooking Boston Common. He sent down for Budweiser beer and a club sandwich, and stood looking across the park. "I used to have an apartment just over there. The first time I really made any money as an actor was in Boston, a hundred and twenty-five dollars a week. I thought I had it made, man." Pensive, he placed a hand on his forehead and said he didn't feel so good. "I'm kind of low right now, anyway . . . personal problems."

"My love life is what's important to me," Pacino continued. "That's number one, even before acting. But I guess it all goes together. Mostly I spend a couple of years or more with one girl, making a home. I seem to need that. When you arrive where I am right now in this business, people are always laying girls on you. It's weird. On location out West, I'd get messages in my room, phone calls. One girl left a vial of dope in my coat pocket in a restaurant, with a note signed 'Love, Susan.' Another time in Denver this chick offered me a ride back to my hotel—I'd had a few, but I wasn't drunk—and after a half hour or so I realized we were heading out of town. I said what the hell is this, and she said: I'm kidnapping you. Jesus! I finally talked her into taking me to my hotel."

Talk of love and sex reminded Pacino of a favorite story about Nabokov explaining to a friend that he had reached a point in life where he can admire an attractive young woman without lusting after her, because he's had all that. Pacino loves the story. "You like to think you'll have had it, too, when you get where Nabokov is. You don't want to be one of those dirty old men, slavering at the mouth when it's all over. . . ." Still, he saw hopeful signs in a writer like Henry Miller, or maybe Picasso, painting erotic pictures and breeding at an advanced age. "Man, that's what encourages you—" Pacino lifted his beer exuberantly, and threw himself back in his chair, feet off the floor. "Imagine—forty more years of *fucking.*"

That's Pacino the man. Meanwhile Pacino the actor reasserts himself: "Actually, I figure in the next ten years I should have the energy to do all the things that are important to me. I'm thirty-two. Just getting there—the career struggle—is behind me, but I don't want to play it safe, you have to dare to fail at something . . . like *Peer Gynt* or *Oedipus* or *Macbeth.* I guess I'm not a real movie star, in the sense of being a personality. I have a lot of work to do."

[1973]

Molly Haskell

GREGORY PECK

His voice conveys both authority and vulnerability, intelligence and sensuality held carefully in check.

There was a time in our lives when my mother and I could agree on only one thing: we both loved Gregory Peck. . . . Coming as he did between the Golden Oldies (Grant, Astaire, Cooper, et al.) and a new generation of stars, Peck was the only male idol for whom we experienced overlapping crushes. Naturally, even in this rare entente were the seeds of further conflict. . . .

Still, though I've now met him in the flesh, Mother *did* see him first. She was lucky enough to be a grown-up when that quietly brooding presence sent its first muted tremors of excitement across the black-and-white screen, to hear that controlled but voluptuous baritone that sent young girls into raptures. The voice, conveying both authority and vulnerability, intelligence and a sensuality held carefully in check, is Peck's defining trademark, and has more to do with the way we think of him than anything else.

In contrast to the actors who would follow him, Peck was a gentleman. Even in the Westerns, anti-Westerns, and war pictures to which he increasingly devoted himself, he was fundamentally decent, and even at his most violent and "villainous" (as in *The Gunfighter* and *12 O'Clock High*), he was somehow trying to do the "right thing."

So while my friends flocked to see Brando and James Dean flail against fate and expose their psychic wounds, I remained true to an ideal of a fleeting-but-perfect male-female partnership as I had seen it in *Roman Holiday*. I was in love with *both* Audrey Hepburn and Gregory Peck, but it was Peck who led me into believing it might not be so bad to grow up after all. Led me to believe that perhaps the boys who were a head shorter than us in the eighth grade might indeed (as our parents assured us) grow tall as oak trees; that men could be both extraordinarily good-looking on the one hand and sweet and considerate and normal on the other; that men could be paternal *and* fraternal *and* sexy. Or, failing that, that Peck himself would be around, at least in movies, to satisfy our fantasy needs.

But there were few such romantic Peck films in the fifties and sixties, and as time wore on, he became more paternal than sexy. The image of Peck as the kindly and concerned liberal, beginning with *Gentleman's Agreement*, was crystallized in *To Kill a Mockingbird* and finally institutionalized.

The ambassador to England in *The Omen* is but an extension of the roles Peck has played in films and in real life, as an active champion of liberal causes. (His first film as producer was *The Trial of the Catonsville Nine*.) So what is a good liberal like Peck doing in the arrogant posture and militaristic role of Douglas MacArthur? When the opportunity arose to ask Peck myself—and, not incidentally, to make my dear mother mad with envy—I naturally took the first plane to California.

"Because I thought MacArthur was a great character and a great opportunity," said Peck, "and because early on in my career I was indoctrinated with the idea that an actor should try every kind of part, within reason."

We are sitting in folding chairs at a card table, the only furniture in the basement-playroom of Peck's new house in Holmby (next to Beverly) Hills. It is a vast Norman structure nestled against the top of a hill overlooking what must, even in these classy parts, be one of the most splendid estates. The lush lawn is steeply landscaped, bordered by flowers and hedges and leading down to an Olympic-size pool on one side and, on the other, a tennis court and white tennis pavilion backed by huge pines. It is paradise on earth. If anyone else owned it, I couldn't help feeling a twinge of resentment, yet somehow I don't begrudge Peck anything.

The late-afternoon sun is streaming in the French windows, the workmen who are remodeling the upstairs are gone. Veronique, Peck's French-born wife, is playing tennis with her brother. All is quiet except for the plop, plop of the tennis ball and the sound of Peck's voice, its relaxed, measured cadences speaking just for me!

"My picture of MacArthur," says Peck, "was formed by the usual liberal prejudices, and was based on mannerisms like the arrogance, the funny costumes, the pipe, the affectations, the flowery Victorian speech. I vaguely remembered he clashed with President Truman and I thought he wanted to start World War Three. But he was discharged for one reason alone, for insubordination. And Truman was probably right. He couldn't have a honcho general out there [in the Far East] dictating foreign policy. But MacArthur's stand was taken out of a deep conviction, a hatred of appeasement, and my investigation of the issues suggests that he may have been right.

"According to many people in the State Department—and granted, most of this is hindsight—the Chinese were not ready to wage a war in 1951. If we had taken a strong stand and established our authority in Korea, many things would be different today. It's too bad that MacArthur and Truman, who both wanted peace in the Far East, couldn't sit down together and air their differences."

"Was MacArthur like Patton?" I ask Peck, "and will the movie take the *Patton* approach?"

"No, not at all," Peck replies. "MacArthur, unlike Patton, was a very cultivated, very intellectual man, not blood and guts, but very concerned about his men, and proud of his low casualty rate—in World War One as well as World War Two. This was one reason he was so frustrated by the restrictions the Joint Chiefs of Staff were placing on him—he was sacrificing human lives and not getting anywhere.

"He was very vain, too, and said outrageous things. Like: 'Alexander, Caesar, and Napoleon all failed as occupiers of foreign cultures because of the harshness of their policies, but I won't.' He saw himself as their peer, even as a kind of Christ figure, equating American-style democracy with Christianity."

I think, as I listen, that it is precisely because Peck is a true liberal rather than a knee-jerk liberal, one who can entertain ideas that seem contrary to his own beliefs, that he can see, and play, MacArthur in a fresh light.

We talk about *The Omen*. Peck has no illusions about its merit, and no hard feelings toward the critics who lambasted it. He had fun doing it and is utterly delighted with its success.

"It's crazy," he says. "I saw it as a kind of movie equivalent to a drugstore paperback. It has made over a hundred million dollars—more than any of my other pictures.

"I know *The Omen* is cleverly contrived claptrap, but what this picture has done for me is to give me a new lease on life. Frankly, I was pretty much on the fringe out here, based on the things I've done recently. Then one huge success, and the phones start ringing. It's the nature of the business. They want somebody who's made money, because they hope it'll rub off on them."

Peck is refreshingly candid about his career. He is neither apologetic nor defensive, unlike so many actors who suggest that they are superior to their material or that they have been victimized—by Hollywood, by critics, even by their mothers and fathers! There is no false bravado in Peck, who seems to enjoy a story at his own expense, and will often bend one in that direction.

"Sophia [Loren] was a little inclined to scene-stealing," Peck begins, in reply to my question about such occurrences. "Not out of any meanness but from her natural energy and high spirits. I used to kid her that I had to stay on my toes to keep up with her. We were shooting *Arabesque*, and there was a

Gregory Peck: A star who brought infinite grace to the movie screen.

scene where we had to crawl on our hands and knees through a cornfield. We were being chased by a harvester that was meant to mow us down. Now, Sophia can run faster than I can, and she can crawl faster than I can, but I was supposed to be the hero rescuing her. So I was scrambling like mad to keep up with her and she was always a nose ahead of me, like a racehorse who wants to get in first. I kept saying, 'Slow down, Sophia, slow down so I can save you.' "

We talk about some other actors Peck has known and admired. "Walter Huston was another wonderful scene stealer. He would seize your hand in a grip of iron" (Peck stands up and acts it out) "and force you into a position with your back to the camera. You either had to wrestle your way out of it and spoil the scene or stay still and lose your place within what the camera was filming. With him, I didn't care, I was completely taken with him, and admired him as much as any man I've ever known.

"Gary Cooper was another actor I admired," Peck says. "And you know, he was not at all the drawling cowboy he pretended to be. He was extremely shrewd, and knew exactly what he was doing. Jimmy Stewart was the same way. It was a kind of protective armor. Cooper had such a well-defined screen personality he was a prototype. People expected him to behave in a certain way and if he didn't sound like Gary Cooper, they would be furious. So he made it his business to sound and act like Gary Cooper. Same with Tracy and Bogart and Cagney.

"My orientation, on the other hand, was toward versatility. I rejected the idea of getting typed, so that when they offered me parts like ones I'd already done—the martinet with the heart of gold in *12 O'Clock High* for example—I turned them down. I was offered a number of those parts—the hard-driving man, dedicated and a bit neurotic. If it weren't for the noble objective, he would be a little bit masochistic. If I had played it three or four more times, I might have gotten into it."

Peck opted for well-roundedness, for the wholesome, better-face-of-America side of himself over the self-doubting neurotic. Whether this is an act of will or instinct, it seems to have become the axis of his family life as well.

I meet Veronique, looking young and unmade-up after an afternoon of athletics, and wearing a Princeton sweatshirt (where their daughter is a sophomore). She doesn't look old enough to have been married to Peck for over twenty years. I also meet, and like, Veronique's mother, a small, striking, slow-moving, gray-haired woman who speaks imperfect English and yet has a California driver's license—thanks to her son-in-law, who, with what I imagine to be unbelievable patience, taught her to drive.

I suppose it is this (told to me not by Peck but by Veronique) that touches me more than anything else. And Peck's obvious feeling for his family—the boy and girl from his marriage with Veronique, and two older sons from a former marriage. Of these, one is living in Los Angeles with his wife, raising horses, and trying to get into film production. The other, an aspiring politician, is an assistant to Senator Claiborne Pell of Rhode Island, in Washington. Both are doing just what they want to do and in the ways they want to do it. A great comfort to Peck who has suffered immeasurably since the 1975 suicide of his thirty-year-old son Jonathan. Peck shows me a photo of Jonathan, taken when he was in the Peace Corps, teaching in Africa. He is tanned and wearing a dashiki and smiling slightly. Yet even there, in what his father believes was the happiest time of his life, there is a brooding quality in the dark-brown eyes, the sense of a deep wound, a lost quality that one has occasionally seen in Peck. The very quality, perhaps, that Peck rejected in turning down those scripts.

"Jonathan wanted eventually to be a news commentator, a sort of Eric Sevareid," Peck says when I ask him about his eldest son. "When he came back from New York, he got a job with a small television station in Santa Barbara. He was the Santa Barbara stringer, and he was required to send in three news stories a day. It was backbreaking work—he had to do the whole thing, dig up the stories, film them, then run around in front of the camera and do the commentary. There weren't three important stories a day to *do* in Santa Barbara, but the station didn't realize what they were asking for. I kept telling him, just do two stories, but he was determined to do the three.

"Once he told me they didn't want him using any extra film because it was so expensive, that they didn't understand you had to use extra footage to get what you wanted. I told him to let me send him some cans of film so he would feel he had something to fall back on. He said no, but I sent them anyway. Twelve cans. We went to Europe for the summer, and a month later he was dead. They found the twelve cans of film in his apartment, untouched.

"He was not in good physical shape. They performed an autopsy and found he had hardened arteries and high cholesterol. He had an enlarged heart—he had been a long-distance runner in school—and should have kept up with his jogging, but hadn't.

"I'll tell you a story about him," says Peck. "Once he was in a cross-country race, when he was a teenager. We all went to see him. One boy was out front, but Jonathan, who was second, suddenly surged ahead and passed him and won. When he came over afterward, we hugged and congratulated him. He seemed very down, very exhausted. I assumed it was the natural end-of-race fatigue, but later he said to me, 'You know, I shouldn't have won that race.' 'What do you mean?' I asked him. 'I let the other guy set the pace, and then I passed him at the last minute. That was wrong. I should have set the pace,' he said. 'But that's what racing is,' I said. I don't think I convinced him."

We talked about the very American conflict that Jonathan's life and death so tragically expresses between a competitive drive and the guilt that drive inspires. How terrible that not even a father's love could save him, that love itself is impotent before the collision course of contradictory ideals.

One feels that the same conflicts exist, in a less exaggerated form, in many of us, not least in Peck himself. But that it was Jonathan, driven and unwell, who died for them.

"Where is *your* protective armor?" I asked him, "where is your actor's ego?"

"Oh, I have one," says Peck, "but it's in my work. Maybe I'm not typical. My wife says I am less an actor off the set than anyone she knows. She says her doctor is more of an actor than I am. Or the television-repair man!"

It's possible that in ultimate terms Peck hasn't the arrogance or egocentricity to make a consummate ham. But if his extraordinarily lovely disposition has kept him from being one of the world's greatest actors, it has made him something rarer: a human being worth knowing and admiring. And a star who will be remembered not so much for specific roles but as one who brought infinite grace to the movie screen. A gentle man. Let us hope that Gregory Peck does not represent the last of a dying breed, but the first of a new.

[1977]

Gary Arnold

MARY PICKFORD

Audiences feel better smiling at these vanished, old-fashioned pieties than groaning at the insistent, new-fashioned ones.

Reviewing Mary Pickford in *A Romance of the Redwoods* (directed by Cecil B. De Mille) for *The New Republic* of July 7, 1917, Vachel Lindsay recalled—lyrically—the way she became a star:

> There is an old vaudeville song, "Every American Girl Is a Queen." O. Henry believed that, and we have his shop-girl stories. Democracy crowns those it loves.

Mary is a queen in especial, born from an all-conquering machine. The story of her rise is so romantic the fans have almost forgiven her fish-eyed exploiters.

When the nickelodeon was a black and stinking conspiracy, with a sagging sheet for a screen, with few lights but the lantern itself, the films were scratched till they looked like a rainstorm of pitchforks and hay wagons. They were hurried through for the sake of blurring the storm.

Someone dashed past the pitchforks to our hearts. There she stayed. The would-be Bowery tough who took the tickets wrote to a similar person higher up. A portrait was put in front of the cave, when all other actors were anonymous. "Little Mary." Not the full name. Just "Little Mary."

After reigning alone a long time in her cave of Adullam, suddenly the child was gone. She was a Broadway star, the first one made by the outlawed films. She had the leading part of Belasco's production of *In the Bishop's Carriage*. We found her full name was Mary Pickford. In due season Mary came back to her people, and such a shout went up from the backwoods that all Broadway was moved with envy. A hundred queens plunged into the films, disputing the first, but we remembered Mary from the days of old. . . .

Mary Pickford was born Gladys Marie Smith in Toronto in 1893 and made her theatrical debut in a touring company at the age of five, as Baby Gladys Smith. She had her first Broadway success in David Belasco's production of *The Warrens of Virginia,* and Belasco was the one who christened her "Mary Pickford," after ruminating over various family names. (Her mother's maiden name was Charlotte Mary Catherine Pickford Hennessey.)

Between 1909 and 1913 the teenage Miss Pickford appeared in 141 one-reel motion pictures, primarily for American Biograph, under the direction of a young ex-actor and unsuccessful playwright named D. W. Griffith, and for Carl Laemmle's "IMP" Company, under the direction of Thomas H. Ince. Between 1913 and 1933 she starred in fifty-two feature films, first for Adolph Zukor's Famous Players (later Paramount), then First National, and finally United Artists, the partnership formed in 1919 by Griffith, Chaplin, Pickford, and her first husband, Douglas Fairbanks.

(It was the creation of United Artists, by the way, that led to the remark, "The lunatics have taken charge of the asylum!" by Richard Rowland, the head of Metro. As it turned out, Fairbanks and Pickford were unusually canny keepers of the asylum.)

So it's been thirty-seven years since Mary Pickford made her last film. There are millions of moviegoers for whom the period of the early talkies represent "the days of old" just as much as the 1909–13 period that Vachel Lindsay was trying to recapture. One has heard that Miss Pickford was the first and most popular movie star of them all; one knows of "Little Mary" and "America's Sweetheart" and "The Glad Girl" and "the little character with the golden curls" by reputation and hearsay. But what were her movies actually like? And what was Pickford the actress actually like? A fine businessman, Pickford had retained control of most of her films. But, fearing that contemporary audiences would find them hopelessly old-fashioned, she had also kept most of her work out of circulation.

The period of seclusion comes to an end with the opening of the series, "A Tribute to Mary Pickford" at the American Film Institute Theatre. The first film on the program is her last silent feature, the charming 1927 romantic comedy *My Best Girl*. Miss Pickford's suitor in *My Best Girl* was played by a remarkably personable, tactful young actor named Charles ("Buddy") Rogers, who eventually became her second husband.

Most of the other features in the series will be accompanied by one-reelers from Miss Pickford's Biograph period. She recently donated negatives of the latter to the American Film Institute Collection at the Library of Congress.

As of this writing, four pictures in the series have been screened for the press—*My Best Girl*, *Sparrows*, *Poor Little Rich Girl*, and *Daddy Long Legs*. I had never seen a Pickford feature before, and these left me with a mixed impression. I much preferred her in *My Best Girl* and the last half of *Daddy Long Legs*, when she was playing more or less mature heroines; there were some rather trying aspects to her little-girl impersonation in *Poor Little Rich Girl* and her adolescent in *Sparrows*.

From this brief exposure, I think it would be wise to mistrust all extreme bits of hearsay and interpretation about Pickford's style. The commonplace misconception that she played nothing but infantile, insipid, goody-goody heroines is certainly refuted. If anything, one is taxed by excessive *irrepressibility* rather than excessive sweetness. The scenarios may, indeed, go overboard on sentimentality, but Miss Pickford is more likely to overdo it on the side of cleverness and high spirits, making her tomboys so rambunctious and florid of gesture that they become a bit *too* gauche.

However, there is no reason to rush to the misconception that the series brochure, written by Bob Cushman, seems to be fostering. Like a lot of documents intended to correct false impressions, this one makes such an ardent case that it can't admit imperfection. Miss Pickford is pictured as such a colossal pioneer and consummate artist that one is quite intimidated, ready to credit her with the discovery of everything from pantomime to the electric light bulb.

It should be possible to reevaluate an artist without getting too patronizing one way or another. From what I've seen, Miss Pickford was an engaging and gifted actress, but there were obviously occasions when she overdid it and when everybody took gross advantage of the audience's pious and sentimental feelings. This will be unusually upsetting only if you believe that filmmakers no longer take such advantage. Anyone who has seen recent movies like *Getting Straight* and *The Strawberry Statement* will know better. Moreover, audiences will probably feel better smiling at these vanished, old-fashioned pieties than groaning at the insistent, new-fashioned ones, which seem harder to dismiss.

Anyway, the feeling that Pickford had better days and inspirations and then lesser days and inspirations hasn't made me any the less curious about her performances in *Pollyanna* or *Rebecca of Sunnybrook Farm* or *Stella Maris* or *The Taming of the Shrew,* a 1929 talkie in which she and Fairbanks co-starred for the first and only time (and got a big jump on the Burtons). Kevin Brownlow's interview with Miss Pickford in his book *The Parade's Gone By . . .* indicates that, proud as she is of her achievement, she does not consider it flawless. She knows that that "little girl," who did wonders for her, also "typed" her.

An unprejudiced look at the Pickford series should reveal not only a great popular career but also a prototypal career for the movies. A contemporary critic like Lindsay is probably a more reliable source of information than either hearsay or Cushman's brochure. Although he admired her work greatly, Lindsay also commented that "in some ways she was the little Eva of this generation" and that her directors encouraged too much in the way of "winsome monkeyshines." One suspects that he was right in wanting fewer "handsprings to keep the people staring" and more of Miss Pickford's "delicate self."

[1970]

Pauline Kael

SIDNEY POITIER

You could sense the pressures, the intelligence, and the tension of self-control in his characters.

Let's Do It Again is like a black child's version of *The Sting*—an innocent, cheerful farce about an Atlanta milkman (Sidney Poitier) and a factory worker (Bill Cosby) who go to New Orleans and pull off a great scam. They outwit the black mobsters (John Amos, Julius Harris, and Calvin Lockhart) and win enough money for their lodge back home, The Sons and Daughters of Shaka, to put up a new meeting hall. Nobody is hurt, and everybody who deserves a comeuppance gets it. Their con involves hypnotizing a spindly prizefighter, played by Jimmie Walker, of television's *Good Times*, in his first screen role. The elder of their lodge (it's their church, too—as if it were the Benevolent and Protective Order of Muslim Elks) is played by Ossie Davis; and the cast also includes such well-known black performers as Mel Stewart, playing the fighter's manager, Denise Nicholas and Lee Chamberlin, as the heroes' wives, and George Foreman. The film was scored by Curtis Mayfield, and the rather patchy script was written by a black scenarist, Richard Wesley.

It's apparent why Sidney Poitier set this project in motion and directed it: he's making films for black audiences that aren't exploitation films. *Let's Do It Again* is a warm, throwaway slapstick, and the two leads are conceived as black versions of Bing Crosby and Bob Hope in the *Road* series. Poitier is trying to make it possible for ordinary, lower-middle-class black people to see themselves on the screen and have a good time. The only thing that makes the film remarkable is that Poitier—who has been such a confident actor in the dozens of roles he has played under other people's direction since his first film, in 1949—gives an embarrassed, inhibited performance. As casual, lighthearted straight man to Bill Cosby, he is trying to be something alien to his nature. He has too much pride and too much reserve for low comedy.

Clearly Poitier is doing something that he profoundly believes in, and there can't be any doubt that he is giving the black audience entertainment that it wants and has never had before. Probably there was no one else who was in a position to accomplish this. One cannot simply say that he is wrong to do it. Many groups have been demanding fantasies in their own image, and if this often seems a demand for a debased pop culture, still it comes out of a sense of deprivation. But for an actor of Sidney Poitier's intensity and grace to provide this kind of entertainment is the sacrifice of a major screen artist. In a larger sense, he's doing what the milkman is doing in the movie: swindling like a Robin Hood, for the good of his lodge, his church. But it's himself Poitier is robbing.

For Bill Cosby, snug in a beard, there's no sacrifice. Cosby doesn't feel that the hipster he's playing is a degrading stereotype, and so the way he plays it it isn't. He has to be a family-picture hipster, but Cosby is spaced out on his own innocent amiability anyway. He's so little-boy antsy that when he stands still he can't resist mugging; it's all right, though, because he's floating along. The format here is too repressive for him to fly, but Poitier lets him run away with the show; maybe he's allowed to be a little too disarming, too droll—which is always a danger for Cosby. As a director, Poitier is overly generous with the actors: he isn't skilled enough to shape sequences so that the actors can benefit from their close-ups (nobody could benefit from all those tacky reaction shots). Jimmie Walker is used unimaginatively, but he's well cast—you can't help wanting him to win his fights, and he has a Muhammad Ali routine in his dressing room, shouting "I am the champ," that is very funny. Ossie Davis has one lush moment: at the feast celebrating the opening of the new meeting hall, he eats his chicken with ceremonial pleasure, and in his great rumbling basso announces, "I tell you, I knew this bird from another life."

It's not a disgraceful movie—I liked the people on the screen better than I liked the people in *The Sting*—but what I can't get out of my head is the image of Sidney Poitier doing primitive-fear double takes, like Willie Best in the old days, only more woodenly. For the fact is that black audiences roar in delight at the very same stereotypes that have been denounced in recent years. It's true that the context is different in these movies, but the frozen, saucer-eyed expressions when Poitier and Cosby are caught doing something naughty or something they can't explain go right back to little Farina in the *Our Gang* comedies. *Let's Do It Again* isn't the first of Poitier's two-black-buddies features: he also directed and appeared in *Buck and the Preacher* and *Uptown Saturday Night*. It amounts to a doggedly persistent skewering of his own talent. What a strange phenomenon it is that the actor who rose through sheer skill and became as elegant as a black Cary Grant should now, out of his deepest conviction, be playing milkman, bug-eyed with comic terror, hanging outside a window by a sheet. And looking sick with humiliation. If Ralph Ellison were to found a new, black-oriented *Saturday Evening Post* and write innocuous stories for it, he might find that he had less talent for light fiction than dozens of writers who couldn't write anything else. Poitier is fighting what he's doing with every muscle of his body; he's fighting his own actor's instinct, which is telling him that this cartoon role is all wrong for him.

Poitier has always had drama going on under the surface of his roles—you could sense the pressures, the intelligence, and the tension of self-control in his characters; that's part of why he became the idealized representative of black people. Now he's trying to make himself an ordinary black man, in comic fantasies for black audiences. But in low comedy you have to abandon yourself and be totally what you are; you can't have a sense of responsibility under the character—or banked fires, either—and be funny. And so this vivid, beautiful actor casts himself as the square, because he knows that in slapstick he comes across unhip. He can't even hold the screen: He loses the dynamism that made him a star. Sidney Poitier, who was able to bring new, angry dignity to black screen acting because of the angry dignity inside him, is violating his very essence as a gift to his people.

[1975]

Pauline Kael

RICHARD PRYOR

He needs to take off into a character in order to be funny.

When Richard Pryor appears on a television talk show and he's asked questions, sometimes you can see that his squirming isn't simple contempt for the host, it's more like boredom and frustration—creative impatience. He knows he is trapped and isn't using the best part of himself: he's being forced to speak in his own voice, and he needs to take off into a character in order to be funny. We're not after the real Richard Pryor (whoever that might be), any more than we were ever eager for the real Peter Sellers to stand up. Pryor's demons are what make people laugh. If he had played the sheriff in *Blazing Saddles,* he'd have made him *crazy*—threatening and funny, both. Pryor shouldn't be cast at all—he should be realized. He has desperate, mad characters coming out his pores, and we want to see how far he can go with them.

Pryor's comedy isn't based on suspiciousness about whites, or an anger, either; he's gone way past that. Whites are *unbelievable* to him. Playing a thief in the new mystery comedy *Silver Streak,* he's stupefied at the ignorance of the hero (Gene Wilder), and he can't believe the way this white man moves. For about fifteen minutes, Pryor gives the picture some of his craziness. Not much of it, but some—enough to make you realize how lethargic it was without him. This movie not only casts him, though—it casts him as a friend to good-guy whites. We're supposed to be touched when he returns Wilder's wallet to him and affectionately advises him to "stay loose." But when he's soft-hearted about his buddy Gene Wilder, he's a bad actor. These moments come at the tag ends of scenes and could easily have been cut. Are they the moviemakers' unconscious revenge on Pryor's craziness? He saves their picture for a few minutes—he gives it some potency and turns

(LEFT) Vanessa Redgrave:
The spirit of eccentric heroism.
(From the motion picture
The Loves of Isadora.
Courtesy of Universal Pictures.)

(BELOW) Sidney Poitier:
Drama under the surface.
(*Uptown Saturday Night.*
© Warner Bros. Inc. All rights
reserved. Used by permission.)

it into the comedy they hoped for—and they emasculate him, turn him into a lovable black man whose craziness is only a put-on. Interracial brotherly love is probably the one thing that Richard Pryor should never be required to express. It violates his demonic, frazzled blackness. The suspense built into watching him is that we don't know what's coming out of him next, or where it's coming from. Those deep-set, somewhere-else eyes and that private giggle don't tell us much, but they do tell us this: his comedy doesn't come from love-thy-white-neighbor. . . .

[1977]

Richard Corliss

VANESSA REDGRAVE

Will Redgrave the activist continue to embarrass Redgrave the actress?

Look into the face; see the soul. That's the assumption that informs the tradition of naturalist acting. It's also the reason star-crossed moviegoers from the days of Gish and Pickford to today have been obsessed, and in love, with movie performers. Now, though, we stare into the faces of stars like Jane Fonda and Vanessa Redgrave to discover how much of their private and political lives are revealed. There are similarities. Both actresses have the sensitive mannishness that we take for intelligence in a woman's face; both have brought life to roles that exploit that aggressive, questioning intelligence; both are icons of sixties radicalism that reflects their screen personalities. By now, their surfaces are so identified with their substances that we assume some special kinship between each actress and her performances. Look into the face; see the role.

Somehow, Jane Fonda has both kept true to her political beliefs and endeared herself to the American moderate—perhaps because, however apologetic her rhetoric may sound for Hanoi dictators, her face and demeanor radiate the good sense and good breeding of the garden-club liberal. (As Tracy Young wrote of Fonda, "You can take the girl out of Vassar . . .") But in Redgrave's stern, shining face, there is not an eyelash of compromise. Is she perceived as the PLO's own La Pasionaria? Yes, she might reply, and so be it. Will Redgrave the activist continue to embarrass Redgrave the actress by passing out radical leaflets to racist workingmen, and by running for office under the frayed banner of a leftist splinter group? Yes, and to hell with Redgrave the actress.

To hell, that is, with the actress's public image. As an artist, she gives everything to her roles; there's no husbanding of her intensity for next week's Hyde Park harangue. That Joan-of-Arc light shines from her eyes— off to a spot just above the film frame, toward a Second Front or the Second Coming—and through her characters, illuminating them with an idealist's ethereal glow. As Isadora, as Julia, as Agatha Christie, as Fania Fenelon, Redgrave embodies the spirit of eccentric heroism. And because her acting style includes the shy, almost clumsy gestures of a sweet schoolgirl in the back row of a class on the Lake Poets, she can play the realists as well as idealists, and with as much conviction. The role of the ordinary, upper-class wife in *Yanks,* which might seem outside (or beneath) her range, becomes a challenge to her gift for suggesting understated goodness. The modest, reluctant smile with which the *Yanks* Redgrave responds to a compliment looks incandescent on the screen, because she knows precisely how to pitch a performance. Which is to say: She knows that the camera loves her face— that it would find her even if she were in the middle of a million May Day marchers—and she respects the camera's ability to transmit the passion, the purity, the fey courage suggested by an almost motionless, utterly beautiful face.

Then again, it could simply be that it's the viewer or critic who loves that face, and who imagines that a unique soul shines through that two-dimensional configuration of light and shadow.

[1980]

Molly Haskell

BURT REYNOLDS

In him we see that blend of the real and the artificial which is the essence of movie stardom.

Burt Reynolds is a man not necessarily for all seasons, but surely for summer, for sunshine, beer, and ice-cream sodas, for drive-ins, and long, lazy nights. I continue to find him one of the more interesting and appealing male stars for those very qualities that others condescend to—the bright, even antiseptic, high gloss and a genuine light touch. There's a glistening, "Draw Me" cartoon quality to his looks: the jet-black hair, the bushy eyebrows, the smooth, round contours of the baby face, the square physique, and the denim outfits that always look lemon-clean, as if his mom had just used a new miracle detergent in the wash. When he pops up in some sweaty, unsavory locale—a bed of corruption, a prison, a men's locker room—he's a little out of place, like a "gosh darn!" in a chorus of "motherfucker!"s, and for better or worse, he sanitizes the milieu and tone accordingly.

In him we see that blend of the real and the artificial which is the essence of movie stardom, but which it has long been fashionable to denigrate. Artifice, including all the perquisites of glamour, was a casualty of the sincere sixties—except as transmuted and theatricalized into camp (which may be one good reason for the shortage of women stars during this period and the durability of Elizabeth Taylor).

Reynolds is made for certain types of comedy—romantic comedy, musical comedy, lightweight adventure, sex farce—a flair to which he is turning more and more as he takes his career in hand. He has always been more aware of his strengths and limitations than he has been given credit for. The most engaging episode of the overrated *Silent Movie* is the cameo in which he takes a gleeful poke at his own superstud image, as it has evolved from the Cosmo cheesecake to *Deliverance* and *The Longest Yard*—all of which, incidentally, were less "macho" for the self-irony Reynolds brought to them.

Gator marks his directorial debut, but in name only. Like Eastwood, Redford, and many of today's studioless stars, he has managed, consciously or unconsciously, to develop his own persona through various forms of control—of projects, of directors, and of direction—previously uncredited.

[1976]

Rex Reed

GEORGE C. SCOTT

"I have never really learned anything from *any* critic."

Somebody once wrote that it is impossible to sit in the same room with George C. Scott without eventually getting punched in the nose, but you can't prove it by me. Out here on his farm, where folks call him G.C. and there is nothing to punch but a bunch of chickens, he seems more like a friendly fertilizer salesman than a slugger. Dark has fallen early and a raw wind moans up from the birch trees on the farm road below. Beams sigh, floors creak, and a warm fire cuts invitingly through the logs he has just brought in from the woodshed. His two sons are doing their homework. G.C. settles down in front of the fire with a bottle of brandy. His straight black hair, which was shaved off everyday during the filming of *Patton,* has grown back and he is wearing a wool sweater, baggy pants, and black-rimmed history-professor spectacles. Red Van Johnson socks peer over the tops of his lumber boots and when he looks at you his eyes are like small cumulus clouds that make tiny swirls of hypnotic vertigo if you look into their direct focus.

"You should see him on regular days, when we don't have company," says his son Alexander, nine, who looks like a young Huck Finn. "I'll leave my *Mad* comics for you, Dad," says his other son, Campbell, eight, who looks like a young Alain Delon. Then, after being promised a ball game at West Point, they both go up to bed. He is left alone with the fire and his bottle of brandy.

In the corner of the room a white dove of peace given to him by Joanne Woodward makes a gurgling sound. He covers the cage with a quilt and the other two doves in the cage begin to flap their wings noisily. "Those doves of peace are going to kill each other," he says with a dirty-old-man chuckle. He was once quite a hawk himself, but then he went to Vietnam and wrote a story about it for *Esquire* and now, since his magnificent performance in *Patton,* he's pretty much of a dove, too. I don't blame him. He takes over the film and for three hours, he owns it—with no love interest, no subplots, and no other noteworthy performances to distract from his own personal fireworks display. It is one of the most brilliant acting triumphs of the decade. He has a lot to be peaceful about.

But one thing troubles. Patton was a psychopath, yet Scott has sometimes been accused of whitewashing the general in his recent interviews. True? "False," he insists. "From the beginning, all I asked was that we show him as multifaceted as he really was. It caused trouble. Conflicts grew out of trying to serve too many masters. We had to serve the Pentagon, we had to serve General Omar Bradley and his book, we had to serve the Zanucks. If you ride that many horses at the same time, you're going to have problems. I simply refused to play George Patton as the standard cliché you could get from newspaper clips of the time. I didn't want to play him as a hero just to please the Pentagon, and I didn't want to play him as an obvious, gung-ho bully, either. I wanted to play every conceivable facet of the man. There were three basic scripts and several revisions before I got the character I wanted. Francis Coppola wrote the first one, which was a combination of Bradley's book, *A Soldier's Story,* and Ladislas Farago's *Ordeal and Triumph.* Then there were memory differences—one guy remembers one thing, another guy says 'He wasn't like that at all!' Then Bradley got into the act and we had the problem of pleasing *him.* He got credit for being a technical adviser on the picture, but it was really General Harkins—who had the best memory about Patton, who was with us every day in Spain—who did all the work. Then the James Webb script came out and I yelled and just said 'Forget the whole thing,' and negotiations came to a screaming halt. It lacked color and imagination and I felt it was just another conventional Hollywood screen biography. Three months later they called back and we kicked around the Coppola script again. Then a third version by Eddie North came out of those talks and became the basis for the shooting script. We reworked it the whole time we were shooting and I kept screaming a lot and now I think it has flaws in it, it has lies in it, it has license in it—but, basically, I think the film captures the essence of Patton, which is the point of the whole goddamn thing.

"I ran three thousand feet of film here at home and really studied the man. I watched the way he moved and talked. Some of it I absorbed, some I threw out. For instance, he had a high, squeaky voice, like a football coach. The more excited he got, the higher it got. I didn't use that. People are used to my gravel voice and if I tried to use a high little voice it would be silly. I also tried not to editorialize about his beliefs or the things he said. Hell, you get paid for acting, for giving the *illusion* of believing, not for *actually* believing. Shit no, I didn't believe in what he did any more than I'd believe in the Marquis de Sade or Frank Merriwell! This is a schizoid business to start with. The biggest mistake an actor can make is to try to resolve all the differences between himself and the characters he plays. Patton actually believed what he was doing was right. So did Hitler. The face-slapping scene? Hell, he really struck *two* men. We only had time to put *one* in the movie. But he wasn't a hypocrite. Even though war was all he cared about, it was what he did for a living. It was a profession. Patton's war was unavoidable, not like Vietnam, which is an obscenity. At least he had no political ambitions, which is more than you can say for our generals today. I told Frank McCarthy, the producer, 'I don't want to play another *Strangelove.* I already played that fucking part.' But on the other hand, I rejected the glory-hunter cliché. Patton was a mean son of a bitch, but he was also generous to his men. Even making it as fair and objective as we did, his family washed their hands of the project. His wife even had an injunction in court against his biography being published. I guess they've lived with enough black eyes. To my knowledge, none of them have seen the film. But now that it is over, I feel we did right by the man. There are still things about him I hate and things I admire—which makes him a human being, I guess. On the whole, it was one of the best working situations I've ever had and it came wholly from my interest in Patton."

It didn't always seem so rosy. There were reports sifting back through the press of drunken brawls and angry disappearances which held up production in Spain. Scott denies the rumors. "There were times when I got frightened. Things weren't going right, so I just went out and got shit-faced. That's me. Something goes wrong, I find a bottle. I don't like it about myself but I've done it before and I'll do it again. But I never vanished for days or held up shooting or quit the picture. All actors feel insecure at times. Just try doing a play eight times a week and you'll find out how good and how bad you can be. There's no guarantee in this business that things will go right. You're on top one minute and the next minute—*zappo!* It's a cruel and capricious profession and you've got *nothing* to fall back on. So actors find shields to hide from their insecurity and pain. Sometimes mine is a bottle. Once somebody asked Patton why he wore his helmet and swaggered around and carried on all the B.S. and he said, 'Because, if I don't people will think the old man is over the hill.' So in a sense he created his own monster."

And in a sense, so has Scott. Ever since he began his remarkable career, playing the meanest Richard III ever seen by human eyes in Joe Papp's 1957 Shakespeare Festival, people have been calling him "the wild man of Broadway." He has one of the great tempers of the age. His nose has been broken five times in barroom brawls. He once smashed in a Hollywood set because he didn't like the way a scene was going, and when they posted the closing-night notice for his first Broadway play, *Comes a Day,* he went into a drunken rage, threw his fist through a glass window, and played the last act bleeding into a rubber glove before being forced into a hospital where he required twenty-two stitches.

Today he is mellower, with the aid of Alcoholics Anonymous and Colleen Dewhurst, who was his third wife, a fine actress, and lone pine of a woman whom one friend describes as "able to survive anything—if the day ever comes when there's a problem too big for Colleen to solve, we might as well *all* give up." G.C. is the first one to admit he has changed since the days when his co-actors feared he would murder them all onstage. "I think of myself as a fairly decent human being and it gives me great pain to be considered for all the mean SOB's that come along. I've played bird decapitators, puppy stranglers, woman beaters, wife poisoners, child molesters—every goddamn thing you can think of. It was quite a scene there for a while. But I think the image is changing. My television series, *East Side, West Side*, helped, *Plaza Suite* helped, the man I played in *Petulia* helped. I hope to God the old image is fading from people's minds."

His old mama dog is having a bad dream in front of the fire. He scratches her head and the tough-guy logo seems no more real than the drivel you read in gossip columns. He loves animals, especially German shepherds. He has one dog who once had a litter of pups and a simultaneous nervous breakdown and is now the family neurotic, and another who was nursed back to health by G.C. and his bodyguard after being poisoned in the Hilton Hotel in Cairo during the filming of *The Bible*. Watching him with his animals, you can see that he is a gentle man. A sour green apple with a soft core hounded by the furies all his life.

He was born in Wise, Virginia (population 1200), in 1927. His dad was a surveyor in a coal mine. His grandfather, who is still alive at eighty-nine, spent forty years in the mines. His people were rural mountain folks, hillside farmers, and coal miners. ("Your basic Appalachia." G.C. grins.) When the stock market crashed, his father went to Michigan, got a job in a tool crib at General Motors for thirty cents an hour, and G.C. grew up in Detroit. He was strong as an ox and full of muscle, but inside, he was a sensitive boy who wrote short stories and dreamed of becoming a writer.

After a hitch in the Marine Corps he attended journalism classes at the University of Missouri on the GI Bill, but after three years, he felt he didn't have what it took to be a newspaperman, so he quit and bummed around for a while. In college he had met a campus actress who married him and planted the seeds of his acting career. They were divorced three years later, and he drove a car to Hollywood with two friends, trying to find himself. "I got a job as a short-order cook, made some rounds, went to the studios, but mostly sat around in MacArthur Park watching the drunks," he says. Then he lived with his sister in Washington, D.C., for a while. Her husband, who was in the construction business, got him a job puddling concrete and driving a truck. He met his second wife, singer Pat Scott, and they moved to a cold-water flat in New York. He worked in a bank from midnight until 10 a.m., "shoveling checks into a registering machine," and during the day he made the rounds of casting offices. He auditioned for *Richard III* three times and got the job with no reputation or anything, playing the entire run while still working at the bank. ("To this day," confides one of the friends who knew him then, "G.C. despises banks. He probably keeps all of his money from *Patton* in a shoe box guarded by one of his German shepherds.")

In 1958 José Quintero hired him to play a wife poisoner in the third act of

Children of Darkness down at the old Circle in the Square. J. D. Cannon and an unknown named Colleen Dewhurst had the leads. She was married, Scott was married, and they were off and running. With all the divorces and legalities, it was 1960 before they got married. They've been divorced and remarried three times since, and are currently divorced. "We couldn't live together and we couldn't live apart," says G.C. "That's about the size of it. I guess I'm just the marriageable type." He is now married to actress Trish Van Devere.

As for movie critics, he has no use for them at all. "Over a period of time you learn who is destructive and who isn't. Most critics are necessary, but years ago I gave up being affected by them. They do their thing and I do mine. The only critics you can learn anything from at all are theater critics, because if they give you valuable advice you can still do something about it. In a film, it's too late. Good or bad, your performance is cemented forever. But I have never really learned anything from *any* critic and I don't know any other actor who has, either. They have more value for writers and maybe even for the public, but not for actors. The thing an actor learns from is the audience. I don't know anything about acting teachers, either. I never had a lesson in my life. I don't think it can be taught."

He is violent on the subject of the "method" and his comments on Sandy Dennis, with whom he once appeared in a disastrous London production of *Three Sisters,* were unprintable. "Cagney and Bogart taught me how to act. During the depressing periods of most actors' lives, they sleep a lot. I went to the movies. Movies kept me off the streets and taught me everything I know. I'm probably one of the few actors in the fifties who never once auditioned for the Actors Studio. It performed one of the greatest disservices to the theater in its entire history and probably ruined the potential of more good actors than any other force. Most method actors work their way out of my heart in no time at all." He also has little in his heart but larceny for British actors.

What he *does* love is the stage and he makes no secret of the fact that "I make movies largely for the money and always have. It's a tedious, deadly, boring way to make a living. I *have* to work in the theater to stay sane. It costs me money to do a play, but I have to do it. You can attack the stage fresh every night, you can say, 'Goddammit, it isn't right yet,' and go on working on it. It's living all the time. What's happening now in both mediums is appalling. This nudity crap. Most of it is trash and in spite of all those naked actors' claims, there is very little freedom in it. I don't think that kind of tastelessness will pay off for long. Dirty jokes are only fun for half an hour. I have not seen *Oh! Calcutta!* or *Che!* or any of that garbage. I have no interest in it. I've seen all the stag films I want to see. They're like the old Moon Mullins books we used to hide in our desks at school. It's called turning a fast buck. But it's changing. I'm encouraged to learn that the Swedish film industry has taken a big drop in the last six months. Nobody's going to the movies anymore in Sweden. They've orgied themselves right out of business. It's the same in the theater. How many times can you watch people doing everything in the book to each other before it begins to look like a short-arm inspection and you wanna yell 'Cough'?"

He once directed a play called *General Seegar* which ran for two performances on Broadway ("I lost all my money and several thousand of some other people's money as well") and last year he directed *Dr. Cook's Garden*, from which he withdrew a week before the opening ("I wanted to get rid of Burl Ives and I couldn't get rid of him, so I got rid of myself"). But he still wants to join that growing list of actors-turned-directors. He directed a television version of *The Andersonville Trial* and a movie called *Rage*. He should be an interesting director. He's certainly had enough experience working *for* them. All kinds:

Richard Lester: "I don't know what the hell was going on in *Petulia* and I don't really think he gives a damn about actors as much as he does about camerawork, but I really liked him. He makes it so much fun you don't worry somehow. I can't ever recall having a close-up in *Petulia*. They were all from fifty feet away. None of that B.S. about a master, then a reverse, then a medium shot. If I was going to emulate anyone, it'd be him."

Kubrick: "He has a brilliant eye; he sees more than the camera does. He walks in in the morning and says 'This is awful!' and you get used to changing things around. I used to kid him by saying I should've gotten screen credit for *Dr. Strangelove* because I wrote half the fucking picture. There's no bullshit with him, no pomposity, no vanity. The refreshing thing is he hates *everything.*"

Otto Preminger: "He lent me money on *Anatomy of a Murder* when I was broke. So I like him. I was never one of his whipping boys. He's not a great director, but he's a great promoter."

Anthony Asquith: "On *The Yellow Rolls-Royce* I couldn't understand a fucking word he said. He was very fey, very nice, wore a red jump suit and a red bandanna and everybody called him Puffin. But I never understood a fucking word he said throughout the entire picture."

Irvin Kershner: "He shot a good picture with *The Flim-Flam Man*, then he went mad in the cutting room and butchered the whole thing. Some of these guys get Jehovah complexes."

Mike Nichols: "He glows. Inside he may be going through the tortures of the damned, but it never shows. He creates an atmosphere for an actor to work in that is so easy you can't believe it. I loved working in *Plaza Suite* and I'd work for him again anytime anywhere—provided I liked the script, of course. He called me up and asked me to do *Catch-22* and after I read the script, I just said, 'No way . . . it's just awful!' "

His greatest ambition for the future is to have a live theater group of his own, like Orson Welles's Mercury group, combining a stage and television situation. "That would be the best of two possible worlds—an ensemble working together with no economic pressures, where you could make money by working out a play on the stage for a live audience until it was perfect, then put it on tape and start all over again with a brand-new project. Richard Boone had a similar situation, but he was under the gun having to do a new play every six days. I wouldn't want a weekly time slot like I had on *East Side, West Side,* just a guarantee to do things when they were ready. Television has got to realize it can't all stop with *Petticoat Junction.* It is going to either be the savior of the world or send us all to hell fast. It's the most powerful communications device since the discovery of language and it is full of shit. We're still in the horse-and buggy stage with television. In the next decade, I believe the networks as we know them now will be obsolete just as the Hollywood studios crumbled under the changing of the times. Too many forces are hammering at them now. The marketplace is too competitive for them to stay in control. The Mike Danns of the world will become as archaic as dinosaurs."

He completed the movie *They Might Be Giants* with Joanne Woodward and is now planning ideas for two television series. "Writing is still something I'd like desperately to succeed at and my favorite idea now is a historical anthology series using events and people from history in theatrical terms. People get hooked on characters—look at *Peyton Place*—so there's no reason why they couldn't get just as excited about Abraham Lincoln, for chrissakes! History is fascinating, man, yet every time it is shown on television it is so dry, pompous, lifeless. There's a kind of reverence about historical figures that puts people off, but nobody expected this kind of wild reaction to a man like Patton, so why not tell the truth about Lincoln or somebody like *him*? Granted, *Patton* is a fairly good film, but to me, it's the *man* that grabs people!"

He is excited now. His voice, like Stromboli struggling to life, begins to widen. He grabs his son's *Mad* comics and whacks the sofa hard. Then he settles back again, his rasping Rasputin of a voice chipping away in a series of lecherous heh-heh-hehs. In 1962 he rocked Hollywood by being the first actor in history to refuse an Oscar nomination for *The Hustler.* Before he won one for *Patton,* he claimed, "They won't nominate me anyway. They're not *that* stupid. Besides, I want to get back to the stage. Colleen Dewhurst and I are planning a new version of *Macbeth.* She'll be a great Lady Macbeth. We won't do it in the nude! I don't want to subject the audience to that sight." His eyes gleam behind the spectacles. "Unless . . . How about me as Macbeth, Colleen as Lady Macbeth, and, on the opposite side of the stage, Steve Reeves and Raquel Welch as our alter egos?"

Somewhere in the night, a dog barks at the moon, but it doesn't have a chance. The brandy bottle is empty and all you can hear is that famous dirty-old-man laugh, rich and healthy, crackling through the dark old house.

[1970]

David Ansen

PETER SELLERS

The most versatile comic actor of his generation.

"I have no personality of my own. I reached my present position by working hard and not following Socrates' advice—know thyself. . . . To me, I am a complete stranger."

It was the complaint of a master dissembler, a note repeatedly struck whenever Peter Sellers talked about himself: the actor had vanished into his role. Yet he was a stranger only to himself. To millions of movie fans who roared at his prolific gallery of comic characters, Sellers was unmistakable and inimitable, a fount of mirth in any guise. By the time of his death in 1980, after suffering his third major heart attack at fifty-four, the great impersonator had proven himself the most versatile comic actor of his generation.

Sellers' sudden emergence in 1959 in *The Mouse that Roared* and *I'm All Right, Jack*, established him as a pivotal figure in British comedy. His three roles in *Mouse* evoked comparison with Alec Guinness in *Kind Hearts and Coronets* and the vintage English comedies of the forties and fifties. The rigidly leftist labor leader he played in *I'm All Right, Jack* showed a subtler side to his satiric touch, and his spoofy skits on British radio's zanily irreverent *Goon Show* presaged the antiestablishment comedy of the sixties. The absurdist humor later popularized by director Richard Lester and Monty Python's Flying Circus is foretold in a classic short that Sellers and the Goon squad made in 1959 called *The Running, Jumping and Standing Still Film.*

Sellers made more than fifty films, and frequently his vehicles were unworthy of his talent. In such forgettable efforts as *Undercovers Hero* and *The Bobo,* his virtuosity is spinning in a void. Only under the direction of Stanley Kubrick and Blake Edwards did Sellers' talent blossom into comic immortality. In his tripartite stardom in Kubrick's *Dr. Strangelove,* Sellers sent up Wernher von Braun as the eponymous mad scientist, spoofed Stevensonian liberals as U.S. President Merkin Muffley and paid homage to Alec Guinness as the unflappable British Group Captain Mandrake. Perhaps his most brilliant and original performance was as the lascivious, oft-disguised playwright Clare Quilty in Kubrick's earlier *Lolita.* Masquerading as a hearty but sinister cop on vacation, Sellers terrorizes James Mason's Humbert Humbert with a monologue of Nabokovian innuendo that is one of the most unnervingly funny set pieces in movie history.

But it was as the imperturbable Gallic schlemiel, Inspector Clouseau, in Edwards' five *Pink Panther* movies that Sellers won his greatest following. Nonchalantly leaning against a spinning globe that in turn spun him out of the room, he proved a rival of great silent clowns in physical slapstick, and he fractured the language (*rheeum* for room, *beump* for bump) with the most hilariously unlikely accent of his myriad-voiced career. Clouseau made Sellers a millionaire, but he came to feel constricted by the character. It was the tricky role of Chauncey Gardiner in last year's *Being There* that brought him back into the critical limelight.

Chauncey was obviously a creature close to Sellers' heart, a chameleon whose personality is totally formed by the media-drenched environment. There was a ghostly pathos in Sellers' affectless portrayal, a tinge of melancholy that was an essential part of his own makeup. A 1969 BBC documentary on the actor, called *Will the Real Peter Sellers . . . ?* portrayed him as a lonely, lost soul. It is said that Sellers cried when the film was screened for him.

Half-Jewish (on his mother's side), half-Protestant, Sellers was the son of variety-show troupers, spending much of his childhood in theatrical boardinghouses. His mother coached him and nursed his ambition: after she died in 1967 he said he remained in psychic communication with her, consulting her for advice. In his stardom, he became an eccentric, often controversial figure, shy and reclusive in private, whose love affairs and four marriages nonetheless made him a staple of the scandal sheets. On the set, his perfectionism and superstitions earned him a reputation for difficulty—no one, for

(RIGHT) Burt Reynolds:
*A bright, even antiseptic high gloss
and a genuine light touch.*

(BELOW) Peter Sellers:
"I have nothing to project."
(*The Pink Panther.* Copyright © 1964
Mirisch–G&E Productions.
All rights reserved. Released
through United Artists Corporation.)

example, was allowed to wear green or purple ("the color of death") in his presence.

A gadget and car lover (he once described himelf as "auto-erotic"), he was the extravagant owner of more than a hundred automobiles. He was also the father of four children (including one illegitimate daughter he never saw) and a man increasingly disenchanted with the world of show business. He kept his distance at his home in Gstaad, Switzerland, but the compulsion to work continually drew him back to the movie set. Though doctors warned him that his weak heart required rest, Sellers could never slow down. For his last movie, *The Fiendish Plot of Dr. Fu Manchu*, he not only played multiple characters but took over the direction of the film.

"I can't do anything [from] within myself," Sellers once said. "I have nothing to project. I've got so many inhibitions that I sometimes wonder whether I exist at all." These are not the words of a clown hiding behind his masks, but of a man who only found himself in his masks. In an era in which self-expression has been the artist's *cri de coeur,* Sellers' curiously egoless esthetic strikes a classical chord. He gave himself to his droll, beleaguered, lovably idiotic characters, and gave moviegoers uncounted laughs. He was comedy's most famous unknown soldier.

[1980]

Richard Corliss

BARBARA STANWYCK

Her personality was so strong that the studios stopped trying to pair her with macho men.

Boy, was she smart! She played cowgirls and faith healers, wives and mistresses, schemers and victims—and informing all these characters was the iron-spined spunk of Ruby Stevens, the kid from Brooklyn, with a profile cut by a hacksaw and the urban wit and grace of a Cagney. "Take a good look," she taunted in the film that made her a star, Frank Capra's 1930 melodrama *Ladies of Leisure,* "it's free." It was never free, but it always seemed reasonable. The challenge Stanwyck offered her leading men wasn't primarily sexual; it was part of a very serious tug-of-wills, which, finally, the best man and the best woman could win together.

Her voice (made for the talkies) was both alluring and all business; its throaty undertone warned of the scam at the end of the rainbow. Stanwyck's screen personality was so strong, her native intelligence so corrosive, that by the end of the thirties the studios had stopped trying to pair her with macho men, and instead were playing off her aggressive, experienced "maleness" against some of the screen's most engaging wimps (Fred Mac-Murray in *Remember the Night*, Henry Fonda in *The Lady Eve*, Gary Cooper in *Meet John Doe* and *Ball of Fire*). Stanwyck's range was surprising for a star with so clearly defined an image—she impressed, and occasionally convinced, as Annie Oakley, Stella Dallas, and the Aimee Semple MacPherson of Capra's *The Miracle Woman*—but it was to comedy she could bring all her gifts.

Came the voluptuous antifeminism of *film noir*, and Stanwyck's save-your-own-ass resilience flowered into her great performance: as Phyllis Dietrichson in Billy Wilder's *Double Indemnity*. When MacMurray played the all-American boy with the Norman Rockwell family (in *Remember the Night*), a Stanwyck character could relax her guard and fall in love. But when he played tough—angling for the Black Widow *and* her insurance money—she had to show him who was boss, and shoot him down. Her men had to provide a window to a simpler, nobler world, rather than a mirror of her own main-chance amorality. One look could be fatal, as MacMurray and a bunch of postwar punks (Burt Lancaster in *Sorry, Wrong Number*, Kirk Douglas in *The Strange Love of Martha Ivers*, Robert Ryan in *Clash by Night*) discovered to their ultimate regret.

If any man was to be her equal, it had to be a man out of the past—out of an American myth. So Stanwyck spent much of the fifties on a horse, looking for love with the proper ranger. In *The Maverick Queen* and Samuel Fuller's *Forty Guns*, she was an outright outlaw who meets her match in . . . well, Barry Sullivan. It took her just one long stride to be established as head of the Barkley clan in the sixties television series *The Big Valley*—where she proved a more convincing patriarch than ponderous Lorne Greene over on the Cartwright spread.

By this time it was difficult to see the soft glow in her eyes illuminated by cinematographer Gregg Toland in the "confession scene" from *Ball of Fire*; only the glint remained. But it was the glint of a steely intelligence that never deserted her—an intelligence that saw more than one side to a nice-guy–bad-girl Hollywood story. Advising an unwary Henry Fonda about women in *The Lady Eve*, she says: "The best ones aren't as good as you think they are, and the bad ones aren't as bad—not nearly as bad." In her best films, Stanwyck was like the little girl with the curl right in the middle of

Barbara Stanwyck: *The glint of steely intelligence.*

her brain. When she was good, she was very very good. And when she was bad, she was terrific.

[1979]

Andrew Sarris

JAMES STEWART

The cumulative effect of all his performances is to transcend acting with being, the noblest and subtlest form of screen acting.

I have been commissioned to write a piece about James Stewart on the basis of a cryptic remark which appears in a book of mine entitled *The American Cinema:* "The eight films [Anthony] Mann made with James Stewart are especially interesting today for their insights into the uneasy relationships between men and women in a world of violence and action. Stewart, the most complete actor-personality in the American cinema, is particularly gifted in expressing the emotional ambivalence of the action hero."

"The most complete actor-personality in the American cinema"? Now what could I have possibly meant by that? Perhaps simply that Stewart has incarnated and articulated a uniquely American presence on the screen throughout his long career, and a presence moreover that is more complex than it seems at first glance. I would add that Stewart is primarily a screen actor and a Hollywood screen actor at that. His few forays on the stage have not been of such a quality as to challenge the Gielguds, the Oliviers, the Richardsons, the Redgraves, and the Scofields. Still, he is their better on the screen, where behavioral consistency in a world of objects and vistas is more important than the vocal realization of a character from a printed page. This judgment would probably cause more gnashing of teeth in New York with its long tradition of mindless Anglophilia in the theater than in London with its perverse appreciation of American vitality and physicality.

Indeed, I recently had a quarrel with the British editors of a reference work I was preparing, they arguing that Burt Lancaster and Kirk Douglas were more crucial entries than Laurence Olivier and Ralph Richardson and I arguing the opposite. Actually, my first intimations of Stewart's having been grossly underrated came in Paris in 1961 at screenings of Alfred Hitchcock's *The Man Who Knew Too Much* and John Ford's *Two Rode To-*

gether. Two sequences stand out in my mind, and in both there is an unforgettable image of Stewart's long legs awkwardly stretched out as a metaphorical confirmation of his quizzical countenance. The excessively cerebral French, of course, know a good physical thing when they see it, and François Truffaut has acknowledged the influence of the riverbank sequence in *Two Rode Together* in which Stewart sits and talks with Richard Widmark on a similar Truffaut sequence in *Jules and Jim.*

However, Stewart's lanky physicality was not so much a key as a clue to the deeper meaning of his acting personality. To get to these deeper meanings requires an examination of the artistic contexts in which he has functioned most effectively. After all, feelings on the screen are expressed not so much *by* actors as *through* them. Hence, we can't really trace Stewart's contribution without dragging in such directors as George Stevens (*Vivacious Lady*), Frank Capra (*You Can't Take It with You, Mr. Smith Goes to Washington,* and *It's a Wonderful Life*), Ernst Lubitsch (*The Shop Around the Corner*), Frank Borzage (*The Mortal Storm*), George Cukor (*The Philadelphia Story*), Alfred Hitchcock (*Rope, Rear Window, The Man Who Knew Too Much,* and *Vertigo*), Otto Preminger (*Anatomy of a Murder*), John Ford (*Two Rode Together* and *The Man Who Shot Liberty Valance*), Robert Aldrich (*Flight of the Phoenix*), and the aforementioned Anthony Mann. But Stewart has never really let down even in bad movies, and this unrelenting professionalism and tenacity are qualities often lacking in even the greatest stage actors when they venture into the relatively fragmented screen.

All in all, Stewart has appeared in over seventy movies since his screen debut in 1935 in some forgotten Metro trifle tagged *Murder Man.* He was twenty-seven then—lean, gangling, idealistic to the point of being neurotic, thoughtful to the point of being tongue-tied. The powers-that-be at M-G-M were slow to recognize his star potential. Through the thirties Stewart made his biggest impact on loan-out to other studios, to Columbia for the Capras with Jean Arthur, to RKO for the Stevens with Ginger Rogers, to United Artists for *Made for Each Other* with Carole Lombard, to Universal for *Destry Rides Again* with Marlene Dietrich.

By the time M-G-M realized they had a prodigy on their hands, Stewart was off to the war for five years during World War II, and when he came back he had had enough of Leo the Lion and began free-lancing. He already had an Oscar for *The Philadelphia Story* and an award from the New York Film Critics for *Mr. Smith Goes to Washington.* But somehow he never regained his stride with critics and audiences. His extraordinarily emotional performance in *It's a Wonderful Life* was overlooked in a year galvanized by the classical grandeur of Laurence Olivier in *Henry V* and the sociological scope of the wildly overrated *The Best Years of Our Lives. Magic Town* was an out-and-out flop, *Call Northside 777* a stolid semidocumentary, *On Our Merry Way* the occasion of a reunion with old buddy Henry Fonda in a John O'Hara sketch. Stewart later played a cameo in clown makeup for Cecil B. De Mille in *The Greatest Show on Earth*, but he was drifting more and more to action pictures and wacky farce comedies. In *Rope*, he was miscast somewhat as an irresponsible intellectual and submerged both by the lurid subject and Hitchcock's single-take technique sans visible cuts.

But in *Rear Window, The Man Who Knew Too Much*, and *Vertigo*, Stewart supplied Hitchcock with three of the most morbidly passionate performances in the history of the cinema, and again he was overlooked by critics hypnotized by the dreary Philco Playhouse realism of Paddy Chayefsky's *Marty* and Terence Rattigan's *Separate Tables*. This was an era in which feeble talents like Ernest Borgnine and David Niven were winning Oscars for characterizations that proclaimed their own drabness. Stewart never changed type. As he became older, he tried to look younger. Unfortunately, the best way to win awards in Hollywood is to plaster a young face with old-age makeup. Artificial aging, however grotesque it may seem to the bored camera, is an infallible sign of "character" for those who confuse the art of acting with the art of disguise.

Stewart, alas, was always Stewart, and he gradually slipped out of the cultural mainstream. In his personal life he fell afoul of the redoubtable Margaret Chase Smith when he was mentioned for a general's commission in the Air Force Reserve. In England, actors are knighted for their services. In America, they are suspected of lurid frivolity. *Strategic Air Command* expressed his devotion to the Air Force at a time when hawkdom was beginning to be viewed in many quarters as a potentially dangerous outlet for patriotism. *The FBI Story* was sickeningly reverent toward J. Edgar Hoover, and *The Spirit of St. Louis* somewhat pointlessly proud of Charles Lindbergh. Besides, Stewart was embarrassingly old for a part the unlamented John Kerr had turned down out of political scruples.

Through the fifties and sixties, Stewart had his share of clinkers. He was no happier doing the Rex Harrison stage role in *Bell, Book and Candle* than he had been a generation earlier doing the Laurence Olivier role in *No Time for Comedy*. His performance in *Harvey* was less effective than Frank Fay's on the stage, and Fay operated on a fey vaudeville level over which Stewart's screen persona usually towered. But put Stewart in the middle of good English players in *No Highway in the Sky* and *Flight of the Phoenix* and *The Man Who Knew Too Much*, and he dominated the proceedings as only the greatest star personalities were capable of doing. And put him in a Western, and he gave it a gritty grandeur worthy of the Waynes and the Fondas and the Scotts and the Coopers.

Indeed, it was when Stewart became too old to be fashionable that he became too good to be appreciated. Suddenly his whole career came into focus as one steady stream of moral anguish. Hitchcock brought out the overt madness in him, the voyeurism (*Rear Window*), the vengefulness (*The Man Who Knew Too Much*), the obsessive romanticism (*Vertigo*). Ford brought out the cynic and opportunist in him. Mann brought out the vulnerable pilgrim in quest of the unknown. Otto Preminger's glazed gaze in *Anatomy of a Murder* reminded us once again of Stewart's dogged tenacity.

That Stewart even had the opportunity to enrich and expand his mythical persona into his sixties and our seventies is a fortunate accident of film history. But enriched and expanded he has become through the steady pull of his personality which has evolved over four decades from American gangly to American Gothic. If we take care of the small matter of preserving his seventy-odd films for posterity, he shall truly belong to the ages, perhaps as a relic of the moral fervor that once shaped even the more intelligent among us. In any event, the cumulative effect of all his performances is to transcend acting with being, the noblest and subtlest form of screen acting.

[1971]

Janet Maslin

BARBRA STREISAND

She amplifies her glamour by revealing, even flaunting, the tremendous skill and effort required to fabricate beauty.

Early on in *Funny Lady* James Caan (who is supposed to be impresario Billy Rose) has persuaded Barbra Streisand (who is supposedly portraying Fanny Brice) to appear in his first major show. He has also coaxed a buffalo into the cast, along with perhaps six hundred singing and dancing extras, and so things become unwieldy and go amusingly awry on opening night. Streisand, who incurs some comic injuries during the debacle, pronounces the whole show "overproduced"—and she ought to know. How else can you describe a film in which, when Billy sneaks into Fanny's bedroom to apologize late that same evening, Fanny's peachy-pink shiner is perfectly matched by her miraculously unrumpled negligee?

Streisand is indubitably a movie star, but she either cannot or will not metamorphose into an actress. Indeed, the only thing that makes *Funny Lady* interesting is the ingenuity with which she ducks the story's serious moments, hiding behind a crust of Pan-Cake and a wall of song. And what makes *Funny Lady* disappointing is its ossifying of a screen image that Streisand, in a few of the pictures that preceded it, had expressed some faint interest in relaxing.

Though it goes without saying that Streisand always plays herself, she has had several different selves from which to choose. Barbra-the-homebody reared her good-natured head in *For Pete's Sake*, turning a mishmash of formulaic high jinks into a moderate commercial success, but the personality was unconvincing and indistinct. Serious Barbra, the beleaguered housewife of *Up the Sandbox*, began the picture looking appropriately (and surprisingly) drab and conveying an earnest despair, but she could brook such realism for only about twenty minutes before wandering off into a series of asinine fantasy episodes. (I am assuming, here and elsewhere, that when something happens in a Barbra Streisand picture it does so with the star's approval and blessing, and that no director ever really tells her what to do.) The romantic, vulnerable, hard-headed Katie of *The Way We Were* was her most provocative persona, easily outshining Singing Barbra of *Funny Girl* and *Hello Dolly!* fame. However, part of Katie's appeal seemed involuntary, and far beyond the understanding of Barbra the Star.

In *The Way We Were*, as in all of her films, Streisand was lavishly coiffed and painted and costumed—only this time, for once, the makeup had meaning. The character was a woman who had grown up unlovely and unloved to become belligerently defensive and insecure. She was also extremely willful, so much so that by the time her romance with Redford was in full bloom she had managed to make herself far more beautiful than nature intended. Through much of the picture Streisand looks immensely attractive, for the very reason that we can see how hard she's had to work at it; like Cher Bono, she amplifies her glamour by revealing, even flaunting, the tremendous skill and effort required to fabricate beauty, making us simultaneously ponder the process and marvel at the finished product. Streisand's bagging of Redford, which takes place midway through the story, is all the more involving because it's her determination, not kismet, that brings them together; her strength has proven a match for his physical appeal. And Streisand is marvelous in much of the film, whenever she can suggest that Katie, no matter how good she looks, will never quite shake off the memory of having been plain.

Streisand conveys this so clearly and poignantly that it feels like an accident, a trace of the real woman glimpsed through the star's careful veneer. Though it may be a disservice to deem her most persuasive performance more ingenuous than deliberate, there are so many attempts to bolster Streisand's vanity throughout the picture that one has to assume she wasn't consciously willing to risk much. For me, the picture collapses when, in the midst of a quarrel, Streisand accuses Redford of thinking she just isn't pretty enough. It could be a tremendously convincing moment; whether he feels that way is almost immaterial, not nearly as important as the fact that she *thinks he might.* But she won't leave it at that; she immediately undermines the whole interchange by adding that she knows she's attractive, albeit in an unusual way. That line isn't Katie's, it's Barbra's. At a moment like this, Katie would be neither so blustery nor so sure.

Still, *The Way We Were* remained ambiguous much of the time, while *Funny Lady* spends over two hours and several million dollars catering to her indomitable vanity. When Omar Sharif, as the slimy Nicky Arnstein who married Brice in *Funny Girl,* first reappears in the sequel, Streisand is called upon by the screenplay to melt; she blurts out something about wanting to crawl into Nicky's hip pocket and stay there all the time. Then she takes his hand, in close-up, and we notice . . . what? Her fingernails. That they are long and perfect and bright-red goes without saying, but they are painted peculiarly, with a straight line rather than a curve at the cuticle, so that the little half-moon of the nail is bare. Only after this delicious detail has been fully digested do we detect Sharif's wedding ring—presumably what prompted the close-up in the first place.

The audience with which I saw *Funny Lady* spent the intermission remarking on how nice Streisand looked, and by the time the thing ended a good many of them were snuffling. But this is a testament to the unfortunate aspects of Brice's love life, not to the abilities or sincerity of the celebrity who plays her. According to the film's rather jumbled narrative, Brice married Billy Rose before she was fully over Arnstein, then fell in love with her second husband when it was too late. The situation is only a slight variation on your basic Scarlett, Rhett, and shades-of-Ashley triangle, and as such it's guaranteed to jerk tears. However, Streisand does her best to keep it from having any emotional immediacy or making any sense. Her big love scene with Caan is a masterpiece of obfuscation: they got married because they were "in like," she says, and they're spatting in a cramped train compartment on their honeymoon when suddenly they kiss. Cut—immediately—to Streisand in bed, setting her postcoital reflections to music ("Now I am calm / Safe and serene / Heartache and hurt are no longer a part of the scene"). The blue glow in the room is presumably moonlight, and

Caan—who has until now been hamming like there's no tomorrow as a coarse little hustler—lies sleeping on her sheet-shrouded bosom. The lighting makes his forehead a perfect match for the tiny satin pillow that completes the tableau. Ostensible message: they're really in love, even if they do mask their tenderness with antagonism. (This, incidentally, is the only moment of hard-core romance in the picture; they begin fighting again immediately afterward.) Real message: even if this man ever *was* a sexual threat, he has now been defused and tamed, turned into just one more of those impeccable props with which Barbra likes to surround herself.

Streisand slips into melody almost as cravenly as she hides behind excessive elegance; the few moments that might put her on the spot prove to be lead-ins for songs. But even if one makes extraordinary allowances for the "original" compositions of John Kander and Fred Ebb ("I walked out / He didn't walk out / It was me who walked out . . ."), their inappropriateness is staggering. "Let's Hear It For Me," a curiously unmotivated song of triumph, comes after Brice refuses to leave Rose for Arnstein, even though Sharif's Arnstein, with a five-o'clock shadow and all the sex appeal of smelt, looks extremely easy to resist.

A Streisand performance never lets you forget for a minute whom you're watching—in one scene here, as the aged Fanny, she wears a grayish wig and fake-looking facial lines that practically spell out her horror of actually appearing old (the makeup is never allowed to interfere with her radiant complexion). Streisand's ability to expose her imperfections without wallowing in them (for an example of the homely-girl-gone-overboard syndrome, *vide* Liza Minnelli), and to transcend them without fully leaving them behind, has a lot to do with the breadth of her appeal. But on the evidence of *Funny Lady*, she may be losing sight of what makes her attractive in taking her glamour as a given. She still clowns, sure, but she really isn't willing to look foolish anymore. When she jokes now, she does it too prettily; no matter how crude a line like "Doncha tryta hussle me, ya little bum" may be, she seems much more conscious of her fur wrap in this particular scene than she does of her delivery. Streisand is a unique composite of familiar qualities, and so much a natural, that it's a pity to see her success transform her into exactly the sort of slick, insulated *grande dame* to which she once provided such refreshing contrast.

[1975]

Bernard Drew

GLORIA SWANSON

"My hair had been cut short because I'd had a fever, so, of course, it became a new style."

Impossible to believe Gloria Swanson's first picture came out in 1915, impossible to believe a year later she married Wallace Beery, and then four other gentlemen including the Marquis de la Falaise de la Coudraye, to say nothing of passionate friendships with such as Joseph P. Kennedy and Herbert Marshall, impossible to believe even her sensational comeback as Norma Desmond in *Sunset Boulevard* is already twenty-two years old.

We all grow old, we fade and wither and stop caring, but not Glorious Gloria, as they called her in her salad days, which are still going on. She is a star like no other star. She invented the business, and if you don't believe it, just watch her make an entrance.

Last week, at the opening of the retrospective of sixty years of Paramount Pictures at the Museum of Modern Art, I watched her descend the steps to the Sculpture Garden as the band struck up "Love, Your Magic Spell Is Everywhere," which she introduced in *The Trespasser* in 1929. It was just a few steps, but she made a drama out of it, the kind of drama movies could use right now.

"How does Gloria do it? She's a miracle," her former boss, Adolph Zukor, told me last fall and he will turn one hundred this winter. "I'll tell you," he added. "She keeps busy, she can't sit still, she never could."

And then a couple of nights ago, Bill Kenly, who programmed the retrospective, arranged to screen Cecil B. De Mille's *The Affairs of Anatol* for Gloria and invited me to sit in. Gloria made that in 1921, along with Wallace Reid, Bebe Daniels, and Agnes Ayres. She hadn't seen it in fifty-one years and thought it might be time to see it again.

She arrived promptly at nine. We were introduced, and she took the seat next to me. I am not going to even attempt to describe her because she must be the most described woman of the century. Everyone knows she's tiny. Everyone knows she's glamorous. Everyone knows she's in her seventies and looks twenty years younger. Maybe it's the organic vegetables she eats and maybe it's something else.

The lights went down, the picture came on, and she chattered, vastly amused, throughout, "My God, will you look at that fat face? I'd just had a baby. . . . Well, I'm glad to see Agnes Ayres is fat too, I feel better. . . . Wallace Reid has more makeup on than I do. I wanted his eyebrows, so they plucked mine and arched them, see! . . . I was scared of Wally because I'd heard he took dope. . . . What are those things on my feet? . . . You know, I can't remember a single scene of this picture. . . . How innocent we were. Well we were kids, all of us. I was a couple of years older than the girls and a couple of years younger than the boys. . . . Isn't that Monte Blue? . . . And what is Bebe doing with her lips? . . . Is anyone still alive, I wonder? . . . Am I the only survivor? I guess so. Where's wood? I'd better knock. . . . You mean this isn't over yet? Another reel? Good God! . . ."

Finally it was over, the lights came on, and she told Bill, "I wish you had shown *Madame Sans-Gêne*. I cannot, will not believe every single print of that is gone. There must be one somewhere."

The premiere of that film is one of the movies' great spectaculars and I had read about it in countless books. She had made the picture in France, where she had married the Marquis. At the New York opening, her name in lights had occupied the entire two-story front of the Rivoli Theatre, with the American and French flags flying above. I asked her to tell it in her own words.

"I'd be glad to," she said. "Those old tales all tend to become exaggerated or diminished with the years, but that was fantastic, all of it, and there were reasons for all that hysteria. You see, I had almost died in France, they had saved space for my obituary in the papers, and then Cinderella comes up from the grave to marry the prince . . . or the marquis.

"It was the first title for Hollywood, you see, and you know how the world loves titles. I'm not even talking about mine. How long did I have it? Two minutes?"

She laughed and went on: "And there was still another reason. This was 1925, my contract with Paramount had only a year more to run and they wanted me to sign again. My pictures made lots of money, they covered the losses of other duds and they knew I was flirting with United Artists and thinking of producing my own pictures.

"So they went to work and set up this thing, and let me tell you, in those days, the publicity people knew their business. They knew act one, act two, act three.

"They had the biggest sign Times Square had ever seen," she recalled. "The mobs were so huge, the trolleys on Broadway had to stop running. Even as soon as the boat came into the harbor, quarantine was jammed with people. And there were ten days of this in New York. I cannot describe those days, there wasn't a moment of privacy, we'd find maids hiding in the clothes closet.

"And then we went to California and Paramount hired not a car, but an entire train, which would pause at every whistle-stop while I went out on that—what is that thing?—and waved and blew kisses. My hair had been cut short because I'd had a fever, so, of course, it became a new style, and everywhere, everywhere, mobs of people.

"You know, we were considered royalty. Not just me, all of us, and all over the world. They put us in tin cans, like sardines, and shipped us out all over the universe.

"We finally got to Los Angeles and there was a brass band to greet us, and all of the United Artists waiting at the station . . . Mary Pickford, Doug Fairbanks, Charlie Chaplin, and Joe Schenck. They were wooing me too.

"And then the night of the premiere at Sid Grauman's theater, our car could hardly move. There were people on the running board, people on top of the car, and as I stepped out, the usherettes threw flowers at us. Here I'm a convalescent, a zombie, and I'm hit on the head with flowers."

She giggled and went on: "As I arrived at the entrance of the theater, the entire place exploded into light. As I was led to my seat between Mack Sennett, who gave me my first job, and Cecil B. De Mille, everyone rose and sang, 'Home Sweet Home.' "

She smiled a little sadly now, remembering, and said, "Going back in the car, I sat with Henri, my husband, and my mother, and I don't know which one of them said, 'Why are you so silent and sad? This should be the happiest night of your life.'

"And then I said, 'I'm sad because all this happened not because I'm a great actress, but because Lazarus rose again, because Cinderella married the prince and because the prodigal returned. I'm sad because from now on, I'll have a problem. Where can I possibly go from here?'

"I was right," Gloria said. "That night was the peak and I saw the handwriting. After that I began to produce my own pictures and there was nothing but trouble. Problems and troubles. Life became very difficult for me, I had to keep moving, I couldn't stay in one place, but I'll tell you something, life also became interesting, far more so than if I just stayed in Hollywood.

"I broke all—well many—of the rules." She smiled. "I was the first to have a child, the first to broadcast from Europe, the first . . . well, why go on? The past has never been as interesting to me as the future. I had bad times, but I wouldn't have changed any of it. I have no regrets, I consider myself blessed."

And now, Gloria?

"Now, I'm off to my farm in Portugal." She laughed. "And then, I may direct a picture for Andy Warhol."

That doesn't shock me. I wouldn't be shocked if she had a baby next year.

[1972]

THE MOVIE STAR | 367

Richard Schickel

ELIZABETH TAYLOR

Since the age of eight she has had no identity but as an actress.

Elizabeth Taylor receives the highest salary any actor has ever attained. It is fitting, for since the age of eight Miss Taylor has had no identity but as an actress or, more accurately, as a public personality. For good or ill, her entire life has been devoted to living a dream peculiar to her time and place. She was even so unlucky as to have no adolescent awkward age which would have given her respite, however temporary, from life in public. In short, she was, is, and will forever be a movie star. There is no other significant fact to record about her life—for that fact has informed nearly every waking moment of her every day.

George Stevens, the director for whom she gave two of her best performances (in *A Place in the Sun* and in *Giant*), has said that "She was kept in a cocoon by her mother, by her studio, by the fact that she was the adored child who had had everything she wanted since she was eight years old. What most people don't know is that there has been a smoldering spirit of revolt in Elizabeth for a long time."

Her mother had once had a modest acting career herself, but it had been cut short by her marriage to Francis Taylor, an art dealer. Eventually they settled in Los Angeles. "It was almost impossible to believe—finding myself in the film capital with my children," said Mrs. Taylor. She determinedly set about making them into stars. Elizabeth's brother, Howard, would have none of it. He went so far as to shave his head on the eve of one screen test.

Elizabeth, however, was not so strong—though she has frequently placed on public record her admiration for her brother's independence. She had one small part at Universal before her option was dropped. Then, in 1942, during a blackout, her air-raid-warden father fell into conversation with a fellow warden, producer Sam Marx, who was looking for a child to appear opposite Roddy MacDowell in *Lassie Come Home*. Elizabeth read for the part and got it. Two years later, at age twelve, she had the lead in the memorable *National Velvet*.

Two years after that she could have played a mature woman. Even as a child star she had a fascinating air of experience about her. The casting director who had dropped her said, "Her eyes are too old. She doesn't have the face of a kid." It is a quality which has persisted, a major part of the excitement she creates, though now the eyes give the illusion not of age but of ageless womanly wisdom.

In the forties and fifties Elizabeth Taylor endured, though it could not be said that she prevailed. She began to hate the Hollywood that had robbed her of her childhood, sullenly played her parts with no more than rudimentary grace. She could not act, she could only give the illusion of existence. Cast as a willful child-woman, the natural development of the womanly child she had been, she was adequate, but it was her perfect beauty that kept her steadily, uninterestingly, before the cameras.

Then came her marriage to Mike Todd. "More than anyone realizes, Mike was responsible for the intellectual and emotional awakening of this girl," director Joseph Mankiewicz said. "For all his flamboyance, he was a man of an infinite variety of interests . . . she had been a sort of Sleeping Beauty in an isolated castle. Mike took her through the cobweb to the other world. . . ."

In touch with reality of a sort, Elizabeth Taylor began to add new dimensions to her screen presence. Her roles were very much in the mode that had become customary for her, but now they were touched by life—especially after the deeply felt tragedy of Todd's death in a plane crash. The rest is current history—the loss of public affection when she broke up the Eddie Fisher–Debbie Reynolds marriage, the regaining of that affection (and an Academy Award) in the sentimental orgy surrounding her near death in London, the epochal offscreen romance during the making of *Cleopatra,* and the ending of her marriage to Fisher. In her work she may now be able to touch reality as never before. But her life itself, that curious compound of legend and unreality, will never seem anything but a fantasy, an inextricable tangle of the real and the unreal which she, least of all, seems capable of sorting out.

In a sense, Elizabeth Taylor is a reversion to the superromantic stars of the silent screen, deliberately out of touch with common mortality. If that is true, then there will never be another movie star like her, for the system that produced them and, in its dying hours, produced Elizabeth Taylor, is now gone forever.

[1962]

Richard Schickel

RUDOLPH VALENTINO

His chief crime was against the American concept of ideal manhood.

It may be, after all these years, that we should readmit Rudolph Valentino to the human race. He was a man inordinately ill-served by everyone—the public, the press, the people who created and marketed his films, himself. His chief crime, in which all of these forces participated, was against the standard American concept of ideal manhood. He was too graceful and too beautiful—that was clear—but worse than that, he seemed weak. His weakness was merely sensed, sensed and commented upon by the American male, who did not like him, sensed and not admitted by the women, who did like him.

In the still-lingering afterglow of the hysteria he generated, he has become a kind of comic symbol of the excesses of his time and, indeed, there was much that was extremely funny about Valentino. There were, to begin with, the absurdly exotic settings in which his screen character was generally placed, not to mention the ludicrous costumes and decor with which they were freighted. But more important was the gap between the style he was forced to adopt in these films and the style that might have been natural to this rather shy and passive personality. The result was a terrible strain on him, and it is largely this strain, which has been captured in the still photographs, which are this generation's chief link with him. Adolph Zukor, who employed The Sheik, wrote that his acting "was largely confined to protruding his large, almost occult, eyes until vast areas of white were visible, drawing back the lips of his wide, sensuous mouth to bare his gleaming teeth, and flaring his nostrils." In other words, to indicate the outbursts of a smoldering flame that did not, in fact, exist, Valentino resorted to heroic Thespian exertions, defying all the laws of successful screen performance. The miracle is that he triumphed despite this nonsense.

For this triumph he could thank the sensibilities of the women who detected beneath the fakery the real Valentino. If you are not distracted by his wildly flailing attempts to indicate a quality quite beyond him, you can still detect this essential Valentino at odd moments in his films. There is, to begin with, the softness of his mouth when he forgets to set it in a hard, determined line, when he is not forcing it to leer. There is, in addition, the withdrawn sadness of his eyes in their unpopped condition. Finally, and most important, there is the insinuating gracefulness of his movements when they are unencumbered by period costumes. It is not the grace of an athlete—it is quite un-Fairbanksian—it is the grace of, frankly, a seducer, perhaps even a gigolo. It is grace directed toward a single end—the smooth transfer of a woman from an upright to a reclining position. To waste such grace on a high jump or a pole vault would have been madness. To use it as he did was an insult to all the Anglo-Saxon traditions of male-female relations, refreshing to women, despicable to men. He was, in short, that infinitely attractive thing—a boy in man's clothing and a boy, what's more, with an obvious talent for sensuality, a talent which any woman might wish first to test and then to develop to a man's full-scale sexuality.

There has never been a movie star in whose presence women more wanted to be, no star they more wanted to touch. There seemed to spring in his fans an eternal hope that one of them would awaken the real forces that slumbered (as they thought) within him. They could see the strain which posing as a man of action caused him, they knew the gap between the pretenses his scenarios forced upon him and the real Valentino, and all of them thought they just might be the woman—if only he would just notice—through whom he could bridge the gap.

Undoubtedly they sensed the truth about the real man, that he was fatally attracted to women stronger than he was. The one he chose as his wife very nearly succeeded in wrecking his career before his sudden death in 1926 ended it. She was a Salt Lake City girl named Winifred Shaunessy, stepdaughter of cosmetician Richard Hudnut. She was a designer and actress and in pursuit of these professions chose the cognomen Natacha Rambova. She began supervising Valentino's pictures and she emphasized the softness of his character, putting him into foppish items like *Monsieur Beaucaire,* presenting him with a slave bracelet that he wore to the great derision of the masculine American.

It was at this point that the Chicago *Tribune* called him a "pink powder puff" and suggested that he was setting a terrible example for American youth. Even the women began to desert him. For what Natacha didn't realize was that it was essential for Valentino to continue his brave attempts at strongly masculine behavior in his films. They served to remind his audience that there was a man within, a man waiting for release through love. The obligatory moment in his films where he threatened to—and sometimes actually did—take his heroine by force was, for his fans, a moment of high deliciousness. Beneath his demands, they sensed his gentleness. Once he had

(ABOVE) Rudolph Valentino:
A boy in man's clothing.
(*The Eagle.*)

(RIGHT) Elizabeth Taylor:
Deliberately out of touch with common mortality.
(From the MGM release *Butterfield 8.*
© Metro-Goldwyn-Mayer Inc. and
Afton-Linebrook Productions.
Copyright renewed 1960 by
Metro-Goldwyn-Mayer Inc.)

broken down resistance by its use they knew he would be gentle and kindly, a perfect lover. Without the tension between this fradulent force and this real gentleness, Valentino was just a pretty profile, and that was what Natacha was reducing him to before they separated and he began his much publicized affair with Pola Negri.

Valentino himself sensed the discrepancy between his screen self and his real self, and as false film followed false film, he complained: "I am beginning to look more and more like my miserable imitators." Many of them were indeed better at playing the Valentino character than was Valentino. Perhaps he so willingly followed Natacha's suggestions because he could no longer bear his pretense. He was, in any case, neither a stupid nor an insensitive man—despite the counterlegend his detractors created in the attempt to debunk him. He came from a relatively prosperous and educated provincial Italian family. He had a diploma from a college of landscape architecture, and he had come to America not as an immigrant seeking relief from oppression but out of curiosity. He was a natural dancer, danced for pleasure in the hours after work as a gardener, then turned professional, taking over from Clifton Webb as Bonnie Glass's partner, touring with her until the act broke up in Los Angeles, where he found work as a minor movie player. Screenwriter June Mathis sensed his appeal and brought him to Rex Ingram, who took a big chance by putting him into his arty superproduction, *The Four Horsemen of the Apocalypse* at Metro, which, with notable lack of foresight, signed him only for that picture. Zukor picked him up before Metro quite realized what it had. The first film was a solid hit; *The Sheik*, made for Paramount, was a sensation, and the mold was cast.

You could not say that Valentino was an intellectual, but he did have a natural sensitivity, which was his undoing. Lacking the strength to assert himself, even to be cynical, he buried his resentments inside himself, devoted himself with a surprisingly professional attitude to trying, somehow, to make himself believable. Of his physical strength he was more sure, but it was not enough, especially when the attacks on his masculinity reached their late heights. Some of his personal idiosyncrasies, his foppish dress, the womanish quality of his temper, served his enemies better than they did Valentino. More and more, toward the end, he talked of the tragic heroes he wanted to play—especially Pirandello's men in search of identity. "A man should control his life," he said once, "mine is controlling me. I don't like it." The screen role he loved best was the one in *The Four Horsemen.* "Julio was a man who allowed his weakness to dictate his circumstances—myself," he once said. His death, creating the awesome outburst of madness which marred his memory irrevocably, was caused by a perforated ulcer, that classic affliction of a man in debt to circumstance and unable to live with the debt.

[1962]

Jack Kroll

JOHN WAYNE

His sincerity becomes an aesthetic and moral force in his best acting and an exasperating complacency in his ill-fitting role as public ideologue.

"I am proud of every day in my life I wake up in the United States of America," John Wayne used to say. Now big Duke will awaken—at least in the United States—no longer, but John Wayne the legend will certainly prove as deathless as any figure of popular culture in the history of his beloved republic. ("Republic—I like the sound of the word," said Wayne in *The Alamo*. "It's one of those words that makes me tight in the throat.")

His death at seventy-two from cancer triggered a massive nationwide reaction to the man, the movie star, and the legend that was more than a tribute to a fifty-year career spanning more than two hundred movies that grossed more than four hundred million dollars. It was a moment for America, the greatest producer of mass fantasy in human history, to take a close look at one of its biggest, most ambiguous embodiments of such fantasy. Celebrating the dead John Wayne, America was celebrating one of its gallant dead dreams—a dream of unflagging national virility, courage, moral righteousness, and stone-fisted sincerity.

Or was the dream gallant? The president of the Republic thought so. "John Wayne was bigger than life," said Jimmy Carter. "In an age of few heroes, he was the genuine article." On Wayne's seventy-second birthday, the president had signed a bill authorizing a special medal, approved by the Congress, to honor Wayne.

The day before Wayne died, the acerbic Briton Henry Fairlie protested the medal: "John Wayne has contributed nothing to the welfare or progress of the American people beyond what has been demanded of him in the normal pursuit of his career and its pecuniary rewards." And Pete Hamill in the New York *Daily News* said: "John Wayne was not a hero. He was an actor who played heroes," and noted that, unlike such stars as James Stewart and

374 | THE MOVIE STAR

Clark Gable, Wayne did not enter the armed forces in World War II. Wayne's film company said that Wayne "had four children. He was over-age, and he had a perforated eardrum." At the time of Pearl Harbor, Wayne was thirty-four, Stewart (who flew twenty combat missions) was thirty-three and Gable was forty.

There is no question here of John Wayne's courage. His fifteen-year struggle against illness—the cancer that cost him a lung and his stomach, his open-heart surgery and gallbladder operation—testified to that. It is rather a question of myth vs. reality. The brilliant French director Jean-Luc Godard, whose politics are as far left as Wayne's were far right, once wondered how he could "hate John Wayne upholding Goldwater and love him tenderly when abruptly he takes Natalie Wood into his arms in the next-to-last reel of *The Searchers.*"

For fifty years—my God, fifty years!—Wayne created such epiphanies on the screen, moments and passages of resonant, emblematic behavior that are not reality and that are not even what is commonly meant by "acting." In his novel *The Moviegoer,* Walker Percy wrote: "Other people . . . treasure memorable moments in their lives: the time one climbed the Parthenon at sunrise, the summer night one met a lonely girl in Central Park. . . . What I remember is the time John Wayne killed three men with a carbine as he was falling to the dusty street in *Stagecoach.*"

Although this is a scene of violence, and John Wayne no doubt played more violent scenes than any actor who ever lived, it's not the violence that's being treasured in the memory of Percy's Moviegoer. It's the drastic grace, the flickering mythic rhythm that dissolves a triple killing into some Utopian gesture that kills nothing but the mediocrity of our ordinary behavior. There's nothing highbrow or pretentious about this: all good art triggers transcendence, and the great thing about the movies is that they turned transcendence into fun—whether it was the Olympian grace of Fred Astaire, the explosive solemnity of Buster Keaton, or the toppling locomotion of John Wayne, leaning into every stride like a dancer falling into arabesque after arabesque. It's Ernest Hemingway's "grace under pressure," and the pressure is our own need for a quick myth-fix that has turned movie stars into behavioral pushers.

If it seems odd to talk about supertough guy, supermacho, superpatriot John Wayne in such Apollonian terms, it must be remembered that he had this mythic quality from the beginning, and it's this quality that will keep him in our pop pantheon.

The radiant and brainy Louise Brooks, who was second only to Garbo as a screen beauty of the twenties and thirties, recalled meeting Wayne in

1938, in the twilight of her career and just before Wayne's comet was to gallop off in *Stagecoach*. Arriving on the set of a cheapie Republic Pictures Western, Brooks saw two figures approaching through the dust. "One was a cherub," she wrote, "five feet tall, carrying a bound script; the other was a cowboy, six feet four inches tall, wearing a lovely smile. The cherub, who was the director, George Sherman, introduced me to the cowboy, who was John Wayne, the star. Looking up at him I thought, This is no actor but the hero of all mythology, miraculously brought to life."

Throughout his career, people had this sense of portent when they met up with John Wayne. Visiting the set of a Wayne movie, writer Joan Didion felt that "the face across the table was in certain ways more familiar than my husband's." When John Ford hired Wayne as a prop boy in 1927, he was still Marion Morrison, a big shy fella from Winterset, Iowa, who played football for the University of Southern California. The great director promptly tried to intimidate the kid in a roughhouse but Duke calmly kicked him in the chest, forever earning Ford's respect.

Three years later director Raoul Walsh met Duke Morrison (the nickname came from a pet Airedale) and signed him to star as John Wayne in an epic Western, *The Big Trail*. "Dammit, the son of a bitch looked like a man," said Walsh. Marlene Dietrich thought so too. She met Wayne in a studio commissary, "looked him up and down as though he were a prime rib at Chasen's," recalled director Tay Garnett, and whispered in Garnett's ear, "Daddy, buy me that!"

Wayne was, as President Carter said, larger than life, and this mythic quality led to the paradox of his career, the conflict and the confusion between illusion and reality. His popularity was truly amazing: in an annual poll of exhibitors to select the year's top moneymaking stars, Wayne was listed a record twenty-five times and, in 1977, *Photoplay* magazine chose Wayne as the top movie star of all time.

And yet many critics, moviegoers, and movie-industry people never took him seriously as an actor, while taking his reactionary image very seriously. The formidable John Simon once defined Wayne as "a cross between a face on Mount Rushmore and a head on Easter Island atop a Doric column that moves with a swagger, talks in a monotone to which a drawl adds a slight curlicue, and looks at you with a lazy gaze that starts out downward but then curves slowly upward. Oh, hell: the last century had its Iron Duke, Wellington; this century has its Granite Duke, Wayne. Every era gets the leader it deserves; John Wayne is ours."

This kind of thing bothered Wayne. "The poor fella, he would tell me time and again, 'Jesus, I got terrible write-ups from those critics in New

York,' " recalls Walsh. "It kinda hurt him a bit. I said, 'Never mind New York. You're a big hit in Cincinnati.' " But the Wayne paradox wasn't a simple matter of Eastern "liberal" highbrows despising what the American "conservative" heartland loved.

Wayne and Ford have been accused of racist distortion for their depiction of Indians in their classic U.S. Cavalry Westerns like *Fort Apache* and *She Wore a Yellow Ribbon*, in which Wayne outsmarts, outfights, but never outrages the Indians, who are sometimes heroic, sometimes brutal. But Vine Deloria told Ford's biographer Andrew Sinclair that the portrayal of the Indians in these movies was a true one, even if it sometimes seemed hard to believe. It would have been false, said Deloria, to deny the eruptions of brutality by the Indians or to exaggerate them.

It's the question of his influence that took John Wayne out of the normal ruck of movie stars and made him a public force to reckon with and ponder over. When Emperor Hirohito of Japan visited the United States in 1975 he asked to visit John Wayne, as if he wished to see the personification of the power and determination that had defeated his country in World War II. And it's likely that Wayne came to think of himself in this way.

Wayne wrote to President Johnson in 1965 about his wish to make a movie on the Green Berets, the Special Forces fighting in Vietnam. Wayne told LBJ that he thought it was "extremely important that not only the people of the United States but those all over the world should know why it is necessary for us to be there." He said he wanted to "tell the story of our fighting men in Vietnam . . . in a manner that will inspire a patriotic attitude on the part of fellow Americans—a feeling which we have always had in this country in the past during times of stress and trouble."

Ironically, Wayne's vision of the Vietnam war was a bit strong even for the administration. The Army rejected the initial script because Wayne's Green Berets were too gung ho in their anti-Communist enthusiasm. Wayne's son Michael, the film's producer, didn't tell his father about this hassle. "I was actually afraid to," said Michael, "because he would have said, 'You dumb son of a bitch!' " Jack Valenti, then a presidential assistant and now president of the Motion Picture Association of America, told LBJ that "Wayne's politics [were] wrong, but insofar as Vietnam is concerned, his views are right. If he made the picture he would be saying the things we want said."

The Green Berets was made, with Wayne playing a colonel assigned to kidnap a North Vietnamese general and uttering such lines as, "Out here, due process is a bullet." It's a crummy movie, a brutalizing travesty of Wayne's genuine mythic Westerns, but it ranks second only to *True Grit* (which won him his only Oscar) as a Wayne moneymaker. Wayne was angered by the review in *The New York Times,* which called the movie "Unspeakable . . . stupid . . . rotten . . . false . . ." But *Times* critic Renata Adler raised the crucial issue when she bewailed what had "happened to the fantasy-making apparatus in this country."

More than any other star, John Wayne provided not only fantasies to beguile the imagination but role models for thousands of young Americans. In his book *Born on the Fourth of July,* Ron Kovic tells how he and his buddy watched Wayne's movie *Sands of Iwo Jima.* "We sat glued to our seats . . . watching Sergeant Stryker, played by John Wayne, charge up the hill and get killed just before he reached the top. And then they showed the men raising the flag on Iwo Jima with the Marines' hymn still playing, and Castiglia and I cried in our seats . . . and every time I heard it I would think of John Wayne and the brave men who raised the flag on Iwo Jima that day." Later Kovic tells how he felt after he had enlisted in the Marines, gone to Vietnam, and been wounded and paralyzed. "Nobody ever told me I was going to come back from this war without a penis. . . .Oh God, oh god, I want it back! I gave it for the whole country . . . I gave [it] for John Wayne . . ."

This is a heavy burden to lay on a movie star, but it testifies dramatically to Wayne's great authority as troop leader of the American dream. The interview he gave to *Playboy* in 1971 was a hair-raising catalogue of rightist righteousness. "I believe in white supremacy until the blacks are educated to a point of responsibility," said Wayne, adding that slavery was "just a fact of life, like the kid who gets infantile paralysis and has to wear braces so he can't play football with the rest of us." About Edward Dmytryk, who directed him in *Back to Bataan*: "When he used the word 'masses,' he exposed himself. The word is not a part of Western terminology. So I knew he was a Commie." Asked if he had helped to blacklist left-wingers in Hollywood: "There was no blacklist. . . . That was a lot of horse—— The only thing our side did that was anywhere near blacklisting was just running a lot of people out of the business."

Wayne has spoken of the movies as "a medium where we used illusion to set off reality." The paradox is that it's the world defined by his comic-aria political opinions that is illusory, and the world and persona of his best movies are the real John Wayne. Tragically, a Ron Kovic is inspired by the sight of Wayne being killed in a Marine charge rather than by the divided, complicated, self-questioning humanity of his great roles. In *She Wore a Yellow Ribbon,* the forty-two-year-old Wayne played Nathan Brittles, an aging cavalry officer who defeats the Indians by guile rather than by bloodshed,

John Wayne: *The last movie lover to make respect sexy.*

and who speaks to his dead wife and daughters with a quiet emotion that shames sentimentality. After the picture, Wayne proudly recalled, John Ford "sent me a cake, with one candle, that said 'You're an actor now.' "

Wayne is even better in Ford's *The Searchers*, which has become a cult masterwork for many movie buffs and critics. Wayne's Ethan Edwards, an unreconstructed Confederate and violent Indian hater who tracks down the niece (Natalie Wood) who was kidnapped years ago by the Indians, is a wonderful piece of acting, the emotions played big, strong, and movingly uncertain as Wayne fights his impulse to kill the niece who doesn't want to leave the Indians who have "defiled her." The final reconciliation with the girl, which Godard remembered so lovingly, is worthy of D. W. Griffith, the great master of partings and reunions.

Best of all is Wayne in Howard Hawks's *Red River*, a Western so filled with rich mythic detail that I keep remembering it in color and am shocked every time it turns up on television in its native black and white. Wayne's Thomas Dunson is one of the great Western characters, a bullying fool who finds his humanity by slugging it out with his wiser adoptive son—Montgomery Clift in his first film. *Red River* is the strongest instance of Wayne's natural ability to literally punch nuances out of the most primal feelings, and clinches the point that he was strongest when he played a "wrongo" instead of the white-hatted or green-bereted Galahad.

The supposedly macho Wayne actually has a more extensive sexual range than younger, ostensibly hipper studs like Paul Newman and Robert Redford. (Wayne didn't marry three Latin ladies to get free tequila.) There's plenty of eroticism in the Duke, but it's a friendly eroticism that takes any woman on her own terms and can explode into combat with a fiery Maureen O'Hara in *The Quiet Man* or slide into a gallant banter with the nice hooker played by Angie Dickinson in *Rio Bravo*. John Wayne is the last movie lover to make respect sexy. In *The Quiet Man*, he and O'Hara are caught in a violent rainstorm. The wind howls, their wet clothing clings to their skin and they are both seized by a beautifully abashed desire that achieves elemental intensity and sweetness in their unsophisticated confusion. Nicest of all are the relationships with older women—with Lauren Bacall in *The Shootist* and Katharine Hepburn in *Rooster Cogburn*, in which the sunset shimmer of sensuality fades into the sweet finality of friendship.

Sincerity is the key to Wayne, a sincerity that becomes an aesthetic and moral force in his best acting and an exasperating complacency in his ill-fitting role as public ideologue. Early in his career John Ford, whose feeling for Wayne was like a sculptor's feeling for clay, told him: "Duke, you're going to get a lot of scenes during your life. They're going to seem corny to you. Play 'em. Play 'em to the hilt. If it's *East Lynne*, play it. You'll get by with it, but if you start trying to play it with your tongue in your cheek and getting cute, you'll lose sight of yourself . . . and the scene will be lost."

The technical devices Wayne developed as an actor are perfectly geared to express this sincerity—the portentous but oddly delicate walk ("He walks like a fairy," said director William Wellman. "He's the only man in the world who can do it"), the emphatic monotone that encases each word in its own candid space. There's another Wayne device that you can practice, and that will make you feel this John Wayne sincerity flushing through you. Look in the mirror. Now raise your eyebrows suddenly. Your forehead crinkles with sincerity, your nostrils flare slightly, your ears tighten and you look like a man who's just been told by a woman that she loves him, or by a man that you're full of bull. Notice how satisfyingly simple and honest you feel; now you know what John Wayne meant all those years when he insisted, "I don't act. I react."

The paradox of John Wayne is the paradox of the conservatism that the country—maybe the entire West—seems to be groping toward. How to recapture the classical virtues and energies, integrity and even a righteous forcefulness of individualism, without losing the passion of an extended fraternity or abandoning the complicated covenants that alone can hold the discordant forces of our time in balance.

Wayne, says his longtime acting colleague Ben Johnson, "was real. He was honest, he was an American. If he tells you tomorrow's Christmas, you can get your sock ready. He was that kind of person." Yes, but he was also unthinking, uncharitable, and arrogant in an excess of pride that swamped that honest grace of his. Only under the real pressure of his art, not the fake pressure of his reality, did that grace operate in a shifting, human balance that touched, amused, and thrilled you. He lied to Ron Kovic because he lied to himself. Maybe he knew that at the end, playing *The Shootist,* like himself a battered old pro, violent and warm, dying. What the hell. Let Wayne be a hero. Maybe a hero is someone you never forget.

[1979]

ABOUT THE
CONTRIBUTORS

David Ansen is a film critic and a general editor at *Newsweek*. Formerly he was film critic at *The Real Paper*.

Gary Arnold is film critic of *The Washington Post*.

Joy Gould Boyum writes on film for *The Wall Street Journal*. She also teaches literature and film at New York University, where she is professor of English.

Vincent Canby, film critic of *The New York Times*, was a critic and reporter for *Variety* from 1960 until 1965. An associate fellow of Pierson College, Yale, he is author of two novels, *Living Quarters* and *Unnatural Scenery*, and several plays including *The End of the War*.

Charles Champlin is film critic of *The Los Angeles Times;* he was host of the *Film Odyssey* series for NET.

Richard Corliss is film and television critic for *Time* magazine and the editor of *Film Comment*. He has been film critic for *New Times, The Soho Weekly News,* and *Maclean's* magazines, and has written for *The New York Times,* the *Village Voice, Commonweal, The Real Paper,* and most of the major specialized film magazines. He is the editor of *The Hollywood Screenwriter* and the author of *Talking Pictures* and *Greta Garbo*.

Judith Crist is film critic of *TV Guide, L'Officiel/USA,* and *50 Plus.* She has been film critic of the New York *Herald Tribune, The World Journal Tribune, New York* magazine, *Saturday Review,* the New York *Post,* and NBC-TV's *Today* show. Her reviews were collected in *The Private Eye, the Cowboy and the Very Naked Girl* and *Judith Crist's TV Guide to the Movies.* She is an adjunct professor at the Columbia University Graduate School of Journalism.

Bernard Drew, film critic and feature writer for the Gannett News Service, has written original material for movies and television.

Roger Ebert, film critic of the *Chicago Sun-Times,* won the 1975 Pulitzer Prize for criticism. His pieces have appeared in *Esquire, The New York Times, Film Comment,* and *The Critic.* He is lecturer in film at the University of Chicago and he wrote the original screenplay for *Beyond the Valley of the Dolls.* He is co-host of the PBS network film-review program *Sneak Previews.*

Stephen Farber is film critic and contributing editor of *New West.* He has also written for *The New York Times, The Los Angeles Times, Partisan Review, Film Quarterly, Film Comment,* and other publications. He is the author of *The Movie Rating Game.*

Penelope Gilliatt, formerly film critic of the London *Observer,* has written fiction and film criticism for *The New Yorker.* She is a Fellow of the Royal Society of Literature. Her latest works are *Nobody's Business,* a collection of short fiction; *The Cutting Edge,* a novel; many television and radio plays for the BBC; *Unholy Fools* and *Three-Quarter Face,* two collections of criticism; *Jean Renoir;* and *Jacques Tati.* She has written two other novels, *One by One* and *A State of Change,* and three previous collections of stories, *Come Back If It Doesn't Get Better, Splendid Lives,* and *Penguin Modern Stories No. 5.* Her original screenplay for *Sunday, Bloody Sunday* is available in hardcover and paperback. She has just finished the libretto for an original three-act opera commissioned by the English National Opera Company and is close to completing two new works of fiction.

Stephen Harvey, film critic of *Saturday Review* and theater critic of *Inquiry* magazine, is also the coordinator of special film projects for the Museum of Modern Art. An instructor at the New School for Social Research, he has written two books, *Fred Astaire* and *Joan Crawford.*

Molly Haskell has been film critic for the *Village Voice* and *New York* magazine. Her pieces have appeared in *Vogue, Saturday Review, Intellectual Digest, Show, USA, Film Comment, Film Heritage, Inter/VIEW, Cahiers du Cinéma in English, American Film,* and *MS.* She is the author of *From Reverence to Rape: The Treatment of Women in the Movies.*

Pauline Kael, film critic for *The New Yorker,* has written for *Partisan Review, Sight and Sound, Film Quarterly, Atlantic, McCall's, New Republic,* and *Harper's.* Her criticism has been collected in *I Lost It at the Movies, Kiss Kiss Bang Bang, Going Steady, Deeper Into Movies* (which won the National Book Award for Arts and Letters in 1973), *Reeling,* and *When the Lights Go Down.* Her long essay "Raising Kane" appears in *The Citizen Kane Book.*

Dave Kehr writes about movies for Chicago's alternative weekly, *The Reader.* He also contributes a monthly column to *Chicago* magazine and frequently appears in *Film Comment.*

Jack Kroll is a film and theater critic for *Newsweek.*

Janet Maslin, a film critic for *The New York Times,* was formerly a critic of film, theater, and music for *Newsweek,* film editor of *The Boston Phoenix,* and music columnist for *New Times.* Her pieces have also appeared in the *Village Voice, Rolling Stone,* and *Film Comment.*

George Morris is film critic for *The Texas Monthly.* He teaches film at the New School for Social Research and the University of Bridgeport and is author of *John Garfield* and *Errol Flynn.*

William S. Pechter has written on films for a number of magazines. Two collections of his criticism have been published: *Twenty-Four Times a Second* in 1971 and

Movies Plus One in 1981. From 1970 to 1977 he was film critic for *Commentary*.

Peter Rainer, film critic and columnist for *Mademoiselle* magazine, is also a regular staff film critic and feature writer for the *Los Angeles Herald Examiner*. His pieces have appeared in *National Review, The Boston Phoenix, Film Society Review,* and King Features syndication, and on KPFK-FM.

Rex Reed is the film critic for the New York *Daily News* and *Vogue*. He has been the film critic for *Women's Wear Daily, Holiday,* and *Cosmopolitan* in past years, and his reviews and articles on film have appeared in most major publications. He is the author of six books: *Do You Sleep in the Nude?; Conversations in the Raw; Big Screen, Little Screen; People Are Crazy Here; Valentines and Vitriol;* and *Travolta to Keaton.*

Frank Rich, theater critic of *The New York Times,* was formerly film critic of *Time* magazine, the New York *Post,* and *New Times.* His journalism has also appeared in *Esquire,* the *Village Voice, TV Guide,* the *Washington Monthly,* and, in England, the *Guardian* and *Harper's Bazaar & Queen.*

Andrew Sarris is film critic of the *Village Voice* and associate professor of cinema at Columbia University. His books are: *The Films of Josef von Sternberg; Interviews with Film Directors; The Film; The American Cinema: Directors and Directions, 1929–1968; Film 68/69,* co-edited with Hollis Alpert; *Confessions of a Cultist: On the Cinema 1955–1969; The Primal Screen; The John Ford Movie Mystery;* and *Politics and Cinema.*

Richard Schickel reviews films for *Time* magazine, as he did for *Life* from 1965 until it ceased weekly publication in 1972. His books include *The Disney Version, His Picture in the Papers, Second Sight,* and, most recently, a novel, *Another I, Another You.* In recent years he has produced, written, and directed for television, and his credits include *The Men Who Made the Movies* series for PBS (which was published in book form as well), *Life Goes to the Movies, Funny Business, The Horror Show,* and *Into the Morning: Willa Cather's America.*

Elisabeth Weis, who serves as secretary of the National Society of Film Critics, is associate professor of film at Brooklyn College of the City University of New York. She has written a book, *The Silent Scream: Alfred Hitchcock's Sound Track* and film criticism for the *Village Voice* and other publications. She co-edited, with Stuart Byron, the Society's earlier anthology, *The National Society of Film Critics on Movie Comedy.*

Colin L. Westerbeck is film critic for *Commonweal*. His articles on movies and still photography have appeared in *Sight and Sound* and *Artforum.*

Bruce Williamson is film critic and contributing editor of *Playboy* magazine and teaches at St. John's University, Long Island; he attended Columbia University, was a film critic at *Time* from 1963 to 1967, and before that a free-lance contributor to various periodicals and satirical revues in New York and London.

INDEX

ACKNOWLEDGMENTS

Grateful acknowledgment is made to the following for permission to reprint copyrighted material:

American Film, Bernard Drew, and Andrew Sarris: "The Basic Training of Jill Clayburgh" (retitled: "Jill Clayburgh") by Bernard Drew, from *American Film* magazine, April 1979, © 1979 The American Film Institute. "Lord Laurence Olivier as Nazi Hunter" (retitled: "Laurence Olivier") by Bernard Drew, from *American Film* magazine, August 1978, © 1978 by The American Film Institute. "The Actor as Auteur" by Andrew Sarris, from *American Film* magazine, May 1977, © 1977 The American Film Institute, J. F. Kennedy Center, Washington, D.C. 20566.

Atlantic Cable Television Publishing Corporation: "Katharine the Great: Woman, Actress, Star and Personality" (retitled: "Katharine Hepburn") by Judith Crist, from the January 1978 Cablevision guide.

Berkley Publishing Corporation: Introduction by George Morris to *Errol Flynn,* copyright © 1975 by Pyramid Communications. Introduction by Stephen Harvey to *Fred Astaire,* copyright © 1975 by Pyramid Communications. Revised and expanded Introduction by Richard Corliss to *Greta Garbo,* copyright © 1974 by Pyramid Communications.

Georges Borchardt, Inc.: Selections ("Marilyn Monroe" and "Charles Chaplin") from *Unholy Fools* by Penelope Gilliatt, copyright © 1961, 1963, 1966 by Penelope Gilliatt. Selections from "To W. C. Fields, Dyspeptic Mumbler Who Invented His Own Way Out" (retitled: "W. C. Fields") by Penelope Gilliatt, from *The New Yorker,* June 21, 1969.

The Boston Phoenix: "That Was No Funny Lady . . ." (retitled: "Barbra Streisand") by Janet Maslin, from *The Boston Phoenix,* April 15, 1975.

Chicago Reader: A review of *The Gauntlet,* "Caught in the Middle" (retitled: "Clint Eastwood") by Dave Kehr, from the *Chicago Reader,* January 13, 1978, copyright © 1978 by Chicago Reader, Inc.

Commentary, William S. Pechter, and Richard Schickel: "Cagney and Other Movie Stars" (retitled: "Cagney vs. Allen vs. Brooks") by William S. Pechter, from *Commentary,* May 1974. "Stars and Celebrities" (retitled: "Stars vs. Celebrities") by Richard Schickel, from *Commentary,* August 1971.

Commonweal: "The Importance of Being Oscar" (retitled: "Stars vs. Actors") by Colin L. Westerbeck, Jr., from *Commonweal,* April 16, 1971.

Bernard Drew: Gannett Newspaper interviews by Bernard Drew with Gloria Swanson, *Reporter-Dispatch,* July 25, 1972; with Burt Lancaster, *Herald-Statesman,* March 6, 1973; and with Glenda Jackson, *Reporter-Dispatch,* November 9, 1976.

Esquire: "Kirk Douglas at Large" (retitled: "Kirk Douglas") by Roger Ebert, from *Esquire,* February 1970, copyright © 1970 by Esquire, Inc.

Field Enterprises, Inc.: Interview with Robert Mitchum by Roger Ebert, from the *Chicago Sun-Times,* November 11, 1969. Used by permission. Further reproduction is prohibited.

Film Comment: "In Memoriam: Joan Crawford" (retitled: "Joan Crawford") by Stephen Harvey, from *Film Comment,* July/August 1977, copyright © 1977 by The Film Society of Lincoln Center.